Assessing Bilingual Children in Context

SCHOOL PSYCHOLOGY BOOK SERIES

Assessing Bilingual Children in Context

An Integrated Approach

Edited by **Amanda B. Clinton**

American Psychological Association • Washington, DC

Published by
American Psychological Association
750 First Street, NE
Washington, DC 20002
www.apa.org

To order
APA Order Department
P.O. Box 92984
Washington, DC 20090-2984
Tel: (800) 374-2721; Direct: (202) 336-5510
Fax: (202) 336-5502; TDD/TTY: (202) 336-6123
Online: www.apa.org/pubs/books
E-mail: order@apa.org

In the U.K., Europe, Africa, and the Middle East, copies may be ordered from
American Psychological Association
3 Henrietta Street
Covent Garden, London
WC2E 8LU England

Typeset in Goudy by Circle Graphics, Inc., Columbia, MD

Printer: United Book Press, Baltimore, MD
Cover Designer: Mercury Publishing Services, Inc., Rockville, MD

The opinions and statements published are the responsibility of the authors, and such opinions and statements do not necessarily represent the policies of the American Psychological Association.

Library of Congress Cataloging-in-Publication Data
Assessing bilingual children in context : an integrated approach / Edited by Amanda B. Clinton. — First Edition.
       pages cm
  Includes bibliographical references and index.
  ISBN-13: 978-1-4338-1565-2
  ISBN-10: 1-4338-1565-6
  1. Bilingualism in children. 2. Children—Language—Evaluation. 3. Children—Language—Psychological aspects. 4. Language acquisition—Psychological aspects. 5. Cognitive grammar. 6. Psycholinguistics. I. Clinton, Amanda B. editor.
  P115.2.A88 2014
  306.44'6071—dc23
                                   2013027828

British Library Cataloguing-in-Publication Data
A CIP record is available from the British Library.

Printed in the United States of America
First Edition

http://dx.doi.org/10.1037/14320-000

CONTENTS

CONTRIBUTORS

Jennifer Branscome, PhD, Department of Psychology and Counseling, Valdosta State University, Valdosta, GA

Elsa Cárdenas-Hagan, EdD, Texas Institute for Measurement Evaluation, University of Houston

Catherine Christo, PhD, Department of Professional and Graduate Studies in Education, College of Education, California State University, Sacramento

Amanda B. Clinton, PhD, Department of Social Sciences, Psychology Program, University of Puerto Rico, Mayagüez

Erin Crosby, EdS, Department of Professional and Graduate Studies in Education, College of Education, California State University, Sacramento

Jill Fitzgerald, PhD, MetaMetrics and School of Education, The University of North Carolina at Chapel Hill

Sandra G. Garcia, MA, School of Education, The University of North Carolina at Chapel Hill

Lino Gómez-Cerrillo, PsyD, Chaffey Joint Union High School District, Ontario, CA

Korah La Serna Guilar, MA, San Carlos Charter Learning Center, San Carlos, CA

Michael R. Hass, PhD, College of Educational Studies, Counseling and School Psychology, Chapman University, Orange, CA

Kelly S. Kennedy, PhD, College of Educational Studies, Counseling and School Psychology, Chapman University, Orange, CA

Catherine McBride-Chang, PhD, Department of Psychology, Chinese University of Hong Kong, Shatin

Jianhong Mo, Department of Psychology, Chinese University of Hong Kong, Shatin

Elisabeth C. O'Bryon, PhD, Department of Psychology, Yale University, New Haven, CT

Carol B. Olson, PhD, School of Education, University of California at Irvine

Pedro Olvera, PsyD, Department of School Counseling and Psychology, Azusa Pacific University, Azusa, CA

Wanda R. Ortiz, University of Puerto Rico, Mayagüez

Sharolyn D. Pollard-Durodola, EdD, Department of School and Counseling Psychology, University of Denver, Denver, CO

Rachel W. Robillard, PhD, Department of Counseling, Leadership, Adult Education and School Psychology, Texas State University, San Marcos

Patricio A. Romero, PsyD, Department of Education, Queens College, City University of New York, Queens

Robin C. Scarcella, PhD, School of Humanities, University of California at Irvine

Karen Lee Seymour, Department of Education, Perth, Western Australia

Fuhui Tong, PhD, Department of Educational Psychology, Texas A&M University, College Station

Xiuhong Tong, Department of Psychology, Chinese University of Hong Kong, Shatin

Yanling Zhou, PhD, Department of Early Childhood Education, The Hong Kong Institute of Education, Tai Po

Michelle Zozaya, EdS, Department of Professional and Graduate Studies in Education, College of Education, California State University, Sacramento

SERIES FOREWORD

Outside of their homes, children spend more time in schools than in any other settings. From tragedies such as Sandy Hook and Columbine to more hopeful developments such as the movement toward improved mental health, physical health, and academic achievement, there is an ongoing need for high-quality writing that explains how children, families, and communities associated with schools worldwide can be supported through the application of sound psychological research, theory, and practice.

Thus, for the past several years the American Psychological Association (APA) Books and APA Division 16 (School Psychology) have partnered to produce the School Psychology Book Series. The mission of this series is to increase the visibility of psychological science, practice, and policy for those who work with children and adolescents in schools and communities. The result has been a strong collection of scholarly work that appeals not only to psychologists but also to individuals from all fields who have reason to seek and use what psychology has to offer in schools.

Many individuals have made significant contributions to the School Psychology Book Series. First, we would like to acknowledge the dedication of past series editors: Sandra L. Christensen, Jan Hughes, R. Steve McCallum, David McIntosh, LeAdelle Phelps, Susan Sheridan, and Christopher H. Skinner.

We would like to extend special thanks to Catherine Christo for her dedicated service as series editor on this volume as well as on previous volumes in the series. Second, we would like to acknowledge the outstanding editorial vision of the scholars who have edited or authored books for the series. The work of these scholars has significantly advanced psychological science and practice for children and adolescents worldwide.

We welcome your comments about this volume and other topics you would like to see explored in this series. To share your thoughts, please visit the Division 16 website at www.apadivisions.org/division-16.

Linda A. Reddy, PhD
Series Editor

Assessing Bilingual Children in Context

INTRODUCTION

AMANDA B. CLINTON

Multidimensional. Complex. Diverse. These descriptors apply not only to the challenges of bilingual assessment but also to bilingual children themselves. Children who are learning a second language and are referred for psychological assessment in the United States and elsewhere frequently present with unique personal backgrounds and far-ranging experiences. Numerous factors in their histories can have long-term implications for learning, behavior, and social–emotional development. These are children like Lu, who grew up in a refugee camp in Thailand prior to relocation to Minnesota; they are children like Elena, who spent days in the desert while crossing into the United States from Mexico with her parents, who were hoping to alleviate a situation of dire poverty; and Magnus, a biracial child born in the United States to parents who are native speakers of two different languages and who attends his neighborhood school and receives instruction in English. These are just three examples of second language learners—yet with this small number of cases a world of

http://dx.doi.org/10.1037/14320-001

Assessing Bilingual Children in Context: An Integrated Approach, A. B. Clinton (Editor)

challenges arises in terms of best practice for valid and meaningful assessment that can, ultimately, inform intervention.

The complex cases of second language acquisition presented in this book, along with the varying degrees of bilingualism demonstrated by the children who are referred for assessment, represent the clinical realities and challenges faced by practitioners. What, then, is bilingualism? In simple terms, *bilingualism* is defined as "the ability to speak two languages" (http://www.merriam-webster.com/dictionary/bilingualism). Many popular approaches to bilingualism consider dual languages as an "all-or-nothing" skill: You speak two languages, or you do not (Brutt-Griffler & Varghese, 2004). This volume aims to address complexities in second language learning and assessment, however, and acknowledges that human behavior and its measurement are rarely, if ever, a binary question that might be defined in black and white.

Bilingualism is a highly complex phenomenon that is influenced by myriad factors and, as such, is best considered along a continuum. The degree of fluency demonstrated by a child may be affected by variables such as age of acquisition of each language, the contextual factors in which a native and second language are learned, the domains in which each language is used, and the structural similarities between the two languages (Gottardo & Grant, 2008). The chapters that follow were conceptualized in an effort to inform clinicians and educators working with children and youth who demonstrate variability in knowledge and fluency in either one or both of their two languages—that is, to help address the gray areas associated with dual language learning, assessment, and intervention.

The impetus for this volume came from my personal and professional experiences and, quite simply, frustration regarding the apparent lack of a context-oriented, integrated approach to considering second language learners during the assessment process. As a bilingual and bicultural licensed psychologist and credentialed school psychologist, I yearned—as did many of my colleagues—for means of understanding in a more profound manner children referred for "bilingual assessment." This book came to fruition in an effort to take into consideration the multitude of factors that are concordant with the bilingual child's experience.

Clearly, psychologists need to understand how and where the factors that contribute to molding a child into a whole person intersect. This volume, which is intended for mental health professionals (psychologists, social workers, therapists), educational professionals (counselors, teachers), and even physical health professionals (nurses, case managers), moves beyond the standard approach of discussing tests—their uses, interpretation, and limits—to address the interplay of factors that make assessing bilingual children so challenging.

This volume considers interactions between experience, biological, and cultural/societal factors as key influences in the evaluation of the second language learner who has been referred for assessment. The content of this book, although not exhaustive and still tied to the standard format of thematic division by chapters, aims to provide an integrated approach and a series of insights into the complexities of bilingual children and their evaluation. That is, the implications of historical factors such as immigration or refugee experiences are explored. In addition, more direct systems influences, such as poverty, stress, and family/community considerations, are addressed. Certainly, particular areas of emphasis in evaluation, such as cognitive, academic or social–emotional, are reviewed. The established techniques of norm-referenced measures are not the focus, however. Instead, the text incorporates options for evaluation ranging from response to intervention to testing the limits. Consideration of the fluid nature of child development in a context that incorporates myriad significant influences, particularly when a bilingual child is referred for assessment, is the objective.

To aid the reader in understanding the relevant research and applying best practices, the chapters contain two important tools. First, case studies illustrate the application of the principles discussed. Second, concise graphic tools, such as checklists and charts, provide readers with a succinct reference for salient points outlined in the chapter. Thus, in addition to being meaningful for practicing professionals, this book will be useful in training programs that prepare professionals to provide assessments and in training programs for professionals who need to increase their understanding of the many factors that affect the development and learning of bilingual children.

The volume consists of 10 chapters. Chapter 1 frames the rest of the book by providing an overview of the complex issues that influence the needs of bilingual children, particularly in a country such as the United States. Chapters 2 through 4 discuss cross-language transfer—that is, how the structure of one's native language may (or may not) affect second language acquisition, as well as the biological bases of normative and aberrant language development. These are critical points because a bilingual child's second language acquisition process is informed by prior language learning and neuropsychological processes, all of which can be affected by environmental factors.

Beginning with Chapter 5 and continuing through Chapter 10, specific types of assessment are addressed. This section includes chapters addressing the use of norm-referenced measures in bilingual assessment, the use of response to intervention techniques, and social–emotional evaluation in a bilingual–bicultural context. Assessment of acculturation factors is discussed as well. Chapters 9 and 10 review data specific to key areas of learning that may be affected by second language acquisition processes: reading and writing. Finally, Chapter 11 considers the special case of refugee children whose uniquely significant experiences, in addition to requiring specialized consideration in the assessment process, provide an example of the complex interplay between biology, experience, and culture.

This is not a book about tests. Rather, it is a book about children and the complexity of evaluating their functioning when they are acquiring a second language and, often, adapting to a new culture. Hence, this volume provides readers with a broader lens than have traditional texts on assessment of bilingual children. By including chapters written by both practitioners and researchers hailing from a broad range of disciplines and backgrounds, this volume allows readers a greater understanding of the multiple factors that must be considered in the assessment process and, subsequently, the design of interventions for bilingual children. *Assessing Bilingual Children in Context: An Integrated Approach* considers the ways in which biological inclinations and life experiences interact to mold the cognitive, social, and emotional skills and knowledge that combine to create unique multidimensional, complex, and diverse human beings.

REFERENCES

Brutt-Griffler, J., & Varghese, M. (2004). *Bilingualism and language pedagogy*. Clevedon, England: Multilingual Matters.

Gottardo, A., & Grant, A. (2008). Defining bilingualism. *Encyclopedia of language and learning development*. Retrieved from http://literacyencyclopedia.ca/index.php?fa=items.show&topicId=236

1

CHALLENGES AND COMPLEXITIES IN THE ASSESSMENT OF THE BILINGUAL STUDENT

ELISABETH C. O'BRYON

As the number of Americans who speak a language at home other than English steadily rises (Shin & Kominski, 2010), there is a corresponding increase in the number of bilingual students attending U.S. schools. Bilingual students are an exceedingly heterogeneous group with diverse backgrounds and experiences. For example, bilingual students are both foreign and native born; some have learned two languages simultaneously, whereas others have learned a second language after a first language was established; bilingual students display variable abilities in terms of listening, reading, speaking, and writing in both their native and second languages (Calderón, Slavin, & Sanchez, 2011; National Council of Teachers of English, 2008). Unfortunately, the process of second language learning contributes to the array of academic difficulties, particularly when coupled with additional challenges, such as immigration, acculturation, and low socioeconomic status (SES), that may affect bilingual students' educational experiences.

http://dx.doi.org/10.1037/14320-002
Assessing Bilingual Children in Context: An Integrated Approach, A. B. Clinton (Editor)

Bilingual students who struggle academically are likely to be referred for a psychoeducational assessment. The evaluation process enables psychologists to gather additional information about students' current levels of functioning and what may be affecting their educational performance. However, assessing bilingual students often is not a straightforward process and can thus be an extremely challenging task. Unlike the assessment of monolingual, English-dominant peers, evaluators who are assessing bilingual students must recognize and appropriately consider a number of factors that uniquely affect students from diverse cultural and linguistic backgrounds.

This chapter sheds light on many of the challenges associated with appropriately assessing bilingual students. The chapter begins with an examination of how language learning can complicate the assessment process for bilingual students who exhibit academic difficulties. Next, immigration, low SES, and how the process of acculturation can further complicate the assessment process by creating an even more complex profile of the bilingual student are discussed. Additional relevant assessment considerations are also addressed, including language transfer uniqueness and the limitations of available assessment tools.

SECOND LANGUAGE LEARNING

Professionals who are assessing bilingual students often face the difficult task of distinguishing between academic concerns that are indicative of a disability and academic concerns that are a function of characteristics associated with a student's cultural and linguistic background (Klingner & Harry, 2006). Given how complex the assessment process can be, it is not surprising that the disproportionate representation of students from diverse backgrounds who are diagnosed with learning disabilities can manifest itself in two distinct ways (Shifrer, Muller, & Callahan, 2011). First, overidentified diverse students qualify for special education services as a result of other factors that are at play, and second, underidentified diverse students do not qualify for, nor receive, the special education services that they need (Shifrer et al., 2011). In addition to creating a serious misallocation of resources, the issue of misidentification of linguistic minority students highlights an overarching need for professional guidance related to appropriately assessing bilingual students.

Available research has suggested that a number of issues at play during the assessment process contribute to the inappropriate special education classification of bilingual students (Klingner, Artiles, & Barletta, 2006). A key issue involves effectively determining the language proficiency of the referred student in both the native and second language. A challenge emerges for psychologists given that second language learners who display well-developed conversational skills in their second language can appear deceptively proficient in their second language, even though they are actually in the early stages of language development. That is, students may display basic interpersonal communication skills (BICS) in English, for example, although they have yet to develop cognitive academic language proficiency (CALP; Cummins, 1981). Conversational language, which is context-embedded and cognitively undemanding, is distinct from academic language, which is context-reduced and cognitively demanding; thus, although it may take 2 years to establish BICS, it may take 5 to 7 years to acquire CALP, which is necessary for success in demanding academic contexts (Cummins, 1984, 2000).

Cummins (2000) used a quadrant framework with two dimensions—the degree of cognitive involvement and degree of contextual support—to expand on the distinction between conversational (BICS) and academic (CALP) language. His framework classifies language tasks and activities as falling into four quadrants: context-embedded and cognitively undemanding, context-embedded and cognitively demanding, context-reduced and cognitively undemanding, and context-reduced and cognitively demanding (Cummins, 2000). The framework demonstrates the impact of language proficiency on a student's ability to successfully complete tasks and activities that vary in terms of their cognitive involvement and contextual support (Cummins, 2000). For example, bilingual students who have conversational language skills in their second language can succeed in carrying out context-embedded cognitively undemanding activities (e.g., copying from the board) but will struggle when faced with classroom tasks that offer fewer context clues and are increasingly cognitively complex (e.g., completing math word problems).

It is important that psychologists who evaluate bilingual students understand the distinction between BICS and CALP as well as the importance of accurately assessing a bilingual student's language proficiency during the evaluation process. Given the confusion that can develop regarding the degree to which a student has developed language proficiency in a second language, it is not surprising that psychologists conducting bilingual assessments have been found to overuse English language tests with English language learners who are referred for special education (Klingner et al., 2006). That is, psychologists often fail to appropriately consider students' native language abilities and how the process of learning English is likely to influence students' test scores.

In addition to appropriately considering the role of language, psychologists who conduct thorough, comprehensive bilingual evaluations also engage in the time-intensive process of acquiring relevant background information about their students. When conducting bilingual assessments, psychologists should gather information regarding the previous schooling the student has received, including the type of educational placement (public vs. private), relevant classroom variables (e.g., number of students per class, average educational level of teachers), whether there were disruptions in the student's schooling, and the amount of exposure the student has had to both the first language and the second language. It is also important to examine the student's parents' level of education, literacy level of family members, the language(s) spoken at home, as well as relevant cultural characteristics (Blatchley & Lau, 2010; M. A. Evans, Shaw, & Bell, 2000; Saracho, 2007; Wilkinson, Ortiz, Robertson, & Kushner, 2006). Stressors related to immigration, such as whether the student experienced family separations as a result of immigration, can also affect children's functioning and should be examined (Mitrani, Santisteban, & Muir, 2004). Psychologists must then use this background information to inform decisions made during the assessment process. Furthermore, the bilingual student's assessment results should be considered in light of these factors. Appendix 1.1 provides a checklist for assessing students' background information.

It is important to note that the assessment process that is traditionally used to diagnose learning disabilities falls short both in its attempt to appropriately consider the role of second language learning and in its attempt to adequately consider the role of environmental and institutional factors that may contribute to a student's display of academic concerns (Klingner et al., 2006). It is critical that professionals who assess bilingual students consider the interaction between individual student characteristics and the cultural contexts and environments in which students live. Although challenging, best practice assessment of bilingual students necessitates the consideration and integration of student variables in addition to that of relevant environmental factors.

IMMIGRATION

When assessing bilingual students, it is critical to understand the influence of factors associated with immigration, given that the display of academic difficulties may be directly linked to the student's status as an immigrant. Students who have immigrated to the United States may be unfamiliar with the culture of American schools, and this unfamiliarity can affect their academic performance and success. For example, not having experienced similar educational environments, immigrant students may maintain different expectations for classroom behavior than their native-born peers, and they may not be familiar with the type of formal testing that is conducted in American schools, such as in the use of multiple-choice test items (Solano-Flores, 2008). Furthermore, immigrant students hail from diverse countries, and as a result, their previous schooling experiences may vary and may include interruptions in their formal schooling. These experiences can affect their ability to succeed academically and socially in U.S. schools, often promoting feelings of isolation and low levels of school belonging (Wells, 2009).

It is also important for psychologists evaluating linguistic minority students to understand that the process of immigration can be a challenging and stressful time for bilingual students and their families. In addition to sometimes difficult and dangerous journeys, immigrant families often also experience stress associated with the sudden need to learn a new language, secure employment, and locate housing (Ruiz, Kabler, & Sugarman, 2011). It also can be a difficult process to attain legal status in the United States, and immigrant families who do not attain legal status face a host of additional challenges and difficulties. For example, families who have not achieved legal status are not able to access a number of benefits, which often serves to promote poor health outcomes for immigrants (Ruiz et al., 2011). Psychologists who understand these and other factors associated with immigration will be more likely to appropriately consider how broader environmental influences affect bilingual students' behavior and academic success.

Importantly, U.S. census data reveal that immigration status is associated with poverty status (U.S. Census Bureau, 2010). Specifically, 31.8% of first-generation, foreign-born children and youth live below the poverty level, compared with 27.2% of second-generation children who have at least one foreign-born parent and 18.4% of children who are third generation and higher, which includes those with two native U.S. parents (U.S. Census Bureau, 2010). Furthermore, a relationship has been uncovered between citizenship and poverty status. Data indicate that 26% of families in which both partners are not U.S. citizens are living below the poverty level, compared with 9.9% of families in which both partners are naturalized U.S. citizens (U.S. Census Bureau, 2010). These findings warrant attention given that immigrant students are also at risk of educational difficulties that are associated with low SES, such as lower levels of parental school involvement and decreased access to books and computers (G. W. Evans, 2004). The following case study illustrates the importance of examining factors associated with immigration during the assessment process. Assessment considerations associated with SES are discussed next.

CASE STUDY

Gabriela is an 11-year-old student who has entered fifth grade in a U.S. school[1]. She and her mother recently emigrated from a rural town in El Salvador to a small city in the United States. They left behind

---

[1]The details of the case studies have been changed to protect the confidentiality of the individuals involved.

Gabriela's father, in addition to other extended family members. Gabriela and her mother currently live with her aunt and uncle and three cousins in a small apartment. Gabriela's mother, aunt, and uncle have not achieved legal status in the United States, and they have a difficult time making rent payments each month.

Gabriela's mother has been looking for work in the community and ultimately hopes to move with Gabriela out of her sister's apartment. Although financial resources are scarce, Gabriela's mother is reluctant to access federal assistance such as food stamps or housing assistance for fear of being deported. She hopes to become a U.S. citizen, but she is confused about the steps that she needs to take to attain legal status.

Gabriela's mother has noticed that discussions of deportation are causing significant anxiety for Gabriela. Furthermore, Gabriela often communicates to her mother that she misses her father, who she has not had contact with since she and her mother moved. Gabriela often appears withdrawn and sad. Language barriers, a lack of health insurance, as well as a reluctance to approach public institutions for health care are preventing her mother from accessing mental health services for Gabriela.

Gabriela's previous school experiences consisted of largely unstructured time spent in a class with children of various ages. She is not accustomed to the classroom rules in the American school she attends. She has a difficult time following the teacher's instructions, and she often spends class time worrying about her family. Her teacher has expressed concerns around inattention, noting that Gabriela appears distracted.

A school psychologist knowledgeable about stressors associated with immigration spoke with Gabriela about her family and her experience thus far in a U.S. school. Gabriela communicated the stress and anxiety that she experiences daily. The psychologist recommended that social–emotional supports be put into place.

SOCIOECONOMIC STATUS

SES is a well-established academic risk factor for students, and unfortunately, students learning a second language are more likely to come from low-income and less educated families than students in the general school-age population (Ballantyne, Sanderman, & Levy, 2008). Given these data, professionals assessing bilingual students must take great care in determining whether economic factors distinguish a struggling bilingual student from his or her nonstruggling peers or whether there are other factors at play, such as a true disability (Wilkinson et al., 2006). To appropriately assess bilingual students and make this distinction, it is important to understand the types of academic risks that are associated with low SES and that may affect bilingual students' functioning.

A number of factors associated with low SES may adversely affect students' educational performance. For example, students' access to basic needs is affected by their SES. Specifically, SES can affect a student's access to medical and dental care, healthy food, and reliable housing (Berliner, 2006). Furthermore, many students from low socioeconomic backgrounds live in unstable neighborhood environments that are ridden with violence. These characteristics undoubtedly affect students' feelings of security and may make it difficult for students to focus in the classroom and excel academically (Berliner, 2006).

In addition, research has revealed that in comparison with their high SES peers, children growing up in poverty are less likely to be exposed to cognitively stimulating home environments, less likely to have parents who are involved in their schooling, and less likely to have highly qualified teachers (G. W. Evans, 2004). Not surprisingly, academic outcome data have revealed that children living in households below the poverty threshold exhibit lower levels of proficiency in reading and mathematics than children living at or above the poverty threshold (U.S. Department of Education, National Center for Education Statistics, 2007).

SES is also a key variable to consider during the assessment process because it has been identified as a major contributor to the disproportionate identification of learning disabilities in minority students (Shifrer et al., 2011). Research has reliably demonstrated that students from higher socioeconomic backgrounds are less likely to be in special education than students from lower socioeconomic backgrounds (Samson & Lesaux, 2009; Shifrer et al., 2011). This line of research further emphasized the meaningful impact that SES has on student test performance and, ultimately, on referral and placement in special education. Furthermore, the consistent relationship between sociodemographic characteristics and the display of learning difficulties suggests that social differences may be affecting special education classification more than true learning differences (Shifrer et al., 2011). Given these effects, evaluators have a challenging, yet critical, responsibility to try to tease apart how socioeconomic variables may be affecting their test results. The case study that follows provides an example of the influence of socioeconomic variables.

CASE STUDY

Jon, a middle school student, lives with his mother, stepfather, and two siblings in a small apartment that the family recently moved to. Jon's stepfather has been unable to maintain a stable job, and the family has been forced to move between multiple apartment complexes during the past year. Jon's mother has a high school education, and she currently works two part-time jobs. She is not at home in the afternoons and evenings and hence Jon is responsible for his younger siblings after school each day. He and his siblings spend a significant amount of time each day watching television. The family does not own a computer, and Jon does not have access to many books in the home.

Jon's teacher is concerned about his reading performance. The middle school that he attends has recently adopted a response-to-intervention framework, and progress-monitoring data have revealed that Jon is not progressing at the same rate as his classmates. His teacher hopes to schedule a meeting with his mother to speak about in-home supports that can be put into place to promote Jon's literacy skills (e.g., increased reading at home in English and/or the family's native language). The teacher has had a difficult time connecting with Jon's mother, given the demands of his mother's work schedule. Jon's teacher plans to continue her efforts to speak with his mother. She also plans to implement a small group-reading intervention with Jon and to continue regular progress monitoring.

ACCULTURATION

The process of *acculturation*—defined as change that occurs as a result of contact with a different culture—can affect bilingual students in many complex ways. Rivera (2008) summarized the concept of acculturation as a "dynamic process of change and adaptation that individuals undergo as a result of contact with members of different cultures" (p. 76). The acculturation process affects an individual's attitudes and beliefs and, in turn, affects an individual's functioning within a new culture (Rivera, 2008). Given the complex effects of acculturation, it is critical that professionals who assess bilingual students examine and appropriately consider a student's level of acculturation and how the process of acculturation may be influencing a student's display of academic difficulties.

Examining a student's level of acculturation during the bilingual assessment process provides an indication of how comfortable a student is with the dominant culture, how closely the student identifies with values upheld by members of the dominant culture (Rhodes, Ochoa, & Ortiz, 2005), and the degree to which students have retained their original culture and assimilated into the majority culture (Jacob, Decker, & Hartshorne, 2011). With this information, psychologists have a better understanding of key factors that may be influencing a student's behavior and academic performance. For example, a student who exhibits low levels of acculturation and is unfamiliar with the cultural "rules" of the classroom is likely to experience certain difficulties and challenges. Similarly, given that tests are subject to cultural bias, a student's level of acculturation is likely to affect his or her performance (Blatchley & Lau, 2010). Psychologists can and should use student acculturation data to inform the test selection process, the interpretation of test scores, and future treatment planning (Jacob et al., 2011).

It is also important to acknowledge that the level of acculturation exhibited by a bilingual student's parents may affect the student's functioning (Ruiz et al., 2011). For example, parents may experience stress associated with maintaining cultural beliefs that are incompatible with the mainstream culture, as well as stress caused by the challenges associated with learning a new language (Ruiz et al., 2011). Acculturative stress experienced by bilingual students' parents may also lead to increased levels of family conflict in the home because children often assimilate into U.S. culture at a faster rate than their parents (Smokowski & Bacallao, 2007). Serafica and Vargas (2006) explained that making sense of the apparent discord between native cultural norms and U.S. cultural norms can be a difficult and stressful experience for diverse students and their families.

Psychologists who understand the process of acculturation can support students who are experiencing acculturative stress. They can advocate for appropriate service delivery that reflects a student's level of acculturation. For example, psychologists can design a social skills intervention to assist students who are displaying difficulty socializing with peers. In addition, they can make assessment recommendations that communicate to teachers and other service providers how acculturation is likely to affect a student's functioning within the classroom. The next case study illustrates how acculturation may affect a student's functioning.

CASE STUDY

Asad, an 11-year-old sixth-grade student, is a Somali refugee who has recently moved to the United States. Previously, Asad lived in a refugee camp where basic resources were extremely limited, including access to safe drinking water. Formal schooling was largely unavailable for children at the refugee camp. Furthermore, Asad was repeatedly exposed to violence in his community.

Currently, Asad lives with his parents and sister in a crowded apartment complex in a low-income, diverse neighborhood. His neighborhood is ridden with crime and violence, which often reignites feelings of fear that he experienced in his native country. Asad's parents have had a difficult time securing employment in the United States. Asad's mother had not previously worked outside the home, and she is having a particularly difficult time finding work in her new community.

Adjusting to school in the United States has been challenging for Asad. He has exhibited a number of behavioral problems and has come to the attention of his teachers and a number of school administrators. He displays disruptive behavior in class, which has included a number of violent outbursts. He has had physical altercations with students who tease him about his accent and his clothing. At home, Asad has been getting into frequent disagreements with his parents. His parents feel that he has become less respectful since moving to the United States. The psychologist in Asad's school has been reaching out to cultural brokers who may be able to provide her with additional information about refugee students and ways to support Asad's assimilation into the school community.

LANGUAGE TRANSFER

When assessing bilingual students, it is important for evaluators to be cognizant of the effects of language transfer from a student's native language (L1) to his or her second language (L2). *Language transfer* refers to the use of one language's semantic or syntactic structures (e.g., that of L1) while speaking a different language (Marian & Kaushanskaya, 2007). Language transfer is likely to occur as students learn a new language and rely on their preexisting linguistic knowledge (Paradis, Genesee, & Crago, 2011). However, depending on the similarities between L1 and L2, the influence of L1 can either promote L2 language learning or serve as a source of error (Paradis et al., 2011).

Psychologists working with bilingual students are likely to observe the effects of language transfer from L1 to L2 in their students. For example, Spanish–English bilingual individuals who have learned Spanish first may transfer phonological or pronunciation rules to English, such as saying "estop" rather than "stop" (Paradis et al., 2011). Furthermore, morphological differences, as well as differences in gender markings and word order, exist between Spanish and English and may be observed in Spanish speakers who are learning English (Silliman, Bahr, Brea, Hnath-Chisolm, & Mahecha, 2002). A variety of language transfer effects are observed with different languages, such as morphosyntactic issues for students who know Chinese languages and are learning English, as well as word order rule issues for students who speak Dutch and are learning English as their L2 (Paradis et al., 2011).

It is valuable for psychologists to understand how certain pairs of contact languages are likely to affect one another such that language transfer is interpreted as a function of L2 development as opposed to a manifestation of a disability. By understanding the relationships between certain languages, psychologists can anticipate certain positive or negative transfer effects (Ping & Liow, 2011). Importantly, psychologists who have knowledge of language transfer effects have valuable information regarding the process of L2 development, which can valuably inform the assessment process.

LIMITATIONS OF ASSESSMENT TOOLS

Professionals who assess bilingual students have numerous assessment options available to them; however, given the various limitations associated with each, it is important that they are approached with caution. Commonly used assessment options with students from culturally and linguistically diverse backgrounds include modified testing or altering traditionally used measures, using nonverbal measures, native language testing, and providing standardized traditional assessment measures. The shortcomings associated with each of these assessment options are discussed next.

Psychologists who choose to modify an assessment measure's testing procedures, thus breaking standardization, face certain pitfalls when assessing bilingual students. For example, breaking standardization by rewording questions or providing additional task explanations to bilingual students can ultimately produce test results that are neither valid nor reliable. In addition, psychologists are advised to use caution when using interpreters during the assessment process, given that assessment measures are not standardized with interpreters. Furthermore, the results of the assessment are often compromised by the use of interpreters, given that the training interpreters receive in psychoeducational assessment is variable, interpreters may have previous relationships with bilingual students in communities where few people speak a student's native language (American Educational Research Association, American Psychological Association, & National Council on Measurement in Education, 1999), and some words and concepts may not accurately translate from English to a student's native language (Lopez, 2002). Research suggests that many psychologists who conduct bilingual assessments and use interpreters have not received the training needed to do so and that this has serious implications for service delivery to culturally and linguistically diverse students (O'Bryon & Rogers, 2010). It is critical that psychologists seek out continuing education opportunities and identify and access relevant resources within their communities (e.g., cultural brokers, local experts in bilingual assessment) to improve their skill sets and ability to effectively assess bilingual students.

Another widely used approach to bilingual assessment is the use of nonverbal measures. Although nonverbal tests may be less culturally loaded options for assessing students from culturally and linguistically diverse backgrounds, they are not without their own weaknesses and drawbacks (Blatchley & Lau, 2010). First, it is important to note that nonverbal tests still represent mainstream culture and values. For example, nonverbal tests may rely on the use of pictures or other graphics that are culturally loaded (Mpofu & Ortiz, 2009). Second, nonverbal tests are limited by the fact that they naturally allow for a narrow range of information to be assessed. A third drawback associated with the use of nonverbal measures is that some type of communication and language is inherently necessary during the assessment process—for example, evaluators often must use language to communicate the meaning of gestures that are to be used during the assessment (Mpofu & Ortiz, 2009).

Native language testing provides another potentially limited assessment option when working with bilingual students. For example, native language testing may not be a viable option given that it necessitates the use of examiners who are fluent and trained to assess in the student's L1 (Mpofu & Ortiz, 2009). This becomes a particular issue given the myriad languages spoken by linguistically diverse youth and the shortage of trained bilingual school psychologists. In fact, only 10.7% of practicing school psychologists in the United States speak a language other than English fluently, and only 6.2% provide psychological services in a language other than English (Charvat, 2008). Furthermore, native language testing can be an inappropriate choice during bilingual assessments, given the native language loss that may occur during the process of learning a second language (Mpofu & Ortiz, 2009).

Last, administering standardized assessment measures in a student's L2 can present a number of concerns in terms of the validity of the assessment results. Language factors affect students' understanding of test items and contribute to measurement error variance (Solano-Flores & Trumbull, 2003). Accordingly, research has shown that the performance gap between English language learners and language majority peers is largest in reading (highest language demands) and smallest in math calculation (lowest language demand; Abedi, 2004). Furthermore, the standardization sample may not be representative of the bilingual student who is being assessed, which affects the value and utility of the normative scores that are gathered during the assessment process (Blatchley & Lau, 2010).

Given the aforementioned limitations of assessment tools, it is critical that psychologists avoid using the results of one tool to identify students' strengths and weaknesses and to inform future service delivery. Assessments should be multidimensional and should appropriately consider the student's functioning in multiple contexts, relevant background characteristics, and environmental variables that may be affecting a student's ability to succeed within the educational setting (Blatchley & Lau, 2010).

CONCLUSION

To provide teachers and other service providers with information that can effectively inform instruction and intervention, professionals who assess bilingual students must have the knowledge and skills needed to appropriately assess bilingual students. More important, they must have knowledge and skills that will enable the fair and equitable assessment of bilingual students if high-quality, appropriate educational decisions are to made with their assessment results (Mpofu & Ortiz, 2009). Assessments that purport to examine a student's cognitive or academic abilities, but instead provide a measure of language proficiency or the influence of immigration, acculturation, and low SES, are neither fair nor equitable, and they ultimately provide a biased evaluation of a student's strengths and weaknesses.

It is a psychologist's ethical and professional responsibility to engage in assessment practices that are both fair and equitable (Jacob et al., 2011). These standards for professional competence and training are clearly articulated in the American Psychological Association's (2010) *Ethical Principles of Psychologists and Code of Conduct* (see Standard 2). Furthermore, equitable assessment is truly essential, given that it serves social justice aims by facilitating diverse and often marginalized students' access to appropriate resources within school settings (Mpofu & Ortiz, 2009). Although it can be both a complex and challenging process, equitable bilingual assessment is a critically important process that involves examining bilingual students' functioning through a lens that considers factors within the student and the student's environment.

APPENDIX 1.1: BACKGROUND INFORMATION CHECKLIST

Language proficiency:

- What is the student's language proficiency in his/her native language?
  - Fluent/semifluent/not fluent in (language): _____
    Reading skills: ☐ Beginner ☐ Intermediate ☐ Advanced
    Writing skills: ☐ Beginner ☐ Intermediate ☐ Advanced
    Oral expression: ☐ Beginner ☐ Intermediate ☐ Advanced
    Oral comprehension: ☐ Beginner ☐ Intermediate ☐ Advanced

- What is the student's language proficiency in L2?
  - Fluent/semifluent/not fluent in (language): _____
    Reading skills: ☐ Beginner ☐ Intermediate ☐ Advanced
    Writing skills: ☐ Beginner ☐ Intermediate ☐ Advanced
    Oral expression: ☐ Beginner ☐ Intermediate ☐ Advanced
    Oral comprehension: ☐ Beginner ☐ Intermediate ☐ Advanced

Previous schooling:

- How many years has the child attended U.S. schools?_____
- What type of previous language support has the student received?
  _____
- How many years has the child attended non-U.S. schools?_____
- Were there disruptions in the student's schooling?
  ☐ Yes   ☐ No
  If yes, for how long? _____
- What type of school did the student attend in his or her native country?
  ☐ Private school
  ☐ Public school
- Average number of students per class: _____
- Average educational level of teachers: _____

Home/family characteristics:

- How long have the student's family members been living in the United States: _____
- Are there family members who are still residing in the student's native country?
  ☐ Yes   ☐ No

- Was the student separated from primary caregivers during immigration?
  - ☐ Yes   ☐ No
- Language(s) spoken at home: _____
- Parental level of education:
  - ☐ No formal schooling
  - ☐ Some formal schooling
  - ☐ High school education
  - ☐ College-level education
  - ☐ Post-college level education
  - Parents' literacy skills: _____

REFERENCES

Abedi, J. (2004). The No Child Left Behind Act and English language learners: Assessment and accountability issues. *Educational Researcher, 33*, 4–14. doi:10.3102/0013189X033001004

American Educational Research Association, American Psychological Association, & National Council on Measurement in Education. (1999). *Standards for educational and psychological testing.* Washington, DC: Author.

American Psychological Association. (2010). *Ethical principles of psychologists and code of conduct* (2002, amended June 1, 2010). Retrieved from http://www.apa.org/ethics/code/index.aspx

Ballantyne, K. G., Sanderman, A. R., & Levy, J. (2008). *Educating English language learners: Building teacher capacity.* Retrieved from http://www.ncela.gwu.edu/files/uploads/3/EducatingELLsBuildingTeacherCapacityVol1.pdf

Berliner, D. (2006). Our impoverished view of educational reform. *Teachers College Record, 108*, 949–995. doi:10.1111/j.1467-9620.2006.00682.x

Blatchley, L. A., & Lau, M. Y. (2010). *Culturally competent assessment of English language learners for special education services.* Retrieved from http://www.nasponline.org/publications/cq/pdf/V38N7_CulturallyCompetentAssessment.pdf

Calderón, M., Slavin, R., & Sanchez, M. (2011). Effective instruction for English learners. *The Future of Children, 21*, 103–127. doi:10.1353/foc.2011.0007

Charvat, J. L. (2008). *Fluency and use of languages other than English among school psychologists: Data from the NASP membership survey.* Retrieved from http://www.nasponline.org/advocacy/LanguageFluency_NASPSurvey05.pdf

Cummins, J. (1981). Empirical and theoretical underpinnings of bilingual education. *Journal of Education, 163*, 16–21.

Cummins, J. (1984). *Bilingualism and special education: Issues in assessment and pedagogy.* San Diego, CA: College Hill Press.

Cummins, J. (2000). *Language, power, and pedagogy: Bilingual children in the crossfire.* Clevedon, England: Multilingual Matters.

Evans, G. W. (2004). The environment of childhood poverty. *American Psychologist, 59*, 77–92. doi:10.1037/0003-066X.59.2.77

Evans, M. A., Shaw, D., & Bell, M. (2000). Home literacy activities and their influence on early literacy skills. *Canadian Journal of Experimental Psychology/Revue canadienne de psychologie expérimentale, 54*, 65–75. doi:10.1037/h0087330

Jacob, S., Decker, D. M., & Hartshorne, T. S. (2011). *Ethics and law for school psychologists* (6th ed.). Hoboken, NJ: Wiley.

Klingner, J. K., Artiles, A. J., & Barletta, L. M. (2006). English language learners who struggle with reading: Language acquisition or LD? *Journal of Learning Disabilities, 39*, 108–128. doi:10.1177/00222194060390020101

Klingner, J. K., & Harry, B. (2006). The special education referral and decision-making process for English language learners: Child study team meetings and placement conferences. *Teachers College Record, 108,* 2247–2281. doi:10.1111/j.1467-9620.2006.00781.x

Lopez, E. C. (2002). Best practices in working with school interpreters to deliver psychological services to children and families. In A. Thomas & J. Grimes (Eds.), *Best practices in school psychology IV* (pp. 1419–1432). Washington, DC: National Association of School Psychologists.

Marian, V., & Kaushanskaya, M. (2007). Cross-linguistic transfer and borrowing in bilinguals. *Applied Psycholinguistics, 28,* 369–390. doi:10.1017/S014271640707018X

Mitrani, V. B., Santisteban, D. A., & Muir, J. A. (2004). Addressing immigration-related separations in Hispanic families with a behavior-problem adolescent. *American Journal of Orthopsychiatry, 74,* 219–229. doi:10.1037/0002-9432.74.3.219

Mpofu, E., & Ortiz, S. O. (2009). Equitable assessment practices in diverse contexts. In E. L. Griorenko (Ed.), *Multicultural psychoeducational assessment* (pp. 41–76). New York, NY: Springer.

National Council of Teachers of English. (2008). *English language learners: A policy research brief produced by the National Council of Teachers of English.* Retrieved from http://www.ncte.org/library/nctefiles/resources/policyresearch/ell researchbrief.pdf

O'Bryon, E. C., & Rogers, M. R. (2010). Bilingual school psychologists' assessment practices with English language learners. *Psychology in the Schools, 47,* 1018–1034. doi:10.1002/pits.20521

Paradis, J., Genesee, F., & Crago, M. B. (Eds.). (2011). *Dual language development and disorders: A handbook on bilingualism and second language learning.* Baltimore, MD: Paul H. Brooks.

Ping, S. W., & Liow, S. J. R. (2011). Morphophonemic transfer in English second language learners. *Bilingualism: Language and Cognition, 14,* 423–432. doi:10.1017/S1366728910000283

Rhodes, R. L., Ochoa, S. H., & Ortiz, S. O. (2005). *Assessing culturally and linguistically diverse students: A practical guide.* New York, NY: Guilford Press.

Rivera, L. M. (2008). Acculturation and multicultural assessment: Issues, trends, and practice. In L. A. Suzuki & J. G. Ponterrotto (Eds.), *Handbook of multicultural assessment: Clinical, psychological, and educational applications* (3rd ed., pp. 73–91). San Francisco, CA: Wiley.

Ruiz, M., Kabler, B., & Sugarman, M. (2011). *Understanding the plight of immigrant and refugee students.* Retrieved from http://www.nasponline.org/publications/cq/39/5/understandingtheplight.aspx

Samson, J. F., & Lesaux, N. K. (2009). Language-minority learners in special education: Rates and predictors of identification for services. *Journal of Learning Disabilities, 42,* 148–162. doi:10.1177/0022219408326221

Saracho, O. N. (2007). Hispanic families as facilitators of their children's literacy development. *Journal of Hispanic Higher Education, 6*, 103–117. doi:10.1177/1538192706299009

Serafica, F. C., & Vargas, L. A. (2006). Cultural diversity in the development of child psychopathology. In D. Ciccetti & D. K. Cohen (Eds.), *Developmental psychopathology: Vol. 1. Theory and method* (pp. 588–626). Hoboken, NJ: Wiley.

Shifrer, D., Muller, C., & Callahan, R. (2011). Disproportionality and learning disabilities: Parsing apart race, socioeconomic status, and language. *Journal of Learning Disabilities, 44*, 246–257. doi:10.1177/0022219410374236

Shin, H. B., & Kominski, R. A. (2010). *Language use in the United States: 2007. American survey reports.* Retrieved from http://www.census.gov/hhes/socdemo/language/data/acs/ACS-12.pdf

Silliman, E. R., Bahr, R. H., Brea, M. R., Hnath-Chisolm, T., & Mahecha, N. R. (2002). Spanish and English proficiency in the linguistic encoding of mental states in narrative retellings. *Linguistics and Education, 13*, 199–234. doi:10.1016/S0898-5898(01)00062-6

Smokowski, P. R., & Bacallao, M. L. (2007). Acculturation, internalizing mental health symptoms, and self-esteem: Cultural experiences of Latino adolescents in North Carolina. *Child Psychiatry and Human Development, 37*, 273–292. doi:10.1007/s10578-006-0035-4

Solano-Flores, G. (2008). Who is given tests in what language by whom, when, and where? The need for probabilistic views of language in the testing of English language learners. *Educational Researcher, 37*, 189–199. doi:10.3102/0013189X08319569

Solano-Flores, G., & Trumbull, E. (2003). Examining language in context: The need for new research and practice paradigms in the testing of English-language learners. *Educational Researcher, 32*, 3–13. doi:10.3102/0013189X032002003

U.S. Census Bureau. (2010). *Characteristics of the foreign-born population by nativity and U.S. citizenship status.* Retrieved from http://www.census.gov/population/foreign/data/cps2010.html

U.S. Department of Education, National Center for Education Statistics. (2007). *The condition of education 2007.* Washington, DC: U.S. Government Printing Office.

Wells, R. (2009). Segregation and immigration: An examination of school composition for children of immigrants. *Equity & Excellence in Education, 42*, 130–151. doi:10.1080/10665680902779853

Wilkinson, C. Y., Ortiz, A. A., Robertson, P. M., & Kushner, M. I. (2006). English language learners with reading-related LD: Linking data from multiple sources to make eligibility determinations. *Journal of Learning Disabilities, 39*, 129–141. doi:10.1177/00222194060390020201

I

INSIGHTS FROM NEUROSCIENCE AND COGNITIVE PSYCHOLOGY ON CROSS-LANGUAGE TRANSFER

2

CROSS-LANGUAGE TRANSFER IN BILINGUAL STUDENTS

YANLING ZHOU, XIUHONG TONG, JIANHONG MO,
AND CATHERINE McBRIDE-CHANG

Transfer as a learning mechanism has been studied for more than a century (e.g., Brown & Kane, 1988; Thorndike, 1913). Thorndike (1913) concluded that transfer of learning takes place when the original learning situation and the transfer situation share "identical elements." Initially, transfer was regarded as the ability to identify these shared elements and apply them to novel but related situations. Brown and Kane (1988) argued that what is important for transfer is the mastering of "underlying commonalities." They demonstrated that even 3- and 4-year-old preschool children could develop analogous solutions to solve problems that share commonalities in terms of deeper relational features but that differ in terms of surface features. As such, Brown and Kane's definition of transfer therefore emphasized acquisition and awareness of implicit structures.

We are grateful to the Research Grants Council of the Hong Kong Special Administrative Region (project reference: 451811) for support of this research.

http://dx.doi.org/10.1037/14320-003
Assessing Bilingual Children in Context: An Integrated Approach, A. B. Clinton (Editor)

Among linguists, there is not a unanimous definition for the term *transfer* in second language acquisition studies (see Corder, 1983, for a review; Odlin, 1989). Corder (1983) argued that transfer evolves "from the mental structure which is the implicit knowledge of the mother tongue to the separate and independently developing knowledge of the target language" (p. 92). The emphasis on implicit knowledge of the mother tongue is the key in second language transfer, whereas little is mentioned about any possible reverse influence from the target language to the mother tongue. In contrast, Odlin (1989) regarded transfer as mere "influence resulting from similarities and differences between the target language and any other language that has been previously acquired" (p. 27). This definition implies more flexibility than the first one. That is, Odlin argued that, indeed, the target language can influence the mother tongue. Because both similarities and differences of the target language and the previously acquired language are included in the transfer process, there can be both positive and negative influences (Gass & Selinker, 1992). This chapter, however, focuses primarily on specific aspects of positive transfer in second language learning (L2).

Taken together, the Corder (1983) and Odlin (1989) definitions suggest that transfer in L2 acquisition during childhood takes place when children start to make use of the implicit linguistic structure shared by both their mother tongue and the target language. Children apply their implicit knowledge of linguistic structures as they acquire L2. In the process, they also reinforce the target language, or their previously learned native language (L1).

This definition of language transfer in childhood as a reciprocal process emphasizes three important features that are discussed in this chapter. First, transfer in L2 acquisition can be bidirectional. The underlying implicit linguistic knowledge can be used in L2 learning but can also strengthen the L1, given that both languages share a particular feature. Second, implicit linguistic knowledge goes beyond perceptual similarities. Some metalinguistic skills, such as word awareness, syntactic awareness, and phonological and morphological awareness, that facilitate language learning but are not constrained by different orthographies exert a positive learning influence. Third, oral language and reading development cannot truly be separated during the L2 acquisition process in childhood. Therefore, in addition to providing some new evidence from neuroimaging studies to support the view of cross-linguistic transfer, this chapter concerns three areas of implicit language knowledge related to both oral and written language development in L2 acquisition: phonological awareness, morphological awareness, and orthographic awareness.

Phonological awareness skills can be defined as metalinguistic skills that enable learners to be both sensitive to and able to manipulate phonological units (Wagner & Torgesen, 1987). *Morphological awareness* is defined as the ability to reflect on and manipulate *morphemes*, the smallest phonological unit that carries meaning, and to use word formation rules in a language (Carlisle, 1995). *Orthographic processing skills* refer to those abilities that "form, store and access orthographic representations" (Stanovich & West, 1989, p. 402) or efficiently recognize visual patterns in one's language.

PHONOLOGICAL AWARENESS TRANSFER

Learning to read requires mastery of the process of mapping speech sounds to *print*, or graphic representations in the form of symbols and letters. Across different languages, including both alphabetic and nonalphabetic languages, phonological awareness skills play an important role in this mapping process (Anthony & Francis, 2005; Ho & Bryant, 1997; Hu & Catts, 1993; Lafrance & Gottardo, 2005; Luk & Bialystok, 2008; McBride-Chang, Bialystok, Chong, & Li, 2004; Stahl & Murray, 1994; Ziegler & Goswami, 2006). Phonological awareness skills at the syllable and onset-rime levels are involved in the child's development of a foundation for mapping speech to print in the majority of languages (Ziegler & Goswami, 2005). Syllable and onset-rime skills tend to develop prior to phoneme awareness skills, the latter typically being acquired through formal literacy instruction. Phoneme awareness skills are relevant to learning both transparent languages, such as Spanish, German, and Italian, which have rather consistent grapheme–phoneme correspondences, and learning more opaque alphabetic languages such as English, which has much less consistent grapheme–phoneme correspondences (Ziegler & Goswami, 2006).

Transfer of phonological awareness skills has been extensively examined between L1 and L2 alphabetic language pairs. Phonological awareness skills at the syllable, onset-rime, and phoneme levels appear to transfer across transparent and opaque alphabetic languages depending on the similarity of their phonological systems (Cárdenas-Hagan, Carlson, & Pollard-Durodola, 2007; Sparks, Patton, Ganschow, Humbach, & Javorsky, 2008; Verhoeven, 2007). A majority of studies have found strong associations among phonological awareness skills at all levels (Cárdenas-Hagan et al., 2007; Durgunoğlu, 2002; Sparks et al., 2008; Sparks, Patton, Ganschow, & Humbach, 2009; Verhoeven, 2007). A meta-analysis by Melby-Lervåg and Lervåg (2011) found that among 47 studies that have examined transfer effects between L1 and L2, phonological awareness combined with decoding skills showed major transfer effects across alphabetic languages. Some intervention studies have even demonstrated that training of phonological awareness skills in one language can significantly enhance children's L2 phonological awareness skills and, therefore, improve decoding skills in both languages (Durgunoğlu, Nagy, Hancin-Bhatt, 1993).

For example, Korean Hangul is an alphabetic language that has 14 basic consonants (C) and 10 basic vowels (V), which have distinct visual features. Korean syllables have simple sound structures including CV and CVC, and most Korean words have one to three syllables. The word *tea* in Korean is 차, which consists of phonemes ㅊ as a consonant *ch* and ㅏ as a vowel *a*. The similar phonological and orthographical structures to that of English make Korean children with rich L1 experiences able to transfer the awareness that phonemes are manipulable and separable within an English syllable or syllables in a similar way to that in their L1. Indeed, in Kang's (2012) study, she found that Korean children's L1 phonological awareness significantly correlated with English phonological awareness skills and English pseudoword reading.

However, for nonalphabetic languages such as Chinese, phonological awareness at the phoneme level has a relatively minimal influence on Chinese word reading (e.g., Gottardo, Chiappe, Yan, Siegel, & Gu, 2006; McBride-Chang et al., 2004; McBride-Chang, Cheung, Chow, Chow, & Choi, 2006; McBride-Chang & Ho, 2000), although phonological awareness skills at the syllable, onset-rime, and lexical tone levels make important contributions to reading Chinese words (e.g., Chow, McBride-Chang, & Burgess, 2005; Ho & Bryant, 1997; McBride-Chang & Kail, 2002; McBride-Chang, Tong, Shu, Wong, Leung, & Tardif, 2008; Shu, Peng, & McBride-Chang, 2008; Siok & Fletcher, 2001; Yin et al., 2011).

The phonological system of the Chinese language can be characterized as *morphosyllabic:* The sound-to-print mapping occurs at the syllable-to-character level. Further analysis at the phoneme level is therefore not required in the process of learning to read Chinese characters or words. Huang and Hanley (1995) compared the phonological correlates of English and Chinese in native-speaking children. They found that although English phoneme awareness contributed uniquely to English word reading in native English-speaking children, Chinese phoneme awareness did not contribute to Chinese word reading but had a relatively strong association with vocabulary knowledge. McBride-Chang and her colleagues (2008) partly replicated these results and further demonstrated that, even within the same group of children from Hong Kong, phoneme awareness was salient to reading English words whereas phonological awareness sensitivity at the lexical tone level is vital in Chinese character recognition. These empirical findings suggest that phonological awareness skills were important to both English and Chinese word reading, but at different levels.

A focus on Chinese children learning an L2 that is an alphabetic language has demonstrated transfer of phonological awareness skills predominantly at the syllable and onset-rime awareness levels (Gottardo, Yan, Siegel, & Wade-Woolley, 2001; Wang, Perfetti, & Liu, 2005). Although Chinese phoneme awareness skills tend not to be particularly important for reading Chinese characters or words—particularly for Chinese, children from Hong Kong are taught Chinese in a "whole language" approach without phonological coding systems, such as *Pinyin* or *Zhu-Yin-Fu-Hao*—phoneme awareness skills have been shown to be transferable to reading English words for children whose L1 is Chinese (McBride-Chang et al., 2008). Chinese phoneme awareness skills are particularly well-developed in Chinese societies such as mainland China and Taiwan where phonological coding systems (Pinyin and Zhu-Yin-Fu-Hao, respectively) are used to teach Chinese characters to children (Chen & Yuen, 1991; Huang & Hanley, 1997; Lin et al., 2010; McBride-Chang et al., 2004).

A typical Pinyin or Zhu-Yin-Fu-Hao syllable is composed of an onset, a coda, and a lexical tone. In Mandarin Chinese there are four tones, whereas Cantonese has six to nine tones. A change of lexical tone for a particular syllable alters the meaning of the syllable completely. Training in Pinyin or Zhu-Yin-Fu-Hao helps unpack phonological units at the syllable, onset-rime, tone, and phoneme levels (Lin et al., 2010). Even the lexical tone level, which is unique to the Chinese language, has been found to have strong correlations with English pseudoword reading (Wang et al., 2005). Wang and colleagues (2005) interpreted their findings to mean that general auditory processing skills facilitate lexical tone awareness transfer to English pseudoword reading. Therefore, it can be surmised that strengthening phonological awareness at all levels, which is important for L1 learning, may have a significant influence on L2 learning.

This, however, raises questions for alphabetic readers who learn to speak and read Chinese as a second language. There is little research about phonological awareness transfer in alphabetic learners learning nonalphabetic languages as an L2. In a cross-cultural study (McBride-Chang et al., 2004), Chinese children from Xi'an with Pinyin training demonstrated significantly stronger phoneme awareness skills in both Chinese and English than Hong Kong children who did not have Pinyin training. Although phoneme awareness skills were not significant predictors of Chinese word reading, they were highly correlated with English word reading in both groups of Chinese children.

MORPHOLOGICAL AWARENESS TRANSFER

In alphabetic languages, research has mainly focused on three types of morphological structures: compounding, inflectional, and derivational. In English, all three types of word formation rules make morphologically complex words (Carlisle, 2003). *Inflections* usually change a word's grammatical nature (e.g., *writes* is the present tense of *write*). *Derivations* often create new meanings from a base word using a suffix or affix. For example, *painter* derives from *paint*, which has a different meaning. Compared with inflections and derivations, *compounds* are less common in the English language. They are usually the combination of two base words—for example, *barefoot* and *sleepwalk*. Accordingly, morphological awareness itself can be measured from three aspects: awareness of compounds, inflections, and derivations.

The prevalence of these three aspects of morphology is quite different in alphabetic languages as compared with Chinese. Inflections and derivations, which are the main word formation methods in alphabetic languages, are not as frequent as in the Chinese language. However, Chinese has a high frequency of compounding words. For example, *television* is 电视 (*diàn shì*) in Chinese; its literal translation would be *electronic* (电) *vision* (视). Similarly, *battery* in Chinese is 电池 (*diàn chí*)—*electric pool*—whereas *computer* is 电脑 (*diàn nǎo*) or *electronic brain* in Chinese.

Over 75% of words are formed through two or three character compounding words in Chinese; there are few inflectional and derivational words in the language overall (Kuo & Anderson, 2006). The few inflectional examples include morphemes such as 了 or *lè* (equivalent to *ed* in English, indicating past tenses) and 着 or *zhe* (equivalent to *ing* in English, indicating present tense). For example the morpheme 吃 or *chī* means *eat* in English, whereas 吃了 or *chī le* means *ate* or *have eaten*. The morpheme 着 or *zhe* usually comes after verbs as well. For example, 听 or *ting* means *listen* in English, and 听着 or *ting zhe* means *listening*. It may appear to be similar to the inflectional words (e.g., work, worked, working) in English, but these morphemes serve as only grammatical markers in a sentence; they do not affect the morpheme structure of verbs. Thus, such variant linguistic features across languages create a challenge of comparing morphological awareness between Chinese and alphabetic languages.

Chinese is thought to obey the *grapheme–morpheme rule* (Kuo & Anderson, 2008). Virtually every character, the individual written unit in Chinese, plays the role of a morpheme. In 1997, Shu and Anderson proposed that written Chinese has two levels of morphological structure: the radical level and the character level, and each character is also an individual morpheme that has a pronunciation attached to it. The *radical* is a unique component in Chinese script. There are two kinds of radicals, phonetic and semantic, within a Chinese character. *Semantic radicals* imply the meaning of characters, whereas *phonetic radicals* provide some cues to characters' pronunciation.

Although semantic radicals can be seen as the smallest meaning unit in the Chinese orthography, they are not associated with a pronunciation. For example, the semantic radical ⺌ usually indicates that a character means a kind of plant, so the character 花 *huā* means *flower* in English, and the character 草 *cǎo* means *grass* in English. The most significant distinction is that semantic radical information, in itself, is insufficient for character recognition. In other words, it is impossible to get the meaning of the whole character by merely deriving the meaning of the semantic radical of the character. The role of the semantic radical is quite limited, typically just signaling the semantic category or a physical attribute of the referent of the character. For example, a character with a 钅 radical usually is a kind of metal or something made of metal.

Indeed, compounding morphology is an area in which Chinese and alphabetic languages (mainly English) share similarity in word formation. Also, it has been established that compound awareness is a significant predictor of literacy development among Chinese children in monolingual studies (Pasquarella, Chen, Lam, Luo, & Ramirez, 2011). Thus, compound awareness could be chosen as a window to examine the transfer effect between Chinese and English. Roughly speaking, such transfer could happen at two levels: first, directly through association of morphological awareness in L1 and morphological awareness in L2 and, second, through the impact of L1 morphological awareness on L2 reading and L2 morphological awareness on L1 (e.g., McBride-Chang et al., 2006; Wang, Chen, & Cheng, 2006; Wang, Yang, & Cheng, 2009; Zhang, Anderson, Li, Dong, Wu, & Zhang, 2010).

To date, a few studies have been conducted on morphological awareness transfer between Chinese and English. These studies yielded positive results on Chinese–English compound morphological transfer. One of the first quasi-experimental studies to test cross-language transfer of compound morphological awareness studied native Chinese-speaking children learning English (Zhang et al., 2010). Zhang and his colleagues (2010) demonstrated a bidirectional cross-language transfer of L1 and L2 compound morphological awareness. In this study, children were given instructions in both Chinese and English compound morphology as interventions. Children learned that noun, verb, and particle are the form classes of morpheme constituents and that there are four basic types of compound structures: noun + noun (e.g., 风扇, or *fēng shàn*, literally meaning *wind fan*), verb + particle (e.g., 坐下, or *zuò xià*, meaning *sit down*), verb + noun (e.g., 读书, or *dú shū*, literally meaning *read books*), and noun + verb (e.g., 目睹, or *mù dǔ*, meaning *eye witness*). Through activities such as compound structure match, compound structure oddity, and classification and production, these children experienced how morphemes can be manipulated in word formation and the significance of change of morpheme in change of word meanings. As a result, they were more aware of this structure in both languages, and that facilitated their reading abilities in both languages.

In contrast, Wang and her colleagues (Wang, Cheng, & Chen, 2006, 2009) demonstrated reverse transfer of morphological awareness but no straightforward transfer of English compound morphological awareness to Chinese character reading and reading comprehension in a sample of young Chinese immigrant children in the United States. This remained true even after controlling for vocabulary and phonological awareness in Chinese. This result was consistent with previous findings showing that Chinese morphological awareness explained unique variance in Chinese vocabulary but not in English vocabulary, suggesting limited or no transfer of compound awareness for Chinese L1 children learning English as their L2 (McBride-Chang et al., 2006). One possible explanation for this finding is that reading in Chinese requires more compound awareness than does reading in English. Thus, it may be easier to detect transfer of compound awareness from English to Chinese than in reverse. Some studies have also included derivational awareness, but the results suggest no cross-language transfer effect, given the rare occurrence of derivational morphology in Chinese (Wang, Cheng, & Chen, 2006).

Discrepancies in results across studies of morphological transfer between L1 and L2 can be considered from several perspectives. First, the groups sometimes differed by sample. For example, in a study of Chinese bilingual individuals (Zhang et al., 2010), all the participants were from mainland China and had limited exposure to English learning environments. Indeed, the researchers mentioned this limitation in explaining why reverse transfer was restricted by language proficiency in L2. In contrast, another study of Chinese bilingual individuals (Wang, Cheng, Chen, 2006) recruited participants who were immigrant children immersed in an English-speaking environment. Thus, the reverse transfer may have been due to the rapid increasing resources of the L2. In fact, it is possible that the L2 became their dominant language as a result of the intensive L2 language environment. So for this sample group, the morphological awareness transfer from a strong language to a weak language is consistently more obvious and easier to detect.

ORTHOGRAPHIC AWARENESS TRANSFER

Orthographic processing is another important step for a learner to map sounds onto script for different languages. For alphabetic languages, the mapping between sounds to script can take place at the phoneme level as well as at the syllable, rime, and word levels. During the process of literacy acquisition, children gradually master certain patterns of letter combinations, which can always be possible in their written language (e.g., in English, *at* in *fat* or *nat*) even when these combinations are embedded in fake words. Children also recognize letter combinations that are not possible in their language (e.g., in English, the letters *aa* or *fg* cannot be placed immediately adjacent to one another in a word). The sensitivity to such conventions—that is, how letters are configured for an alphabetic language—can therefore be regarded as orthographic awareness (Vellutino, Fletcher, Snowling, & Scanlon, 2004).

Orthographic processing develops from the earliest stages of literacy acquisition (e.g., Thompson, Cottrell, & Fletcher-Flinn, 1996) and continuously influences reading acquisition in later stages of development (Barker, Torgesen, & Wagner, 1992; Bowey & Muller, 2005). Some researchers have argued that orthographic processing skills develop from exposure to print and are, therefore, independent from phonological processing (Cunningham, Perry, & Stanovich, 2001). Indeed, children's awareness of sublexical relations between orthography and phonology are already established prior to formal literacy acquisition because of their early exposure and experience with printed words (Thompson et al., 1996). They can transfer such orthographic skills in learning new words, and this self-teaching process is more apparent during silent reading (Cunningham, Perry, Stanovich, & Share, 2002; de Jong & Share, 2007). Others argue that orthographic processing is closely intertwined with phonological processing (Savage, Deault, Daki, & Aouad, 2011; Savage & Stuart, 2001; Sprenger-Charolles, Siegel, Béchennec & Serniclaes, 2003). Once formal literacy acquisition starts it seems difficult to entirely disentangle orthographic processing from phonological processing because of the nature of phoneme–grapheme mapping for alphabetic languages.

Transfer of orthographic awareness between alphabetic languages is relatively transparent (Commissaire, Duncan, & Casalis, 2011; Deacon & Cain, 2011; Sun-Alperin & Wang, 2011). At least to a certain extent, these languages share certain cognates that provide significant orthographic cues for learning a second language (Brenders, van Hell, & Dijkstra, 2011). Fashola, Drum, Mayer, and Kang (1996) analyzed English spelling errors of native Spanish-speaking children and found that children rely on their knowledge of native language Spanish orthography in attempting to spell English words. This demonstrates the influence of the orthography of one's first language (Spanish) on a related second language (English).

Deacon and Cain (2011) reached similar conclusions by examining the impact of native English children's orthographic skills on second language French learning. Commissaire et al. (2011) found that among native French-speaking children who learned English as a second language, the transfer of orthographic skills remained at the word level but did reach the sublexical level. This demonstrates that orthographic processing is not parallel to phonological processing. Even though transfer is at the word level, this reflects some similarity between the two orthographies. It could also be argued that as both languages are relatively opaque in terms of spelling, children might adopt a more holistic approach rather than an analytical one

(Ziegler & Goswami, 2005) in reading the two orthographies. Particularly, because English is the most opaque Indo–European language in the language spectrum, the grapheme–phoneme decoding strategies are not efficient for reading English words such as *knock* or *yacht*.

Other than learning the sublexical strategies in reading words, English children also learn to master orthographic skills in recognizing whole words and for letter sequences such as onsets and rhymes (Goswami, Ziegler, Dalton, & Schneider, 2001). Because German and English share many cognates and come from the same language family, German children can already transfer some German orthographic skills into reading English words automatically and then gradually developing their orthographic skills in reading words that are unique to English orthography. Thus, German children who learn to read English as a second language may apply similar orthographic skills in reading English words.

Evidence for orthographic transfer between two alphabetic languages from distinct language families has been in many ways inconclusive. Research that directly examined the associations of orthographic skills of two unrelated alphabetic languages, such as Russian and English (Abu Rabia, 2001), Persian and English (Arab-Moghaddam & Senechal, 2001), and Korean and English (Wang, Park, & Lee, 2006), found no orthographic awareness transfer. However, other studies identified moderately strong associations between L1 orthographic awareness—even to the point of predicting L2 (usually English)—on tasks of pseudoword reading and spelling (Abu-Rabia & Siegel, 2002). Abu-Rabia and Siegel (2002) argued that it is the similar grapheme–phoneme mapping rules that underlie reading Arabic and English, for example, that make the orthographic transfer possible. It seems that in the case of two unrelated alphabetic languages, orthographic awareness transfer should be possible because all alphabetic languages share the same phoneme–grapheme mapping rules.

As a nonalphabetic language, however, Chinese orthographic awareness usually refers to one's sensitivity to conventions of how characters are configured by radicals (Leong, 2011). The majority of Chinese characters are composed of phonological and semantic radicals. Many of these radicals have distinct visual features that can, however, readily be confused with a similar looking radical. For example, the character 汤 (*tāng* in Pinyin, or *soup* in English) and the character 场 (*hǎng* in Pinyin, or *field* or *stage* in English) share the same radical on the right side, but on the left side the two radicals are different. Another example is that for the character 目 (*mù* in Pinyin, which means *eye* in English): Inside the square shape there are two horizontal lines, but sometimes children erroneously perceive three horizontal lines. Children's recognition of individual characters and words are, therefore, vitally important to reading in any language. Their orthographic awareness in Chinese may be measured by identifying legal and illegal radicals, radical combinations, and orthographic awareness; all of these skills have been found to be predictive of Chinese character and word reading even after controlling for phonological awareness and morphological awareness (Tong, McBride-Chang, Shu, & Wong, 2009).

Similar results were found in Korean children who learn English as an L2 (Wang, Park, & Lee, 2006). In this research, Korean children's orthographic skills assessed through orthographic legality judgment tasks in both L1 Korean and L2 English were significant predictors of word reading in the two languages. Orthographic skills also explained greater variances than did phonological skills in English word reading. Although Korean is an alphabetic language, its orthography is visually distinct from English. Though orthographic skills in the two languages were not correlated in any way, they had significant impact on word reading of both L1 and L2.

However, similar orthographic awareness transfer between Chinese and English was not identified and remains to be further delineated. The studies that have examined orthographic transfer between Chinese and English in children have used orthographic sensitivity tasks (Wang et al., 2005, 2009). Children were also asked to identify the legality of the radical position and the radical form for Chinese and to identify possible legal words from a list of English language pseudowords. No associations between the orthographic skills across languages have been found. In addition, orthographic awareness skills in Chinese did not explain English real or pseudoword reading.

Wang and Geva (2003), by examining lexical and orthographic processing in spelling of L1 Chinese children learning English, found that Chinese children learning English as their L2 and L1 English-speaking children performed similarly on spelling real words but not pseudowords. They suggested that such a phenomenon reflected both positive and negative transfer of orthographic skills. Although Chinese children learning English as an L2 applied orthographic cues in spelling real words, they lacked a phonological route for spelling pseudowords. Similarly, another study by Li, McBride-Chang, Wong, and Shu (2012) examined orthographic transfer in Chinese–English bilingual children and identified strong associations between Chinese and English spelling. They argued that such an orthographic transfer effect may have resulted from the "look and say" method or "whole language" approach to word learning for both Chinese and English. Such transfer may entail other cognitive skills, including memory, within orthographic processes particularly because Chinese children typically learn Chinese characters by rote learning. This process itself may facilitate orthographic memory for L2.

Although some have argued that orthographic patterns are language specific (Durgunoğlu, 2002), orthographic transfer may actually involve two layers. Transfer of orthographic awareness might not be based solely on the similarities of orthographic forms across two languages. Rather, children's understanding and sense of legal and illegal orthographic features for one language might prompt them to detect and capture the legal and illegal orthographic trends for an L2. During the language learning process, orthographic awareness might remind them to actively sensitize orthographic information for the language, no matter whether it is the general principles of sound and print mapping or orthographic memory that is trained from learning L1.

MORPHOLOGICAL, PHONOLOGICAL, AND ORTHOGRAPHIC ASPECTS OF LANGUAGE TRANSFER

Phonological, morphological, and orthographic awareness skills are important basic reading-related skills that play a significant role in the bilingual student's L2 language and reading development because it is usually the case that L2 students learn to read at the same time as they develop their oral language skills. The three aspects of language transfer form a solid base for word reading. Phonological and morphological awareness skills can be developed through oral language acquisition, and these skills prepare children to later learn to map phonological units onto orthography. The development of orthographic awareness skills also facilitates the mapping process in learning to read.

The three aspects of language transfer may be more direct between languages that share similar language roots (e.g., English–German or French–English) than those language pairs that are from distinct language families (e.g., Arabic–English, Chinese–English, Korean–English). However, the transfer of these metalinguistic skills between the unassociated languages is disputed. Perhaps it may be particularly important for educators to recognize and make use of these potential transferrable skills in children in the process of L2 language acquisition.

BRAIN ACTIVATION IN THE BILINGUAL CHILD

This review was focused primarily on phonological, orthographic, and morphological transfer between languages in children, with particular attention to Chinese, a logographic language, as L1 and English, an alphabetic script, as L2. In this final section of the chapter, we briefly review another fundamental question: How do bilingual individuals organize two (written) languages in their brain? For example, are the two languages represented in separate neural networks or in an overlapping brain region? In the past half-century, a large number of neuroimaging and neurophysiological investigations have been conducted using a variety of techniques such as event-related potentials, positron emission tomography (PET), magnetic resonance imaging, and functional magnetic resonance imaging (fMRI). These investigations have used tasks (e.g., word generation, word translation, semantic judgment, semantic categorization, picture naming, lexical decision, semantic or syntactic acceptance) relating to whole language performance, including phonological, semantic, and syntactic processes, to examine the issue of whether two languages are represented in common or distinct cortical areas in bilingual individuals. The results to date are quite mixed.

A majority of studies have suggested that the two languages spoken by bilingual individuals activate common brain regions, irrespective of the age at which learners begin to acquire L2 (Briellmann et al., 2004; Frenck-Mestre, Anton, Roth, Vaid, & Viallet, 2005; Gandour et al., 2007; Halsband, Krause, Sipilä, Teräs, & Laihinen, 2002; Hasegawa, Carpenter, & Just, 2002; Hernandez, Martinez, & Kohnert, 2000; Illes et al., 1999; Klein, Milner, Zatorre, Meyer, & Evans, 1995; Klein, Milner, Zatorre, Zhao, & Nikelski, 1999; Klein, Watkins, Zatorre, & Milner, 2006; Klein, Zatorre, Milner, Meyer, & Evans, 1994; Mahendra, Plante, Magloire, Milman, & Trouard, 2003; Perani et al., 1998; Yokoyama et al., 2006). In a PET study using semantic and phonological tasks with French–English bilingual individuals, common activations were observed in the left inferior frontal gyrus for both L1 and L2 (Klein et al., 1995). Similarly, overlapping activation in the frontal lobe region for L1 and L2 in Spanish–English bilingual individuals completing semantic versus nonsemantic decision tasks was reported in an fMRI study (Illes et al., 1999). Perani et al. (1998), using PET analyses during a story comprehension task, found that fluent Italian–English and Spanish–Catalán bilingual individuals showed nearly identical activations for L1 and L2. For bilingual individuals who speak Indo–European languages (e.g., English, Spanish, French), it may not be surprising that L1 and L2 shared common cortical areas when considering the similar structural properties between Indo–European languages.

Interestingly, studies of Chinese–English bilingual individuals, in spite of the remarkably different orthography, phonology, and syntax of the two languages, also found similar patterns of cortical activation for L1 and L2 (Chee, Soon, & Lee, 2003; Chee, Tan, & Thiel, 1999; Chee et al., 2000; Pu et al., 2001; Xue, Dong, Jin, Zhang, & Wang, 2004). Using an fMRI measure, Chee et al. (1999) examined the cortical organization of language of both early and late Mandarin–English bilingual individuals using a word stem completion task. They found that in both languages, activations were observed in the prefrontal, temporal, and parietal regions, as well as the supplementary motor area of the brain. Chee and colleagues further observed that early and late bilingual individuals presented a similar pattern of over-lapping activations. Thus, Chee and colleagues suggested that common corti-cal areas are activated among fluent Mandarin–English bilingual individuals in a cued word generation task, irrespective of age of acquisition of either language. Similarly, using a PET measure, Klein et al. (1999) found that flu-ent Mandarin–English speakers who acquired English later in life showed common cortical activation in a lexical search task at a single word level. This was typically localized in the left frontal, parietal, and temporal cortices for both L1 and L2.

In contrast, some studies have demonstrated that each of the two lan-guages in bilingual individuals might involve language-specific brain areas. That is, the brain areas recruited for processing L1 are different from those recruited for L2 even in bilingual individuals who speak Indo–European lan-guages (Blumenfeld & Marian, 2007; Dehaene et al., 1997; Ding et al., 2003; J.-J. Kim et al., 2002; K. H. S. Kim, Relkin, Lee, & Hirsch, 1997; Kovelman, Baker, & Petitto, 2008; Perani et al., 2003, 1996; Tan et al., 2003; Tham et al., 2005; Yetkin, Zerrin Yetkin, Haughton, & Cox, 1996). For example, using an fMRI measure, K. H. S. Kim and colleagues (1997) found that the brain activation for native English speakers and late-acquired French bilin-gual speakers showed distinct activations in Broca's area. Specifically, the sep-aration between centroids of activity ranged from ~ 4.5 mm to 9.0 mm within one slice. Dehaene et al. (1997) also reported that the L2 tended to have more diffuse representations in the left hemisphere than did the L1. In addi-tion, Ding et al. (2003) applied an orthographic search and a semantic clas-sification task with fluent Chinese–English bilingual individuals and found that English words caused more right hemisphere activation than Chinese characters in both the orthographic search and semantic classification task, suggesting that L2 may be more right hemisphere dominant than L1. Tan et al. (2003) proposed that "language experience tunes the cortex" (p. 158), meaning that reading involves language-specific brain activation in which L2 reading is shaped by L1 for bilingual individuals.

Meanwhile, some critical factors have been found to contribute to mod-ulating the neural patterns of the L1 and L2 language in bilingual subjects. The degree of proficiency in L2 is suggested to be a critical factor that affects the activation patterns of L2 relative to L1 (Chee et al., 1999; Klein et al., 1999; Perani & Abutalebi, 2005; Perani et al., 1996, 1998; van Heuven & Dijkstra, 2010). It has been proposed that an increase in proficiency of L2 for bilingual individuals results in increased similarities between L1 and L2 in the cortical representation of language processes (Illes et al., 1999). There is increasing evidence to support this hypothesis. Highly fluent bilingual indi-viduals activate similar left temporal areas for L1 and L2 (Perani et al., 1998). In contrast, less fluent subjects using an L2 often show more extensive or higher levels of brain activation, including more right hemisphere activation (Briellmann et al., 2004; Chee, Hon, Lee, & Soon, 2001; De Bleser et al., 2003; Ding et al., 2003; Perani et al., 1996; Pillai et al., 2003).

The age of L2 acquisition is another variable that may exert pervasive influence on the organization of the L1 and L2 in bilingual individuals (K. H. S. Kim et al., 1997; Neville et al., 1997; Weber-Fox & Neville, 1996). For example, two nonoverlapping subregions of Broca's area were found in late bilingual individuals, whereas for early bilingual individuals who received equal practice with their two languages from birth, there was common brain activation for L1 and L2 (K. H. S. Kim et al., 1997). Moreover, the exposure to L2, in terms of L1 and L2 daily usage, has been found to affect the cerebral representations in multilinguals, even when the degree of proficiency is kept constant (Perani et al., 2003).

Thus, the different pattern of activation found in bilingual individuals might be ascribed to differences in the degree of proficiency or the age of acquisition or the exposure to L2 (for a review, please see Perani & Abutalebi, 2005). Differences in brain activations for L1 and L2 might also be associated with differences in processing effort (van Heuven & Dijkstra, 2010). For example, the greater the difficulty of the task, the more brain activation that may be found in bilingual individuals (Hasegawa et al., 2002). The increasing or additional executive control demands also elicit different brain activation for particular tasks (Crinion et al., 2006; Hernandez, Dapretto, Mazziotta, & Bookheimer, 2001). The increased effort in linking motor codes with visual codes may also elicit additional brain activations (Meschyan & Hernandez, 2006).

The evidence reviewed so far indicates that the issue of how two languages are represented in bilingual individuals remains a matter of debate: separate versus integrated. More research that considers the factors mentioned (e.g., proficiency level of L2, the age of L2 acquisition, the usage of L2 in daily life as well as extra cognitive or task-related factors) that may modulate the brain activation patterns of L1 and L2 should be carried out to further explore the language organization in the bilingual brain. In addition, longitudinal studies may be helpful to investigate this issue, with adequate controls for the difference in age of acquisition, proficiency level, and other individual differences in cognitive abilities.

CONCLUSION

We have reviewed behavioral and neuroimaging studies concerning cross-linguistic transfer in bilingual students, particularly for bilingual students whose first language is Chinese. From three aspects of metalinguistic skills, namely, phonological awareness skills, morphological awareness skills, and orthographic skills, which are all potentially important for L2 language and reading development, we identified some universal transfer of phonological awareness skills, a possible partial transfer of morphological awareness skills, and an ambiguous transfer of orthographic awareness skills. In addition, brain activity of bilingual individuals is related to several factors. It may be possible to conclude that these individuals share the same brain region or have separate brain activations for L1 and L2 without considering those extraneous factors as reviewed earlier, such as proficiency of L2. We propose that in the process of L2 language and reading development, it is particularly important to address the potential transfer of L1 phonological, morphological, and orthographic awareness skills in bilingual students. A checklist for cross-language transfer in bilingual students appears in Appendix 2.1.

The neurophysiological studies echo behavioral studies and inform educators and practitioners that it is not only a bilingual child's age of acquisition, exposure, and proficiency in their two languages but also the orthographic similarities and differences between L1 and L2 that are important factors affecting bilingual and biliteracy development. One of the implications for this work is that educators and practitioners should take into consideration a bilingual child's L1 experience when teaching or assessing the child's L2 language and literacy skills. Investigating the aforementioned metalinguistic skills in L1 could help educators and practitioners gain understanding and insights into underlying cognitive difficulties, potential deficits, or linguistic links of the two languages in bilingual children. If a bilingual child manifests difficulties in L1 acquisition, it is likely that it will affect his or her L2 acquisition. Therefore, it is important to address the issues not only in L2 but also similar issues in L1 to ensure a positive transfer from L1 to L2 and perhaps equally positive countertransfer experience from L2 to L1. Raising the awareness of the transfer effect between L1 and L2 could empower educators and practitioners to identify any possible learning opportunities that facilitate bilingual children in making connections or differentiating between L1 and L2 in the process of bilingual and biliteracy acquisitions.

APPENDIX 2.1: CHECKLIST FOR CROSS-LANGUAGE TRANSFER IN BILINGUAL STUDENTS

Age of acquisition of L1 and L2

Language exposure to L1 and L2 at home and in school

Language proficiencies of L1 and L2

Phonological awareness transfer
- ☐ Sensibility and manipulation of phonological units in L1 and L2
  - ○ Syllable skills, onset-rime skills, phoneme levels, and lexical tone levels

Morphological awareness transfer
- ☐ Reflection and manipulation of morphemes in L1 and L2
- ☐ Use of word formation rules in language
  - ○ Morphological structures: awareness of compounds, inflections, and derivations

Orthographic awareness transfer
- ☐ Efficiently recognize orthographic representations in L1 and L2
  - ○ Legally and illegally spelled pseudowords

REFERENCES

Abu-Rabia, S. (2001). Testing the interdependence hypothesis among native adult bilingual Russian–English students. *Journal of Psycholinguistic Research, 30*, 437–455. doi:10.1023/A:1010425825251

Abu-Rabia, S., & Siegel, L. S. (2002). Reading, syntactic, orthographic, and working memory skills of bilingual Arabic–English speaking Canadian children. *Journal of Psycholinguistic Research, 31*, 661–678. doi:10.1023/A:1021221206119

Anthony, J. L., & Francis, D. J. (2005). Development of phonological awareness. *Current Directions in Psychological Science, 14*, 255–259. doi:10.1111/j.0963-7214.2005.00376.x

Arab-Moghaddam, N., & Senechal, M. (2001). Orthographic and phonological processing skills in reading and spelling in Persian/English bilinguals. *International Journal of Behavioral Development, 25*, 140–147. doi:10.1080/01650250042000320

Barker, T. A., Torgesen, J. K., & Wagner, R. K. (1992). The role of orthographic processing skills on five different reading tasks. *Reading Research Quarterly, 27*, 334–345. doi:10.2307/747673

Blumenfeld, H. K., & Marian, V. (2007). Constraints on parallel activation in bilingual spoken language processing: Examining proficiency and lexical status using eye-tracking. *Language and Cognitive Processes, 22*, 633–660. doi:10.1080/01690960601000746

Bowey, J. A., & Muller, D. (2005). Phonological recoding and rapid orthographic learning in third-graders' silent reading: A critical test of the self-teaching hypothesis. *Journal of Experimental Child Psychology, 92*, 203–219. doi:10.1016/j.jecp.2005.06.005

Brenders, P., van Hell, J. G., & Dijkstra, T. (2011). Word recognition in child second language learners: Evidence from cognates and false friends. *Journal of Experimental Child Psychology, 109*, 383–396. doi:10.1016/j.jecp.2011.03.012

Briellmann, R. S., Saling, M. M., Connell, A. B., Waites, A. B., Abbott, D. F., & Jackson, G. D. (2004). A high-field functional MRI study of quadri-lingual subjects. *Brain and Language, 89*, 531–542. doi:10.1016/j.bandl.2004.01.008

Brown, A. L., & Kane, M. J. (1988). Preschool children can learn to transfer: Learning to learn and learning from example. *Cognitive Psychology, 20*, 493–523. doi:10.1016/0010-0285(88)90014-X

Cárdenas-Hagan, E., Carlson, C., & Pollard-Durodola, S. D. (2007). The cross-linguistic transfer of early literacy skills: The role of initial L1 and L2 skills and language of instruction. *Language, Speech, and Hearing Services in Schools, 38*, 249–259. doi:10.1044/0161-1461(2007/026)

Carlisle, J. F. (1995). Morphological awareness and early reading achievement. In L. Feldman (Ed.), *Morphological aspects of language processing* (pp. 189–209). Hillsdale, NJ: Erlbaum.

Carlisle, J. F. (2003). Morphology matters in learning to read: A commentary. *Reading Psychology, 24*, 291–322. doi.org/10.1080/02702710390227369

Chee, M. W., Tan, E., & Thiel, T. (1999). Mandarin and English single word processing studies with functional magnetic resonance imaging. *The Journal of Neuroscience, 19*, 3050–3056.

Chee, M. W. L., Hon, N., Lee, H. L., & Soon, C. S. (2001). Relative language proficiency modulates BOLD signal change when bilinguals perform semantic judgments. *NeuroImage, 13*, 1155–1163. doi:10.1006/nimg.2001.0781

Chee, M. W. L., Soon, C. S., & Lee, H. L. (2003). Common and segregated neuronal networks for different languages revealed using functional magnetic resonance adaptation. *Journal of Cognitive Neuroscience, 15*(1), 85–97. doi:10.1162/089892903321107846

Chee, M. W. L., Weekes, B., Lee, K. M., Soon, C. S., Schreiber, A., Hoon, J. J., & Chee, M. (2000). Overlap and dissociation of semantic processing of Chinese characters, English words, and pictures: Evidence from fMRI. *NeuroImage, 12*, 392–403. doi:10.1006/nimg.2000.0631

Chen, M. J., & Yuen, J. C.-K. (1991). Effects of pinyin and script type on verbal processing: Comparisons of China, Taiwan, and Hong Kong experience. *International Journal of Behavioral Development, 14*, 429–448. doi:10.1177/016502549101400405

Chow, B. W.-Y., McBride-Chang, C., & Burgess, S. (2005). Phonological processing skills and early reading abilities in Hong Kong Chinese kindergarteners learning to read English as a second language. *Journal of Educational Psychology, 97*, 81–87. doi:10.1037/0022-0663.97.1.81

Commissaire, E., Duncan, L. G., & Casalis, S. (2011). Cross-language transfer of orthographic processing skills: A study of French children who learn English at school. *Journal of Research in Reading, 34*(1), 59–76. doi:10.1111/j.1467-9817.2010.01473.x

Corder, S. P. (1983). A role for the mother tongue. In S. Gass & L. Selinker (Eds.), *Language transfer in language learning* (pp. 85–97). Rowley, MA: Newbury House.

Crinion, J., Turner, R., Grogan, A., Hanakawa, T., Noppeney, U., Devlin, J. T., . . . Price, C. J. (2006). Language control in the bilingual brain. *Science, 312*, 1537–1540. doi:10.1126/science.1127761

Cunningham, A. E., Perry, K. E., & Stanovich, K. E. (2001). Converging evidence for the concept of orthographic processing. *Reading and Writing, 14*, 549–568. doi:10.1023/A:1011100226798

Cunningham, A. E., Perry, K. E., Stanovich, K. E., & Share, D. L. (2002). Orthographic learning during reading: Examining the role of self-teaching. *Journal of Experimental Child Psychology, 82*, 185–199. doi:10.1016/S0022-0965(02)00008-5

Deacon, H., & Cain, K. (2011). What we have learned from "learning to read in more than one language." *Journal of Research in Reading, 34*(1), 1–5. doi:10.1111/j.1467-9817.2010.01487.x

De Bleser, R., Dupont, P., Postler, J., Bormans, G., Speelman, D., Mortelmans, L., & Debrock, M. (2003). The organisation of the bilingual lexicon: A PET study. *Journal of Neurolinguistics, 16*, 439–456. doi:10.1016/S0911-6044(03)00022-8

Dehaene, S., Dupoux, E., Mehler, J., Cohen, L., Paulesu, E., Perani, D., . . . Le Bihan, D. (1997). Anatomical variability in the cortical representation of first and second language. *NeuroReport, 8*, 3809–3815. doi:10.1097/00001756-199712010-00030

de Jong, P. F., & Share, D. L. (2007). Orthographic learning during oral and silent reading. *Scientific Studies of Reading, 11*, 55–71.

Ding, G., Perry, C., Peng, D., Ma, L., Li, D., Xu, S., . . . Yang, J. (2003). Neural mechanisms underlying semantic and orthographic processing in Chinese–English bilinguals. *NeuroReport, 14*, 1557–1562.

Durgunoğlu, A. Y. (2002). Cross-linguistic transfer in literacy development and implications for language learners. *Annals of Dyslexia, 52*, 189–204.

Durgunoğlu, A. Y., Nagy, W. E., & Hancin-Bhatt, B. J. (1993). Cross-language transfer of phonological awareness. *Journal of Educational Psychology, 85*, 453–465. doi:10.1037/0022-0663.85.3.453

Fashola, O. S., Drum, P. A., Mayer, R. E., & Kang, S.-J. (1996). A cognitive theory of orthographic transitioning: Predictable errors in how Spanish-speaking children spell English words. *American Educational Research Journal, 33*, 825–843. doi:10.3102/00028312033004825

Frenck-Mestre, C., Anton, J. L., Roth, M., Vaid, J., & Viallet, F. (2005). Articulation in early and late bilinguals' two languages: Evidence from functional magnetic resonance imaging. *NeuroReport, 16*, 761–765. doi:10.1097/00001756-200505120-00021

Gandour, J., Tong, Y., Talavage, T., Wong, D., Dzemidzic, M., Xu, Y., . . . Lowe, M. (2007). Neural basis of first and second language processing of sentence-level linguistic prosody. *Human Brain Mapping, 28*, 94–108. doi:10.1002/hbm.20255

Gass, S., & Selinker, L. (1992). *Language transfer in language learning.* Philadelphia, PA: John Benjamins.

Goswami, U., Ziegler, J. C., Dalton, L., & Schneider, W. (2001). Pseudohomophone effects and phonological recoding procedures in reading development in English and German. *Journal of Memory and Language, 45*, 648–664. doi:10.1006/jmla.2001.2790

Gottardo, A., Chiappe, P., Yan, B., Siegel, L., & Gu, Y. (2006). Relationships between first and second language phonological processing skills and reading in Chinese–English speakers living in English-speaking contexts. *Educational Psychology, 26*, 367–393. doi:10.1080/01443410500341098

Gottardo, A., Yan, B., Siegel, L., & Wade-Woolley, L. (2001). Factors related to English reading performance in children with Chinese as a first language: More evidence of cross-language transfer of phonological processing. *Journal of Educational Psychology, 93*, 530–542. doi:10.1037/0022-0663.93.3.530

Halsband, U., Krause, B. J., Sipilä, H., Teräs, M., & Laihinen, A. (2002). PET studies on the memory processing of word pairs in bilingual Finnish–English subjects. *Behavioural Brain Research, 132*(1), 47–57. doi:10.1016/S0166-4328(01)00386-2

Hasegawa, M., Carpenter, P. A., & Just, M. A. (2002). An fMRI study of bilingual sentence comprehension and workload. *NeuroImage, 15*, 647–660. doi:10.1006/nimg.2001.1001

Hernandez, A. E., Dapretto, M., Mazziotta, J., & Bookheimer, S. (2001). Language switching and language representation in Spanish–English bilinguals: An fMRI study. *NeuroImage, 14*, 510–520. doi:10.1006/nimg.2001.0810

Hernandez, A. E., Martinez, A., & Kohnert, K. (2000). In search of the language switch: An fMRI study of picture naming in Spanish–English bilinguals. *Brain and Language, 73*, 421–431. doi:10.1006/brln.1999.2278

Ho, C. S.-H., & Bryant, P. (1997). Learning to read Chinese beyond the logographic phrase. *Reading Research Quarterly, 32*, 276–289. doi:10.1598/RRQ.32.3.3

Hu, C.-F., & Catts, H. W. (1993). Phonological recoding as a universal process? Evidence from beginning readers of Chinese. *Reading and Writing, 5*, 325–337. doi:10.1007/BF01027395

Huang, H. S., & Hanley, J. R. (1995). Phonological awareness and visual skills in learning to read Chinese and English. *Cognition, 54*, 73–98. doi:10.1016/0010-0277(94)00641-W

Huang, H. S., & Hanley, J. R. (1997). A longitudinal study of phonological awareness, visual skills, and Chinese reading acquisition among first-graders in Taiwan. *International Journal of Behavioral Development, 20*, 249–268. doi:10.1080/016502597385324

Illes, J., Francis, W. S., Desmond, J. E., Gabrieli, J. D. E., Glover, G. H., Poldrack, R., . . . Wagner, A. D. (1999). Convergent cortical representation of semantic processing in bilinguals. *Brain and Language, 70*, 347–363. doi:10.1006/brln.1999.2186

Kang, J. (2012). Bilingual PA and its influence on biliteracy for Korean English as a foreign language learners. *Reading and Writing, 25*, 1307–1326. doi:10.1007/s11145-011-9319-6

Kim, J.-J., Kim, M. S., Lee, J. S., Lee, D. S., Lee, M. C., & Kwon, J. S. (2002). Dissociation of working memory processing associated with native and second languages: PET investigation. *NeuroImage, 15*, 879–891. doi:10.1006/nimg.2001.1025

Kim, K. H. S., Relkin, N. R..Lee, K.-M., & Hirsch, J. (1997). Distinct cortical areas associated with native and second languages. *Nature, 388*, 171–174. doi:10.1038/40623

Klein, D., Milner, B., Zatorre, R. J., Meyer, E., & Evans, A. C. (1995). The neural substrates underlying word generation: A bilingual functional-imaging study. *Proceedings of the National Academy of Sciences of the United States of America, 92*, 2899–2903. doi:10.1073/pnas.92.7.2899

Klein, D., Milner, B., Zatorre, R. J., Zhao, V., & Nikelski, J. (1999). Cerebral organization in bilinguals: A PET study of Chinese–English verb generation. *NeuroReport, 10*, 2841–2845. doi:10.1097/00001756-199909090-00026

Klein, D., Watkins, K. E., Zatorre, R. J., & Milner, B. (2006). Word and nonword repetition in bilingual subjects: A PET study. *Human Brain Mapping, 27*, 153–161. doi:10.1002/hbm.20174

Klein, D., Zatorre, R. J., Milner, B., Meyer, E., & Evans, A. C. (1994). Left putaminal activation when speaking a second language: Evidence from PET. *NeuroReport, 5*, 2295–2297. doi:10.1097/00001756-199411000-00022

Kovelman, I., Baker, S. A., & Petitto, L.-A. (2008). Bilingual and monolingual brains compared: A functional magnetic resonance imaging investigation of syntactic processing and a possible "neural signature" of bilingualism. *Journal of Cognitive Neuroscience, 20*, 153–169. doi:10.1162/jocn.2008.20011

Kuo, L., & Anderson, R. C. (2006). Morphological awareness and learning to read: A cross-language perspective. *Educational Psychologist, 41*, 161–180. doi:10.1207/s15326985ep4103_3

Kuo, L. J., & Anderson, R. C. (2008). Conceptual and methodological issues in comparing metalinguistic awareness across languages. In K. Koda & A. Zehler (Eds.), *Learning to read across languages: Cross-linguistic relationships in first- and second-language literacy development* (pp. 39–67). New York, NY: Routledge.

Lafrance, A., & Gottardo, A. (2005). A longitudinal study of phonological processing skills and reading in bilingual children. *Applied Psycholinguistics, 26*, 559–578. doi:10.1017/S0142716405050307

Leong, C. K. (2011). Chinese language learners of English use more orthographic–lexical than phonological strategies in English word recognition and spelling. In A. Y. Durgunoğlu & C. Goldenberg (Eds.), *Language and literacy development in bilingual setting* (pp. 188–209). New York, NY: Guilford Press.

Li, T., McBride-Chang, C., Wong, A., & Shu, H. (2012). Longitudinal predictors of spelling and reading comprehension in Chinese as an L1 and English as an L2 in Hong Kong Chinese children. *Journal of Educational Psychology, 104*, 286–301. doi.org/10.1037/a0026445

Lin, D., McBride-Chang, C., Shu, H., Zhang, Y., Li, H., Zhang, J., . . . Levin, I. (2010). Small wins big: Analytic pinyin skills promote Chinese word reading. *Psychological Science, 21*, 1117–1122. doi:10.1177/0956797610375447

Luk, G., & Bialystok, E. (2008). Common and distinct cognitive bases for reading in English–Cantonese bilinguals. *Applied Psycholinguistics, 29*, 269–289. doi:10.1017/S0142716407080125

Mahendra, N., Plante, E., Magloire, J., Milman, L., & Trouard, T. P. (2003). fMRI variability and the localization of languages in the bilingual brain. *NeuroReport, 14*, 1225–1228. doi:10.1097/00001756-200307010-00007

McBride-Chang, C., Bialystok, E., Chong, K. K. Y., & Li, Y. (2004). Levels of phonological awareness in three cultures. *Journal of Experimental Child Psychology, 89*, 93–111. doi:10.1016/j.jecp.2004.05.001

McBride-Chang, C., Cheung, H., Chow, B. W.-Y., Chow, C. S.-L., & Choi, L. (2006). Metalinguistic skills and vocabulary knowledge in Chinese (L1) and English (L2). *Reading and Writing, 19*, 695–716. doi:10.1007/s11145-005-5742-x

McBride-Chang, C., & Ho, C. S.-H. (2000). Developmental issues in Chinese children's character acquisition. *Journal of Educational Psychology, 92*, 50–55. doi:10.1037/0022-0663.92.1.50

McBride-Chang, C., & Kail, R. V. (2002). Cross-cultural similarities in the predictors of reading acquisition. *Child Development, 73*, 1392–1407. doi:10.1111/1467-8624.00479

McBride-Chang, C., Tong, X., Shu, H., Wong, A. M.-Y., Leung, K.-w., & Tardif, T. (2008). Syllable, phoneme, and tone: Psycholinguistic units in early Chinese and English word recognition. *Scientific Studies of Reading, 12*, 171–194. doi:10.1080/10888430801917290

Melby-Lervåg, M., & Lervåg, A. (2011). Cross-linguistic transfer of oral language, decoding, phonological awareness and reading comprehension: A meta-analysis of the correlational evidence. *Journal of Research in Reading, 34*(1), 114–135. doi:10.1111/j.1467-9817.2010.01477.x

Meschyan, G., & Hernandez, A. E. (2006). Impact of language proficiency and orthographic transparency on bilingual word reading: An fMRI investigation. *NeuroImage, 29*, 1135–1140. doi:10.1016/j.neuroimage.2005.08.055

Neville, H. J., Coffey, S. A., Lawson, D. S., Fischer, A., Emmorey, K., & Bellugi, U. (1997). Neural systems mediating American Sign Language: Effects of sensory experience and age of acquisition. *Brain and Language, 57*, 285–308. doi:10.1006/brln.1997.1739

Odlin, T. (1989). *Language transfer: Cross-linguistic influence in language learning.* West Nyack, NY: Cambridge University Press. doi:10.1017/CBO9781139524537

Pasquarella, A., Chen, X., Lam, K., Luo, Y. C., & Ramirez, G. (2011). Cross-language transfer of morphological awareness in Chinese–English bilinguals. *Journal of Research in Reading, 34*(1), 23–42. doi:10.1111/j.1467-9817.2010.01484.x

Perani, D., & Abutalebi, J. (2005). The neural basis of first and second language processing. *Current Opinion in Neurobiology, 15*, 202–206. doi:10.1016/j.conb.2005.03.007

Perani, D., Abutalebi, J., Paulesu, E., Brambati, S., Scifo, P., Cappa, S. F., & Fazio, F. (2003). The role of age of acquisition and language usage in early, high-proficient bilinguals: An fMRI study during verbal fluency. *Human Brain Mapping, 19*, 170–182. doi:10.1002/hbm.10110

Perani, D., Dehaene, S., Grassi, F., Cohen, L., Cappa, S. F., Dupoux, E., . . . Mehler, J. (1996). Brain processing of native and foreign languages. *NeuroReport, 7*, 2439–2444. doi:10.1097/00001756-199611040-00007

Perani, D., Paulesu, E., Galles, N. S., Dupoux, E., Dehaene, S., Bettinardi, V., . . . Mehler, J. (1998). The bilingual brain. Proficiency and age of acquisition of the second language. *Brain: A Journal of Neurology, 121*, 1841–1852. doi:10.1093/brain/121.10.1841

Pillai, J. J., Araque, J. M., Allison, J. D., Sethuraman, S., Loring, D. W., Thiruvaiyaru, D., & Lavin, T. (2003). Functional MRI study of semantic and phonological language processing in bilingual subjects: Preliminary findings. *NeuroImage, 19*, 565–576. doi:10.1016/S1053-8119(03)00151-4

Pu, Y., Liu, H.-L., Spinks, J. A., Mahankali, S., Xiong, J., Feng, C.-M., . . . Gao, J.-H. (2001). Cerebral hemodynamic response in Chinese (first) and English (second) language processing revealed by event-related functional MRI. *Magnetic Resonance Imaging, 19*, 643–647. doi:10.1016/S0730-725X(01)00379-4

Savage, R., & Stuart, M. (2001). Orthographic analogies and early reading: Explorations of performance and variation in two transfer tasks. *Reading and Writing, 14*, 571–598. doi:10.1023/A:1012052631557

Savage, R. S., Deault, L., Daki, J., & Aouad, J. (2011). Orthographic analogies and early reading: Evidence from a multiple clue word paradigm. *Journal of Educational Psychology, 103*, 190–205. doi:10.1037/a0021621

Shu, H., & Anderson, R. C. (1997). Role of radical awareness in the character and word acquisition of Chinese children. *Reading Research Quarterly, 32*, 78–89. doi:10.1598/RRQ.32.1.5

Shu, H., Peng, H., & McBride-Chang, C. (2008). Phonological awareness in young Chinese children. *Developmental Science, 11*, 171–181. doi:10.1111/j.1467-7687.2007.00654.x

Siok, W. T., & Fletcher, P. (2001). The role of phonological awareness and visual–orthographic skills in Chinese reading. *Developmental Psychology, 37*, 886–899. doi:10.1037/0012-1649.37.6.886

Sparks, R., Patton, J., Ganschow, L., & Humbach, N. (2009). Long-term crosslinguistic transfer of skills from L1 to L2. *Language Learning, 59*, 203–243. doi:10.1111/j.1467-9922.2009.00504.x

Sparks, R. L., Patton, J., Ganschow, L., Humbach, N., & Javorsky, J. (2008). Early first-language reading and spelling skills predict later second-language reading and spelling skills. *Journal of Educational Psychology, 100*, 162–174. doi:10.1037/0022-0663.100.1.162

Sprenger-Charolles, L., Siegel, L. S., Béchennec, D., & Serniclaes, W. (2003). Development of phonological and orthographic processing in reading aloud, in silent reading, and in spelling: A four-year longitudinal study. *Journal of Experimental Child Psychology, 84*, 194–217. doi:10.1016/S0022-0965(03)00024-9

Stahl, S. A., & Murray, B. A. (1994). Defining phonological awareness and its relationship to early reading. *Journal of Educational Psychology, 86*, 221–234. doi:10.1037/0022-0663.86.2.221

Stanovich, K. E., & West, R. F. (1989). Exposure to print and orthographic processing. *Reading Research Quarterly, 24*, 402–433. doi:10.2307/747605

Sun-Alperin, M., & Wang, M. (2011). Cross-language transfer of phonological and orthographic processing skills from Spanish L1 to English L2. *Reading and Writing, 24*, 591–614. doi:10.1007/s11145-009-9221-7

Tan, L. H., Spinks, J. A., Feng, C.-M., Siok, W. T., Perfetti, C. A., Xiong, J., . . . Gao, J.-H. (2003). Neural systems of second language reading are shaped by native language. *Human Brain Mapping, 18*, 158–166. doi:10.1002/hbm.10089

Tham, W. W. P., Rickard Liow, S. J., Rajapakse, J. C., Choong Leong, T., Ng, S. E. S., Lim, W. E. H., & Ho, L. G. (2005). Phonological processing in Chinese–English bilingual biscriptals: An fMRI study. *NeuroImage, 28*, 579–587. doi:10.1016/j.neuroimage.2005.06.057

Thompson, G. B., Cottrell, D. S., & Fletcher-Flinn, C. M. (1996). Sublexical orthographic–phonological relations early in the acquisition of reading: The knowledge sources account. *Journal of Experimental Child Psychology, 62*, 190–222. doi:10.1006/jecp.1996.0028

Thorndike, E. L. (1913). *Educational psychology* (Vol. 2). New York, NY: Teachers College, Columbia University.

Tong, X., McBride-Chang, C., Shu, H., & Wong, A. M.-Y. (2009). Morphological awareness, orthographic knowledge, and spelling errors: Keys to understanding early Chinese literacy acquisition. *Scientific Studies of Reading, 13*, 426–452. doi:10.1080/10888430903162910

van Heuven, W. J. B., & Dijkstra, T. (2010). Language comprehension in the bilingual brain: fMRI and ERP support for psycholinguistic models. *Brain Research Reviews, 64*(1), 104–122. doi:10.1016/j.brainresrev.2010.03.002

Vellutino, F. R., Fletcher, J. M., Snowling, M. J., & Scanlon, D. M. (2004). Specific reading disability (dyslexia): What have we learned in the past four decades? *Journal of Child Psychology and Psychiatry, 45*(1), 2–40. doi:10.1046/j.0021-9630.2003.00305.x

Verhoeven, L. (2007). Early bilingualism, language transfer and phonological awareness. *Applied Psycholinguistics, 28*, 425–439. doi:10.1017/S0142716407070233

Wagner, R. K., & Torgesen, J. K. (1987). The nature of phonological processing and its causal role in the acquisition of reading skills. *Psychological Bulletin, 101*, 192–212. doi:10.1037/0033-2909.101.2.192

Wang, M., Cheng, C., & Chen, S.-W. (2006). Contribution of morphological awareness to Chinese–English biliteracy acquisition. *Journal of Educational Psychology, 98*, 542–553. doi:10.1037/0022-0663.98.3.542

Wang, M., & Geva, E. (2003). Spelling performance of Chinese children using English as a second language: Lexical and visual–orthographic processes. *Applied Psycholinguistics, 24*, 1–25. doi:10.1017/S0142716403000018

Wang, M., Park, Y., & Lee, K. R. (2006). Korean–English biliteracy acquisition: Cross-language phonological and orthographic transfer. *Journal of Educational Psychology, 98*, 148–158. doi:10.1037/0022-0663.98.1.148

Wang, M., Perfetti, C. A., & Liu, Y. (2005). Chinese–English biliteracy acquisition: Cross-language and writing system transfer. *Cognition, 97*, 67–88. doi:10.1016/j.cognition.2004.10.001

Wang, M., Yang, C., & Cheng, C. (2009). The contributions of phonology, orthography, and morphology in Chinese–English biliteracy acquisition. *Applied Psycholinguistics, 30*, 291–314. doi:10.1017/S0142716409090122

Weber-Fox, C. M., & Neville, H. J. (1996). Maturational constraints on functional specializations for language processing: ERP and behavioral evidence in bilingual speakers. *Journal of Cognitive Neuroscience, 8*, 231–256. doi:10.1162/jocn.1996.8.3.231

Xue, G., Dong, Q., Jin, Z., Zhang, L., & Wang, Y. (2004). An fMRI study with semantic access in low proficiency second language learners. *NeuroReport, 15*, 791–796. doi:10.1097/00001756-200404090-00010

Yetkin, O., Zerrin Yetkin, F., Haughton, V. M., & Cox, R. W. (1996). Use of functional MRI to map language in multilingual volunteers. *American Journal of Neuroradiology, 17*, 473–477.

Yin, L., Li, W., Chen, X., Anderson, R. C., Zhang, J., Shu, H., & Jiang, W. (2011). The role of tone awareness and pinyin knowledge in Chinese reading. *Writing Systems Research, 3*(1), 59–68. doi:10.1093/wsr/wsr010

Yokoyama, S., Okamoto, H., Miyamoto, T., Yoshimoto, K., Kim, J., Iwata, K., . . . Kawashima, R. (2006). Cortical activation in the processing of passive sentences in L1 and L2: An fMRI study. *NeuroImage, 30*, 570–579. doi:10.1016/j.neuroimage.2005.09.066

Zhang, J., Anderson, R. C., Li, H., Dong, Q., Wu, X. C., & Zhang, Y. (2010). Cross-language transfer of insight into the structure of compound words. *Reading and Writing, 23*, 311–336. doi:10.1007/s11145-009-9205-7

Ziegler, J. C., & Goswami, U. (2005). Reading acquisition, developmental dyslexia, and skilled reading across languages: A psycholinguistic grain size theory. *Psychological Bulletin, 131*, 3–29. doi:10.1037/0033-2909.131.1.3

Ziegler, J. C., & Goswami, U. (2006). Becoming literate in different languages: Similar problems, different solutions. *Developmental Science, 9*, 429–436. doi:10.1111/j.1467-7687.2006.00509.x

3

NEUROPSYCHOLOGICAL CONSIDERATIONS IN BILINGUAL ASSESSMENT: THE UNDERLYING BASIS OF LANGUAGE DISABILITY

RACHEL W. ROBILLARD

The challenges and complexities related to assessment of the bilingual student that are described in the chapters of this book also apply to the assessment and understanding of the neuropsychological underpinnings of language disorders, particularly those of bilingual individuals. When considering the best approach to assessment of the bilingual child in terms of language processing, it is important to first understand the brain structures and cognitive functions involved in processing language for both monolingual and multilingual children. A significant amount of research has explained these processes for monolingual English-speaking individuals. Similarly, our understanding of the mechanisms involved in processing language for several other letter–phoneme based languages is growing. Less is known, however, about the neuropsychology of a second language imposed on a dominant language and how the age of acquisition and the proficiency of each may mitigate fluency in both or either. This chapter reviews the current fund of information across these areas to help

http://dx.doi.org/10.1037/14320-004
Assessing Bilingual Children in Context: An Integrated Approach, A. B. Clinton (Editor)

the practitioner by providing a foundation for understanding what is needed to evaluate language difficulties in bilingual children.

NEUROPSYCHOLOGY OF LANGUAGE PROCESSING: DEVELOPMENTAL CONSIDERATIONS

A basic understanding of typical language development is important when considering issues of atypical development underlying language difficulties for bilingual children. Fortunately, we now have a more robust array of information related to typical development of language, including neuroimaging, as well as traditional language-focused and neuropsychological evaluations (Mindt et al., 2008). Homae, Watanabe, Nakano, and Taga (2011) examined the large-scale brain networks involved in language acquisition in early infancy. Using 94-channel near-infrared spectroscopy, the authors studied functional neural networks in the brains of 21 sleeping 3-month-old infants while presenting speech sounds through spoken sentences in Japanese, the infants' native language. Probes were placed over the bilateral frontal, temporal, temporoparietal, and occipital regions of infants' brains, and three measurements were taken. During the first, spontaneous fluctuation of activity in the brain was measured while the infants slept. During the second, the experimenters provided stimuli by playing Japanese sentences for 3 minutes and then measuring brain activation for another 3 minutes, without providing the stimulus. In the third experiment, in which they measured the brain activation without the stimulus, the activation findings were similar to those of the first measurement.

Changes in oxygenated and deoxygenated hemoglobin signals, as well as mapping of the functional connectivity during each measured period, provided results suggesting that 3-month-old infants register spontaneous brain activity and hemodynamic responses to speech sounds in both the left and right hemispheres. The temporal, temporoparietal, and occipital regions showed remarkable signal changes from the baseline to when sounds (sentences) were presented. Results suggested that the activations produced in the extensive cortical regions are not global systemic effects but reflect region-specific cortical activity. This was the case not only in the bilateral temporal and temporoparietal regions, as previous research has suggested, but also in the prefrontal and occipital regions where specific signal increases and decreases were produced when speech sounds were presented to the infants. Although the bilateral regions were responsive to speech sounds, a hemispheric difference was marked in the frontotemporal networks. An increase in correlations was found between the right temporoparietal region and the right prefrontal region during the period of time when the sounds were presented. This suggests that the prosodic information in normal speech is likely processed in the right-lateralized network. The research by Homae and colleagues (2011) suggests that the critical issue in both the developmental and language disciplines is whether the frontal and temporal regions of the preverbal infant work as a functional network, because this is likely the primary focus for the neural foundation of language acquisition. These results are consistent with the hypothesis that the frontotemporal networks begin to function in infancy and may play a role in the processing of speech sounds and eventually in the production and comprehension of spoken language.

Research on the neural basis of language development has also been conducted with samples of children at developmental periods in which speech and language are typically evolving at an active and rapid rate. Friederici, Brauer, and Lohmann (2011) used functional magnetic resonance imaging (fMRI) to investigate the functional properties of language networks by comparing 6-year-olds with adults. They analyzed correlations based on the analysis of low frequency fluctuations (LFF). LFF amplitude (< 0.1 Hz) represents a large portion of the overall signal variance of the blood oxygen level–dependent response as measured by fMRI. This approach was used to determine the default language network in the different age groups, independent of the various aspects examined in the experimental conditions. Two conditions comprised correct sentences, one with semantically incorrect structure and one with syntactically incorrect structure. These sentences were presented aloud, in a random fashion. Participants were asked to judge the acceptability of the sentences. Subjects were right-handed German native speakers without neurological history and with normal language development.

A developmental difference was observed between the two age groups in the default language network underlying sentence processing. Adults displayed a network clearly lateralized in the left hemisphere, whereas 6-year-old children demonstrated stronger interhemispheric correlation to contralateral cortices. The data from this study suggest that functional connectivity between brain regions and their respective structures does not appear to solidify by age 6, despite measurable activity in specific regions. Children's default language network seems to be characterized by functional interhemispheric connections, mainly between the superior temporal regions. Furthermore, the frontal-to-temporal connectivity between the language areas within the left hemisphere appears to be a prerequisite for the processing of syntactically complex sentences. Data from this study also suggest both structural and functional reorganization of the neural network underlying language development, suggesting that as the child's language abilities mature, she or he is moving toward a system that allows close interactions between frontal and temporal regions within the left hemisphere. These data correspond to the view of organization of the developing brain that assumes a shift in network architecture from being locally organized to a more diffusely distributed pattern that evolves as the child's brain matures through life experiences and learning.

In sum, neuropsychological research has suggested that language development relies on the establishment of connections between specific cortical regions. Intercommunication between regions, particularly frontal and temporal areas, supports the understanding of speech sounds, which in turn leads to meaningful language use and comprehension of oral and written language. Regional connections vary by hemisphere and developmental level. The most basic aspects of sound recognition and rhythm in language processing in the infant brain appear to be lateralized to the right hemisphere, as contrasted by language lateralization largely to the left hemisphere in the adult brain. Solid language development, however, incorporates interhemispheric activity at least through 6 years of age, highlighting the complexities in language development from infancy to adulthood.

BILINGUAL LANGUAGE DEVELOPMENT

Research on bilingualism has typically focused on two key cognitive mechanisms: frequency of language-specific use and competition or interference between the two languages in question. A review of these mechanisms, as well as of possible advantages and disadvantages of bilingualism, is needed to understand how bilingualism may affect overall neuropsychological performance.

Neuropsychological data have indicated that bilingual subjects tend to have a disadvantage on verbal tasks, yet benefit from subtle advantages on some measures of cognitive control. Disadvantages include the likelihood that the simultaneous bilingual child (one who learns two languages at the same time) may initially acquire language more slowly than the monolingual child, and relatively more slowly than the bilingual child who learns one language followed by a second language later in life (sequential bilingual). These differences tend to diminish quickly after entering school (Collier, 1995; Hamayan & Damico, 1991). However, proficiency in a second language for basic interpersonal communication skills may put students at risk of being tested prematurely in the nondominant language (L2) for academic purposes. In addition, the strongest predictor of academic achievement in L2 is years of formal schooling in the native, dominant language (L1; Thomas & Collier, 2002), suggesting that greater proficiency in L1 facilitates proficiency in the subsequent language(s). These findings suggest that children in immersion classrooms may lose ground in both languages, requiring them to make more gains than the average native-English speaker every year for several years to catch up to grade level.

Both younger and older bilinguals have been found to be at a disadvantage on verbal fluency tests, with a greater disadvantage found on measures of semantic verbal fluency rather than on letter fluency (Gollan, Montoya, & Werner, 2002). In addition, within each additional language, bilinguals are reported to have a smaller vocabulary size relative to monolinguals' vocabulary in their one respective language; however, bilingual students may catch up to monolinguals in vocabulary knowledge by the time they reach adulthood (Hamers & Blanc, 2000). Bilingual young adults recognize fewer difficult vocabulary words than monolingual individuals on measures of receptive vocabulary and have more tip-of-the-tongue (just-cannot-remember-the-word) retrieval failures than monolingual individuals. They may also name pictures more slowly than those who are monolingual (Gollan & Brown, 2006), and they may name fewer pictures correctly on standardized naming tests (Roberts, Garcia, Desrochers, & Hernandez, 2002). These disadvantages appear to remain static even when bilinguals are tested exclusively in their first, acquired, and dominant languages (Ivanova & Costa, 2008).

Advantages associated with bilingualism include the early opportunity to practice inhibitory control, making it easier to use the executive functions often used to control the attention and inhibition used to suppress one language while expressing the other. Bilingualism appears to improve executive function throughout the life span, as evidenced in several studies in which bilingual children outperform monolingual children on tasks of inhibitory control of attention (Bialystok, 2001; Festman, Rodriguez-Fornells, & Münte, 2010; Zelazo, Muller, Frye, & Marcovitch, 2003; Zied et al., 2004). The literature on neural development has suggested that neural processes involved in language acquisition and speech disorders are similar in many ways across individuals, regardless of mono- or bilingualism (Holm, Dodd, Stow, & Pert, 1999), and there is a growing body of research supporting the notion that L2 is primarily stored in the same neural network as L1 (Abutalebi & Green, 2007; Miozzo, Costa, Hernández, & Rapp, 2010).

The executive function advantage is also supported by studies involving *language switching*, or moving between two languages within the same conversation. Language switching has been associated with greater activation of the dorsolateral prefrontal cortex, a region of the brain that has been associated with conflict control, higher order attentional processes (including selective attention), and inhibition, among others (Chen, Wei, & Zhou, 2006). It has also been suggested that a lack of proficiency in L2 is associated with recruitment of additional regions, specifically prefrontal areas (Briellmann et al., 2004; Meschyan & Hernandez, 2006), and an increase in the density of gray matter in the left inferior parietal cortex (Mechelli et al., 2004); however, this left hemisphere effect was found to be more pronounced in early, rather than late, bilingual individuals. Similar results have been obtained imaging

Chinese–English speakers to understand local and global inhibition in bilingual word production (Guo, Liu, Misra, & Kroll, 2011).

Although less research has been completed concerning the language development of bilingual individuals during childhood, there are a few studies that contribute to our understanding of the neuropsychology of the developing bilingual brain. A study by Lehtonen et al. (2009) was one of the first to examine the young bilingual brain across languages. The study used fMRI to explore how the visual recognition of inflected nouns can recruit different processing routes in morphologically rich versus morphologically limited languages by studying the neuronal correlates of the processing routes using a visual lexical decision task. Subjects were Finnish–Swedish early bilingual individuals. Results suggested a language-specific processing difference in the brain that was reflective of the morphological differences between the two languages.

In 2011, Wang et al. examined word processing in bilingual adults using magnetoencephalography to investigate the spatiotemporal and frequency characteristics of bilingual (Mandarin–English) and monolingual (English) subjects during a word-match paradigm. The experiment was designed to determine whether the subjects could distinguish simultaneously presented audio and visual stimuli that did or did not match. There were no significant differences between bilingual and monolingual individuals in the left inferior frontal cortex (Brodmann's Area [BA] 44/45) when they were processing their L1. The images indicated there were significantly stronger activations in this same region for monolingual individuals when compared with bilingual individuals when they were processing English, however. This finding suggests that it is possible that bilingual individuals process L1 in a similar manner to monolingual individuals processing L1, with some distinct activation patterns, such as high involvement in the right supramarginal gyrus (BA 40) of the parietal lobe. These distinctions may be, in part, due to the differences between Chinese and English (Xue, Chen, Jin, & Dong, 2006); encoding of audiovisually presented Chinese words takes more time than audiovisual processing of English words. However, the findings indicated that it also took a longer time for bilingual individuals to process both L1 and L2, whereas it took a shorter time for monolingual individuals to process L1. Although bilingual individuals also produced significantly stronger activations in BA 39/40 of the right hemisphere as compared with English monolingual individuals when both were processing the L1, monolinguals showed significantly stronger activations in the inferior frontal cortex (BA 44/45) of the left hemisphere than bilingual individuals when both were processing English. In addition, the Mandarin–English bilingual speakers produced stronger beta-band power suppression in the right supramarginal area when processing Mandarin, and there was significantly stronger beta-band power suppression in the right inferior parietal lobe covering the supramarginal gyrus (BA 40) and angular gyrus (BA 39) for bilingual individuals when processing Mandarin versus English. Results of this study are potentially beneficial in determining language lateralization in bilingual speakers. These results supported the view that Mandarin–English bilingual speakers have a shared neural system for word processing in both L1 and L2, which is highly similar to that of monolingual speakers but with stronger right hemisphere involvement.

Additional research has more directly addressed the question concerning whether the neuroanatomical organization of the bilingual mental lexicon may also be affected by neural maturation (development) and the developmental level at which a bilingual individual's two languages become interconnected (Isel, Baumgaertner, Thrän, Meisel, & Büchel, 2010; Saur et al., 2009). These studies examined the level of interconnection on a conceptual level, with particular attention to whether the two languages shared the same underlying neural representation. They were most focused on understanding the extent to which the age of acquisition (AoA) of the L2 affects the conceptual representations between the two languages. In particular, Isel et al. (2010) investigated whether the semantic–conceptual representation of concrete nouns in L2 differs from that of the representation in L1 depending on the AoA of L2. "Early" (French–German) bilinguals (before age 3) were distinguished from proficient "late" bilinguals (L2 acquired after age 10). Reaction time and accuracy, as well as functional neuroimaging data, were recorded during a semantic organization task in which the subjects were presented visually with French–German pairs of concrete nouns.

Results (Isel et al., 2010) indicated that correct response times for the semantic categorization task were significantly faster for early bilingual s than late bilinguals. In addition, on average, early bilingual speakers were more accurate than late bilingual speakers in assigning a semantic category to the German target words. A larger repetition effect was observed for late bilinguals in specific brain structures, including the left mid-insula and the right middle frontal gyrus, with larger repetition effects for early bilingual speakers in other areas of the brain, including the left superior temporal gyrus, the bilateral superior frontal gyrus, and the right posterior insula. The authors speculated that the primed condition in late bilingual speakers might have led the brain to spontaneously produce more images, voices, thoughts, and feelings, all of which constitute a more stimulus-independent response that is often associated with a specific concept. In addition, a significant correlation was found between behavioral data and the neural priming findings in the left middle frontal gyrus of the dorsolateral prefrontal cortex, indicating that this area of the brain may directly contribute to behavioral priming in bilinguals.

The frequency of language-specific use and competition or interference between two languages are factors that must be addressed when working with bilingual individuals with language-related difficulties. When evaluating someone who is bilingual, it is necessary to understand these mechanisms, as well as the individual's patterns of strength and weakness, particularly those due to their bilingualism, to best understand how these factors may affect overall neuropsychological performance.

NEUROPSYCHOLOGY OF READING DISABILITIES

Processing language through reading involves a variety of brain structures. Key among these are the corpus callosum (CC) and a network of left hemisphere temporal, parietal, and frontal regions, including the left central temporal gyrus; the left inferoventral frontal, temporal, and retrosplenial cingulate areas; the prefrontal cortex; and Broca's area (Pinel, 2010). In addition, molecular diffusion of the CC has been measured to assess interhemispheric connectivity with results indicating there is a difference in molecular diffusion but not in the size of the CC, which may be interpreted to reflect a stronger and/or faster interhemispheric connection in strongly left-lateralized subjects as compared with moderately left-lateralized, bilateral, or moderately right-lateralized subjects (Westerhausen et al., 2006). As noted by Westerhausen and colleagues (2006), macrostructural measures in healthy subjects are too insensitive to assess the interindividual variations in the CC that are related to language lateralization; however, in diseased individuals (i.e., those with epilepsy) variations are more pronounced and more easily detectable, suggesting that the main function of the CC is to inhibit the contralateral hemisphere while the ipsilateral hemisphere is working on its specialized task (i.e., word generation).

Although information concerning diseased individuals' brains is useful, understanding differences in typically developing brains is also essential for understanding the difficulties inherent in the neural mechanisms of those that are not. Mapping the neural pathways of typically developing readers has helped us understand the difficulties the dyslexic reader must face (S. E. Shaywitz & Shaywitz, 2008). Dyslexia has been associated with low activation in the posterior occipitotemporal and temporoparietal regions (i.e., angular gyrus) through imaging studies completed with subjects using alphabetic writing systems, such as English (Hu et al., 2010). Decreased activation in these areas causes dyslexic readers to have considerably more difficulty analyzing words and transforming letters into sounds, resulting in less fluid reading, and loss of fluency negatively affects reading comprehension and written expression, causing dyslexic readers to often become frustrated with the processes of reading and writing (S. Shaywitz, 2005).

An unexpected difficulty in reading, when cognitive ability and motivation are measured to be within normal limits and reasonable reading instruction has been provided, is defined as *developmental dyslexia* (Odegard, Ring, Smith, Biggan, & Black, 2008). Identifying the specific factors associated with impaired reading development has implications for diagnosis, intervention, and prevention. In 2010, Ferrer, Shaywitz, Holahan, Marchione, and Shaywitz completed an analysis of data collected from a sample of 232 Connecticut schoolchildren in a 15-year longitudinal study. They compared a composite reading score, which included sight-word, phonemic awareness, and reading comprehensions scores, with cognitive scores over time. Findings indicated that reading and intellectual development appear to be dynamically linked over time for typically developing readers, but these relationships are not readily perceptible in dyslexic readers. This suggests that reading and cognition develop more independently in dyslexic individuals than they do in typically developing children, which is central to understanding how to address this learning disability.

Advances in technology, particularly the less invasive forms of imaging such as fMRI, have provided evidence for a neurobiological understanding of dyslexia, specifically as a disruption of two left hemisphere posterior brain systems. These two systems, one that is parietal–temporal and the other occipital–temporal, are coupled with the compensatory engagement of anterior systems centering on the inferior frontal gyrus and the right occipital–temporal (posterior) system. In addition, fMRI studies of young adults with reading difficulties followed prospectively and longitudinally from the age of 5 have suggested that there may be two types of reading difficulties, one primarily reflecting a genetic basis and the other reflecting environmental influences. Overall, research has suggested that brain systems implicated in reading are malleable, and their disruption in children diagnosed with dyslexia may be remediated using an evidence-based reading intervention that is delivered with fidelity (B. A. Shaywitz, Lyon, & Shaywitz, 2006).

More recently, Lebel et al. (2013) used diffusion tensor imaging (DTI) and voxel-based analysis to examine correlations between reading ability and tissue structure in 136 healthy adolescents and young adults with a wide range of reading ability. Three reading scores (word reading, decoding, and reading fluency) yielded positive correlations with *fractional anisotropy* (FA; a scaled value between 0 and 1 that describes the property of being directionally dependent) that spanned bilateral brain regions. FA is a measure often used in DTI, where it is thought to reflect fiber density, axonal diameter, and myelination in white matter. These FA correlations included the frontal lobes, as expected, but also included the thalamus and parietal and temporal areas. An analysis of the unique effects of each of the three reading assessments revealed that most of the variance in FA values could be attributed to sight-word reading ability, suggesting that this is an area of significant functional difference for individuals with dyslexia.

Developmental dyslexia has been found to have a different neural basis in Chinese and English speakers due to the processing demands of the differing writing systems. Hu et al. (2010) used fMRI to examine this phenomenon in a study comparing semantic decisions on written words between dyslexic Chinese- and English-speaking subjects and typically developing Chinese- and English-speaking subjects. Results indicated that dyslexia, for both languages, produced less activation in the left angular gyrus and the middle frontal, posterior temporal, and occipitotemporal regions. Normal readers produced increased activation in the left inferior frontal sulcus for Chinese relative to English. For normal readers of English relative to Chinese, increased activations were noted in the left posterior superior temporal sulcus. These cultural differences were not noted in the dyslexic subjects for each language; however, activations were noted for both left inferior frontal sulcus and left posterior superior temporal sulcus for both Chinese and English dyslexics. By removing the effects of dyslexia from noted differences in normal readers for both languages, the results validated the influence of cognitive ability and the learning environment on a common neural system used for reading.

To become a skilled reader in alphabetic languages, one must learn to associate auditory information of speech sounds with the visual information provided by letters in an automated manner. Blau et al. (2010) used fMRI to begin to understand the neural networks associated with this process in children with and without dyslexia. Their results show reduced neural integration of letters and speech sounds in the planum temporale/Heschl sulcus and the superior temporal sulcus for dyslexic readers. Fluent readers were able to strongly suppress effects for incongruent letters while demonstrating positive cortical responses to speech sounds that were modulated by letter–speech sound congruency, a finding not noted in dyslexic children. They also performed whole-brain analyses of unisensory visual and auditory group differences that indicated dyslexic readers had reduced unisensory responses to letters in the fusiform gyrus and reduced activity for processing speech sounds in the anterior superior temporal gyrus, planum temporale/Heschl sulcus, and superior temporal sulcus. The differences in the integration of letters and speech sounds in the planum temporale/Heschl sulcus and the neural response to letters in the fusiform gyrus explained 40% of the variance in the individual subjects' reading performance. This team's contributions indicate there is an interrelated network of visual, auditory, and heteromodal brain areas that contribute to skilled use (fluency) of letter–speech sound associations necessary for learning to read. The findings suggest that the letter–speech sound integration necessary for learning to read develops inadequately in dyslexic readers as a result of a malfunctioning of the interactive neural systems for processing auditory and visual input.

The recent extraordinary and rapid progress in functional brain imaging has allowed us to better understand the neural systems used in processing written language and how these systems differ in dyslexic readers. Thus far, contributions in identifying the neural signature of dyslexia have made this previously hidden disability more visible, allowing for progress in identification and intervention for children at risk of the disability at a young age.

USING NEUROPSYCHOLOGY TO INFORM ASSESSMENT OF LANGUAGE DISORDER IN BILINGUAL INDIVIDUALS

To address the neuropsychological underpinnings and evaluation of language disorders in bilingual children, it is important to also understand language assessment of the monolingual child. The assessment of language disorders even with monolingual speakers can be a complicated process. Traditionally, language disorders are evaluated by speech and language pathologists, with the focus of an evaluation on receptive language, expressive language, intelligibility of language, and socially appropriate language. To be referred for a speech and language assessment, concerns must become significant enough to be apparent to either the parent, the school- or community-based professional, or both. Some of these referral concerns include the inability to follow oral directions, disorganization, difficulties completing tasks, the inability to understand information read aloud on a developmentally appropriate level, difficulties writing or speaking in short utterances, confusing speech production, the inability to answer questions, and difficulties retaining information (American Speech–Language–Hearing Association, 2007).

Receptive, expressive, and pragmatic aspects of language disorders are typically assessed using formal and informal sources, and these data may be incorporated into other evaluations, including, but not limited to, cognitive, academic, psychological, and behavioral reports. The informal sources of data may include work samples, observations of the child, reading and writing samples, interviews, and informal conversation. Informal data are important to collect along with formal assessment data because they may suggest to the evaluator additional areas to examine more thoroughly during the formal assessment and may provide examples of specific difficulties particular to each child.

If receptive language is a concern, the psychologist may notice informally that the student has difficulty following a conversation and pays limited attention to the speaker, showing poor listening skills (difficulties facing the speaker, waiting to speak until the speaker is finished, maintaining focus on the exchange). These informal observations are subjective but are typically useful supplementary information when interpreting data collected through formal means. Formal data collection usually involves the use of standardized assessments that are chosen on the basis of the referral question but typically include tests of cognitive ability, as well as specific tests of articulation and expressive, receptive, and pragmatic language in the child's native language.

Expressive language is assessed by evaluating a student's ability to report information in oral or written format. The practitioner evaluates the child's ability to use words and language conventions appropriately. In an informal assessment, the focus is on what and how the student is communicating. When assessing the bilingual child in particular, it is important to take extensive notes or record what the student says. These quotes are helpful in providing information to assist in determinations when a difficult differential diagnosis is to be made. For example, the running record may be useful in determining whether a student is having repeated, but similar, difficulties in subject–verb agreement or whether the patterns of error are more random. Using direct quotes within a language assessment also helps the clinician describe specific issues that may need to be addressed during therapy and intervention. Formal assessment of expressive language usually takes the format of providing the child with a prompt that he or she can talk or write about. The child might also narrate a wordless picture book or tell a story based on a picture. In addition, single words and phrases that are repeated are included in the evaluation of expressive language, although care should be taken in their interpretation because there is an element of attention that is also measured with this type of tool.

Pragmatic language, the combination of language components into functional and socially acceptable communication, involves both receptive and expressive language and is often neglected in language evaluation. However, with the bilingual child, this is an essential component of the assessment and is necessary to better understand inherent difficulties in both expressive and receptive language and to diagnose whether the student has a language disorder or is negotiating language acquisition (Marrero, Golden, & Espe-Pfeifer, 2002). Pragmatics concern the way words and sentences are used to communicate implicit and explicit meaning at an expected level based on age, maturity, education, and exposure related to socioeconomic status.

Pragmatic language can be assessed informally through conversation. The ability to contribute to a fluid conversation with equal participation, show an interest in the content of another person's conversation, pick up on social nuances, and understand when another person is serious or joking are all included in the use and understanding of pragmatic language. Formally assessing pragmatic language can be difficult, because it is, in essence, a social form of communication. The social aspect of pragmatic language also makes it difficult to create standardized assessments that can be used to evaluate it. Therefore, formal assessment usually consists of conducting observations and completing checklists made up of age-appropriate characteristics. Again, the need for the evaluator to be familiar, if not fully fluent, in the child's native language is essential in the evaluation of this language skill.

In the native language, evaluation of pragmatic language may often take the form of asking the child to interpret an idiom (e.g., "A stitch in time saves nine") appropriately. Cieslicka and Heredia (2011) began looking at the neuropsychology involved in the processing of these idioms, noting that hemispheric asymmetries in processing L1 and L2 idioms appear to depend on the effects of salience and context for each language. Studies such as these further support the need to be sure that the evaluator of the bilingual child has a good understanding of the implicit and explicit meaning of each language in question when attempting to measure the child's use of pragmatic language.

When evaluating the language of the bilingual child, it is important not only to keep in mind the need to explore each of these areas of ability but also to remember that, for the child who may be processing two very different languages in terms of inflection and sound as well as in terms of visual and visuospatial complexity, there may be significantly different cognitive processes occurring simultaneously that should be taken into account. For instance, Kumar and colleagues (2010) noted that when comparing the processes involved in reading Hindi and English, which differ significantly in terms of orthography, it would be important to understand that English is alphabetic linear (vowels and consonants are arranged sequentially) and Hindi is alphasyllabary and nonlinear (vowels are placed around consonants making it a visually complex script). Their study of the orthographies of late Hindi–English bilingual individuals indicated reading fluency was significantly slowed, and those who were fluent in Hindi (L1) showed left putamen activation when processing in English (L2) and activation in the temporal pole and caudate nucleus of the right hemisphere, areas associated with semantic and visual processing. They attributed these findings to the increased visuospatial demands for processing Hindi that have been documented in other visually complex orthographies. Kumar et al. additionally documented activation in the right superior temporal gyrus, which they attributed to the syllabic rhythm of Hindi.

There are many examples of formal measures that may be used to assess all areas of language in a developmentally appropriate and statistically sound manner. These may include, but are not limited to, the Clinical Evaluation of Language Fundamentals, Fourth Edition (CELF-4; Semel, Wiig, & Secord, 2003), in Spanish and the Clinical Evaluation of Language Fundamentals, Fifth Edition (CELF-5; Semel, Wiig, & Secord, 2013), in English; the Bayley Infant Neurodevelopmental Screener (Aylward, 1995); the CELF–Preschool–

2 test (Semel, Wiig, & Secord, 2004); and the Preschool Language Scale, Fourth Edition, in Spanish (Zimmerman, Steiner, & Pond, 2002b) and English (Zimmerman, Steiner, & Pond, 2002a). (For a complete list of instruments and guidelines, please refer to the website of the American Speech–Language–Hearing Association). A language dominance checklist is provided in Appendix 3.1.

PRACTICAL APPLICATION

The following case studies help depict how a basic understanding of the neuropsychological underpinnings of language and reading development are essential in making an appropriate differential diagnosis for the bilingual child and, subsequently, developing the most effective intervention plan possible. Each of these cases involves Spanish–English bilingual children at various stages of acculturation and with a variety of complicating, but not unusual, mitigating factors. For each case, background information is provided along with data from the neuropsychological evaluation pertinent to the case. The reader will note that the background information is equally as important in the process of diagnosis as the subjective data gathered through the direct evaluation of the child's current abilities; gathering background information should be a practice carried out in all evaluations of the bilingual student.

Case Study: Carlos—Language Disorder With Interhemispheric Involvement

Carlos is a 6-year-old U.S.-born Hispanic boy[1] who was tested at the end of his kindergarten year. He is in a dual language (50–50 Spanish/English) educational program. Prior to kindergarten, he attended a bilingual early childhood program with instruction predominantly in Spanish, his native language.

Carlos's teachers expressed concern about his level of academic achievement. They reported that he struggles to remain focused during class, has difficulty getting organized and turning in work, and seems to misunderstand many of the directions given in either Spanish or English. Carlos's English teacher reported that she believes Carlos understands her directions and communication most of the time, but he rarely follows directions. She indicated that Carlos voluntarily asks her to explain the meaning of unfamiliar words in English. He has been receiving small group instruction and extra time for reading and writing assignments,

---

[1] The details of the case studies have been changed to protect the anonymity of the individuals involved.

and he receives instruction from a reading specialist for work on subject–verb agreement in both languages. However, he has not made measurable progress with these interventions.

Carlos's developmental history is positive for motor impairment, and he received physical therapy from 8 months to 3 years of age. Recently, he has begun receiving occupational therapy at school twice weekly. He continues to exhibit difficulties holding a writing utensil correctly and does not yet have a dominant hand preference. Carlos's parents shared that the family history is negative for difficulties with immigration, socioeconomic issues, or acculturation issues.

Carlos's attention at home is reported as variable. When he is interested in a particular activity, such as watching TV, his mother reported he can maintain focus for as long as he wishes. However, when attention is required for an activity he dislikes, he will resist. This pattern is commensurate with teacher reports of classroom behavior. Carlos has recently begun exhibiting somatic symptoms, complaining of stomachaches when he does not want to go to school or when he hopes to avoid tasks that are difficult for him. His mother indicated concerns that Carlos is often unnecessarily rough with cousins and friends who visit them. At school, his teacher reported that his behaviors often cause other students to withdraw from him because his actions make them feel unsafe. For example, instead of greeting his peers with a soft handshake at the morning meeting, he will purposely slap a student's hand. When teachers remind him how to properly greet his peers, he may laugh in response.

Carlos's evaluation was conducted in Spanish, his native and dominant language. Limits were tested through subsequent evaluation for academic achievement in English. Results showed overall cognitive ability in the low average range, with little difference between index scores for verbal, perceptual reasoning, processing speed, working memory, long-term memory, and fluid processing. Adaptive measures yielded scores commensurate with measured cognitive ability. His receptive language scores were in the borderline range, with expressive language measured in the mildly impaired range in both languages. Additional cognitive evaluation indicated nonverbal reasoning was an area of relative strength.

Achievement scores ranged from average to moderately impaired. He scored in the moderately impaired range on broad reading tasks, with significant difficulties in reading fluency and comprehension and low average skills in areas including phonics and sight-word reading. Math scores were impaired, as were scores in written expression. He performed significantly better on tasks of oral expression when they were embedded in context, and appeared to retain this information for long-term retrieval. Parents and teachers reported functional communication is mildly impaired, with articulation difficulties noted in both Spanish and English.

When the limits were tested in English, Carlos performed similarly to what was measured in Spanish, with differences in scores for receptive language and basic reading skills. In English, receptive language was measured as slightly better developed than what was measured in Spanish; however, basic reading skills (phonics and sight word reading) were somewhat less developed in English.

Although this case may not initially appear to be significant for language-based difficulties due to the many complicating factors (lower cognitive ability, history of motor difficulties, attentional problems), data from Carlos's evaluation indicated the presence of an expressive–receptive language disorder, with difficulties measured in both Spanish and English. From a neuropsychological perspective, his difficulties in motor development, as well as his attentional difficulties, both associated with frontal lobe dysfunction, are likely contributing to his inability to process language effectively. He is at an age where research would indicate his default language network would be characterized by incomplete functional interhemispheric connections, mainly between the superior temporal regions.

Both structural and functional reorganization of the neural network underlying language development are in formation at this stage of development, suggesting that intense and immediate intervention may help him develop more functional language abilities. As he matures and moves toward a system that allows close interactions between frontal and temporal regions within the left hemisphere, compensatory structures and function, including his relatively better developed processing speed and visual–spatial abilities, may be recruited through intervention to improve language and reading ability. In addition to speech, language, and reading intervention, it is likely Carlos will benefit from intervention that focuses on attention and fine motor development as well.

Case Study: Inez—Dyslexia or Bilingual Language Transition?

Inez is a 7-year-old girl in the first grade who is receiving instruction in a bilingual classroom. Her multidisciplinary committee requested an evaluation following 8 months of progress monitoring and targeted intervention in English and Spanish for difficulties in reading and writing where limited progress was achieved. At school, Inez is classified as a limited English proficient student, on the basis of a home language survey. Although Spanish is indicated as her native language, she is reported to have more facility in English at school. Inez's family has been in the United States for 18 years, and both parents are employed. Her three older sisters are fully bilingual. Inez's parents speak predominantly Spanish, whereas her sisters speak mainly English. Inez has many friends at school and in her neighborhood.

Inez's health history is insignificant, and her hearing and vision are within normal limits. Inez's mother reported a history of difficulties with attention and concentration during homework completion, particularly on tasks involving reading and writing.

Because Inez's native language is Spanish, but she is reported to be performing better academically in English, testing was completed in both languages. Results indicated she has variable language performance in her native language, with average scores for receptive language, low average scores for expressive language, and borderline to impaired scores for both listening and reading comprehension. English scores indicated she is able to blend sounds in the superior range, with phonetic decoding and language fluency skills in the average range and listening and reading comprehension scores in the borderline impaired range. As with the results of her Spanish language testing, her scores varied greatly.

Achievement scores were obtained in English because she indicated she was more comfortable completing these tasks in that language. Scores for math were in the average to low average range. Reading fluency was in the mildly impaired range, with writing fluency in the borderline range. Spelling and written expression were in the broad average range. Limits were tested in Spanish, showing reading fluency in the borderline range and writing fluency in the mildly impaired range.

Inez's cognitive ability was initially evaluated in Spanish, her native language, because language testing indicated her expressive–receptive abilities were variable for both languages. Due to her variability across languages, limits were subsequently tested using an English language measure, because parents and teachers reported anecdotally that she seems to be functioning better in that language. A different cognitive measure was used, with 21 days between administrations, to guard against practice effect. Results of cognitive testing indicated her verbal ability and knowledge comprehension scores in Spanish were in the mildly impaired range and in the low average range in English.

As with most bilingual assessments, a variety of confounding factors can make definitive diagnosis difficult. Cognitive testing indicated Inez's verbal ability is mildly impaired in Spanish and low average in English. It is critical to determine whether these scores represent Inez's true cognitive ability for verbal tasks or whether the scores reflect a student transitioning from monolingual to bilingual fluency. Regardless, there is an overall (Spanish and English) significant difference between verbal ability and perceptual reasoning abilities, suggesting that verbal skill may be an area of significant cognitive deficit. We have evidence that phonemic awareness skills are developed at least at the average range in Spanish and in English, both better than expected given cognitive–verbal ability scores. However, we need to remember that Inez has had intensive reading intervention in both languages for over 2 years. Expressive language is in the low average range in Spanish and in the average range in English. Listening and reading comprehension are also variable, with borderline-to-impaired scores for both in both languages, but fluency is significantly better developed in English, her preferred academic language. Receptive language in Spanish is in the average range but in the borderline impaired range in English; teachers have indicated she seems to understand their directions better in English. In addition, we cannot discount the mild attentional issues that were noted by parents and teachers and also suggested by her scores. Does her inability to remain focused and on task have to do with a language transition difficulty or an attentional difficulty? How do we make a decision as to what will be the best diagnosis for this student that will then suggest the best process of intervention for her?

As with many cases the school psychologist encounters, best practice would be to obtain collaborating evidence from other sources. Clarity on this case improved when curriculum-based methods supplemented information gathered through formal evaluation. In Inez's case, comprehension (both listening and reading) appeared to be the area of significant deficit. It is unclear whether this is because she has a cognitive deficit in verbal ability (scores were discrepant from other cognitive scores) or that it is just a case of transition from monolingual to bilingual fluency, because there are many indicators she is in transition between languages. When teachers were consulted and assessment took place in a small group or individually using materials she was familiar with in her classroom, Inez performed significantly better in listening comprehension in both languages. When the same methods were used for reading comprehension, her performance remained an area of significant difficulty, allowing for a diagnosis and intervention in reading comprehension. To ensure accuracy of diagnosis, a bilingual speech and language therapist conducted further evaluation, concurring with the diagnosis of a learning disability, rather than a speech and language disorder.

Although there is little doubt Inez is in transition between Spanish and English and not exhibiting fluency in either language, the research shows she presents with a reading comprehension disability. Her ability to function better when given unimodal input (visual or auditory) in either language is indicative of likely dysfunction in the planum temporale/Heschl sulcus and the superior temporal sulcus, which have been found to contribute to lack of reading fluency. In addition, difficulties in reading comprehension, despite improved phonemic awareness, suggest her early and appropriate reading intervention likely improved her ability to suppress effects for incongruent letters while demonstrating positive cortical responses to congruent letter–speech sounds, a task moderated by the planum temporale/Heschl sulcus and the neural response to letters in the fusiform gyrus.

LIMITATIONS IN BILINGUAL NEUROPSYCHOLOGICAL ASSESSMENT

The application of neuropsychology to bilingual assessment in children is still in a formative stage. Although research over the past 10 to 15 years has increased significantly in this area, available information remains insufficient to answer many questions that arise as the practitioner attempts to understand the data gathered during an evaluation of language for a bilingual child. The limitations Ellen Stubbe Kester and Elizabeth Peña (2002) suggested over 10 years ago included a dearth of materials in any language other than Spanish (and those being limited as well), as well as the danger of direct translation of materials meant for monolingual English speakers. These limitations are exacerbated by those practitioners who may have enough command of the second language to be tempted to modify testing materials normed for English speakers, virtually spoiling the usefulness of the instrument.

Different linguistic cues are prominent in every language, and it is likely bilingual individuals use an amalgamated system to make sense of all cues available, thus yielding invalid estimates of language ability in both their native and second languages. Tests that are translated do not retain their original psychometric properties and may become more or less robust than the original as a result. In addition, direct translations may change the order of difficulty for the test items and may not reflect the order of difficulty for development of the target language (Restrepo & Silverman, 2001). Although words may represent the same general concept, they may have significant variation and represent different levels of difficulty across languages. This may be due to their prominence or frequency of use in the native language. The context in which words are learned may also influence category development and may be associated across different languages for different reasons. Contextual variations make direct translations vulnerable to psychometric imbalance in the new "test" document (Peña, Bedore, & Zlatic-Giunta, 2002). Vocabulary differences, grammatical structure, age of second language acquisition, exposure to first language as well as to the second language—including circumstantial exposure as compared with more academic exposure—may all influence the child's approach to the evaluation. Each of these would be difficult to account for in any evaluation of a child's language, but the task is exacerbated when more than one language must be taken into account.

Improving translation practices and awareness of limitations for bilingual evaluation are important short-term goals, whereas developing and norming a wider variety of test instruments for use in a many languages should remain a long-term goal. Information provided through neuropsychological studies of bilingual individuals should help the further development and production of viable instruments for bilingual children. Although additional research is needed to better understand the development and neuropsychology of semantic and syntactic language skills for many bilingual individuals, the information available for several major world languages is likely sufficient to be able to begin developing useful instruments. These may include domain samples that represent cognitive and linguistic features of the target language that are broadly representative of each language (e.g., similarities and differences, categorizations, associations), the selection of appropriate items to attain the maximum amount of information concerning ability in each language, and the use of conceptual scoring systems to best estimate ability in each language. Legitimate guidelines are available to help clinicians identify language impairments in Spanish–English bilingual children, and these models might be used to further develop similar guidelines to be used with children bilingual in other languages as well (Gutiérrez-Clellan & Simon-Cereijido, 2009).

Assessment of a bilingual child should be completed by a psychologist who is bilingual in the child's native and acquired languages. However, it should be noted that training and competency guidelines within the field of neuropsychology fail to provide explicit procedures concerning the parameters of linguistic and professional competency necessary for ethical and competent neuropsychological evaluation of bilingual individuals and other non-English-speaking children. The National Academy of Neuropsychology (NAN) has provided broad guidelines for the evaluation of Hispanic clients (Judd et al., 2009), with direction concerning use of translators and interpreters, levels of competency, language of evaluation, the ethics involved, as well as the interpretation of federal law. Although each of these concerns, as well as the specific qualifications of the neuropsychologist, procedures for the evaluation of acculturation and level of education of the individual assessed, and appropriate use of informed consent, is addressed, the position paper does not specifically speak to the issue of evaluation of children. A branch of NAN, the Hispanic Neuropsychological Society, has provided additional guidelines for patients and their families on their website; however, these guidelines pertain to general neuropsychological evaluation rather than to evaluation of the Hispanic population or of Hispanic children (http://hnps.org).

Whenever possible, it is best to have bilingual examiners evaluate bilingual children in both languages to capture information that is more readily available in each. Evaluation in a single language limits the validity of the assessment results. Ensuring that a bilingual psychologist conducts the evaluation of a bilingual child provides a more comprehensive assessment of functioning. Ultimately, it seems that a cooperative approach, in which the school-based school psychologist and speech–language pathologist combine efforts with the clinical practitioner, will be the best approach when diagnosing these difficult cases.

CONCLUSION

The information from the studies reviewed in this chapter suggests that attainment of lexical knowledge (segmental phonology, inflectional morphology, and syntax) in a second language is affected by neural maturation, at least for Indo–European languages. This hypothesis is supported by the theory proposed by Locke (1997) and reinforced by Paradis (2005) postulating that the organization and use of the mental lexicon must occur during an optimum biological moment (the "right" time developmentally). Neuroimaging data have suggested that the age at which an individual is first exposed to the second language might have an effect on the cortical organization of the mental lexicon of that language, with additional behavioral data indicating that late (older than 10 years) bilingual individuals are likely to be slower to become competent in the second language and may make more errors in the process. These findings lend support to neurocognitive models of bilingual word recognition postulating that for both early and late bilingual individuals, the two languages are interconnected at the conceptual level and will be best approached, for all types of learning, from that standpoint.

Although professionals from distinct backgrounds may complete evaluations and conduct interventions with bilingual children, an understanding of the neuropsychological underpinnings of bilingualism, as well as an awareness of the practitioners' own linguistic competence in a nondominant language, should be reviewed before beginning. Ultimately, it is up to practitioners to decide whether their level of professional competency—including their neuropsychological competency—is adequate to evaluate and treat bilingual children.

APPENDIX 3.1: LANGUAGE DOMINANCE CHECKLIST

Use Prior to Administering Bilingual Neuropsychological Evaluation

Developmental considerations:

Years the child has attended U.S. schools: _____
Any history of language disorder/disability? ☐ Yes ☐ No
Diagnosis: _____
Programs student has participated in (bilingual/ESL/sheltered classroom, etc.):
_____
Number of years student did not attend school after age 5: _____
Years of school in another country/language: _____
Number of years student's family has resided in United States: _____

Language(s) spoken at home: _____

Parental level of education:
  Number of years of formal schooling _____
  High school education?   ☐ Yes ☐ No
  College level education?   ☐ Yes ☐ No
  Post-college level education? ☐ Yes ☐ No

Parents' literacy skills in native language (approximate):
  Reading comprehension: ☐ Beginner ☐ Intermediate ☐ Advanced
  Oral comprehension: ☐ Beginner ☐ Intermediate ☐ Advanced

Parents' literacy skills in second language (approximate):
  Reading comprehension: ☐ Beginner ☐ Intermediate ☐ Advanced
  Oral comprehension: ☐ Beginner ☐ Intermediate ☐ Advanced

Language exposure:
  Birth to 6:   ☐ Only L1 ☐ L1 and > 50% L2 ☐ L1 and < 50% L2
  K to 3rd grades: ☐ Only L1 ☐ L1 and > 50% L2 ☐ L1 and < 50% L2
  3rd to 6th grades: ☐ Only L1 ☐ L1 and > 50% L2 ☐ L1 and < 50% L2
  7th to 12th grades: ☐ Only L1 ☐ L1 and > 50% L2 ☐ L1 and < 50% L2

Language proficiency:

Based on formal measures, including: _____

Based on informal measures, including: _____

What is the student's language proficiency in his/her native language?

Reading skills: ☐ Beginner ☐ Intermediate ☐ Advanced
Writing skills: ☐ Beginner ☐ Intermediate ☐ Advanced
Oral expression: ☐ Beginner ☐ Intermediate ☐ Advanced
Oral comprehension: ☐ Beginner ☐ Intermediate ☐ Advanced

What is the student's language proficiency in L2?

Reading skills: ☐ Beginner ☐ Intermediate ☐ Advanced
Writing skills: ☐ Beginner ☐ Intermediate ☐ Advanced
Oral expression: ☐ Beginner ☐ Intermediate ☐ Advanced
Oral comprehension: ☐ Beginner ☐ Intermediate ☐ Advanced

Making the determination concerning which language to use for assessment: Use the above information to determine whether the student is more proficient in L1 or L2.

- If student's language proficiency/dominance is determined to be in L1: Administer neuropsychological measures in L1 only.
- If student's language proficiency/dominance is determined to be in L2: Administer neuropsychological measures in L2 only.
- If student's language proficiency/dominance is unclear, but student responds to L1 questions using L1: Administer cognitive measures in L1, and follow by testing the limits in L2.
- If student's language proficiency/dominance is unclear, but student responds to L1 questions using L2: Administer cognitive measures in L2, and follow by testing the limits in L1.
- If student's language proficiency/dominance appears well developed in both languages, ask the student which language is most comfortable for evaluation. Begin with that language, but follow up by testing the limits in the other language as well.

REFERENCES

Abutalebi, J., & Green, D. (2007). Bilingual language production: The neurocognition of language representation and control. *Journal of Neurolinguistics, 20,* 242–275. doi.org/10.1016/j.jneuroling.2006.10.003

American Speech–Language–Hearing Association. (2007). *Scope of practice in speech–language pathology.* Retrieved from http://www.asha.org/docs/html/SP2007-00283.html

Aylward, G. P. (1995). *Bayley Infant Neurodevelopmental Screener (BINS).* San Antonio, TX: PsychCorp.

Bialystok, E. (2001). *Bilingualism in development: Language, literacy and cognition.* New York, NY: Cambridge University Press. doi:10.1017/CBO9780511605963

Blau, V., Reithler, J., van Atteveldt, N., Seitz, J., Gerretsen, P., Goebel, R., & Blomert, L. (2010). Deviant processing of letters and speech sounds as proximate cause of reading failure: A functional magnetic resonance imaging study of dyslexic children. *Brain: A Journal of Neurology, 133,* 868–879. doi:10.1093/brain/awp308

Briellmann, R. S., Saling, M. M., Connell, A. B., Waites, A. B., Abbott, D. F., & Jackson, G. D. (2004). A high-field functional MRI study of quadrilingual subjects. *Brain and Language, 89,* 531–542. doi:10.1016/j.bandl.2004.01.008

Chen, Q., Wei, P., & Zhou, X. (2006). Distinct neural correlates for resolving Stroop conflict at inhibited and noninhibited locations in the inhibition of return. *Journal of Cognitive Neuroscience, 18,* 1937–1946. doi:10.1162/jocn.2006.18.11.1937

Cieślicka, A. B., & Heredia, R. R. (2011). Hemispheric asymmetries in processing L1 and L2 idioms: Effects of salience and context. *Brain and Language, 116,* 136–150. doi:10.1016/j.bandl.2010.09.007

Collier, V. P., (1995). Acquiring a second language for school. *Directions in Language and Education, 1,* 1–10.

Ferrer, E., Shaywitz, B. A., Holahan, J. M., Marchione, K., & Shaywitz, S. E. (2010). Uncoupling of reading and IQ over time: Empirical evidence for a definition of dyslexia. *Psychological Science, 21,* 93–101. doi:10.1177/0956797609354084

Festman, J., Rodriguez-Fornells, A., & Münte, T. F. (2010). Individual differences in control of language interference in late bilinguals are mainly related to general executive abilities. *Behavioral and Brain Functions, 6.* doi:10.1186/1744-9081-6-5

Friederici, A. D., Brauer, J., & Lohmann, G. (2011). Maturation of the language network: From inter- to intrahemispheric connectivities. *PLOS ONE, 6*(6), e20726. doi:10.1371/journal.pone.0020726

Gollan, T. H., & Brown, A. S. (2006). From tip-of-the-tongue (TOT) data to theoretical implications in two steps: When more TOTs means better retrieval. *Journal of Experimental Psychology: General, 135,* 462–483. doi:10.1037/0096-3445.135.3.462

Gollan, T. H., Montoya, R. I., & Werner, G. (2002). Semantic and letter fluency in Spanish–English bilinguals. *Neuropsychology, 16,* 562–576. doi:10.1037/0894-4105.16.4.562

Guo, T., Liu, H., Misra, M., & Kroll, J. F. (2011). Local and global inhibition in bilingual word production: fMRI evidence from Chinese–English bilinguals. *NeuroImage, 56,* 2300–2309. doi:10.1016/j.neuroimage.2011.03.049

Gutiérrez-Clellen, V. F., & Simon-Cereijido, G. (2009). Using language sampling in clinical assessments with bilingual children: Challenges and future directions. *Seminars in Speech and Language, 30,* 234–245. doi:10.1055/s-0029-1241722

Hamayan, E. V., & Damico, J. S. (1991). Developing and using a second language. In E. V. Hamayan & J. S. Damico (Eds.), *Limiting bias in the assessment of bilingual students* (pp. 39–75). Austin, TX: Pro-Ed.

Hamers, J., & Blanc, M. (2000). *Bilinguality and bilingualism* (2nd ed.). Cambridge, MA: Cambridge University Press. doi:10.1017/CBO9780511605796

Holm, A., Dodd, B., Stow, C., & Pert, S. (1999). Identification and differential diagnosis of phonological disorder in bilingual children. *Language Testing, 16,* 271–292.

Homae, F., Watanabe, H., Nakano, T., & Taga, G. (2011). Large-scale brain networks underlying language acquisition in early infancy. *Frontiers in Psychology, 2.* doi:10.3389/fpsyg.2011.00093

Hu, W., Lee, H. L., Zhang, Q., Liu, T., Geng, L. B., Seghier, M. L., . . . Price, C. J. (2010). Developmental dyslexia in Chinese and English populations: Dissociating the effect of dyslexia from language differences. *Brain: A Journal of Neurology, 133,* 1694–1706. doi:10.1093/brain/awq106

Isel, F., Baumgaertner, A., Thrän, J., Meisel, J. M., & Büchel, C. (2010). Neural circuitry of the bilingual mental lexicon: Effect of age of second language acquisition. *Brain and Cognition, 72,* 169–180. doi:10.1016/j.bandc.2009.07.008

Ivanova, I., & Costa, A. (2008). Does bilingualism hamper lexical access in speech production? *Acta Psychologica, 127,* 277–288. doi:10.1016/j.actpsy.2007.06.003

Judd, T., Capetillo, D., Carrion-Baralt, J., Marmol, L. M., San Miguel-Montes, L., Navarrete, M. G., . . . the National Academy of Neuropsychology Policy and Planning Committee. (2009). Professional considerations for improving the neuropsychological evaluation of Hispanics: A National Academy of Neuropsychology education paper. *Archives of Clinical Neuropsychology, 24,* 127–135. doi:10.1093/arclin/acp016

Kester, E. S., & Peña, E. D. (2002). Language ability assessment of Spanish–English bilinguals: Future directions. *Practical Assessment, Research & Evaluation, 8*(4). Retrieved from http://pareonline.net/getvn.asp?v=8&n=4

Kumar, U., Das, T., Bapi, R. S., Padakannaya, P., Joshi, R. M., & Singh, N. C. (2010). Reading different orthographies: An fMRI study of phrase reading in Hindi–English bilinguals. *Reading and Writing, 23,* 239–255. doi:10.1007/s11145-009-9176-8

Lebel, C., Shaywitz, B., Holahan, J., Shaywitz, S., Marchione, K., & Beaulieu, C. (2013). Diffusion tensor imaging correlates of reading ability in dysfluent and non-impaired readers. *Brain and Language, 125,* 215–222. doi.org/10.1016/j.bandl.2012.10.009

Lehtonen, M., Vorobyev, V., Soveri, A., Hugdahl, K., Tuokkola, T., & Laine, M. (2009). Language-specific activations in the brain: Evidence from inflectional processing in bilinguals. *Journal of Neurolinguistics, 22,* 495–513. doi:10.1016/j.jneuroling.2009.05.001

Locke, J. L. (1997). A theory of neurolinguistic development. *Brain and Language, 58,* 265–326. doi:10.1006/brln.1997.1791

Marrero, M. Z., Golden, C. J., & Espe-Pfeifer, P. (2002). Bilingualism, brain injury, and recovery: Implications for understanding the bilingual and for therapy. *Clinical Psychology Review, 22,* 463–478. doi:10.1016/S0272-7358(01)00109-X

Mechelli, A., Crinion, J. T., Noppeny, U., O'Doherty, J., Ashburner, J., Frackowiak, R. S., & Price, C. J. (2004). Neurolinguistics: Structural plasticity in the bilingual brain. *Nature, 431,* 757. doi:10.1038/431757a

Meschyan, G., & Hernandez, A. E. (2006). Impact of language proficiency and orthographic transparency on bilingual word reading: An fMRI study. *NeuroImage, 29,* 1135–1140. doi:10.1016/j.neuroimage.2005.08.055

Mindt, M. R., Arentoft, A., Germano, K. K., D'Aquila, E., Scheiner, D., Pizzirusso, M., . . . Gollan, T. H. (2008). Neuropsychological, cognitive, and theoretical considerations for evaluation of bilingual individuals. *Neuropsychology Review, 18,* 255–268. doi:10.1007/s11065-008-9069-7

Miozzo, M., Costa, A., Hernández, M., & Rapp, B. (2010). Lexical processing in the bilingual brain: Evidence from grammatical/morphological deficits. *Aphasiology, 24,* 262–287. doi:10.1080/02687030902958381

Odegard, T. N., Ring, J., Smith, S., Biggan, J., & Black, J. (2008). Differentiating the neural response to intervention in children with developmental dyslexia. *Annals of Dyslexia, 58*(1), 1–14. doi:10.1007/s11881-008-0014-5

Paradis, M. (2005). *A neurolinguistic theory of bilingualism.* Amsterdam, the Netherlands: John Benjamins.

Peña, E. D., Bedore, L. M., & Zlatic-Giunta, R. (2002). Category generation performance of young bilingual children: The influence of condition, category, and language. *Journal of Speech, Language, and Hearing Research, 45,* 938–947. doi:10.1044/1092-4388(2002/076)

Pinel, J. (2010). *Biopsychology.* Upper Saddle River, NJ: Pearson.

Restrepo, M. A., & Silverman, S. W. (2001). Validity of the Spanish Preschool Language Scale-3 for use with bilingual children. *American Journal of Speech–Language Pathology, 10,* 382–393. doi:10.1044/1058-0360(2001/032)

Roberts, P. M., Garcia, L. J., Desrochers, A., & Hernandez, D. (2002). English performance of proficient bilingual adults on the Boston Naming Test. *Aphasiology, 16,* 635–645. doi:10.1080/02687030244000220

Saur, D., Baumgaertner, A., Moehring, A., Büchel, C., Bonneson, M., Rose, M., . . . Meisel, J. M. (2009). Word order processing in the bilingual brain. *Neuropsychologia, 47*, 158–168. doi:10.1016/j.neuropsychologia.2008.08.007

Semel, E., Wiig, E. H., & Secord, W. A. (2003). *Clinical Evaluation of Language Fundamentals—Fourth Edition* (CELF-4). San Antonio, TX: PsychCorp.

Semel, E., Wiig, E. H., & Secord, W. A. (2004). *CELF–Preschool–2*. San Antonio, TX: PsychCorp.

Semel, E., Wiig, E. H., & Secord, W. A. (2013). *Clinical Evaluation of Language Fundamentals—Fifth Edition* (CELF-5). San Antonio, TX: PsychCorp.

Shaywitz, B. A., Lyon, G. R., & Shaywitz, S. E. (2006). The role of functional magnetic resonance imaging in understanding reading and dyslexia. *Developmental Neuropsychology, 30*(1), 613–632. doi:10.1207/s15326942dn3001_5

Shaywitz, S. (2005). *Overcoming dyslexia: A new and complete science-based program for reading problems at any level*. New York, NY: Random House.

Shaywitz, S. E., & Shaywitz, B. A. (2008). Paying attention to reading: The neurobiology of reading and dyslexia. *Development and Psychopathology, 20*, 1329–1349. doi:10.1017/S0954579408000631

Thomas, W. P., & Collier, V. P. (2002). *A national study of school effectiveness for language minority students' long-term academic achievement*. Santa Cruz, CA: Center for Research on Education, Diversity & Excellence.

Wang, Y., Xiang, J., Vannest, J., Holroyd, T., Narmoneva, D., Horn, P., . . . Holland, S. (2011). Neuromagnetic measures of word processing in bilinguals and monolinguals. *Clinical Neurophysiology, 122*, 1706–1717. doi:10.1016/j.clinph.2011.02.008

Westerhausen, R., Kreuder, F., Dos Santos Sequeira, S., Walter, C., Woerner, W., Wittling, R. A., . . . Wittling, W. (2006). The association of macro- and microstructure of the corpus callosum and language lateralization. *Brain and Language, 97*, 80–90. doi:10.1016/j.bandl.2005.07.133

Xue, G., Chen, C., Jin, Z., & Dong, Q. (2006). Cerebral asymmetry in the fusiform areas predicted the efficiency of learning a new writing system. *Journal of Cognitive Neuroscience, 18*, 923–931. doi:10.1162/jocn.2006.18.6.923

Zelazo, P. D., Muller, U., Frye, D., & Marcovitch, S. (2003). The development of executive function. *Monographs of the Society for Research in Child Development, 68*, 11–27.

Zied, K. M., Phillipe, A., Karine, P., Valerie, H. T., Ghislaine, A., Arnaud, R., & Didier, L. G. (2004). Bilingualism and adult differences in inhibitory mechanisms: Evidence from a bilingual Stroop task. *Brain and Cognition, 54*, 254–256. doi:10.1016/j.bandc.2004.02.036

Zimmerman, I. L., Steiner, V. G., & Pond, R. E. (2002a). *Preschool Language Scale, Fourth Edition (PLS-4) English Edition*. San Antonio, TX: PsychCorp.

Zimmerman, I. L., Steiner, V. G., & Pond, R. E. (2002b). *Preschool Language Scale, Fourth Edition (PLS-4) Spanish Edition*. San Antonio, TX: PsychCorp.

4

IMPLICATIONS OF SEMILINGUALISM FOR ASSESSMENT OF THE BILINGUAL CHILD

AMANDA B. CLINTON, WANDA R. ORTIZ,
AND KORAH LA SERNA GUILAR

Modern societies are mobile and global. This reality means that many children will immigrate during their school years or be born to parents who recently immigrated themselves. The conditions of immigration vary, but the primary reasons are economic, social, political, or environmental (Pacheco, Rossouw, & Lewer, 2013). Migration may be a choice, such as when an individual seeks better job opportunities, or forced, as in the case of war or famine. The varying circumstances and distinct groups of people moving from one place to another mean that the bilingual children referred to school psychologists bring complex personal, familial, and educational histories. This chapter addresses one of these complexities, semilingualism, specifically, limited literacy development in both a child's native and, in turn, second language and its implications for assessment by the school psychologist.

The term *semilingual* describes individuals who are considered to possess limited levels of literacy in their native language and their second language

http://dx.doi.org/10.1037/14320-005
Assessing Bilingual Children in Context: An Integrated Approach, A. B. Clinton (Editor)

(Escamilla, 2006). Another term used to indicate the same meaning is *bi-illiteracy*, which has been described as "a socially constructed concept that implies low levels of literacy" (Escamilla, 2006, p. 2330) in both one's native and second languages. In an effort to reduce potential negative connotations suggested when terminology was debated, Cummins (1981) ultimately settled on the term *limited bilingualism* in lieu of semilingualism.

Although some researchers in education and linguistics interpret semilingualism as an indication that non-English languages are problematic or that bilingualism is damaging (e.g., MacSwan, 2000; MacSwan, Rolstad, & Glass, 2002), this is not the interpretation given to bilingualism or semilingualism in this chapter. The term *semilingualism* as used throughout the upcoming pages is largely synonymous with Escamilla's (2006) definition of bi-illiteracy. The term is not intended to be destructive in its use but instead to be helpful in identifying the bilingual child referred for assessment and intervention who demonstrates poor development and knowledge of both their native and second languages.

A significant body of research substantiates the importance of school preparedness as a facilitator of positive educational experiences and long-term, successful life outcomes (e.g., Hart & Risley, 1995; Wagner, Torgesen, & Rashotte, 1994). Children who enter school with low levels of literacy typically establish and continue along a learning trajectory that is persistently below that of their peers (Adams, 1990; Campbell & Ramey, 1994). These are commonly children hailing from low socioeconomic backgrounds and include the majority of first- and second-generation immigrant youth who often live in poverty and whose parents possess limited literacy themselves (U.S. Census Bureau, 2012). As a result, newly arrived families and their children have less access to learning materials such as books and educationally oriented activities (Rodríguez et al., 2009).

One particular example demonstrating the relationship between poverty and language development can be observed in Hart and Risley's (1995) study. In this seminal project, the authors demonstrated that youngsters whose family income levels are below the poverty line enter kindergarten with a vocabulary of approximately 5,000 words, compared with the 20,000-word vocabulary of children from higher income families. Underdevelopment of literacy in language-minority children in the United States has been documented (August, Shanahan, & Escamilla, 2009). Given the relatively high numbers of second language learners who immigrate with their parents to a new country in an effort to escape poverty, the possibility of semilingualism in their native and second languages is clear and its impact significant.

In sum, when we consider assessment of the semilingual child, we are referring to a youngster who commonly presents a highly complicated set of circumstances. These typically include immigration, low parental education levels, and poverty. These types of issues bring additional consequences, such as limited access to high quality education, acculturation stressors, and later, stereotypes, all of which may be confounded by the lack of preparedness of educators to work with bilingual students. Language learning in relation to immigration, parent education, and poverty is explored in the upcoming paragraphs, and ultimately, assessment considerations relevant to helping children who are semilingual improve their academic progress in school will be discussed.

LANGUAGE ACQUISITION

Native Language Acquisition

Learning to speak and, later, to read in one's native language incorporates the acquisition of a series of skills that occur in a largely predictable pattern. As summarized by Feldman (2011), babies initially babble using the sounds from any and all languages. Their babbling increasingly reflects the sounds they hear in their particular language environment, however, until, at about a year of age, children begin speaking their first words. From this point, they progress to two-word combinations, and later, telegraphic speech (i.e., "I drink juice") develops as the child's vocabulary becomes increasingly complex. Around three years of age, children are capable of adding plurals (s) and past tense (-ed) to words. By age 5, the average child possesses the basic rules of language, although subtleties such as double entendre may be difficult for them, and by 8 years of age, even complex language usage is mastered.

The idea of critical periods for language learning posits that children are particularly sensitive to acquiring the sounds and cues related to language early in life (Feldman, 2011). Evidence has suggested that sensitive periods for language learning exist for both one's native language (L1) and a second language (L2) as well, although determination of specific environmental and biological influences occurs later (Shafer & Garrido-Nag, 2007). Extreme environmental deprivation certainly alters brain development, as observed in research with orphans from the former Soviet bloc country of Romania (Bos, Fox, Zeanah, & Nelson, 2009) and in the case of Genie, a victim of abuse who was not exposed to any language from 20 months to 13 years of age and never developed the ability to speak in spite of intensive treatment (Rymer, 1994; Veltman & Browne, 2001). Even in less severe circumstances, it is recognized that limited L1 development negatively affects the potential for complete L2 development (Gutiérrez-Clellen, Simon-Cereijido, & Sweet, 2012), resulting in issues of low literacy in both languages.

Second Language Acquisition

It is common for young children to acquire two languages fluently and with relative ease when they are exposed to them simultaneously, as in cases of bilingual first language acquisition (learning two languages at once). Most of the referrals for children who may be considered semilingual are cases of sequential bilingualism where the child learns their first language to a limited degree and later must acquire a second language. Many bilingual children in schools master their L1 and their L2, having learned two languages either simultaneously or sequentially. However, the process of learning a second language, similar to that of learning one's native language, is not error free even in optimal learning conditions. Instead, normative errors may be observed. These are not indicative of a disability but of learning processes.

A child who is acquiring a second language may access knowledge through his or her first language by mapping the language being acquired onto their first language. Alternatively, the child may learn a second language directly. In the bilingual child whose dual language development is normative, errors tend to be systematic and rule-governed (Paradis, 2005; Paradis, Rice, Crago, & Marquis, 2008). For example, children commonly "overregularize" past tense verbs (Xu & Pinker, 1995). One example would be use of the morpheme *-ed* to convert irregular verbs, such as *run*, to the past tense. In this case, adding *-ed* creates the word *runned* instead of *ran*. Bilingual children may demonstrate even greater frequency of these types of errors while working out linguistic intricacies, in comparison with their monolingual peers who are negotiating the same linguistic structures (Mueller Gathercole, 2007; Paradis, 2010). This has been hypothesized to be due to differential input factors, such as varying degrees of exposure between one's native and second language at home (Paradis, Nicoladis, Crago, & Genesee, 2011). In the case of semilingual children, errors of this type may reflect erroneous language learning or broader levels of low literacy rather than normative errors in second language acquisition.

As with native speakers residing in specific regions or neighborhoods, children learning their second language in a place where a nonstandard version or emergent variety of this language is spoken will likely speak this particular dialect themselves (Benesch, 2008). Benesch (2008) posited that this phenomenon, commonly observed in students whose parents immigrated when they were in elementary school, should be explored as a legitimate linguistic variation and not necessarily a deficit.

In addition to linguistic aspects of language acquisition, other factors, including the environment, are critical to developing fluency in a second language. The child development literature has demonstrated that particular types of interactions between caregivers and children or teachers and children can facilitate language development (Pan, Rowe, Singer, & Snow, 2005; Quiroz,

Snow, & Zhao, 2010). Studies have demonstrated relationships between home literacy environment and a child's later language development (de Jong & Leseman, 2001; Roberts, Jurgens, & Burchinal, 2005; Sénéchal & LeFevre, 2002). Semilingual children may be at a disadvantage in terms of literacy-rich environments because many first- and second-generation immigrant children hail from impoverished families (U.S. Census Bureau, 2012).

Educational issues are also critical in relation to language and literacy in L1 and L2. In cases where poverty was a concern in a bilingual child's country of origin or, if they were born in their country of residence, in their particular neighborhood, it is not unlikely that he or she attended schools where resources and teacher preparation may have been limited. The lack of comprehensive literacy programs is considered critical to closing the literacy gap between rich and poor (Wamba, 2010). Data have shown that bilingual education teachers devalue the ideas and quality of thinking in their students on the basis of language issues (Escamilla, 2006). It is not uncommon for bilingual educators to presume that bilingual children who are struggling have been unable to learn specific aspects of language that teachers believed were previously taught—such as the use of the accent in Spanish—yet not to know that this instruction is relatively late in a child's academic career in foreign school systems (Escamilla, 2006). These assumptions lead to biased interpretations about causation and incorrect conclusions about student abilities, which may negatively affect the quality of their educational experience.

In addition to an appropriately enriched developmental context, motivation and the sociocultural context can make important contributions to second language learning. In fact, in a meta-analysis by Masgoret and Gardner (2003), motivation and achievement in language learning showed stronger correlations than attitudes about the learning situation and level of adaptation to the new culture. Other research has indicated key relationships between affective factors, such as self-confidence and level of anxiety related to language learning, and language acquisition (Gardner, Tremblay, & Masgoret, 1997). Furthermore, positive experiences with the culture of one's L2 combined with communicative competence can increase language-learning success (Masgoret, 2006). Although questions remain regarding specific contributions from unique factors, the importance of motivation in learning a second language cannot be overemphasized. In the case of children who struggle with literacy-based tasks in their native language, it seems reasonable to believe that working toward learning a second language would present a significant challenge and, as such, often be more frustrating than not, potentially having a negative impact on motivation. This may be further complicated by the types of experiences that recent immigrants can encounter, notably feelings of alienation and discrimination, as demonstrated in the case of José, presented next.

Case Study: José

José[1] is a 15-year-old Mexican teenager enrolled as a junior at a public high school in California. José, his mother, and his sibling arrived in the United States approximately one year prior to his referral for assessment. They do not have legal permission to be in the country but came to join his father who immigrated to the United States illegally approximately three years earlier. They are monolingual Spanish speakers.

José's father works in groundskeeping. His mother is not employed. José's parents both earned a sixth-grade education. A home visit revealed no books in the home, and when parents were asked to complete a written developmental questionnaire in Spanish, their literacy levels were so low that they could not respond to items without help explaining questions and assistance with written replies.

Before moving to California, José attended a public school program in his hometown on the Mexico–U.S. border. Classes were given for 4 hours each day to accommodate two rotations of students. According to José's mother, there were typically well over three dozen students in a class with a teacher and an aide.

José was enrolled in English language courses on arriving in the United States, and he receives tutoring in Spanish for all subjects to assist with the transition. The tutor reported that José appears to have a limited Spanish language vocabulary and typically does not understand commonly used terms, such as *valley* (*valle*) or *emotion* (*emoción*) but manages with more basic words such as *feelings* (*sentimientos*), in lieu of *emotion*. He reads slowly in Spanish and still sounds out many words. Often, he becomes frustrated with reading, writing, and other school tasks and acts out by punching his textbook or skipping class and hanging out with friends from nearby towns in Mexico near the school's track.

In an effort to help José, he was referred to the school's monolingual English-speaking school psychologist. This psychologist told José to "shape up or ship out back to his home country" at the initial individualized education plan meeting. Neither of José's parents spoke at all, though the meeting was translated into Spanish for them. José's level of homework completion and class attendance were historically poor and continued to worsen. When referred for therapy to a school-based counselor who speaks Spanish, José spoke little but, when he did, often made angry outbursts punctuated by a mix of English and Spanish profanity.

José experienced significant academic and behavioral difficulties throughout his junior year. His parents, though receptive to help, willingly "conversed" with José about improving his choices. In general, they indicated an inability to control their son or influence his behavior.

---

[1]The details of the case studies have been changed to protect the anonymity of the individuals involved.

Cross-Language Influence

Cross-linguistic transfer refers to the application of the semantic or syntactic structures of one language, typically a child's native language, to another, typically their second language (Kaushanskaya & Marian, 2007). One language does not interfere with another in a normative bilingual context (Escamilla, 2006). Instead, the language learner experiences a generally positive learning benefit on L2 acquisition from his or her L1 knowledge in the form of cross-language transfer contributions. This process is considered bidirectional, in that structural aspects, as well as specific components—such as vocabulary—of both L1 and L2, contribute to the enrichment of the other, rather than simply being a unidirectional process where L1 leads to enhancement in L2 (Paradis et al., 2011; Sparks, Patton, Ganschow, & Humbach, 2012). This effect may be greater when you have a more transparent L2, such as Spanish or Dutch, and a more opaque L1, such as English (DeSousa, Greenop, & Fry, 2011; Sun-Alperin & Wang, 2011; van der Leij, Bekebrede, & Kotterink, 2010).

Bilingual children typically arrive at school having developed language differently from monolingual children. The second language learner typically comes to school with developed oral L1 and sometimes written L1. The degree of transfer from one language to another will vary even when a child is highly literate in their first language and generally relies on existent linguistic knowledge in L1 (Sparks et al., 2012). In terms of basic reading, well-developed phonological awareness skills in Spanish have been shown to be key to learning English words and sound–symbol relationships in nonsense words (Durgunoğlu, Nagy, & Hancin-Bhatt, 1993; Gottardo, 2002). Other studies have indicated that even modest English language knowledge results in greater success in acquiring a second language (Gottardo, 2002). Because semilingual children lack literacy in their native language and acquired language, a reasonable interpretation of these data is that semilinguals do not have the basic skills that facilitate L2 learning.

Semilingualism and Cross-Language Transfer

It is recognized that native language literacy influences second language learning and, in turn, that poor literacy in L1 can affect L2 learning. Cross-language transfer specific to the case of low literacy, or that of semilinguals, becomes more complicated. It makes sense that if a child possesses a relatively shallow linguistic base in L1 to use and apply in the process of learning L2, that transfer will be reduced or minimal. In fact, it seems reasonable to hypothesize that, because L1 is poorly developed, adding the complexities of learning a second language can be particularly challenging. This situation is even further complicated if the child is a recent immigrant who is struggling with a new school system, has limited prior schooling or schooling of poor quality, and has low literacy at home. This is not uncommon for Spanish-dominant children learning English in the United States and may place them at a particular disadvantage.

Some data have shown that an insufficiently enriched L1 learning environment results in distinct growth patterns for both a child's native and acquired language (Gutiérrez-Clellen et al., 2012). As explained by Gutiérrez-Clellen and her colleagues (2012) in regard to Spanish-speaking English language learners,

> Growth in English may be related to individual differences in the development of their Spanish languages skills as well as the child's current level of English proficiency (i.e., how well the child speaks English), exposure (i.e., how much input the child receives in English), or use (i.e., how frequently the child uses English). (p. 64)

The challenges that semilingual children face learning a second language are many. In terms of reading development in L2, children with limited literacy in L1 and virtually no knowledge of their L2 demonstrate insufficient understanding of mapping from grapheme to phoneme from one language to another (Sun-Alperin & Wang, 2011). In L2 English learners whose first language is highly regular, this is particularly problematic and typically results in incorrect pronunciation of words (Sun-Alperin & Wang, 2011). Additional research has indicated the need for L1 literacy to assist L2 language acquisition in terms of the ability to decode and comprehend print and oral language and in terms of overall proficiency in L2 (Sparks et al., 2012). Sparks and his colleagues (2012) specifically concluded that native language reading skills and broad literacy show a strong relationship to L2 proficiency. In the case of a semilingual child who has low literacy in his or her native language, few skills and limited knowledge in the first language are available to contribute to learning their L2, leaving such students at a distinct disadvantage.

The issue of vocabulary is also critical for semilingual children. As highlighted previously, shallow vocabulary development is frequently observed in families in which parent education levels are low and linguistic and educational enrichment is poor (Hart & Risley, 1995). A limited word base reduces a child's access to understanding or comprehension of school-based tasks. This, along with the previously mentioned challenges of learning to decode words or develop fluency in one's L2, would naturally lead to frustration with school-based assignments and the broader school experience. The long-term consequence of low motivation or feeling like a failure at school are significant (Spira, Storch Bracken, & Fischel, 2005) and may include dropping out, increased poverty, increased rates of violence, and addiction. The case of Jessica, presented next, demonstrates issues related to low socioeconomic status and limited parental education on the progress of bilingual children.

Case Study: Jessica

Jessica is an 11-year-old fifth grade Mexican–American girl who was born in northern California and resides with three generations of family members. Spanish is the primary language spoken in the home; however, the younger generations also speak some English. The family's annual income places them at the poverty level by federal standards.

Jessica attended a neighborhood school program for English language learners (ELL) from kindergarten to Grade 2. She had good attendance and her grades indicated academic standards were being met. As a result of a desegregation case in the courts, Jessica transferred to a higher performing school district with no ELL programs in third grade. Records indicate a positive attitude but increasing absences and "disengagement" after her transfer. In fourth grade, Jessica's teacher noted that she needed to improve her English. By fifth grade, Jessica was not performing at grade level, and testing was requested. According to her mother, Jessica's English abilities are beginning to surpass her Spanish; however, she sometimes struggles to communicate clearly in either language.

During assessment, when asked which language she prefers, Jessica responded, "Both. But sometimes in English, I have a hard time—there's words that I don't get." She was observed to code switch. According to Jessica, it is difficult for her to understand all of the words used in class. Behavior rating scales showed clinically significant concerns in the areas of anxiety, depression, self-esteem, attention, and perceived control.

During testing, Jessica demonstrated high-average thinking ability; however, her Spanish verbal ability is considered low. Jessica exclaimed with frustration, "Sometimes I don't like English because I forget Spanish!"

When assessed by the speech and language specialist, Jessica's English vocabulary, auditory memory, and phonological processing were considered average. However, areas of significant deficit were noted in her ability to process complex information, follow complex directions, and use higher order thinking skills in her second language (English). The bilingual school psychologist found that Jessica demonstrated a low average ability to listen to a sequence of complex instructions and then follow the directions in Spanish. The school psychologist determined that Jessica can follow complex instructions more easily in her L1, whereas she is able to retrieve words from her lexicon and express herself more efficiently in her L2. Jessica was enrolled in special education services to help improve her verbal memory and language processing in Spanish and English.

THE NEUROSCIENCE OF LANGUAGE AND POVERTY

Bilingual students who are referred for psychoeducational assessment may frequently be relatively recent immigrants to the country. According to the U.S. Census Bureau (2012), nearly 32% of first-generation and 27% of second-generation immigrant children live below the poverty level, compared with approximately 10% of children from families where both parents are U.S. citizens. The reality in the United States is that the academic achievement of immigrant students continues to fall behind that of native speakers (U.S. Department of Education, 2009). Because poverty has implications for the quality of a child's home environment, and this immediate context has been shown to predict performance on measures of basic processes that affect learning (National Institute of Child Health and Human Development & Early Child Care Research Network [NICHD], 2005), these are critical considerations in assessment of bilingual and semilingual children.

The way in which poverty influences brain development is complex and multifaceted. Individual differences can result from the interaction of one's genetic makeup, the accumulated exposure to risk, and specific aspects of the quality of the child's developmental context (NICHD, 2005). Low socioeconomic status brings with it a number of risk factors, many of which may lead to cumulative effects (Walker et al., 2007). These may include poor nutrition, exposure to infectious disease, poor parental home stimulation, or exposure to toxins, to name a few.

Cognitive neuroscience research has elucidated some specific relationships between an impoverished environment and brain development. Data have shown that children from low socioeconomic backgrounds demonstrate lower proficiency on a number of executive processes, such as attentional focus (Mezzacappa, 2004), inhibition, planning, and cognitive flexibility (Lipina, Martelli, Vuelta, & Colombo, 2005; Lipina, Martelli, Vuelta, Injoque Ricle, & Colombia, 2004). Working memory has also been shown to be affected (Lipina, et al., 2005). These basic processes make significant contributions to academic success, such as learning to read and understand print (Hannon, 2012; Swanson, Orosco, Lussier, Gerber, & Guzman, 2011). Indeed, correlations between frontal lobe function and measures of math and reading have been shown and, more important, these executive functions account for unique variance on these academic tasks (Blair & Razza, 2007). In fact, written language development in children from homes with limited economic resources has specifically been shown to be negatively affected by the consequences of poverty (Noble, Farah, & McCandliss, 2006). This research, then, links an impoverished environment, in which many immigrant children in the United States and across the world grow up, to cognitive development and, in particular, fundamental language processes and skills, in addition to complementary and critical abilities such as paying attention and focusing, to limited skill growth and, in turn, poor performance. It helps elucidate potential contributing factors to semilingualism in children.

Semilingual children in the school system typically hail from backgrounds that present a highly complex set of circumstances. A fundamental aspect of the child's prior experience that would affect their language learning across the life span is that of the impact of poverty on brain development. To be more specific, low socioeconomic status brings issues such as poor nutrition, parents and family members with low education levels, and limited enrichment opportunities. Other stressors that may accompany low resource environments, such as high stress levels and inadequate educational systems, may further contribute to distinct brain development processes that result in differential learning. In addition to the potential long-term impacts of an impoverished environment on a child's biological development, semilingual children frequently cope with additional challenges such as immigration, acculturation, changing schools, and acquiring academic skills in a second language. Taken together, children whose history includes these circumstances may well be semilingual and, as such, need special consideration in terms of assessment procedures and test interpretation, in addition to intervention. In terms of special education qualification, however, obtaining academic enrichment for these children is complicated because the environmental factors that lead to semilingualism typically exclude them from receiving services.

ASSESSMENT

Assessment is particularly complicated in the case of bilingualism and potentially even more so when semilingualism in two languages is a concern. Few measures have been developed for either of these purposes. For this reason, it is important to carefully consider the validity of assessment tools and procedures. In terms of bias, many tests are not appropriate for a variety of reasons—content does not coincide with academic instruction or relevant experience, normative samples are not representative, or task instructions and testing techniques are unfamiliar (Baca & Cervantes, 2004). Even informal assessment tools, such as grading rubrics for writing assessment, are commonly developed in the dominant language according to norms and expectations of the dominant educational system and may, therefore, also be biased in terms of the skills they evaluate and how they are measured (Black & Valenzuela, 2004).

Informal assessment and teacher expectations may also present particular challenges. As demonstrated in a study on writing by Escamilla (2006), educators appear to presume certain skills have been taught at a particular grade level. For example, when surveyed, American teachers of ELL students stated they believed the use of accents is a skill taught in the fourth and fifth grades in Mexico. In reality, this skill is taught in sixth grade. The result was that American ELL teachers believed their Mexican immigrant students were below expected levels in Spanish usage and evaluated them accordingly (below expectations), even though their errors were grade-appropriate.

An adequate assessment of a child who appears to be semilingual will require more time than a typical evaluation. If the student is assessed in both languages, the process will be most informative if it is relatively fluid in terms of language usage. That is, the psychologist will consider responses in either language throughout the process, rather than insist on discrete periods of L1 use ("This test is in English") followed by discrete periods of L2 use ("This test is in Spanish") or vice versa. Many of the procedures discussed as particularly useful for the assessment of the semilingual child are detailed in other chapters of this volume, and the reader is referred to relevant chapters on response to intervention (Chapter 6), use of standardized measures (Chapter 5), and social–emotional assessment (Chapter 7). In addition, Appendix 4.1 provides a checklist to assess semilingualism. It is important to note, however, that semilingualism requires a significant amount of flexibility through combining methods to best ascertain the child's knowledge overall rather than limit understanding of their skills to what they may express in one language or the other.

Context Is Key

Understanding the semilingual child and his or her language development in both their L1 and L2 requires a solid understanding of the context. This includes a detailed family history that addresses (with detailed attention to language) developmental, social, and academic history in addition to specific exploration of parental education levels, interactions (passive or active learning emphasized, type of conversations, etc.), and the child's educational experience in their country of origin, in the case of immigration. A home visit should be considered prerequisite to the evaluation as well. This allows the school psychologist the opportunity to gain a better sense of the environment surrounding the child and put into context responses provided in an interview regarding the aforementioned topics. It also helps clarify many of these areas, such as the kind of verbal interactions that children have with their parents or the degree of enrichment the environment offers.

It is critical to gather information not just about the level of education of the child's parents but also about their beliefs regarding schooling and its relationship to their child's future. Parental beliefs about education have been shown to influence parent–school interactions and, furthermore, can be highly culturally embedded (Durand, 2011). Because parental level of education is related to a child's educational attainment (Hortaçsu, 1995) and poverty, low education levels and immigration are often related. It is particularly important for the school psychologist to understand the family so as to best encourage the semilingual student to remain in school in spite of the difficulties that he or she may face in terms of academic success.

Understanding the nature of interactions between semilingual children and their parents is critical in terms of the child's context. It has been well documented that verbally rich environments facilitate language growth in children (Cohen & Cooper, 1972; Schady, 2011). Do families report reading to their children, talking about the news, or telling stories orally? Are children encouraged to question and explore? Or is learning more passively oriented toward watching TV? The quality of interactions and enrichment in the home setting make a meaningful contribution to the child's learning (Schady, 2011).

Finally, to adequately determine what a child should know, it is critical to ensure that the school psychologist understands the curriculum and instruction of the school the child attended in his country of origin as well as within his country of current residence. It is not uncommon for children to be assessed on the basis of information they have not been taught, particularly when they are bilingual, recently immigrated, or have moved frequently (Escamilla, 2006). Educators often make assumptions about what a child has been taught, but these are frequently erroneous (Escamilla, 2006).

Standardized Batteries

Standardized, norm-referenced tests are those that are developed to be administered and scored in a consistent manner, the results of which are compared with the scores of a group of children who were previously administered the measure and are considered similar in demographics. Several commercial, national, norm-referenced standardized tests have been developed for use with bilingual or multilingual populations.

Recognized measures include tests developed in a specific language, tests with translated items, and others designed specifically to assess vocabulary in more than one language. The Batería III Woodcock–Muñoz (Woodcock, Muñoz-Sandoval, McGrew, & Mather, 2007) was developed in Spanish, rather than translated into Spanish. It was conceptualized as a parallel version of the Woodcock–Johnson tests of cognitive and academic ability and, as such, was based on the Cattell–Horn–Carroll (CHC) model (Woodcock, McGrew, & Mather, 2007). Another measure of intellectual functioning available in Spanish is the Wechsler Intelligence Scale for Children—Fourth Edition (WISC–IV) Spanish (Wechsler, 2005). Norms are based on 851 ELLs with less than 5 years of schooling in the United States and a Spanish reliability sample of 500 children from countries in Mexico, the Caribbean, and Central and South America (Clinton, 2007). The Kaufman Assessment Battery for Children–Second Edition (KABC–2) includes processing, cognitive, and nonverbal indices (Kaufman & Kaufman, 2004). Similar to the Batería, the KABC–2 is based both on the CHC theory of intelligence and Luria's (1966) theory of processing and provides translation of items. The Bilingual Verbal Abilities Test (BVAT; Muñoz-Sandoval, Cummins, Alvarado, & Ruef, 2006) assesses vocabulary and verbal reasoning in two languages, typically English and the examinee's second language, and suggests that these results offer an overall estimate of ability.

Although these tests offer a Spanish language option for assessment, none has been normed using bilingual children in the United States and, as such, their validity is questionable in cases such as referrals of semilingual children who are struggling in their L1 and their L2. Concerns with the aforementioned standardized measures include problems with norms. For example, the WISC–IV Spanish norms were equated to the English version of the Wechsler Scales (Braden & Iribarren, 2007). Norms for the Batería are based on a sample of Spanish-speaking children, rather than bilingual children living in the United States. For this reason, the measure is of limited utility, because regional language and content issues can negatively affect a child's performance. The BVAT purports to measure "ability" but is largely based on word knowledge. This is particularly problematic for semilingual children who may be capable of solving problems in situations that are not heavily loaded with vocabulary.

Nonverbal tests of intellectual functioning are measures that limit the use of oral and written language. Nonverbal tools provide another option but may also be problematic. Although the majority of instructions are mimed in the administration of nonverbal ability tests, these measures are not entirely language free (Ortiz, 2011). They have the benefit of eliminating subtests that require significant vocabulary knowledge, which also reduces the influence of differences in word knowledge but omits information in this critical area of ability. In addition, their norming samples are not based on bilingual children and the testing process is never completely "culture free." A commonly used test of nonverbal intelligence is the Universal Nonverbal Intelligence Test (Bracken & McCallum, 1998).

Testing the limits on a standardized bilingual assessment may include administering items in the language in which the test was initially written and, after doing so, administering items in the child's second language or, more informally, accepting a response in either of the child's two languages to determine the child's knowledge on the basis of a general rather than linguistic level in one specific language. Similar to dynamic assessment procedures (see the following section), the items on which a child made mistakes can be revisited and hints provided to see whether, with some additional information, examinees are able to better understand the item, access existing knowledge, or solve the problem using logic. Naturally, the quantitative scores for measures on which testing the limits is used would be meaningful for the initial assessment only. Other data would provide useful qualitative information. A bilingual examiner should be recruited to administer tests in this manner.

Dynamic Assessment

Dynamic assessment (DA) provides an option for situations in which static testing measures may not be appropriate because of issues of validity or because these measures may provide information that is of limited significance in terms of understanding a child's true potential. DA measures learning potential of the child through examiner–examinee interaction (Grigorenko & Sternberg, 1998). DA is unique in that, instead of accepting a particular answer and determining whether it is correct or incorrect, the examiner provides feedback and instruction to the examinee if he or she experiences difficulty with particular items. Modifications may consist of a change in format; provision of additional response opportunities; cues, hints, or prompts; or the offer of a strategy that the examinee could implement to solve the problem (Swanson & Lussier, 2001). DA may also be used in a pretest–teach–posttest format in which the child is taught how to perform the task and his or her ability to benefit from instruction is evaluated (Grigorenko, 2009). Evidence suggests that DA offers a more effective means of predicting reading difficulties than traditional testing tools, such as norm-referenced measures and even curriculum-based assessment techniques (Sittner Bridges & Catts, 2011; Swanson & Lussier, 2001).

In assessing the semilingual child, DA can be particularly useful in addressing issues related to the floor effect. As with testing younger children, it is not infrequent for semilingual children to struggle with initial items on a test— particularly in their L2—and as a result, a high false-positive rate may be observed. This can be addressed in a meaningful manner using DA, in that DA allows students with "partially developed knowledge the opportunity to demonstrate their potential for reading success while at the same time identifying other children who may have more trouble learning to read" (Sittner Bridges & Catts, 2011, p. 336).

Response to Intervention

Many concerns exist regarding overrepresentation of ELLs identified for special education using traditional discrepancy models (Donovan & Cross,

2002; Fletcher et al., 1994). Indeed, the IQ versus achievement model does not accurately differentiate between ELLs and generally low-achieving students (Vellutino, Scanlon, & Lyon, 2000). Because semilingual children may best be categorized as fitting into the latter category, another method is required. Response to intervention is a promising possibility.

Response to intervention (RTI), as described by Linan-Thompson and Ortiz (2009) is designed to determine a student's ability to benefit from high-quality instruction, either at the classroom or small-group level. Assessment is a process, rather than a discrete event, in which students are evaluated regularly and, in between brief assessments, provided instruction aimed directly at helping remediate academic problems. Typically, RTI is delivered in a three-tier model. Tier 1 is *core instruction*, or classroom-based instruction provided by the student's teacher. Tier 2 is more intense and oriented toward small groups of students with similar academic needs and serves to supplement Tier 1. Tier 3 is the level at which children who do not progress adequately on benchmarks in Tiers 1 and 2 receive even more intensive intervention with more individualized instruction.

The advantage of RTI with semilingual students is twofold. First, and most important, it provides intervention-based assessment. In this way, students whose L1 and L2 are both low can receive classroom and small-group instruction aimed specifically at their vocabulary, reading, and writing needs. It would be optimal if this were provided by a bilingual teacher or aide so that semilingual students could work in both languages, rather than one only. That is, they could provide responses in either their L1 or L2 because uneven development of each would be expected. Furthermore, a bilingual teacher or aide could use knowledge from one language to facilitate learning in the other. In addition, this kind of assessment procedure should reduce placing semilingual children in special education settings if the true problem is a flatter learning curve. Standardized tests will not reflect a learning curve; RTI provides information about progress for semilingual students who are capable of learning (Escamilla 2006), just at a slower pace.

CONCLUSION

Semilingual children are youngsters who have typically confronted numerous obstacles from the beginning of their lives. Poverty is a primary concern in terms of development for semilingual children because lack of nutrition and a poor learning environment can mold biological developmental processes, making learning more difficult. In addition, however, semilingual youth must attempt to cope with two languages, immigration and acculturation issues, and the typical difficulties that school, home, and social lives present.

As should be clear, there is no "perfect" test under the best circumstances in special education assessment. There is certainly no specific measure meant to address bilingual assessment, and no tools are available that differentiate between children with typical second language acquisition and those who are not learning disabled but are, in fact, semilingual in both their L1 and L2. Given the lack of valid assessment tools, a clinician's professional interpretation of numerous pieces of information is key to making a determination about the kind of services the child should receive. To offer a well-developed clinical interpretation of issues surrounding bilingualism and semilingualism in a child referred for special education, significant amounts of information must be obtained.

A best practices assessment that differentiates between a typical second language acquisition and semilingualism would incorporate a detailed developmental, social, school, and family history in addition to a home visit. Classroom observations would be necessary, as would consideration of work samples from the classroom. DA techniques or RTI should be combined with standardized testing that incorporates testing of the limits. This offers the specialist meaningful qualitative and quantitative data, all of which should be interpreted in context, which is necessary for providing educational services that are appropriate for the semilingual child.

APPENDIX 4.1: SEMILINGUALISM ASSESSMENT CHECKLIST

Family History and Context
Parent Interview:
  Years of parent education?
  Parent interest in education? (Enjoyed school? Wanted to continue
  schooling? Disliked school; often absent?)
  Academic goals for their child?
  Literacy level L1 for parent?
  Literacy level L2 for parent?
  Reasons for immigration (professional opportunities, seeking a better
  life, educational opportunities for child, etc.)?

Home Visit:
  Stressors in the environment?
      Noise   Contamination   Threats to safety   Poverty
  Educational enrichment?
      Computers   Books   Puzzles/games
      Other active learning (projects like car repair, cooking, etc.)?
  Parent–child interaction?
      Oriented toward commands?
      Oriented toward increasing vocabulary and information gathering?
      Oriented toward problem solving or compliance?
Developmental History
  Prenatal care received?
  Nutrition during pregnancy?
  Language milestones in L1? (see language acquisition section—
babbling, etc.)

Language Proficiency

  ■ L1 proficiency?
      • Fluent/semifluent/not fluent in (language): _____
        Reading skills: ☐ Beginner ☐ Intermediate ☐ Advanced
        Writing skills: ☐ Beginner ☐ Intermediate ☐ Advanced
        Oral expression: ☐ Beginner ☐ Intermediate ☐ Advanced
        Verbal comprehension: ☐ Beginner ☐ Intermediate ☐ Advanced
        Social interaction: ☐ Below average ☐ Age-appropriate
                            ☐ Advanced
  ■ L2 proficiency?
      • Fluent/semifluent/not fluent in (language): _____
        Reading skills: ☐ Beginner ☐ Intermediate ☐ Advanced
        Writing skills: ☐ Beginner ☐ Intermediate ☐ Advanced

Oral expression: ☐ Beginner ☐ Intermediate ☐ Advanced
Verbal comprehension: ☐ Beginner ☐ Intermediate ☐ Advanced
Social interaction: ☐ Below average ☐ Age-appropriate
                      ☐ Advanced

Language spoken at home
Parents: _____   Child: _____
If parent speaks to child in their native language, does child respond in this language or in English?

If parent asks child to complete a task in their native language, does the child understand the language or the context of the request? Would they understand the request if made in another setting?

Previous Schooling

- Year of school in country of origin (if other than United States): _____

- Curriculum in school? Teacher level of preparation in country of origin? Number of students in class? Hours in school day?
- Grades and performance in school in country of origin?
- Special services in country of origin?

Assessment
        ☐ Nonverbal ability measure
        ☐ Norm-referenced ability measure
        ☐ Testing the limits/flexible use of language
        ☐ Classroom observation
        ☐ Dynamic assessment
        ☐ Response to intervention

REFERENCES

Adams, M. J. (1990). *Beginning to read: Thinking and learning about print*. Cambridge, MA: MIT Press.

August, D., Shanahan, T., & Escamilla, K. (2009). English language learners: Developing literacy in second-language learners—Report of the National Literacy Panel on language-minority children and youth. *Journal of Literacy Research, 41*, 432–452. doi:10.1080/10862960903340165

Baca, L., & Cervantes, C. (2004). *The bilingual special education interface*. Upper Saddle River, NJ: Pearson.

Benesch, S. (2008). "Generation 1.5" and its discourses of partiality: A critical analysis. *Journal of Language, Identity, and Education, 7*, 294–311. doi:10.1080/15348450802237954

Black, B., & Valenzuela, A. (2004). Educational accountability for English language learners in Texas: A retreat from equity. In L. Skrla & J. Scheurich (Eds.), *Educational equity and accountability: Paradigms, policies and politics* (pp. 215–234). Albany, NY: State University of New York Press. doi:10.4324/9780203465615_chapter_16

Blair, C., & Razza, R. P. (2007). Relating effortful control, executive function, and false belief understanding to emerging math and literacy ability in kindergarten. *Child Development, 78*, 647–663. doi:10.1111/j.1467-8624.2007.01019.x

Bos, K. J., Fox, N., Zeanah, C. H., & Nelson, C. (2009). Effects of early psychosocial deprivation on the development of memory and executive function. *Frontiers in Behavioral Neuroscience, 3*. doi:10.3389/neuro.08.016.2009

Bracken, B. A., & McCallum, R. S. (1998). *Universal Nonverbal Intelligence Test*. Itasca, IL: Riverside.

Braden, J. P., & Iribarren, J. A. (2007). Test review: Wechsler, D. (2005). Wechsler Intelligence Scale for Children–Fourth Edition Spanish. San Antonio, TX: Harcourt Assessment. *Journal of Psychoeducational Assessment, 25*, 292–299. doi:10.1177/0734282907302955

Campbell, F. A., & Ramey, C. T. (1994). Effects of early intervention on intellectual and academic achievement: A follow-up study of children from low-income families. *Child Development, 65*, 684–698. doi:10.2307/1131410

Clinton, A. (2007). Test review: Wechsler, D. (2005). Wechsler Intelligence Scale for Children–Fourth Edition Spanish. San Antonio, TX: Psychological Corporation. *Journal of Psychoeducational Assessment, 25*, 285–292. doi:10.1177/0734282907300448

Cohen, A., & Cooper, T. (1972). Fallacies: Reading retardation and the urban disadvantaged beginning reader. *The Reading Teacher, 26*(1), 38–45.

Cummins, J. (1981). The role of primary language development in promoting educational success for language minority students. In California State Department of Education (Ed.), *Schooling and language minority students: A theoretical framework* (1st ed., pp. 3–49). Sacramento, CA: California State Department of Education.

de Jong, P. F., & Leseman, P. P. M. (2001). Lasting effects of home literacy on reading achievement in school. *Journal of School Psychology, 39*, 389–414. doi:10.1016/S0022-4405(01)00080-2

De Sousa, D., Greenop, K., & Fry, J. (2011). Language transfer of spelling strategies in English and Afrikaans. *International Journal of Bilingual Education and Bilingualism, 14*, 49–67. doi:10.1080/13670051003657959

Donovan, M. S., & Cross, C. T. (2002). *Minority students in special and gifted education*. Washington, DC: National Academy Press.

Durand, T. (2011). Latina mothers' cultural beliefs about their children, parental roles, and education: Implications for empowering home-school partnerships. *The Urban Review, 43*, 255–278. doi:10.1007/s11256-010-0167-5

Durgunoğlu, A. Y., Nagy, E., & Hancin-Bhatt, B. J. (1993). Cross-language transfer of phonological awareness. *Journal of Educational Psychology, 85*, 453–465. doi:10.1037/0022-0663.85.3.453

Escamilla, K. (2006). Semilingualism applied to the literacy behaviors of Spanish-speaking emerging bilinguals: Bi-illiteracy or emerging bi-illiteracy? *Teachers College Record, 108*, 2329–2353. doi:10.1111/j.1467-9620.2006.00784.x

Feldman, R. (2011). *Essentials of understanding psychology* (9th ed.). New York, NY: McGraw-Hill.

Fletcher, J. M., Shaywitz, S. D., Shankweiler, D. P., Katz, L., Liberman, I. Y., Stubing, K. K., . . . Shaywitz, B. A. (1994). Cognitive profiles of reading disability: Comparisons of discrepancy and low achievement profiles. *Journal of Educational Psychology, 86*, 6–23. doi:10.1037/0022-0663.86.1.6

Gardner, R. C., Tremblay, P. F., & Masgoret, A.-M. (1997). Towards a full model of second language learning: An empirical investigation. *Modern Language Journal, 81*, 344–362. doi:10.1111/j.1540-4781.1997.tb05495.x

Gottardo, A. (2002). The relationship between language and reading skills in bilingual Spanish–English speakers. *Topics in Language Disorders, 22*, 46–70.

Grigorenko, E. L. (2009). Dynamic assessment and response to intervention: Two sides of one coin. *Journal of Learning Disabilities, 42*, 111–132. doi:10.1177/0022219408326207

Grigorenko, E. L., & Sternberg, R. J. (1998). Dynamic testing. *Psychological Bulletin, 124*, 75–111. doi:10.1037/0033-2909.124.1.75

Gutiérrez-Clellen, V., Simon-Cereijido, G., & Sweet, M. (2012). Predictors of second language acquisition in Latino children with specific language impairment. *American Journal of Speech-Language Pathology, 21*, 64–77. doi:10.1044/1058-0360(2011/10-0090)

Hannon, B. (2012). Understanding the relative contributions of lower-level word processes, higher-level processes, and working memory to reading comprehension performance in proficient adult readers. *Reading Research Quarterly, 47*, 125–152.

Hart, B., & Risley, T. (1995). *Meaningful differences in the everyday experiences of young American children*. Baltimore, MD: Brookes.

Hortaçsu, N. (1995). Parents' education levels, parents' beliefs, and child outcomes. *The Journal of Genetic Psychology: Research and Theory on Human Development, 156*, 373–383. doi:10.1080/00221325.1995.9914830

Kaufman, A. S., & Kaufman, N. L. (2004). *Kaufman Assessment Battery for Children: Technical manual* (2nd ed.). Circle Pines, MN: American Guidance Service.

Kaushanskaya, M., & Marian, V. (2007). Nontarget language recognition and interference in bilinguals: Evidence from eye-tracking and picture naming. *Language Learning, 57*, 119–163. doi:10.1111/j.1467-9922.2007.00401.x

Linan-Thompson, S., & Ortiz, A. (2009). Response to intervention and English-language learners: Instructional and assessment considerations. *Seminars in Speech and Language, 30*, 105–120. doi:10.1055/s-0029-1215718

Lipina, S. J., Martelli, M. I., Vuelta, B., Injoque Ricle, I., & Colombia, J. A. (2004). Pobreza y desempeño ejecutivo en alumnus preescolares de la cuidad de Buenos Aires (Argentina) [Poverty and executive performance in preschoolers from the City of Buenos Aires (Argentina)]. *Interdisciplinaria Revista de Psicología y Ciencias Afines, 21*, 153–193.

Lipina, S. J., Martelli, M. I., Vuelta, B. L., & Colombo, J. A. (2005). Desempeño en la prueba A-no-B de infants Argentinos provenientes de hogares con y sin necesidades Básicas Satisfechas [Performance on the A-not-B task of Argentinean infants from unsatisfied and satisfied basic needs homes]. *Revista Interamericana de Psicología, 39*, 49–60.

Luria, A. R. (1966). *Human brain and psychological processes*. New York, NY: Harper & Row.

MacSwan, J. (2000). The threshold hypothesis, semilingualism, and other contributions to a deficit view of linguistic minorities. *Hispanic Journal of Behavioral Sciences, 22*(1), 3–45. doi:10.1177/0739986300221001

MacSwan, J., Rolstad, K., & Glass, G. (2002). Do some school-age children have no language? Some problems of construct validity in the pre-LAS Español. *Bilingual Research Journal, 26*, 395–420. doi.org/10.1080/15235882.2002.10668718

Masgoret, A.-M. (2006). Examining the role of language attitudes and motivation on the sociocultural adjustment and the job performance of sojourners in Spain. *International Journal of Intercultural Relations, 30*, 311–331. doi:10.1016/j.ijintrel.2005.08.004

Masgoret, A.-M., & Gardner, R. C. (2003). Attitudes, motivation, and second language learning: A meta-analysis of studies conducted by Gardner and Associates. *Language Learning, 53*, 167–210. doi:10.1111/1467-9922.00227

Mezzacappa, E. (2004). Alerting, orienting, and executive attention: Developmental properties and sociodemographic correlates in an epidemiological sample of young, urban children. *Child Development, 75*, 1373–1386. doi:10.1111/j.1467-8624.2004.00746.x

Mueller Gathercole, V. M. (2007). Miami and North Wales, so far and yet so near: A constructivist account of morpho-syntactic development in bilingual children. *International Journal of Bilingual Education and Bilingualism, 10,* 224–247. doi:10.2167/beb442.0

Muñoz-Sandoval, A. F., Cummins, J., Alvarado, C. G., & Ruef, M. L. (2006). *Bilingual Verbal Ability Tests (BVAT) Normative Update.* Rolling Meadows, IL: Riverside.

National Institute of Child Health and Human Development & Early Child Care Research Network. (2005). Predicting individual differences in attention, memory, and planning in first graders from experiences at home, child care, and school. *Developmental Psychology, 41,* 99–114. doi:10.1037/0012-1649.41.1.99

Noble, K. G., Farah, M. J., & McCandliss, B. D. (2006). Socioeconomic background modulates cognition achievement relationships in reading. *Cognitive Development, 21,* 349–368. doi:10.1016/j.cogdev.2006.01.007

Ortiz, S. O. (2011). Separating cultural and linguistic differences (CLD) from specific learning disability in the evaluation of diverse students: Difference or disorder. In D. P. Flanagan & V. C. Alfonso (Eds.), *Essentials of specific learning disability identification* (pp. 299–324). Hoboken, NJ: Wiley.

Pacheco, G. A., Rossouw, S., & Lewer, J. (2013). Do non-economic quality of life factors drive immigration? *Social Indices Research, 110,* 1–15. doi.org/10.1007/s11205-011-9924-4

Pan, B. A., Rowe, M. L., Singer, J. D., & Snow, C. E. (2005). Maternal correlates of growth in toddler vocabulary production in low-income families. *Child Development, 76,* 763–782. doi.org/10.1111/1467-8624.00498-i1

Paradis, J. (2005). Grammatical morphology in children learning English as a second language: Implications of similarities with specific language impairment. *Language, Speech, and Hearing Services in Schools, 36,* 172–187. doi:10.1044/0161-1461(2005/019)

Paradis, J. (2010). Bilingual children's acquisition of English verb morphology: Effects of language exposure, structure complexity, and task type. *Language Learning, 60,* 651–680. doi.org/10.1111/j.1467-9922.2010.00567.x

Paradis, J., Nicoladis, E., Crago, M., & Genesee, F. (2011). Bilingual children's acquisition of the past tense: A usage-based approach. *Journal of Child Language, 38,* 554–578. doi:10.1017/S0305000910000218

Paradis, J., Rice, J. J., Crago, M., & Marquis, J. (2008). The acquisition of tense in English: Distinguishing child second language from first language and specific language impairment. *Applied Psycholinguistics, 29,* 689–722. doi:10.1017/S0142716408080296

Quiroz, B., Snow, C. E., & Zhao, J. (2010). Vocabulary skills of Spanish/English bilinguals: Impact of mother–child language interactions and home language and literacy support. *The International Journal of Bilingualism, 14,* 379–399. doi:10.1177/1367006910370919

Roberts, J., Jurgens, J., & Burchinal, M. (2005). The role of home literacy practices in preschool children's language and emergent literacy skills. *Journal of Speech, Language, and Hearing Research, 48,* 345–359. doi:10.1044/1092-4388(2005/024)

Rodríguez, E. T., Tamis-LeMonda, C. S., Spellmann, M. E., Pan, B. A., Raikes, H., Lugo-Gil, J., & Luze, G. (2009). The formative role of home literacy experiences across the first three years of life in children from low-income families. *Journal of Applied Developmental Psychology, 30,* 677–694. doi:10.1016/j.appdev.2009.01.003

Rymer, R. (1994). *Genie: A scientific tragedy.* New York, NY: Penguin.

Schady, N. (2011). Parents' education, mothers' vocabulary, and cognitive development in early childhood: Longitudinal evidence from Ecuador. *American Journal of Public Health, 101,* 2299–2307. doi:10.2105/AJPH.2011.300253

Sénéchal, M., & LeFevre, J. (2002). Parental involvement in the development of children's reading skill: A five-year longitudinal study. *Child Development, 73,* 445–460. doi:10.1111/1467-8624.00417

Shafer, V. L., & Garrido-Nag, K. (2007). The neurodevelopmental bases of language. In E. Hoff & M. Shatz (Eds.), *Blackwell handbook of language development* (pp. 21–45). Malden, MA: Blackwell. doi:10.1002/9780470757833.ch2

Sittner Bridges, M., & Catts, H. W. (2011). The use of dynamic screening to predict risk for reading disabilities in kindergarten children. *Journal of Learning Disabilities, 44,* 330–338. doi:10.1177/0022219411407863

Sparks, R. L., Patton, J., Ganschow, L., & Humbach, N. (2012). Do L1 reading achievement and L1 print exposure contribute to the prediction of L2 proficiency? *Language Learning, 62,* 473–505. doi:10.1111/j.1467-9922.2012.00694.x

Spira, E. G., Storch Bracken, S., & Fischel, J. E. (2005). Predicting improvement after first-grade reading difficulties: The effects of oral language, emergent literacy, and behavioral skills. *Developmental Psychology, 41,* 225–234. doi:10.1037/0012-1649.41.1.225

Sun-Alperin, M. K., & Wang, M. (2011). Cross-language transfer of phonological and orthographic processing skills from Spanish L1 to English L2. *Reading and Writing, 24,* 591–614. doi:10.1007/s11145-009-9221-7

Swanson, H. L., & Lussier, C. M. (2001). A selective synthesis of experimental literature on dynamic assessment. *Review of Educational Research, 71,* 321–363. doi:10.3102/00346543071002321

Swanson, H. L., Orosco, M. J., Lussier, C. M., Gerber, M. M., & Guzman, D. A. (2011). The influence of working memory and phonological processing on English language learner children's bilingual reading and language acquisition. *Journal of Educational Psychology, 103,* 838–856. doi:10.1037/a0024578

U.S. Census Bureau. (May, 2012). *The foreign-born population in the United States: 2010.* Retrieved from http://www.census.gov/prod/2012pubs/acs-19.pdf

U.S. Department of Education. (2009). *The nation's report card. Reading 2009: National assessment of educational progress at Grades 4 and 8.* Retrieved from http://nces.ed.gov/nationsreportcard/pdf/main2009/2010458.pdf

van der Leij, B., Bekebrede, J., & Kotterink, M. (2010). Acquiring reading and vocabulary in Dutch and English: The effect of concurrent instruction. *Reading and Writing, 23*, 415–434. doi:10.1007/s11145-009-9207-5

Vellutino, F. R., Scanlon, D. M., & Lyon, J. (2000). Differentiating between difficult-to-remediate and readily remediated poor readers: More evidence against the IQ achievement discrepancy definition of reading disability. *Journal of Learning Disabilities, 33*, 223–238. doi:10.1177/002221940003300302

Veltman, M. W., & Browne, K. D. (2001). Three decades of child maltreatment research: Implications for the school years. *Trauma, Violence, & Abuse, 2*, 215–239. doi:10.1177/1524838001002003002

Wagner, R. K., Torgesen, J. K., & Rashotte, C. A. (1994). Development of reading-related phonological processing abilities: New evidence of bidirectional causality from a latent variable longitudinal study. *Developmental Psychology, 30*, 73–87. doi:10.1037/0012-1649.30.1.73

Walker, S. P., Wachs, T., Gardner, J. M., Lozoff, B., Wasserman, G. A., Pollit, E., & Carter, J. A. (2007). Child development: Risk factors for adverse outcomes in developing countries. *The Lancet, 369*, 145–157. doi:10.1016/S0140-6736(07)60076-2

Wamba, N. G. (2010). Poverty and literacy: An introduction. *Reading & Writing Quarterly: Overcoming Learning Difficulties, 26*, 189–194. doi:10.1080/1057356 1003769533

Wechsler, D. (2005). *Wechsler Intelligence Scale for Children–Fourth edition Spanish*. San Antonio, TX: Psychological Corporation.

Woodcock, R. W., McGrew, K. S., & Mather, N. (2007). *Woodcock–Johnson III Normative Update Complete*. Rolling Meadows, IL: Riverside.

Woodcock, R. W., Muñoz-Sandoval, A. F., McGrew, K. S., & Mather, N. (2007). *Batería III Woodcock-Muñoz*. Rolling Meadows, IL: Riverside.

Xu, F., & Pinker, S. (1995). Weird past tense forms. *Journal of Child Language, 22*, 531–556. doi:10.1017/S0305000900009946

II

PRACTICAL IMPLICATIONS
FOR ASSESSMENT

5

INTEGRATED INTELLECTUAL ASSESSMENT OF THE BILINGUAL STUDENT

PEDRO OLVERA AND LINO GÓMEZ-CERRILLO

The intellectual assessment of school-age students has proven to be a complex and multidimensional task. Each student is unique and brings an exceptional range of experiences that take the practitioner beyond an IQ score and into the realm of a student's learning abilities. Knowledge of these complexities can prove helpful in providing a student with needed supports and services. Intellectual assessment becomes even more complex when assessing individuals from non-English and bilingual backgrounds. The examiner is forced to examine and integrate myriad factors (e.g., home language, acculturation, language proficiency, socioeconomic status, educational program of instruction) in combination with the obtained IQ score. In many instances, when these additional variables are not considered, the data can be obscured, which can inadvertently result in inaccurate conclusions. In its consideration of integrated assessment of the bilingual child, this chapter examines contextual factors, such as language ability, family, and school, that

http://dx.doi.org/10.1037/14320-006
Assessing Bilingual Children in Context: An Integrated Approach, A. B. Clinton (Editor)

can affect intellectual test performance. Subsequently, it outlines the steps involved in selecting an appropriate testing approach and battery for children with bilingual backgrounds.

DEMOGRAPHICS

Public School System

The public school system in the United States is becoming progressively more diverse. Data obtained from the National Center for Education Statistics (NCES) in 2010 revealed that 49,293,000 children were enrolled in kindergarten through 12th grade public schools in 2007 (U.S. Department of Education, 2010). Of this total, 43% were reported to be of culturally and linguistically diverse (CLD) backgrounds. As of 2006, the NCES reported that CLD populations in public schools were as follows: non-Hispanic White (57%), Hispanic/Latino (19%), non-Hispanic Black (16%), and Asian and Pacific Islander (4%). The evidence is clear that the United States is at its most diverse point in all its history. Moreover, the trend in diversity will only grow in the coming years.

It follows, then, that school age children are increasingly from non-English backgrounds and may be identified as English language learners (ELLs). ELLs are the fastest growing segment of the population within public schools in the United States (Izquierdo, 2011). In the year 2000 alone, it was estimated that 3.9 million students (about 8% of all students) in U.S. public schools were considered ELLs (Capps et al., 2005). Over 460 languages are presently spoken in the United States (Kindler, 2002). Of those, Kindler (2002) noted that the top five are Spanish (79.2%), Vietnamese (2%), Hmong (1.6%), Cantonese (1%), and Korean (1%). In school systems, students who are classified as ELLs come from non-English-speaking homes and are in the process of acquiring English as a second language (ESL). ELLs require English language development (ELD) services and supports to learn English and demonstrate success in academic settings.

Five states account for 60% of ELLs enrolled at the secondary level in public school systems in the United States: California, Texas, New York, Florida, and Illinois (Capps et al., 2005). Remarkably, states that have not seen significant ELL populations are experiencing noticeable growth in these populations. For example, from 1993 to 2000, North Carolina experienced a 500% growth in ELLs entering their school systems. During that same period, Oregon, Georgia, Colorado, Nevada, Nebraska, and Indiana had 200% growth (Capps et al., 2005). During the 20-year period from 1989 to 2009, Arkansas experienced a growth of 1,200% in their ELL population

(Hobson, 2010). Now, more than ever, practitioners need to develop skills and competencies to work with this unique population.

School Psychologist Demographics

School psychologists, as school-based experts in intellectual assessment, frequently assess children of CLD backgrounds. However, the cultural and linguistic demographics of school psychologists have not kept up with this trend. For example, White non-Hispanic school psychologists presently comprise 92% of total reported practitioners, Latino school psychologists represent 3% of the profession, African American practitioners represent 1.9%, Asian American/Pacific Islanders are estimated at 0.9%, indigenous American school psychologists at 0.8%, and other at 0.8% (Curtis et al., 2008). School psychology, as a profession, has not kept pace with this explosive ELL growth. Although exact figures are unknown, Curtis, Hunley, Walker, and Baker's (1999) survey estimated that one in 10 school psychologists reported proficiency in a language other than English. Proficiency was not directly defined; thus, the extent of the bilingual school psychologists' competence in the other language was not specifically determined. However, given these survey findings, Curtis, Grier, and Hunley (2004) concluded:

> The field of school psychology has been largely Caucasian throughout its history. Although individuals from diverse ethnic backgrounds and those fluent in languages other than English continue to be seriously underrepresented in the field, many school psychologists work in settings in which they serve an increasingly diverse student population (p. 52).

The disparity in the demographic makeup of school psychologists and the cultural and linguistic makeup of public school students is significant considering the mandate for nonbiased assessment practices. A critical need exists for practitioners who are knowledgeable and qualified to conduct intellectual assessments of individuals with varying degrees of English proficiency and who are from non-English or immigrant backgrounds.

MANIFESTATIONS OF BILINGUALISM

One of the most pressing challenges for practitioners who work with CLD children relates to understanding how the bilingual mind affects intellectual functioning and, within the school environment, scholastic achievement. Closing the research–practice gap regarding the relationship between bilingualism and cognitive processing continues to be a challenge. Public policy is a reflective mirror of this challenge, which has been characterized by inconsistent intervention and instruction for bilingual children (Hakuta, 1986). For practitioners to meaningfully address the scholastic needs of bilingual children, the implications of bilingualism across various contexts need to be understood. Historically, researchers such as Hakuta, Ferdman, and Diaz (1987) have noted the complexity of the meaning of bilingualism across settings by applying a multifaceted definition of bilingualism, rather than a unidimensional one. There is a need for practitioners who go beyond simply measuring language proficiency and account for the cultural and intellectual manifestations of bilingualism. In addition, practitioners must improve ecological validity during the assessment process and, in turn, be able to recommend instructional strategies that are more holistic in approach. To assist the reader, a brief summary of the multidisciplinary implications of bilingualism is provided in the following two sections.[1]

Psycholinguistic and Intellectual Implications

Early work on the definition and development of bilingualism had its origins in psycholinguistics. The work of Noam Chomsky and other linguists had a significant impact on the study of bilingualism and intellectual development (de Villiers, Tager-Flusberg, Hakuta, & Cohen, 1979). The manner in which bilingualism may affect language development, therefore, was initially the subject of psycholinguistic research, rather than psychoeducational study (Hakuta & Cancino, 1977). Much inquiry has also focused on the relationship between bilingualism and intellectual functioning (Hakuta & McLaughlin, 1996).

Researchers have studied the relationship between bilingualism and intellectual development to varying degrees since the early 20th century (Hakuta & Cancino, 1977). Although a complete review of the research related to these variables is outside the scope of this chapter, a significant body of literature has addressed the impact of bilingualism on cognition. General themes in the literature include the role of second language acquisition; sociocultural influences; psychometric assessment bias; and types of bilingualism, such as elective versus circumstantial (Valdes & Figueroa, 1996). An overarching theme affecting bilingualism relates to sociocultural implications—namely, cultural beliefs, language attitudes, and choices, which also influence the way children adapt to a new language. The literature has further denoted the potential skills of bilingual children, such as increased cognitive flexibility and improved *metalinguistic awareness*, or the

---

[1]For a thorough review of the history and various definitions of bilingualism, the reader is directed to the works of Hakuta, Valdes, and Figueroa (Hakuta, 1986; Hakuta & Cancino, 1977; Hakuta & Suben, 1985; Valdes & Figueroa, 1996).

ability to think abstractly about language (Hakuta, 1990). However, such findings are to be interpreted with great caution because further research is needed to determine whether the aforementioned skills are evident across all bilingual children.

Sociocultural Perspectives

How children negotiate cultural values, family influences, and their immediate environments (i.e., school, home, and peers) significantly affects how they adopt, learn, and use language. Bilingualism is a reflection not only of the acquisition of grammar, syntax, and knowledge of two languages but also of the fluid process of adaptation to multiple contexts, as in, for example, bilingual interactions with peers on the playground, reading a text for language arts, and contributing to classroom discussions. Consequently, practitioners working with CLD children must assess both language proficiency and cultural competence to determine where they fall on what Valdes and Figueroa (1996) termed the *language continuum* (Rhodes, Ochoa, & Ortiz, 2005).

IMPLICATIONS OF BILINGUALISM FOR ACADEMIC PERFORMANCE

To gather valid and meaningful data, intellectual assessment should always be conducted in the most proficient language(s) of the bilingual examinee. *Bilingualism* refers to the individual's capacity to possess two language systems and his or her ability to function in both (Valdes & Figueroa, 1996). Bilingualism does not always translate into full proficiency in both languages. To establish language proficiency, school psychologists must conduct a language proficiency assessment of students who are classified as bilingual and/or ELL. One issue that is key to understanding bilingualism is that language development, in any language, occurs across a spectrum. Although a student may have exposure to a language other than English at home, this exposure does not necessarily translate into full proficiency. The same is true for knowledge of and/or exposure to the English language in academic settings. Full proficiency includes oral language (expressive and receptive), reading, and writing, all of which are vital to success in an academic setting. To identify where on the continuum of language a bilingual child's abilities fall, practitioners should gather as much information as possible regarding the child's language functioning.

The following discussion provides an overview of steps considered fundamental to address this task as best as possible given the inherent complexities of measuring the language proficiency of bilingual individuals. Available measures are reviewed to help practitioners consider options that may augment a language proficiency assessment. Although use of standardized assessments may further complicate the assessment process because of issues of bias, practitioners may use them as part of a larger collection of language data. Together, these efforts may provide a more valid intellectual assessment.

Development of Language Proficiency

Cummins (1979) conceptualized two separate yet interrelated language skills: basic interpersonal communications skills (BICS) and cognitive academic language proficiency (CALP). Briefly, BICS (context-embedded) is the language skill that facilitates communication in social environments that are typically found in informal settings: socializing with peers, discussing day-to-day interactions, and conversing at recess or lunch. Conversely, CALP (context-reduced) is a more complex language skill, such as that required in academic settings. Cognitively undemanding tasks are those that are generally automatic and involve decreased cognitive strategies. For example, stating a birth date or home address tends to be cognitively undemanding. However, cognitively demanding tasks require higher order and varied cognitive strategies—for instance, reading a text on chemistry or physics or analyzing a complex essay. Figure 5.1 illustrates the interplay between cognitively undemanding or cognitively demanding tasks and context-embedded or context-reduced settings.

A thorough acquisition of CALP involves synthesizing, evaluating, and inferring verbal and written concepts through verbal, reading, and written means. The process of achieving a fully developed CALP ability may take 7 to 10 years of academic exposure. All language development follows a developmental course. Diaz-Rico and Weed (2002) provided an outline and a developmental sequence for CALP stages: CALP 1, preproduction; CALP 2, early production; CALP 3, speech emergence; CALP 4, intermediate fluency; and CALP 5, advanced fluency. Thus, the examiner is advised to understand where the student is on this developmental continuum.

Prior to evaluating the intellectual ability of bilingual children who are classified as ELL, practitioners—typically the school psychologist or speech and language pathologist—must first determine the child's CALP levels, including both the first language (L1) and English (L2), to determine the most appropriate language in which to assess the child. For example, a student may be conversationally proficient in English (BICS) but may not be academically competent in English (CALP). During social conversation, she or he may appear to be proficient in English; however, it might not become obvious until the examiner administers an English language proficiency measure that the student is still ELL—that is, that the student has not developed a rich enough depth in her or his second language to effectively function in academic contexts. Without assessing CALP levels, the examiner may

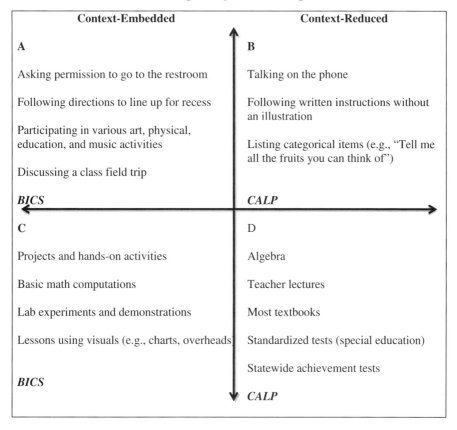

Cognitively Undemanding

Context-Embedded	Context-Reduced
A	**B**
Asking permission to go to the restroom	Talking on the phone
Following directions to line up for recess	Following written instructions without an illustration
Participating in various art, physical, education, and music activities	Listing categorical items (e.g., "Tell me all the fruits you can think of")
Discussing a class field trip	
BICS	*CALP*
C	**D**
Projects and hands-on activities	Algebra
Basic math computations	Teacher lectures
Lab experiments and demonstrations	Most textbooks
Lessons using visuals (e.g., charts, overheads)	Standardized tests (special education)
	Statewide achievement tests
BICS	*CALP*

Cognitively Demanding

Figure 5.1. Cummins's Grid of Cognitive Demands. This grid looks at the degree of complexity of cognitively demanding and undemanding language demands in both academic and nonacademic settings. From *Multicultural Students With Special Language Needs: Practical Strategies for Assessment and Intervention*, by C. Roseberry-McKibbin, 2008, p. 235. Copyright 2008 by Academic Communication Associates. Reprinted with permission.

unknowingly engage in biased practices by assessing the bilingual student in a language in which the student is either limited or not proficient.

As mentioned previously, low CALP levels may indicate limited proficiency in the given language. The following questions may guide the examiner in considering reasons for low CALP scores:

- Can the student's difficulty in acquiring English proficiency be attributed to his or her insufficient development in his or her first language?

- Can the student's academic difficulties or failure in an English-only academic setting be attributed to his or her not having attained CALP in English?
- Was the student given ample instructional time in his or her first language to (a) develop CALP in this language and (b) demonstrate ability within the average range of academic performance (Rhodes et al., 2005, p. 73)?

After considering these questions, the practitioner may use the following section to review the contextual factors that should be considered prior to the intellectual assessment of the bilingual child.

Acculturation and Cognitive Assessment

Acculturation factors must be considered when assessing students from CLD backgrounds. Briefly, *acculturation* refers to acquiring or adopting the dominant culture's values and norms by underrepresented groups living within that society. Acculturation is developmental and occurs across a continuum. Tests that measure cognitive abilities inherently reflect a bias, given that they are based on the values and norms of the culture in which they were created. Intellectual assessments measure the ability to access that culturally influenced information that is embedded in the test itself (Lau & Blatchey, 2009). Thus, relying strictly on norm-referenced assessments may be inappropriate when the examiner is seeking to compare the CLD student's ability to access that information while being compared with a potentially different reference group. The differences, whether significant or not, may yield results that are not meaningful, given that the norm group was not similar to the student in question; the results may consequently be inappropriate for making diagnostic and eligibility decisions. A comprehensive and integrated assessment of a bilingual student will include the need to supplement assessment findings with multiple sources of information, including records, information from parents or caretakers, and thorough observations.

CONTEXTUAL FACTORS AND BILINGUAL INTELLECTUAL ASSESSMENT

Cumulative File Review and Embedded Language Proficiency Data

The assessment process begins with a comprehensive review of the student's cumulative file. In most states, the cumulative file contains the student's ELD level and language of instruction. In cases where the cumulative file does not contain that information, the school psychologist should consult a bilingual specialist for those data. For example, California uses the Home Language Survey (California Department of Education, 2005), which is given to each parent enrolling a student in a public school. This form is included as part of a school district's student enrollment packet and documents the student's home language exposure. Readers are advised to determine whether a similar survey is administered in their geographical area of practice.

On reviewing these test data, the practitioner is encouraged to note the yearly progression of ELD and determine whether a pattern of consistently low performance is evident. This includes reviewing the overall proficiency, which generally includes reading, writing, and language (receptive and expressive). If an ELL student is gradually progressing at his or her ELD level, this may indicate a trajectory of appropriate language development (Valdes & Figueroa, 1996). As a cautionary note, if the student has consistent difficulties across one or more areas, particularly reading and writing, the practitioner must not assume that a disability is present. Instead, other factors that may possibly be contributing to this dynamic must be considered. As mentioned earlier, these may include depth of proficiency in the primary language, fidelity of RTI implementation, appropriateness of the program of instruction (e.g., bilingual instruction or ELD supports), English development support in the family, and community factors, to name a few.

Other sources of information to examine in the cumulative file include, but are not limited to, anecdotal notes, psychological reports, all schools of attendance, retention records, attendance, truancies, grades, behavioral comments, health records, discipline records, and achievement results from state-normed tests. Particular attention should be given to the language of instruction. That is, has the student been educated in a bilingual or an English-only program or exclusively in their native language? A determination of the language of instruction will provide the examiner with information about academic functioning and supports in both their primary and native language. If the practitioner is not familiar with the program of instruction, he or she should consult a bilingual specialist.

Prereferral Team File and Response to Intervention

Another source of data that is integral to all intellectual assessments is the prereferral assessment team file. Prereferral assessment team files are increasingly implementing response to intervention (RTI) data. This should all be documented and incorporated in the interpreting of testing data. As school districts incorporate RTI systems, the information derived from progress monitoring and intervention history will be essential for individual education plan (IEP) teams to make the best decisions for ELL children regarding placement and further intervention. In addition, Lichtenstein (2008) found the incorporation of RTI data within a comprehensive intellectual assessment to be the best practice for the identification of learning disabilities for all children, including ELLs. To facilitate the cumulative file review, we have included the Educational File Language Review Checklist (see Exhibit 5.1). Practitioners assessing bilingual children can use this checklist to guide them in considering contextual factors as part of an integrated intellectual assessment.

Behavioral Observations (School and Home)

Structured observations are crucial aspects of any assessment and should be conducted in the student's natural learning environment (Prasse, 2008). Observations support psychometric potential assessments by contextualizing a student's intellectual functioning and allowing for intangible strengths to be noted (i.e., mode of communication, sensory motor abilities, memory, planning, attention, etc.). Observations should be completed across multiple settings, adopting structured and systematic methods to document a variety of student dynamics, including language preference and usage, behavioral performance, and most important, an estimate of the student's acculturation or process of acquiring mainstream U.S. culture (Rhodes et al., 2005).

Observing the student both inside and outside the school setting allows the practitioner to approximate the student's level of acculturation. Behavioral indicators of acculturation include the preferred language of communication (primary vs. English), the cultural and linguistic backgrounds of those the student prefers to socialize with, retention of native cultural traditions versus the dominant culture, and preferred foods (native vs. dominant culture). Observing the student within the home provides much information regarding family dynamics and the cultural environment. In general, observations in both the home and educational environments can provide data regarding the student's language, cognitive, and scholastic functioning by allowing the examiner to personally observe students in their natural environments. Together, this collection of information helps to rule out exclusionary factors, focuses on understanding the student's cultural and linguistic profile, and provides a foundation for interpreting intellectual assessment results within the context of observation in natural settings.

LANGUAGE PROFICIENCY ASSESSMENT

Standardized Language Proficiency Measures

Language proficiency measures are important because they measure aspects of CALP in a given language. Areas of proficiency typically assessed include speaking, listening, reading, and writing. For example, the California Department of Education (2009) developed the California English Language Development Test (CELDT) to assess public education students' English language proficiency. The CELDT, which parallels Cummins's (1979) model, provides the following stages of ELD: Beginner (CALP 1), Early Intermediate (CALP 2), Intermediate (CALP 3), Early Advanced (CALP 4), and Advanced (CALP 5). Examining state-level assessments such as the CELDT, which is used primarily in California, can be the first step in the data collection process in determining English language proficiency. School district language assessors and/or bilingual specialists generally administer the CELDT. The CELDT, which is normally administered at the beginning of the school year, is given to students who are classified as ELLs or whose home language is not English.

Individual standardized language proficiency measures are also available to help determine the most appropriate language for intellectual assessment. One such measure is the Bilingual Verbal Ability Tests (BVAT; Muñoz-Sandoval, Cummins, Alvarado, & Ruef, 1998). The BVAT, which is available in 16 languages, was developed to assess the verbal abilities of bilingual individuals. The BVAT provides a measure of verbal CALP in English and a combined bilingual score (English + L1). The assessment is based on three tests with origins in the Woodcock–Johnson Tests of Cognitive Ability for ages 5 years to adulthood (Garfinkel & Stansfield, 1998).

The first test of the BVAT is Picture Vocabulary, which asks students to name familiar and unfamiliar objects. The second test is Oral Vocabulary, which asks students to name synonyms and antonyms of selected items. The last of the three is Verbal Analogies, which assesses the ability to comprehend and verbally complete a logical word relationship. All three tests are first administered in English. Next, the items that were answered incorrectly in the English version are repeated in the student's L1 (Garfinkel & Stansfield, 1998).

A benefit of the BVAT is the option to obtain a specific English CALP designation ranging from 1 to 5. According to Garfinkel and Stansfield (1998), the test is aimed at nonbiased placement of learners in or out of special education classes, and sensitivity to sociolinguistic issues is achieved by testing individuals in their home languages. However, caution is urged against depending solely on this tool when making placement decisions. Examiners are urged to incorporate multiple sources of information (e.g., work samples, observations, other sources of information) to augment the data (Garfinkel & Stansfield, 1998). Other considerations include limitations in the normative sample, including systemic control for issues related to acculturation, language proficiency, or type of bilingual or ESL program (Rhodes et al., 2005).

The Woodcock–Muñoz Language Survey (WMLS; Alvarado, Ruef, & Schrank, 2005), like the BVAT, can be used to estimate a student's CALP level (Woodcock & Muñoz-Sandoval, 2001). Many of the subtests are similar to the verbal comprehension tasks of the BVAT, with the addition of a reading and writing cluster. Unlike the BVAT, the WMLS includes single-word reading (Letter Word Identification) and writing (Dictation) to provide both a verbal and an academic measurement of CALP. The WMLS provides English and Spanish CALP level scores for all the various clusters, including language (oral and expression), writing, and reading. Of particular interest is the Applied Language Proficiency score (ALP), which provides a global CALP score across all language domains. Limitations of the WMLS include the following: administration of both English and Spanish versions can be time consuming; administering the tests is complex; scoring can be time consuming and tedious; and the Spanish version is not clear about socioeconomic status, gender, or geographical location of the norm sample (Brown & Ochoa, 2007). Regardless of which language proficiency instrument is used to assess CALP, practitioners should augment findings with other indicators of language functioning, such as observations, work samples, language samples, and other contributing data, when deciding the language modality to be adopted for intellectual assessment. Table 5.1 provides a summary of additional primary language assessments (Olvera & Cerrillo-Gómez, 2011, p. 122).

The following case study illustrates a situation in which a student, though limited in his English verbal skills, demonstrates full proficiency in his primary language. Implications for intellectual assessment are discussed.

Case Study: Sergio

> Sergio is a 12-year-old student in the seventh grade.[2] He arrived in the United States from Mexico as a sixth grader. He is the youngest of three siblings and lives with both of his parents. His language arts teacher is concerned that he is making minimal progress in reading and writing, which was the reason she referred him to the prereferral problem-solving team. At the meeting, the parents informed the school that Sergio had received average to above average grades across all academic areas while attending elementary school in Mexico.

---

[2]The details of the case studies have been changed to protect the anonymity of the individuals involved.

TABLE 5.1
Summary of Primary Language Assessment and Available Languages

Test	Available languages
Bilingual Verbal Abilities Test (Muñoz-Sandoval, Cummins, Alvarado, & Ruef, 1998)	Arabic, Chinese (Simplified and Traditional), English, French, German, Haitian-Creole, Hindi, Italian, Japanese, Korean, Polish, Portuguese, Russian, Spanish, Turkish, Vietnamese
Basic Inventory of Natural Languages (Herbert, 1986)	Arabic, Armenian, Cambodian, Cantonese, Chinese Creole, Dutch, English, Farsi, Filipino, French, German, Greek, Hindi, Hmong, Ilocano, Inupiaq, Italian, Japanese, Korean, Laotian, Navajo, Polish, Portuguese, Russian, Spanish, Tagalog, Taiwanese, Toishanese, Ukrainian, Vietnamese
Woodcock–Muñoz Language Survey–Update (Woodcock & Muñoz-Sandoval, 2001)	English, Spanish
California English Language Development Test (California Department of Education, 2009)	English
IDEIA Oral Language Proficiency Test (Dalton, 1991)	English, Spanish

Note. From "A Bilingual (English and Spanish) Psychoeducational Assessment MODEL Grounded in CHC Theory: A Cross Battery Approach," by P. Olvera and L. Gómez-Cerrillo, *Contemporary School Psychology,* 13, p. 122. Copyright 2011 by California Association of School Psychologists. Reprinted with permission.

The prereferral team requested that an English language proficiency test be administered in both Spanish and English to establish language dominance. The WMLS was administered by the bilingual specialist and the following scores were obtained: Sergio's ALP score in Spanish was equivalent to a CALP level of 5 out of 6, and his English ALP score was equivalent to a CALP level of 2 out of 6.

The team determined that Sergio demonstrated advanced-level proficiency in Spanish and very limited proficiency in English, as evidenced by his performance. Because of his advanced proficiency in his primary language, the team concluded that Sergio needed more intensive ESL services and agreed to meet again in 3 months to assess his progress. The language assessment clarified that a special education referral would not be appropriate.

Informal Language Proficiency Assessment

The use of informal language proficiency assessments is necessary when assessing a student from a low-incidence linguistic background. This option is to be implemented when there are no standardized assessment

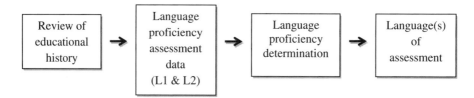

Figure 5.2. Language Proficiency and Cognitive Academic Language Proficiency Data. Using contextual data for the determination of language(s) of assessment of the bilingual student.

tools for the language in question or to supplement obtained standardized assessment findings. Informal language proficiency assessments are usually qualitative and rely on observations, interviews, and work sample analysis. The following informal approaches have been suggested (Rhodes et al., 2005; Roseberry-McKibbin, 2007): observations, questionnaires, teacher rating scales, storytelling, story retelling, cloze techniques, language samples, and dynamic and portfolio-based assessments. Given the subjective nature of this type of assessment, the examiner must ensure that the use of informal assessments remains nonbiased and relies on multiple sources of information.

Using Cognitive Academic Language Proficiency Data for Language Intellectual Assessment

The decision to conduct an intellectual assessment in a specific language will depend, among other sources of information, on the collected CALP data in both languages. First and foremost, the examiner must review the student's educational history (i.e., program and language of instruction, ESL supports, etc.). Once educational history and language exposure have been determined, CALP data from standardized language proficiency measures should be considered. After these data have been collected, the examiner can best make a determination for the language intellectual assessment. Figure 5.2 provides the examiner with the decision-making process.

Each student will present with a unique language profile, which makes generalizability difficult when relying solely on CALP scores from language proficiency assessments. The practitioner must combine CALP levels and multiple sources of information and the integration of language proficiency results to best determine the language of intellectual assessment. The following case study illustrates the use of language proficiency measures and the determination of the language for intellectual assessment.

Case Study: Suzy

Suzy is a third-grade student and is classified as ELL. She was born in the United States to Peruvian-born immigrant parents. Her educational records indicate that she speaks Spanish at home and has been educated in English only. She has been having difficulties in language arts. Specific problems include poor phonemic awareness and fluency. According to her prereferral file, she has been receiving interventions and has been part of the RTI program for the past year and a half. Suzy has made limited progress.

The prereferral team recommended that she be assessed by the IEP team. Because she is still classified as an ELL, the school psychologist administered the oral language sections of the WMLS (English and Spanish). Suzy scored 3 on the English CALP (limited) and 1 on the Spanish CALP (negligible).

Although Suzy's assessment results indicated that her English skills are limited, she is more proficient in English than in Spanish. Her negligible results in Spanish indicated that she has minimal conversation skills in that language. The results led the school psychologist to proceed with assessment in English. Though Suzy speaks Spanish at home, she has been educated only in English. Language proficiency assessment confirmed that she is clearly more proficient in English.

THE PROCESS: ASSESSMENT OF INTELLECTUAL ABILITIES

Once language proficiency has been established, the examiner determines the most appropriate process for conducting an intellectual assessment. Because of the various cultural and linguistic factors involved, examiners must select methods that adhere to nonbiased assessment procedures in order to obtain valid results. Ortiz (2011) indicated possible approaches to the intellectual assessment of students classified as ELL: native language assessment, nonverbal assessment, modified or adapted assessment, and English language assessment, each of which is discussed in the upcoming paragraphs.

Native Language Assessment

Native language assessment is fast becoming a growing specialty among practitioners; however, as mentioned previously, few practitioners are qualified to provide this type of assessment. Simply put, native language assessment involves the assessment of the student in their home language by a psychologist who is proficient in that particular language (Rhodes et al., 2005). This method of assessment is most appropriate for referred children who have had some formal education in the language in which they are being assessed. For example, Spanish assessment of a student from a Spanish-speaking home who has been schooled only in English can produce invalid results. This is the case because the student is being tested on information (e.g., vocabulary) that he or she has never formally learned.

Norms for native language intellectual tests often use monolingual speakers from other countries who are educated in the native language. As such, they do not form an adequately representative normed sample for comparison and will not match an individual who has been educated in the United States (Ortiz, 2008). Thus, great care and caution must be taken when assessing students with native language assessments.

Several native language assessment measures are available to school psychologists. For Spanish speakers, the Batería III Woodcock–Muñoz: Pruebas de Habilidad Cognitivas expands and supplants the Batería Woodcock–Muñoz: Pruebas de Habilidad Cognitiva–Revisada and the Batería Woodcock Psico-Educativa en Español (Doll & LeClair, 2007; Olivarez & Boroda, 2007). The Batería III is based on the Cattell–Horn–Carroll (CHC) model of intellectual processing and uses subtests to formulate cluster scores (Doll & LeClair, 2007; Olivarez & Boroda, 2007). The battery is designed as a parallel Spanish-language version of the Woodcock–Johnson III Tests of Cognitive Ability.

A sample size of only 1,413 subjects was used to calibrate the Spanish-speaking sample of the Batería III, limiting its generalizability and comparability for ELL students in the United States (Doll & LeClair, 2007; Olivarez & Boroda, 2007). Although reliability and validity are considered acceptable given their matched psychometric properties to the Woodcock–Johnson III, caution is warranted when interpreting results with ELL students in the United States. Issues of linguistic bias can become apparent and must be noted by the practitioner if deciding to use the Batería III (Doll & LeClair, 2007; Olivarez & Boroda, 2007). Linguistic bias can be observed in Batería III norming samples of Spanish-proficient children from Latin America in comparison with U.S. student populations. Differences in levels of Spanish proficiency, educational background, and regional dialects can highlight these biases. Nevertheless, the Batería III is the most complete Spanish intellectual assessment tool to date.

The Wechsler Intelligence Scale for Children—Fourth Edition (WISC–IV) Spanish (Wechsler, 2005) has included bilingual Spanish-speaking individuals in its norming sample. It is appropriate for children ages 6 to 16 years. According to the developers (Wechsler, 2005), the purpose was "to ensure that the WISC–IV Spanish was clinically appropriate for use with Spanish-speaking children of diverse backgrounds living in the U.S." (p. 52). For bilingual examiners, this tool provides materials in both English and Spanish to facilitate assessment in both languages. The norming sample included 851 ELLs who had studied in the United States for less than

5 consecutive years and a Spanish reliability sample of 500 individuals (Clinton, 2007). In addition to the United States, regions represented in the norming sample included Mexico, Cuba, Puerto Rico, the Dominican Republic, and Central and South America. The strength of the WISC–IV Spanish is that it was created for students who have recently arrived in the United States and are in the process of learning English. Caution should be noted, however, because the Spanish norms are equated to the WISC–IV English norms; consequently, the WISC–IV Spanish does not have distinct Spanish norms (Braden & Iribarren, 2005).

Nonverbal Assessment

Nonverbal assessment is another approach that can be used in the assessment of children from linguistically different backgrounds. Nonverbal assessments are intended to

> assess all manner of abilities by using formats that minimizes the influence of oral and written language. The instructions can be administered orally or by gestures, pantomime, or sign language; but the content of a nonverbal test and its required method for assessment must not involve words in any way. (Hammill, Pearson, & Wiederholt, 2009, p. 1)

It is important to note, however, that tests can never truly be nonverbal, given the high degree of receptive language that many nonverbal assessments require (Ortiz, 2011). Even tests that are pantomimed or gestured require language and communication. A proposed, possibly more accurate term for this assessment is *language-reduced assessment* (Ortiz, 2011). An immediate benefit of nonverbal measures in general is the absence of linguistically loaded test items; thus, they can accommodate ELL children and those with language–hearing-based disabilities. However, practitioners should still proceed with caution when administering any norm-referenced assessment. Although nonverbal assessments present with reduced linguistic loadings, cultural manifestations of tasks unfamiliar to the student may also negatively affect performance.

Potential challenges or problems associated with relying solely on nonverbal assessments include the following (Ortiz, 2011): (a) They have not demonstrated increased fairness or validity over assessments that incorporate verbal tasks; (b) they measure a more limited range of abilities than verbal tests; (c) most special education referrals for reading problems and underlying abilities are verbal in nature (i.e., auditory processing and crystallized abilities), and nonverbal tests exclude these highly correlated areas; and (d) test norm samples do not control for acculturation or language experience for children of CLD individuals, which can be problematic.

Thus, although nonverbal assessment may contribute to evaluation of a bilingual child, it falls short of addressing the complexities of bilingualism.

Several nonverbal measures commonly used by school psychologists are discussed in the following paragraphs. The Universal Nonverbal Intelligence Test (UNIT; Bracken & McCallum, 1998) is an individually administered nonverbal intelligence test designed to measure "the general intelligence and cognitive abilities of children and adolescents from ages 5 years through 17 years who may be disadvantaged by traditional verbal and language-loaded measures" (Bracken & McCallum, 1998, p. 1). The UNIT consists of a norm sample of 2,100 children based on the 1995 U.S. Census. The norm sample was grouped according to gender, race, Hispanic origin, region, parental educational attainment, community setting, classroom placement (regular or special education), and special education program (e.g., learning and speech and language disabilities, emotional–behavioral disorders, intellectual disability, giftedness, ELLs and bilingual education, general education). Of particular interest for assessing ELLs is that all communication of the UNIT is through gestures that have been standardized by the test developer with the intent of minimizing all modes of language (expressive and receptive).

The Leiter–Revised (Roid & Miller, 1997) provides a theoretically driven, psychometrically sound, and modernized improvement over the previous edition (Marco, 2005; Stinnett, 2005). The authors selected CHC theory as the driving theory behind processing cluster development. Psychometrically, the revised norming sample included over 2,000 children and adolescents (ages 2 years, 0 months–20 years, 11 months), reflecting a wide range of subpopulations, which provides relevancy to a variety of at-risk students. The test provides a Brief IQ and a Full-Scale IQ. The Brief IQ is for tentative or reversible decisions, whereas the Full-Scale is for identification or placement decisions (Roid & Miller, 1997).

The Kaufman Assessment Battery for Children—Second Edition (KABC–2; Kaufman & Kaufman, 2004), in addition to providing a comprehensive estimate of processing and intellectual abilities (Fluid–Crystallized Index and Mental Processing Index), provides a Nonverbal Index (NVI). The KABC–2 is based on the CHC theory of intelligence and Luria's neuropsychological theory of processing. It was normed on a sample of children from 3 to 18 years of age across 39 U.S. states. The NVI has been developed and deemed appropriate for children for whom the Fluid–Crystallized Index and Mental Processing Index may not be, given language demands, and those who may have difficulties with oral communication and/or who have limited English proficiency (Kaufman, Lichtenberger, Fletcher-Janzen, & Kaufman, 2005). The premise underlying the development of the NVI within the KABC–2 was to "facilitate the valid assessment of children who have difficulty understanding verbal stimuli, responding orally, or both" (Kaufman et al., 2005, p. 177).

Modified or Adapted Assessment

Modified or adapted assessment is often referred to as *testing the limits*. This type of assessment approach involves deviating from standardization practices to accommodate linguistic and/or cultural differences. Although this type of assessment can provide valuable qualitative and observational data, the fact remains that the reliability and validity of the assessment results will be compromised. Modification and adaptation practices can involve the following: eliminating items, repeating instructions, and/or accepting responses in both primary and secondary languages (Ortiz, 2011). Beneficial aspects of modified assessment include learning about students learning style, gaining insight into the student's optimal language of performance, and helping during standardized assessment.

One common modification or adaptation used with ELLs involves the use of an interpreter. Often, interpreters are necessary; however, they can significantly affect the validity and reliability of the assessment results. One of the major criticisms of using interpreters involves selecting poorly trained interpreters who can commit errors in terms of omitting important items and/or adding test items that may significantly alter the content and/or the meaning of the task (Gopaul-McNicol & Armour-Thomas, 2002). For best practice guidelines in the use of interpreters within school systems, the reader is directed to Lopez (2002). It should be noted that standardized tests that were not developed with the use of interpreters would compromise the validity and reliability, given that they were not normed in that manner.

English Language Assessment

The final intellectual assessment method involves assessing bilingual or ELL students using English-based assessments. Often this becomes the only feasible option, given the academic experience of the student. However, before undertaking an assessment in which English is the primary mode of communication, assessing CALP levels in both L1 and L2 is necessary. The examiner must establish that the student's CALP in L2 is more dominant before proceeding with English language assessment. As mentioned previously, such standardized measures as the WMLS and the BVAT can provide helpful information in this area.

Though not necessarily exclusionary, the following factors should be considered when low scores are obtained by ELLs and/or bilingual individuals on English language measures (Gopaul-McNicol & Armour-Thomas, 2002): less-than-proficient English language skills, limited proficiency in native and second languages, differential prior educational experiences, and inadequate opportunities and conditions to learn. There is also evidence to suggest that ELLs tend to perform at a lower level than native English speakers on verbal and linguistically loaded tasks and at about the same range on tasks that are minimal in regard to linguistic demands (Ortiz, 2011). Given this information, examiners can understand expected and predicted patterns of performance on English assessments by ELL populations.

To select English language instruments with reduced cultural and linguistic demands, the reader is directed to review the Culture–Language Test Classifications (C–LTC) and the Cultural Language Interpretative Matrix (C–LIM), which are based on the CHC and Cross Battery approach in Flanagan, Ortiz, and Alfonso (2007). To be more specific, the C–LTC is a framework for examining and classifying subtests dimensionally according to cultural loading and linguistic demand variables. Possible rankings are low, moderate, and high. The C–LIM is the related matrix in which the examiner inputs individual subtest assessment data and analyzes and evaluates the emerging pattern for level of linguistic demand and cultural loading. Although the C–LTC and C–LIM are not diagnostic tools (Ortiz, 2011), the utility of this type of framework lies in the need for a system for determining cultural and linguistic demands and for a means to interpret the degree of impact of those variables on a particular assessment profile.

Multiple Approaches

Although four approaches have been presented, it is important to note that these approaches are neither fixed nor inflexible. The examiner may choose one or a combination of the approaches to best understand the student's abilities. For example, a student may require an English-only approach with modifications and/or adaptations. A student from a non-English-speaking home who may have been educated in English, however, has limited English language skills and may require English and nonverbal assessment approaches. The examiner may combine the approaches and tailor them to the individual's needs.

INTEGRATED INTELLECTUAL ASSESSMENT: PUTTING IT ALL TOGETHER

In summary, assessing individuals from linguistically diverse backgrounds involves a multifaceted approach. The goal of an integrated intellectual assessment is to conduct nonbiased assessments through the consideration

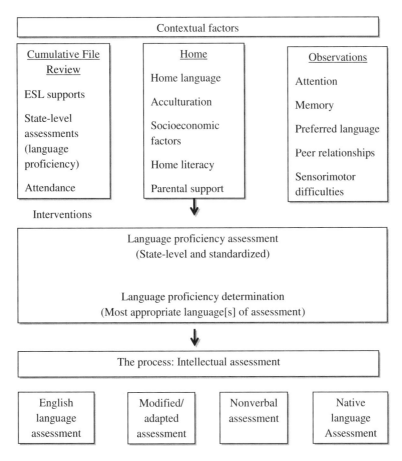

Figure 5.3. Flow chart for the integrated assessment of bilingual students. This flow chart outlines the contextual and linguistic factors to consider when determining the process of intellectual assessment of the bilingual student. ESL = English as a second language.

of contextual factors in light of obtained intelligence scores. The examiner is advised to consider each student's unique assessment needs. Figure 5.3 provides a concise framework outlining the steps and types of data needed to perform this type of assessment.

Similarly, the assessment process should be grounded in a hypothesis-testing approach (Beers, Hammond, & Ryan, 2006). That is, the assessment process is seen as data-driven, flexible, and guided by the upholding or refuting of examiner-generated hypotheses. A hypothesis-testing approach may be useful because new data may surface during the assessment process. The examiner may decide to use a combination of assessment approaches to gather the most accurate and precise data.

CONCLUSION

Assessing cognitive functioning in bilingual individuals is a complex and multifaceted task. Essential to assessing children from ELL and/or bilingual backgrounds is having a thorough understanding of language development (CALP, BICS). This will facilitate the determination of the most appropriate method of language assessment by using nonbiased assessment methods. The consideration of available contextual data will aid the practitioner in selecting the most appropriate approach and, consequently, the most suitable assessment battery, ensuring valid and reliable results. Ultimately, school psychologists will be better able to develop culturally and linguistically appropriate interventions that address the academic and social–emotional needs of children from culturally and linguistically diverse backgrounds.

APPENDIX 5.1: EDUCATIONAL FILE LANGUAGE REVIEW CHECKLIST

Identifying information		
Student name:	School(s) of attendance:	
Grade:	Home language:	

Educational information		
Language (s) of instruction:	Retention(s)— If so, grades:	
Attendance:	Discipline records:	

Language proficiency data		
Language proficiency data (e.g., state-level, WMLS, BVAT)	Year 1	Year 2	Year 3
	Date:	Date:	Date:
	Speaking:	Speaking:	Speaking:
	Listening:	Listening:	Listening:
	Reading:	Reading:	Reading:
	Writing:	Writing:	Writing:
Support in native language:		Language student socializes in:	

Current academics			
Language arts	Current grade(s):	Concerns (L1 &L2):	Interventions:
Math:	Current grade(s):	Concerns (L1 & L2)	Interventions:

Prereferral team information	
Intervention area:	Progress:

REFERENCES

Alvarado, D. G., Ruef, M. L., & Schrank, F. A. (2005). *Comprehensive manual. Woodcock–Muñoz Language Survey—Revised.* Itasca, IL: Riverside.

Beers, S. R., Hammond, K., & Ryan, C. M. (2006). General assessment issues for a pediatric population. In P. D. Nussbaum, D. L. Robins, & P. J. Snyder (Eds.), *Clinical neuropsychology: A pocket handbook for assessment* (pp. 105–123). Washington, DC: American Psychological Association. doi:10.1037/11299-028

Bracken, B. A., & McCallum, R. S. (1998). *Universal Nonverbal Intelligence Test.* Itasca, IL: Riverside.

Braden, J. P., & Iribarren, J. A. (2005). Test review: Wechsler, D. (2005). Wechsler Intelligence Scale for Children—Fourth Edition Spanish. San Antonio, TX: Harcourt Assessment. *Journal of Psychoeducational Assessment, 25,* 292–299.

Brown, J. D., & Ochoa, S. H. (2007). Woodcock–Muñoz language survey revised. In K. Geisinger, R. Spies, J. Carlson, & B. Plake (Eds.), *Mental measurements yearbook* (17th ed., pp. 872–87). Lincoln, NE: Buros Institute of Mental Measurements.

California Department of Education. (2005). *Home Language Survey (HLS).* Sacramento, CA: Author.

California Department of Education. (2009). *California English Language Development Test: Understanding and using 2009–2010 individual results.* Sacramento, CA: Author.

Capps, R., Fix, M., Murray, J., Ost, J., Passel, J. S., & Herwantoro, S. (2005). *The new demography of America's schools: Immigration and the No Child Left Behind Act.* Washington, DC: The Urban Institute. doi:10.1037/e723122011-001

Clinton, A. (2007). Test review: Wechsler, D. (2005). Wechsler Intelligence Scale for Children—Fourth Edition Spanish. San Antonio, TX: Psychological Corporation. *Journal of Psychoeducational Assessment, 25,* 285–292. doi:10.1177/0734282907300448

Cummins, J. (1979). Linguistic interdependence and the educational development of bilingual children. *Review of Educational Research, 49,* 222–251. doi:10.3102/00346543049002222

Curtis, M. J., Grier, J. E. C., & Hunley, S. A. (2004). The changing face of school psychology: Trends in data and projections for the future. *School Psychology Review, 33,* 49–66.

Curtis, M. J., Hunley, S. A., Walker, K. J., & Baker, A. C. (1999). Demographic characteristics and professional practices in school psychology. *School Psychology Review, 28,* 104–116.

Curtis, M. J., Lopez, A. D., Castillo, J. M., Batsche, G. M., Minch, D., & Smith, J. C. (2008). The status of school psychology: Demographic characteristics, employment conditions, professional practices, and continuing professional development. *Communiqué, 36,* 27–29.

Dalton, E. F. (1991). *IPT oral grades K–6 technical manual, IDEA Oral Language Proficiency Test Forms C and D English.* Brea, CA: Ballard & Tighe.

de Villiers, J. G., Tager-Flusberg, H., Hakuta, K., & Cohen, M. (1979). Children's comprehension of English relative clauses. *Journal of Psycholinguistic Research*, 8, 499–518.

Diaz-Rico, L. T., & Weed, K. Z. (2002). *The crosscultural, language, and academic language development handbook: A complete K–12 reference guide.* Boston, MA: Allyn & Bacon.

Doll, B., & LeClair, C. (2007). Review of the Batería III Woodcock–Muñoz. In K. F. Geisinger, R. A. Spies, J. F. Carlson, and B. S. Plake, *The seventeenth mental measurements yearbook* (pp. 56–69). Lincoln, NE: Buros Institute of Mental Measurements.

Flanagan, D. P., Ortiz, S. O., & Alfonso, V. C. (2007). *Essentials of cross-battery assessment* (2nd ed.). Hoboken, NJ: Wiley.

Garfinkel, A., & Stansfield, C.W. (1998). Review of the Bilingual Verbal Ability Tests. In B. S. Plake & J. C. Impara (Eds.), *The fourteenth mental measurements yearbook* (pp. 155–157). Lincoln, NE: Buros Institute of Mental Measurements.

Gopaul-McNicol, S., & Armour-Thomas, E. (2002). *Assessment and culture: Psychological tests with minority populations.* San Diego, CA: Academic Press.

Hakuta, K. (1986). *Mirror of language: The debate on bilingualism.* New York, NY: Basic Books.

Hakuta, K. (1990). Language and cognition in bilingual children. In A. Padilla, C. Valdez, & H. Fairchild (Eds.), *Bilingual education: Issues and strategies* (pp. 47–59). Newbury Park, CA: Sage.

Hakuta, K., & Cancino, H. (1977). Trends in second language acquisition research. *Harvard Educational Review*, 47, 294–316.

Hakuta, K., Ferdman, B. M., & Diaz, R. M. (1987). Bilingualism and cognitive development: Three perspectives. In S. Rosenberg (Ed.), *Advances in applied psycholinguistics: Vol. II. Reading, writing and language learning* (pp. 284–319). Cambridge, MA: Cambridge University Press.

Hakuta, K., & McLaughlin, B. (1996). Bilingualism and second language learning: Seven tensions that define the research. In D. Berliner & R. Calfee (Eds.), *Handbook of educational psychology* (pp. 603–621). New York, NY: Macmillan.

Hakuta, K., & Suben, J. (1985). Bilingualism and cognitive development. *Annual Review of Applied Linguistics*, 6, 35–45. doi:10.1017/S0267190500003044

Hammill, D. D., Pearson, N. A., & Wiederholt, J. L. (2009). *Comprehensive Test of Nonverbal Intelligence, Second Edition: Examiner manual.* Austin, TX: Pro-Ed.

Herbert, C. (1986). *Basic inventory of natural language.* San Bernardino, CA: Checkpoint Systems.

Hobson, J. (2010). *District profiles.* Retrieved from http://springdale.sharpschool.net/cms/One.aspx?portalId=2943042&pageId=5521665

Izquierdo, E. (2011). Two way dual bilingual education. In R. R. Valencia (Ed.), *Chicano school failure and success: Past, present and future* (pp. 160–172). New York, NY: Routledge.

Kaufman, A. S., & Kaufman, N. L. (2004). *Kaufman Assessment Battery for Children: Technical manual* (2nd ed.). Circle Pines, MN: American Guidance Service.

Kaufman, A. S., Lichtenberger, E. O., Fletcher-Janzen, E., & Kaufman, N. L. (2005). *Essentials of KABC-II assessment*. Hoboken, NJ: Wiley.

Kindler, A. L. (2002). *Survey of the states' limited English proficient students and available educational programs and services: 2000–2001*. Washington, DC: Office of English Language Acquisition, Language Enhancement and Academic Achievement for Limited English Proficient Students.

Lau, M. Y., & Blatchey, L. A. (2009). A comprehensive, multidimensional approach to assessment of culturally and linguistically diverse children (pp. 139–171). In J. M. Jones (Ed.), *The psychology of multiculturalism in schools: A primer for practice, training, and research*. Bethesda, MD: National Association of School Psychologists.

Lichtenstein, R. (2008). Best practices in identification of learning disabilities. In A. Thomas & J. Grimes (Eds.), *Best practices in school psychology* (pp. 295–317). Bethesda, MD: National Association of School Psychologists.

Lopez, E. C. (2002). Best practices in working with school interpreters to deliver psychological services to children and families. In A. Thomas & J. Grimes (Eds.), *Best practices in school psychology IV* (pp. 1419–1432). Bethesda, MD: National Association of School Psychologists.

Marco, G. (2005). Review of the Leiter International Performance Scale–Revised. In B. S. Plake & J. C. Impara (Eds.), *The fourteenth mental measurements yearbook* (pp. 683–687). Lincoln, NE: Buros Institute of Mental Measurements.

Muñoz-Sandoval, A. F., Cummins, J., Alvarado, C. G., & Ruef, M. L. (1998). *Bilingual Verbal Ability Tests: Manual*. Rolling Meadows, IL: Riverside.

Olivarez, A., & Boroda, A. (2007). Review of the Batería III Woodcock–Muñoz. In K. F. Geisinger, R. A. Spies, J. F. Carlson, and B. S. Plake, *The seventeenth mental measurements yearbook*. Lincoln, NE: University of Nebraska Press.

Olvera, P., & Cerrillo-Gómez, L. (2011). A bilingual approach (English and Spanish) psychoeducational assessment MODEL grounded in Cattell-Horn Carroll (CHC) theory: A cross battery approach. *Contemporary School Psychology, 13*, 113–123.

Ortiz, S. O. (2008). Best practices in nondiscriminatory assessment. In A. Thomas & J. Grimes (Eds.), *Best practices in school psychology* (pp. 661–678). Bethesda, MD: National Association of School Psychologists.

Ortiz, S. O. (2011). Separating cultural and linguistic differences (CLD) from specific learning disability in the evaluation of diverse students: Difference or disorder. In D. P. Flanagan & V. C. Alfonso (Eds.), *Essentials of specific learning disability identification* (pp. 299–324). Hoboken, NJ: Wiley.

Prasse, D. P. (2008). Best practices in school psychology and the law. In A. Thomas & J. Grimes (Eds.), *Best practices in school psychology* (pp. 1903–1920). Bethesda, MD: National Association of School Psychologists.

Rhodes, R. L., Ochoa, S. H., & Ortiz, S. O. (2005). *Assessing culturally and linguistically diverse students: A practical guide*. New York, NY: Guilford Press.

Roid, G. H., & Miller, L. J. (1997). *Leiter International Performance Scale–Revised*. Wood Dale, IL: Stoelting.

Roseberry-McKibbin, C. (2007). *Language disorders in children: A multicultural and case perspective*. Boston, MA: Allyn & Bacon.

Roseberry-McKibbin, C. (2008). *Multicultural students with special language needs: Practical strategies for assessment and intervention*. Oceanside, CA: Academic Communication Associates.

Stinnett, T. A. (2005). Review of the Leiter International Performance Scale–Revised. In B. S. Plake & J. C. Impara (Eds.), *The fourteenth mental measurements yearbook* (pp. 183–187). Lincoln, NE: Buros Institute of Mental Measurements.

U.S. Department of Education. (2010). The condition of education 2010 (NCES 2010-013). Washington, DC: National Center for Education Statistics.

Valdes, G., & Figueroa, R. A. (1996). *Bilingualism and testing: A special case of bias*. Norwood, NJ: Ablex.

Wechsler, D. (2005). *Wechsler Intelligence Scale for Children—Fourth edition Spanish*. San Antonio, TX: Psychological Corporation.

Woodcock, R. W., & Muñoz-Sandoval, A. F. (2001). *Woodcock–Muñoz Language Survey normative update*. Chicago, IL: Riverside.

6

RESPONSE TO INTERVENTION AND BILINGUAL LEARNERS: PROMISES AND POTENTIAL PROBLEMS

CATHERINE CHRISTO, ERIN CROSBY, AND MICHELLE ZOZAYA

Assessment is performed in schools for both group-based and individual student-based objectives. Group-based objectives include assessments that provide data for school accountability or for evaluating particular programs. Assessment of an individual student is undertaken for a variety of purposes. For example, teachers routinely assess students on content to determine appropriate placement in the curriculum or to ascertain whether a student has mastered the curriculum. Such assessments are considered informal and are often *criterion referenced*; that is, students performing at a certain level are placed in a particular level of the curriculum, or a given criterion is used to indicate mastery of the material. Such assessments may also be used to place students in leveled reading or math programs. In addition, these assessments identify students who may be at risk of academic failure.

Individuals, primarily those considered at risk, are also assessed to determine whether they are making progress and how much progress they are making

http://dx.doi.org/10.1037/14320-007
Assessing Bilingual Children in Context: An Integrated Approach, A. B. Clinton (Editor)

as a result of instruction and intervention. This type of progress monitoring assessment is a component of a response to intervention (RTI; or multiple-tiered service delivery) model. For students who do not appear to be responding to general education instruction and intervention or who present with significant problems, assessment is undertaken to determine whether they are eligible for and need more intensive services, such as special education. Our focus in this chapter is primarily on assessment within an RTI model to determine whether students are responding to a given intervention or instruction.

NEEDS OF ENGLISH LEARNERS

According to data collected in 2010 by the National Clearinghouse for English Language Acquisition, approximately 49.9 million students were enrolled in U.S. public schools in prekindergarten to 12th grade. Of them, 10.7%, or more than 5.3 million students, were English learners (ELs). This holds significant relevance in states such as California, where the number of ELs enrolled in schools was approximately 1.4 million, which was greater than the next five states combined (Batalova & McHugh, 2010): Texas (701,799), Florida (234,934), New York (213,000), Illinois (175,454), and Arizona (166,572).

Because of the expanding presence of ELs in U.S. public schools, it is critical that educators and school personnel address their unique needs. According to data collected by the National Center for Education Statistics (2011), in more than 1,300 U.S. school districts 76% of ELs scored below grade level on tests of English reading. Although this is not surprising given their limited proficiency in English, it is concerning because reading-related difficulties are one of the primary reasons that ELs are referred for special education assessments (McCardle, Mele-McCarthy, Cutting, Leos, & D'Emilio, 2005; Ortiz et al., 2011). Therefore, ELs may be referred to special education at a higher rate than English-only (EO) students because of a lack of English language ability rather than the presence of a learning disability. Generally speaking, critical issues, such as appropriate norm groups, lack of consideration for language proficiency, and school history, exist regarding the assessment of ELs in general education and for special education eligibility (Barrera & Liu, 2010; Chu & Flores, 2011; Dominguez de Ramírez & Shapiro, 2007; Linian-Thompson, Cirino, & Vaughn, 2007; Ortiz et al., 2011; Sandberg & Reschly, 2011).

Assessment Challenges

A primary concern for the assessment of ELs is the inherent difficulty of establishing what is being measured: an EL's English proficiency or the construct a test purports to measure (Chu & Flores, 2011; Ortiz et al., 2011; Sandberg & Reschly, 2011). That is, a student may do poorly on a test because he or she does not thoroughly understand the task instructions (Chu & Flores, 2011). For example, even tests of nonverbal reasoning frequently have verbal directions and require that answers be given verbally. This lack of understanding or confusion regarding procedures and expectations during the assessment process may result in reduced test scores for ELs, which may be a misrepresentation of their true capabilities and skills (Chu & Flores, 2011; Ortiz et al., 2011; Sandberg & Reschly, 2011). As such, a major issue in administering assessments to the EL population is determining whether to assess an EL student in English, in the student's native language, or in both languages (Chu & Flores, 2011).

Language of Assessment

Research has suggested that assessing ELs in their native language may provide a more accurate reflection of students' knowledge and skills, compared with conducting such assessments in English (Chu & Flores, 2011; Wagner, Francis, & Morris, 2005). However, using assessment tools in languages other than English poses practical challenges because these tools can be costly and more difficult to obtain in a school district (Chu & Flores, 2011), and, if they are obtained, a school psychologist fluent in the child's language may not be available to administer them. In these situations, an interpreter may be necessary. Using an interpreter in the assessment process, however, poses unique challenges. For example, interpreters who assist with the assessment process must not only fluently speak the language of the EL student, but they must also understand the educational and assessment context so that they can accurately convey meaning (Chu & Flores, 2011). It is also difficult to assess ELs in their primary languages; they often have limited academic language because they have not received educational instruction in their primary language. Thus, several layers of challenges and considerations must be taken into account when assessing ELs.

Norm-Referenced Tests

The most common method of assessing ELs is through the use of published norm-referenced tests (Dominguez de Ramírez & Shapiro, 2006; Ortiz et al., 2011; Rhodes, Ochoa, & Ortiz, 2005). This method has considerable limitations, however (Dominguez de Ramírez & Shapiro, 2006; Ortiz et al., 2011; Rhodes et al., 2005; Sandberg & Reschly, 2011). First, these tests are often "selected, administered, and then interpreted in a manner that is not guided by the literature on how culture or language influence test performance of individuals from various cultures" (Rhodes et al., 2005, p. 154). Thus, using such tests with ELs may result in a biased assessment.

Standardized norm-referenced tests are developed and normed with certain assumptions in mind, and when such assumptions do not hold true for ELs, the results may be invalid. A major assumption of norm-referenced tests that may not be applicable to the EL population is the lack of the inclusion of ELs in the norm group. This lack of representation may result in an inappropriate interpretation of test scores. In addition, ELs may not have experience with standardized testing, which may place them at a disadvantage due to their unfamiliarity with these tests and their content and negatively affect their scores for reasons other than their abilities (Ortiz et al., 2011; Rhodes et al., 2005; Sandberg & Reschly, 2011).

Special Education Assessment of English Learners

Students from linguistically and culturally diverse backgrounds are overrepresented in special education (Liu, Ortiz, Wilkinson, Robertson, & Kushner, 2008; Rueda & Windmueller, 2006). Research has suggested that this overrepresentation is a reflection of inappropriate assessment of linguistically diverse students (Barrera & Liu, 2010; Donovan & Cross, 2002; Linian-Thompson et al., 2007; Ortiz et al., 2011). As previously mentioned, it is challenging to determine whether an EL's low scores on tests are the result of limited English proficiency, lack of familiarity with the testing process, inadequate norms, test bias, or an actual learning disability (Chu & Flores, 2011; Ortiz et al. 2011; Sandberg & Reschly, 2011). Moreover, it is also difficult to determine whether academic challenges are the result of a learning disability or other possible environmental factors, such as poor academic instruction, lack of language proficiency, lack of language instructional support, culture and acculturation, and/or lack of motivation (Gilbertson, Maxfield, & Hughes, 2007; McCardle et al., 2005). In addition, it is challenging to distinguish between ELs with lower levels of language proficiency and students with learning disabilities because the two groups can often share many of the same characteristics, such as poor comprehension, difficulty following directions, difficulty completing tasks, and a tendency to make grammatical errors (Chu & Flores, 2011; Ortiz & Maldonado-Colon, 1986; Ortiz & Yates, 2001; Sandberg & Reschly, 2011).

Referral Process

The psychoeducational assessment referral process for ELs is also problematic. Although there are many routes to referring a student for an assessment, best practice is to refer a student following the implementation of a problem-solving team or student study team that assists in offering solutions and interventions to aid a student's educational progress and/or to use an RTI approach (Chu & Flores, 2011; Linian-Thompson et al., 2007; Ortiz et al., 2011). In such an approach, students who are classified as academically "at risk" receive research-based academic intervention in their identified area of weakness as part of general education. If after receiving such interventions, a student does not demonstrate appropriate academic growth or progress, he or she may be referred for an evaluation to investigate the presence of a learning disability.

Although some special education referrals for ELs are the result of the previously mentioned best practices (e.g., student study teams, RTI), referrals of ELs often ultimately reflect an educator's personal determination that a student has neither demonstrated academic progress nor benefited from classroom-based interventions. Thus, if an instructor perceives that an EL is not making adequate academic progress, it is likely that the student will be referred for an evaluation. In addition, referrals also tend to reflect a teacher's perception that the underlying cause of academic difficulties is the result of a learning disability (Ortiz et al., 2011). Thus, there appears to be a lack of systematic and structured protocols for appropriately referring ELs for special education assessments.

Studies have indicated that there are serious shortcomings in school districts' implementation of special education referrals, assessments, eligibility determinations, and placement decisions for ELs (Chu & Flores, 2011; Linian-Thompson et al., 2007; Ortiz et al., 2011). In a 2011 study investigating the practices for special education referral and assessment, Ortiz and colleagues found that educators' concerns and the specific nature of students' academic problems were not clearly identified in referral documents. In addition, several students in the sample were receiving reading instruction in a bilingual special education program prior to being evaluated for a learning disability, indicating that students had been placed in a special education setting even before a comprehensive evaluation. Thus, special education in such cases was the initial "early intervention" for the ELs. Moreover, a clinical judgment panel found that 77% of the ELs placed in special education programs did not qualify as learning disabled when information other than an IQ–achievement discrepancy was considered (Ortiz et al., 2011). The panel determined that documentation was sufficient to qualify only 23% of the special education EL sample as having a learning disability.

Of further concern in the referral process is the need to understand the cultural and linguistic context of ELs prior to initiating the process. Many standardized assessments underestimate ELs' skills and abilities because of a lack of cultural and linguistic sensitivity. To tease cultural and linguistic differences apart from learning disabilities, variables such as language, culture, and level of acculturation should be examined before an EL is referred to a special education assessment. Proponents of an RTI model see this as a possible way to ensure that these variables have been addressed.

The following case study illustrates the referral process for Miguel, a third-grade EL. This case study will be revisited in this chapter to demonstrate appropriate referral practices.

Case Study, Part I

> Miguel is a third-grade student who moved to California from Mexico with his family when he was 5 years old.[1] He entered kindergarten in October of the school year and had no preschool experience. Miguel struggled with early reading, having difficulty with learning to recognize common words and with phonics, and he has continued to lag behind other students, though he is doing better in math. His English appears "good" to his teacher, on the basis of conversations with other students on the playground that she has overheard. Therefore, she is not worried about language being an issue; she feels that his use of informal conversational English indicates adequate English language development. In addition, she noted that Miguel has been at the school since kindergarten, and for that reason she thinks he has had sufficient schooling and his reading delays cannot be explained by lack of instruction. Therefore, she has referred him for an evaluation for special education. Educational interventions have consisted of the same reading interventions provided to English speakers, which consisted of a focus on development of phonics.
>
> However, there are various facts not considered in the process of this referral that have affected Miguel's education. His family goes to Mexico to visit family each December. As a result, Miguel misses about one month of school each year. He speaks only Spanish at home, and his after-school playmates are all Spanish speakers. Although Miguel may demonstrate conversational English abilities, he has not developed academic English, which takes much longer to develop (Cummins, 1984). The interventions provided in the classroom have not addressed vocabulary needs or Miguel's need to have instruction in the structure of written English.

RESPONSE TO INTERVENTION

Response to intervention is the name given to a multiple-tiered service delivery model that stresses research-based instruction and intervention and monitoring of student progress to determine the need for more intense interventions. RTI models generally consist of three to four tiers. The first tier involves general education classroom instruction. The second tier includes

---

[1]The details of the case studies have been changed to preserve the anonymity of the individuals involved.

interventions that are targeted toward students who are showing signs of struggle with the curriculum and have been identified as needing some extra support. This support may be in the classroom or outside the classroom. The third tier in most models involves students who need significant support, such as special education services. Each tier can be characterized by the types of assessments and qualities of instruction or intervention that are used. Two themes underlying all tiers of an RTI model are the use of scientific, researched-based curricula (the I for *intervention* in RTI) and progress monitoring (the R for *response* in RTI) to determine how a student is responding to the intervention or instruction implemented.

Instruction and Intervention in a Response to Intervention Model

The quality of the instruction or intervention is critical to a successful RTI model. Not only should the curriculum or intervention have a record of effectiveness, it should also be appropriate for the given student(s). This is particularly important when addressing instruction and intervention for ELs. At each tier, instruction becomes more intense in that there is an effort to increase learning time or provide more instruction in skills that are lacking. Some possible ways to increase the intensity of instruction are (a) reducing the student-to-teacher ratio, (b) increasing the amount of time a student spends on a given topic, and (c) providing instruction focused on particular skills. For example, a first-grade student who is struggling in reading will first be grouped at an appropriate level in the classroom on the basis of information from class or schoolwide screening and an evaluation of academic needs. A student at this level receives whole class instruction as well as group instruction addressing specific aspects of the curriculum. This would be considered Tier 1 instruction or intervention. If that student fails to respond to the classroom instruction, he or she may then be provided with extra support that is more intense (Tier 2). The intensity may be achieved through more time (e.g., a before- or after-school program), a smaller student–teacher ratio (e.g., a small group led by a school support person), or an intervention that targets specific skills (e.g., focusing on just phonics or reading fluency). If these Tier 2 interventions are not effective, the student may be referred for evaluation to determine whether she or he needs special education services. Such services would constitute Tier 3, the most intense level of service available.

As previously stated, the use of appropriate research-based instruction is a critical component of RTI models. There is a large body of research on effective reading instruction and intervention models, particularly for early grades (e.g., Torgesen, 2004). There is much less evidence regarding effective instruction and intervention for older students, in other academic areas, and for ELs. This poses a problem for the application of RTI models beyond reading, the early grades, and for ELs.

Measuring Responsiveness to Intervention

Student progress on key skills, such as reading fluency, is used at each tier to make instructional decisions. At the first tier, school-, grade-, or classwide screening (e.g., benchmark testing administered three times per year) is used to identify students who may be at risk of academic struggles, which informs the classroom teacher as to who may need more support in the classroom. Teachers may also use this information for placing students into appropriate instructional groups. Ongoing progress monitoring (e.g., triannual benchmarking) serves to measure the progress of all students in the general education curriculum.

Students identified through benchmarking as being at risk of academic failure or students receiving interventions are monitored on a more frequent basis. The frequency of monitoring depends on the intensity of the intervention: The more intense the intervention, the more frequent the monitoring. For example, students receiving classroom intervention in Tier 1 may be monitored on a monthly basis, whereas those in a general education intervention in Tier 2 may be monitored two times per month. Regular progress monitoring allows teachers and student support teams to make decisions as to whether an intervention is likely to be effective for a given student. With progress monitoring, a goal may be set for a student at the beginning of an intervention. If a student fails to meet this goal, he or she may be referred for a more intensive intervention or for an evaluation for special education.

Tools used for progress monitoring are generally brief and easy to administer. They are designed to measure small increments of growth (e.g., growth in the span of 1 week). In reading, oral reading fluency is a common progress-monitoring measure. In math, computational fluency is a common measure. Progress monitoring measures for early grades and basic skills are the most well-researched and are widely available (Christo, Davis, & Brock, 2009). It becomes much more difficult to apply these measures to academic progress once students reach the upper grades, unless the intervention is aimed at the development of basic skills.

ELIMINATING THE WAIT-TO-FAIL MODEL FOR SPECIFIC LEARNING DISABILITY IDENTIFICATION

Proponents of the RTI model paint a promising picture of its potential benefits. The most commonly stated benefit of using an RTI approach to assess ELs is the elimination of the discrepancy or *wait-to-fail model* (Haager,

2007; Liu et al., 2008; Xu & Drame, 2008). Historically, to receive specialized services, a student must be classified as learning disabled through the documentation of a severe discrepancy between intellectual ability and one or more areas of achievement (Individuals With Disabilities Education Improvement Act [IDEIA], 2004). However, the reliability and validity of this model for the purpose of identifying learning disabilities have been questioned repeatedly (Liu et al., 2008). First, the definition of a severe discrepancy varies from state to state. Therefore, a student who may be classified as learning disabled in one state may not be in another. Second, a student whose difficulties begin when he or she enters school may not be identified or offered appropriate supports until the second or third grade because it may take several years for the discrepancy to be acquired. Third, relying on an achievement gap alone makes it difficult to differentiate between students with a disability and students who are struggling for other reasons, such as language acquisition or economic disadvantage (Liu et al., 2008). In regard to ELs, these "other reasons" become another barrier to identifying learning disabilities and providing specialized services.

To be identified as learning disabled, a student must not only demonstrate a severe discrepancy but also must not demonstrate any of the exclusionary criteria. These exclusionary criteria include limited school experience or poor school attendance, which may be more common among culturally and linguistically diverse students (IDEIA, 2004). These and other documented shortcomings of the discrepancy model have fostered the belief that using an RTI approach is at least better than the wait-to-fail alternative. This is especially true when assessing ELs because the discrepancy model has been found to contribute to the disproportionate minority representation in special education programs (Xu & Drame, 2008). Liu et al. (2008) explained that "in addition to providing early intervention, RTI approaches are touted as holding promise for resolving disproportionate special education representation of culturally and linguistically diverse learners" (p. 178). This may be due to the emphasis that an RTI model places on empirically based general education practices and differentiated instruction for all students.

Effective Evidence-Based Instruction

The RTI approach has the potential to improve the intervention and instructional appropriateness and effectiveness of education in both general and specialized settings (Xu & Drame, 2008). This is because the RTI approach is congruent with the IDEIA criteria that good evidence-based instruction must be used at all tiers, regardless of disability (Rinaldi & Samson, 2008). The RTI approach places emphasis on curriculum-based measures (CBMs), classroom observations, and work samples in determining the effectiveness of instructional delivery. Because of this emphasis, the RTI approach may improve the quality of instruction at all tiers by increasing the perceived responsibility and accountability of the greater educational team in providing students with differentiated and appropriate access to the curriculum (Orosco, 2010). The nature of the RTI approach encourages strong teaching practices and remedial opportunities across all educational settings to meet the needs of individual students, regardless of whether they have an identified disability. This increased awareness may encourage the members of the education team to work collaboratively, increase communication, and distribute the responsibility for student success across the general education providers, special education providers, English language teachers, administrators, parents, and other service providers (Orosco, 2010; Xu & Drame, 2008).

Appropriate Instruction for English Learners

The question of appropriate instruction is particularly important for ELs and will determine the effectiveness of an RTI model for this population. It is not sufficient that instructional staff understand generally effective instruction; they must know what types of instruction are going to meet the unique needs of any given student under unique conditions (Klingner, McRay-Sorrels, & Barrera, 2007; Saenz, 2008). Teachers should know a variety of strategies to use with different populations (Mathes, Pollard-Durodola, Cárdenas-Hagan, Linan-Thompson, & Vaughn, 2007; Xu & Drame, 2008). Gersten et al. (2006) identified some of the critical elements in interventions for ELs, notably a comprehensive approach that targets all areas of reading (e.g., phonics, fluency, comprehension) along with language development (e.g., vocabulary, sentence structure, narrative) as being the most successful.

Need for Professional Development

Professional development is important to the successful implementation of RTI models for linguistically diverse students. According to Haager (2007), to make significant gains, "EL students need teachers to be using effective instructional techniques in general, adjusting their instruction for individuals having difficulty, engaging their students in interactive and engaging vocabulary and comprehension development, and providing high-quality explicit instruction" (p. 215). To ensure that this is happening, some school districts have adopted criteria to determine the appropriateness of instruction for ELs. For example, the Los Angeles Unified School District developed an *Access to Grade Level Content Observation Checklist* using the principles of specially designed academic instruction in English. This checklist is used to ensure that ELs are afforded appropriate exposure to, and direct instruction in, grade-level content with opportunities for making connections to prior knowledge. This checklist is scored to determine the amount of evidence available in determining the effectiveness of instruction (Los Angeles Unified School District, 2005). Orosco (2010) discussed the importance of considering the social–cultural context of learning for ELs. Instruction must recognize students' cultural and linguistic heritage and incorporate appropriate activities.

Next, we revisit Miguel in light of the information a general education teacher should possess in regard to ELs.

Case Study, Part II

> As previously discussed, Miguel was referred for special education without consideration of factors important to understanding the academic development of ELs. In a school where awareness of the unique needs of ELs was incorporated in the instruction and referral process, the site-based team would first review the referral to determine whether he had received appropriate instruction. With this information the team would be able to decide whether Miguel's lack of progress was due to inappropriate instruction. In addition, they would have more extensive information regarding his attendance and the amount of intervention provided.

Reduction of Special Education Assessment Referrals

The benefits, discussed earlier, of an RTI approach for the general education population suggest that it may also ultimately lead to an overall reduction in special education referrals. Often, referrals for special education are inappropriate because teachers failed to look at previous instruction or primary language. By requiring early, appropriate intervention outside of special education (and prior to consideration for special education), students will receive earlier direct interventions targeting their needs as ELs (Ortiz et al., 2011). The students who respond to this effective early intervention may not need special education services later on, which may prevent ELs from being inappropriately classified as learning disabled (Kamps et al., 2007). In addition, students who do not respond to specialized interventions may be identified as learning disabled earlier, which may allow for more time to be spent addressing students' more intensive needs (Xu & Drame, 2008). Also, identifying learning disabilities earlier in a student's education may lessen the impact of the disability by keeping the achievement gap as narrow as possible (Haager, 2007).

Ecologically Valid Assessment Data

Not only does the RTI approach have the potential to reduce special education referrals, it also offers the potential for ecologically valid information to be used in the assessment process with ELs. The term *ecological validity* refers to assessment that includes the consideration of a student's abilities within their personal contexts and circumstances. Progress-monitoring data within an RTI model provide information about whether a student is struggling academically but does not in itself provide information as to why the student is at risk (National Joint Committee on Learning Disabilities, 2005). Xu and Drame (2008) saw a potential for considering context within RTI: "RTI places emphasis on curriculum-based-assessment, classroom observations and authentic/ecologically valid assessment. Unlike nationally standardized assessments, student output is analyzed within their immediate context" (p. 306).

Data collected within an RTI model must be considered in the context of the student's daily interpersonal experiences and his or her environmental interactions that may affect achievement. This is especially important for students with diverse backgrounds whose manner of interaction may vary significantly from one setting to another (Orosco, 2010). These students may have difficulty meeting the differing expectations for behavior at home versus school or may have difficulty connecting school-based concepts to their own life experiences. These difficulties may in turn prevent them from making adequate progress in the classroom (Xu & Drame, 2008). This type of information provides vital diagnostic data that may be helpful in the assessment process for a student who does not respond to an intervention (Rinaldi & Samson, 2008). The unique circumstances of each student should be considered in determining whether a student is not achieving at an appropriate or expected rate (Saenz, 2008).

The RTI approach also provides progress-monitoring data, most commonly using CBMs. CBMs typically focus on the acquisition of early critical skills, such as phonological awareness in reading. CBMs are useful in monitoring a student's progress because of their ecological validity and their sensitivity to growth over short periods. CBMs can also distinguish between ineffective instruction and inadequate individual learning by constantly comparing students' progress with that of peers in the same environment (Gilbertson et al., 2007).

PROBLEMS WITH RESPONSE TO INTERVENTION MODELS

Although RTI holds the promise of benefit for ELs, its successful implementation has inherent challenges. These include determining appropriate instruction and determining how to use progress-monitoring data. Issues of appropriate instruction include those unique to ELs in general and those unique to individual ELs. Crockett and Brown (2009) suggested an RTI model that incorporates important questions and requirements regarding instructional delivery for ELs. The "guiding questions" at each tier target both the student (e.g., Has the student had interrupted education?) and the classroom (e.g., Are ELs progressing in general?).

Issues With Progress Monitoring

The primary means for monitoring student progress within an RTI model are general outcome measures. These CBMs are short measures that are sensitive to growth and are based on expectations for students (at the school, district, or national level) at the end of a given period. Commonly called *curriculum-based measures*, there are inherent problems in their use for determining academic progress and the need for intervention. First, they are static measures that look at performance at one point in time; second, they do not consider all the reasons for students' given performance; and third, they may sometimes lack content validity for the academic area being assessed (Barrera, 2006). Because of these limitations, researchers continue to explore the necessary frequency for administering CBM and the best ways in which to determine responsiveness. For example, to determine lack of response, one can look at the level of performance, the rate of change in performance, or both. When determining whether a student needs more intensive intervention, one must set cut-off points or criteria for making those decisions. Although there are published national norms and expectations for both level and rate of growth, it may also be appropriate to compare a student with the local population. Decisions as to comparison group and the lack of progress or level of performance that requires intervention are all decisions that schools working to implement an RTI model must make. These questions become more complex when one is working with an EL population.

Setting Expectations for English Learners

When considering ELs, expectations must reflect their language status as well as their cultural context (Barrera & Liu, 2010). Most of the information about ELs and CBMs has focused on reading because that was the original primary focus for all RTI models and the area most likely to be significantly different for ELs. Most studies have found that measures focusing on foundational reading skills can be effective at predicting reading success or difficulties for ELs (Haager, 2007; Ives Wiley & Deno, 2005; Linan-Thompson & Ortiz, 2009). There are, however, limited data on how to determine expectations for growth for ELs. It is not surprising that studies have found that ELs tend to have different growth rates than EO speakers (Dominguez de Ramírez & Shapiro, 2007). Some studies have found that their slope may be the same as for EO speakers, though the level is lower (Linan-Thompson et al., 2007). Therefore, even though they may gain reading proficiency at the same rate, they will not catch up with their EO peers.

Dominguez de Ramírez and Shapiro (2007) suggested that reading fluency measures are useful for monitoring growth for both ELs and EOs, whether learning to read in English or Spanish. However, they noted that the growth curve for ELs in an English classroom may be different than for EO students. For EO students, reading rate typically increases rapidly in the early grades and then slows down. For ELs, the rate is slower in the early grades but may not plateau as much as it does for EO students. This may be due to the effects of continued growth in vocabulary and familiarity with English.

It has also been found that general outcome measures for ELs, though predictive of reading, have a weaker relationship with future reading scores than they do for EO students (Yeo, 2010). Betts, Bolt, Decker, Muyskens, and Marston (2009) found that time in the United States and the language of the home affected the power of oral reading fluency in predicting performance on statewide tests. Klein and Jimerson (2005) also investigated the utility of oral reading fluency measures to identify students who were at risk of poor performance on statewide assessments. They determined that "oral reading fluency probes over predict the reading proficiency (as measured by SAT-9 Total Reading) of Hispanic students whose home language is Spanish and under predict the reading proficiency of Caucasian students whose home language is English" (p. 39).

Use of Curriculum-Based Measures for Educational Decisions for English Learners

Results have been mixed on whether CBMs are equally good at predicting future reading performance for ELs as for EOs. Sandberg and Reschly (2011) reviewed nine studies that examined the use of reading CBMs with ELs. They concluded that oral reading fluency measures are useful in making educational decisions for ELs. However, they also noted areas of concern and areas for future research. For example, they suggested that more research is needed on oral reading fluency and comprehension and the relationship between growth in early and later grades and between languages. The authors also noted that when working with ELs, there are likely more extraneous variables, such as cultural and linguistic background, that can lead to measurement error. For example, ELs may be less familiar with fluency testing than their EO peers.

Linklater, O'Connor, and Palardy (2009) studied the use of phonological processing measures in kindergarten (initial sound fluency, phonemic segmentation) to predict later decoding fluency. They found that early phonemic segmentation fluency did not predict later decoding fluency for ELs; therefore, it would have been a poor measure to use to identify at-risk students. In looking at older readers, Roehrig, Petscher, Nettles, Hudson, and Torgesen (2008) found third-grade reading fluency scores to be good predictors of later reading comprehension scores for ELs. Looking at fifth-grade students, Ives Wiley and Deno (2005) compared the usefulness of oral reading fluency and maze tests in predicting reading comprehension on state-administered tests. Maze tests present the student with a reading passage in which a choice of three words is presented approximately every ninth word. Like fluency measures, the test has a time limit. Therefore, it is a measure of both comprehension and fluency. Ives Wiley and Deno found that maze scores were the best predictors of reading comprehension, as measured on state tests, for non-ELs, whereas oral reading fluency was better for ELs.

Next, we revisit Miguel's case in regard to activities of the child study team.

Case Study, Part III

As previously described, Miguel is a third-grade student who was referred by his teacher for evaluation for special education. We first described a scenario in which a lack of awareness of the needs and unique characteristics of ELs may have led to inappropriate referrals for special education. In "Case Study, Part II," we provided examples of the information that would be considered by a general education teacher with some understanding of ELs. This example provides a scenario in which important factors would be considered before Miguel is evaluated for special education.

Using the checklist in Appendix 6.1, the team would have a more holistic view of Miguel than just teacher opinion and limited classroom data. The team would discover that Miguel's sociocultural context is not the same as his classmates' and that his language proficiency is actually more limited than it appears in informal conversation. In addition, they would be provided with evidence of whether he had received intervention targeting his unique needs as a learner. As a result of taking a more complete look at Miguel, the team would likely determine that the most appropriate intervention for Miguel was in the classroom. Such an intervention should focus on language development and providing the scaffolding necessary to meet his needs. For example, prior to lessons, his teacher should determine whether Miguel has the background knowledge expected of students when interacting with text (e.g., typical community experiences). In addition, the team will likely determine that, within their school, professional development is needed to help teachers appropriately differentiate instruction for ELs.

Variability Among English Learners

As a group, ELs are extremely diverse (Abedi, 2009). Barrera and Liu (2010) noted that the difficulty in using lack of RTIs as a measure of academic failure is the variability in the student population. That is, what may be appropriate instruction for one student is not necessarily so for another. Beyond language differences, ELs vary on such factors as previous schooling, progress in learning English, family factors, and time in the United States. This variability causes difficulties at both the research and practice levels. When using CBMs to determine whether a student is progressing satisfactorily, schools must determine which students are the most appropriate peers for comparison and which group to use to set a median or expected level.

One possibility may be to create norm groups that more closely reflect the EL population. The problem, of course, is that ELs are not homogeneous; they have been exposed to English for varying amounts of time, have been schooled in English for varying amounts of time, and likely have markedly different levels of English proficiency. Therefore, determining an appropriate comparison group and levels of expectation becomes difficult, even when one is looking at ELs only.

CONCLUSION

RTI holds promise for enhanced educational decision making for ELs. The focus is on appropriate instruction for all learners, early intervention, and monitoring student progress. This focus, if implemented with the unique needs of ELs in mind, can lead to better educational outcomes. Implementation of a successful RTI model that will meet the needs of ELs requires a school climate that fosters collaboration among school professionals (e.g., between bilingual educators and general education teachers) and a focus on effective instruction for diverse learners (Linan-Thompson & Ortiz, 2009). A successful RTI model must consider the following important global issues:

- Appropriate instruction must be considered in the context of each child's unique needs. ELs have instructional needs that are different from those of non-ELs as well as different from other ELs. In determining whether a student has had appropriate instruction, language, school history, and sociocultural context must be addressed.

- The results of progress-monitoring assessments (e.g., CBMs) may not mean the same thing for ELs as they do for non-ELs. Therefore, results must be interpreted in accordance with research on ELs, not just with research on non-ELs.

Site-based educational decision-making teams should be aware of these issues and have mechanisms in place to address them during the referral process. Appendix 6.1 provides a checklist that can be used to guide teams in decision making regarding ELs.

APPENDIX 6.1: ASSESSMENT OF ENGLISH LANGUAGE LEARNERS FOR SITE-BASED TEAMS

Student's name: _____   Student's date of birth: _____   Grade: _____

Teacher: _____   Meeting date: _____

Language and culture

Data to gather	Sources of information	Data collected
	Culture	
Student's ethnicity:	Parent interview/records	
Specific region:		
Birthplace:	Parent interview/records	
Number of years in United States:	Parent interview/records	
	Language	
Proficiency in L1 and L2:	Language samples/CELDT scores	
	Parent/teacher/student interview	
Language(s) spoken	Language samples/CELDT scores	
Primary:	Parent/teacher/student interview	
Dominant:		
Language spoken in the home:	Student/parent interview	
Language spoken by parents/siblings:	Student/parent interview	
Exposure to English	Student/parent/teacher interview	
❑ Education ❑ Family ❑ Peers ❑ Media	Records	
Parental language proficiency:	Parent interview	
Parental education:		

If the student is found to have limited English proficiency, he or she should be tested in the native language as much as possible and provided with culturally and linguistically appropriate assessment tools.

	Education
	Educational history
Schooling in other country/duration/quality/ interruptions:	Parent interview/records
Years of formal schooling in L1 and L2:	Parent interview/records
Curriculum used:	
Student progress:	
❑ Previous work samples	
❑ Prior language proficiency levels:	
	Current educational performance
Current classroom performance	Observations, work samples, test scores, portfolio review
Math: ❑ Below ❑ Average ❑ Above	
ELA: ❑ Below ❑ Average ❑ Above	
Compared with other ELs:	
❑ Below ❑ Above average	
Level of participation in comparison with other classmates	Observations, teacher interview
Non-ELs:	
ELs:	
Language usage in the classroom:	Observations, teacher interview
Minutes of ELD per day (at least 30 min to 1 hr recommended):	Teacher interview
Curriculum:	
❑ State-adopted grade level materials are used	
❑ ELs at ELD 1 to 3 are provided	
❑ Content-based ELD to build essential language skills	

(continues)

APPENDIX 6.1: ASSESSMENT OF ENGLISH LANGUAGE LEARNERS FOR SITE-BASED TEAMS (*Continued*)

Student's name: _____ Student's date of birth: _____ Grade: _____

Teacher: _____ Meeting date: _____

Education

Data to gather	Sources of information	Data collected
Teacher's training in teaching ELs:	Teacher interview	
Teaching strategies used: ❑ Direct and systematic instruction Use of: ❑ Visuals ❑ Concrete objects ❑ Opportunities for hands on learning ❑ Scaffolding techniques	Observations, teacher interview	
Interactions in the classroom: ❑ Student-to-student ❑ Teacher-to-student		
Varied instructional grouping: ❑ ELD level ❑ Cooperative group		
Interventions, student progress: ❑ Work samples ❑ Frustration level ❑ Progress monitoring ❑ Research-based interventions	Observations, teacher interview, records	

Social/behavior	
Who the student interacts with: □ Other ELs □ Non-ELs	Observation, teacher interview
Quality of peer interactions: □ Classroom □ Playground □ Home	Observation, teacher/parent interview
Behavior: □ Classroom □ Playground □ Home	Observation, teacher/parent interview
Interaction with adults: □ Classroom □ Home	Observation, teacher/parent interview
Personality: □ Introverted □ Extroverted	Observation, teacher/parent/student interview
Behavior history: □ Documented changes in behavior	Record review/parent interview

Note. CELDT = California English Language Development Test; EL = English learner; ELA = English language arts; ELD = English language development; L1 = native language; L2 = second language. From *Guiding School-Based Teams in the Assessment of English Learners* (p. 45), by H. Linscheid and L. Lopes, 2009, Sacramento, CA: California State University. Copyright 2009 by H. Linscheid and L. Lopes. Reprinted with permission.

REFERENCES

Abedi, J. (2009). English language learners with disabilities: Classification, assessment and accommodation. *Journal of Applied Testing Technology, 10*(3), 1–10.

Barrera, M. (2006). Roles of definitional and assessment models in the identification of new or second language learners of English for special education. *Journal of Learning Disabilities, 39,* 142–156. doi:10.1177/00222194060390020301

Barrera, M., & Liu, K. K. (2010). Challenges of general outcomes measurement in the RTI progress monitoring of linguistically diverse exceptional learners. *Theory Into Practice, 49,* 273–280. doi:10.1080/00405841.2010.510713

Batalova, J., & McHugh, M. (2010). *Number and growth of students in US schools in need of English instruction.* Retrieved from http://www.migrationinformation.org/ellinfo/FactSheet_ELL1.pdf

Betts, J., Bolt, S., Decker, D., Muyskens, P., & Marston, D. (2009). Examining the role of time and language type in reading development for English language learners. *Journal of School Psychology, 47,* 143–166. doi:10.1016/j.jsp.2008.12.002

Christo, C., Davis, J., & Brock, S. E. (2009). *Identifying, assessing, and treating dyslexia at school.* New York, NY: Springer Science and Business Media.

Chu, S., & Flores, S. (2011). Assessment of English language learners with learning disabilities. *Clearing House, 84,* 244–248.

Crockett, D., & Brown, J. (2009). Multicultural practices and response to intervention. In J. M. Jones (Ed.), *The psychology of multiculturalism in the schools: A primer for practice, training, and research* (pp. 117–137). Bethesda, MD: National Association of School Psychologists.

Cummins, J. (1984). *Bilingualism and special education: Issues in assessment and pedagogy.* Clevedon, England: Multilingual Matters.

Dominguez de Ramírez, R., & Shapiro, E. S. (2006). Curriculum-based measurement and the evaluation of reading skills of Spanish-speaking English language learners in bilingual education classrooms. *School Psychology Review, 35,* 356–369.

Dominguez de Ramírez, R. D., & Shapiro, E. S. (2007). Cross-language relationship between Spanish and English oral reading fluency among Spanish-speaking English language learners in bilingual education classrooms. *Psychology in the Schools, 44,* 795–806. doi:10.1002/pits.20266

Donovan, M. S., & Cross, C. T. (2002). *Minority students in special and gifted education.* Washington, DC: National Academy Press.

Gersten, R., Baker, S., Shanahan, T., Linan-Thompson, S., Chiappe, P., & Scarcella, R. (2006). *Effective literacy and language instruction for English learners in the elementary grades: An IES practice guide.* Washington, DC: IES, Department of Education.

Gilbertson, D., Maxfield, J., & Hughes, J. (2007). Evaluating responsiveness to intervention for English-language learners: A comparison of response modes on letter naming rates. *Journal of Behavioral Education, 16,* 259–279. doi:10.1007/s10864-007-9039-9

Haager, D. (2007). Promises and cautions regarding using response to intervention with English language learners. *Learning Disability Quarterly, 30*, 213–218. doi:10.2307/30035565

Individuals With Disabilities Education Improvement Act of 2004, Pub. L. No. 108-446 (2004). Retrieved from http://nichcy.org/wp-content/uploads/docs/IDEA2004regulations.pdf

Ives Wiley, H., & Deno, S. (2005). Oral reading and maze measures as predictors of success for English Learners on a state standards assessment. *Remedial and Special Education, 26*, 207–214. doi:10.1177/07419325050260040301

Kamps, D., Abbott, M., Greenwood, C., Arreaga-Mayer, C., Wills, H., Lonstaff, J., . . . Walton, C. (2007). Use of evidenced-based, small group reading instruction for English language learners in elementary grades; Secondary-tier intervention. *Learning Disability Quarterly, 30*, 153–168. doi:10.2307/30035561

Klein, J., & Jimerson, S. (2005). Examining ethnic, gender, language and socioeconomic bias in oral reading fluency scores among Caucasian and Hispanic students. *School Psychology Quarterly, 20*(1), 23–50. doi:10.1521/scpq.20.1.23.64196

Klingner, J., McRay-Sorrels, A., & Barrera, M. (2007). Considerations when implementing response to intervention with culturally and linguistically diverse students. In D. Haager, J. Klingner, & S. Vaughn (Eds.), *Evidence-based reading practices for response to intervention* (pp. 233–244). Baltimore, MD: Brooks/Cole.

Linan-Thompson, S., Cirino, P. T., & Vaughn, S. (2007). Determining English language learners' response to intervention: Questions and some answers. *Learning Disability Quarterly, 30*, 185–195. doi:10.2307/30035563

Linan-Thompson, S., & Ortiz, A. A. (2009). Response to intervention and English-language learners: Instructional and assessment considerations. *Seminars in Speech and Language, 30*, 105–120. doi:10.1055/s-0029-1215718

Linklater, D. L., O'Connor, R. E., & Palardy, G. J. (2009). Kindergarten literacy assessment of English only and English language learner students: An examination of the predictive validity of three phonemic awareness measures. *Journal of School Psychology, 47*, 369–394. doi:10.1016/j.jsp.2009.08.001

Linscheid, H., & Lopes, L. (2009). *Guiding school-based teams in the assessment of English learners* (Unpublished specialist project). California State University, Sacramento.

Liu, Y., Ortiz, A. A., Wilkinson, C. Y., Robertson, P., & Kushner, M. I. (2008). From early childhood special education to special education resource rooms: Identification, assessment, and eligibility determinations for English language learners with reading-related disabilities. *Assessment for Effective Intervention, 33*, 177–187. doi:10.1177/1534508407313247

Los Angeles Unified School District. Language Acquisition Branch. (2005). *Access to core curriculum—Secondary SDAIE/L1 observation tool*. Retrieved

from http://notebook.lausd.net/pls/ptl/docs/PAGE/CA_LAUSD/FLDR_
ORGANIZATIONS/FLDR_INSTRUCTIONAL_SVCS/INSTRUC
TIONALSUPPORTSERVICES/LANGUAGE_ACQ_HOME_NEW/
LANGUAGE_ACQ_ENGLISH_LEARNERS/LANGUAGE_ACQ_ENG
LISH_LEARNERS_SECONDARY/TAB1181832/HANDOUT6_SEC%20
SDAIE-L1%20TOOL.PDF

Mathes, P. G., Pollard-Durodola, S. D., Cárdenas-Hagan, E., Linan-Thompson, S., & Vaughn, S. (2007). Teaching struggling readers who are native Spanish speakers: What do we know? *Language, Speech, and Hearing Services in Schools, 38,* 260–271. doi:10.1044/0161-1461(2007/027)

McCardle, P., Mele-McCarthy, J., Cutting, L., Leos, K., & D'Emilio, T. (2005). Learning disabilities in English language learners: Identifying the issues. *Learning Disabilities Research & Practice, 20,* 1–5. doi:10.1111/j.1540-5826.2005.00114.x

National Center for Education Statistics. (2011). *The condition of education 2011.* Retrieved from http://nces.ed.gov/pubs2011/2011033.pdf

National Clearinghouse for English Language Acquisition. (2010). *The growing number of English learners.* Retrieved from http://www.ncela.gwu.edu/files/uploads/9/growingLEP_0708.pdf

National Joint Committee on Learning Disabilities. (2005). Responsiveness to intervention and learning disabilities. *Learning Disability Quarterly, 28,* 249–260. doi:10.2307/4126964

Orosco, M. J. (2010). A sociocultural examination of response to intervention with Latino English language learners. *Theory Into Practice, 49,* 265–272. doi:10.108 0/00405841.2010.510703

Ortiz, A. A., & Maldonado-Colon, E. (1986). Reducing inappropriate referrals of language minority students to special education. In A. C. Willig & H. F. Greenberg (Eds.), *Bilingualism and learning disabilities* (pp. 37–50). New York, NY: New American Library.

Ortiz, A. A., Robertson, P. M., Wilkinson, C. Y., Liu, Y. J., McGhee, B. D., & Kushner, M. I. (2011). The role of bilingual education teachers in preventing inappropriate referrals of ELLs to special education: Implications for response to intervention. *Bilingual Research Journal, 34,* 316–333. doi:10.1080/15235882. 2011.628608

Ortiz, A. A., & Yates, J. R. (2001). A framework for serving English language learners with disabilities. *Journal of Special Education Leadership, 14,* 72–80.

Rhodes, R. L., Ochoa, S. H., & Ortiz, S. O. (2005). *Assessing culturally and linguistically diverse students: A practical guide.* New York, NY: Guilford Press.

Rinaldi, C., & Samson, J. (2008). English language learners and response to intervention: Referral considerations. *Teaching Exceptional Children, 40*(5), 6–14.

Roehrig, A. D., Petscher, Y., Nettles, S. M., Hudson, R. F., & Torgesen, J. K. (2008). Accuracy of the DIBELS Oral Reading Fluency Measure for predicting third grade reading comprehension outcomes. *Journal of School Psychology, 46,* 343–366. doi:10.1016/j.jsp.2007.06.006

Rueda, R., & Windmueller, M. P. (2006). English language learners, LD, and over-representation: A multilevel analysis. *Journal of Learning Disabilities, 39*, 99–107. doi:10.1177/00222194060390020801

Saenz, L. (2008). *Using CBM to progress monitor English language learners.* Retrieved from http://www.studentprogress.org/doc/webinars/mar08webinarslides.pdf

Sandberg, K. L., & Reschly, A. L. (2011). English learners: Challenges in assessment and the promise of curriculum-based measurement. *Remedial and Special Education, 32*, 144–154. doi:10.1177/0741932510361260

Torgesen, J. K. (2004). Lessons learned from research on interventions for students who have difficulty learning to read. In V. P. C. McCardle (Ed.), *The voice of evidence in reading research* (pp. 355–382). Baltimore, MD: Brooks.

Wagner, R., Francis, D., & Morris, R. (2005). Identifying English language learners with learning disabilities: Key challenges and possible approaches. *Learning Disabilities Research & Practice, 20*, 6–15. doi:10.1111/j.1540-5826.2005.00115.x

Xu, Y., & Drame, E. (2008). Culturally appropriate context: Unlocking the potential of response to intervention for English language learners. *Early Childhood Education Journal, 35*, 305–311. doi:10.1007/s10643-007-0213-4

Yeo, S. (2010). Predicting performance on state achievement tests using curriculum-based measurement in reading: A multilevel meta-analysis. *Remedial and Special Education, 31*, 412–422. doi:10.1177/0741932508327463

7

INTEGRATED SOCIAL–EMOTIONAL ASSESSMENT OF THE BILINGUAL CHILD

MICHAEL R. HASS AND KELLY S. KENNEDY

This chapter addresses the assessment of the social, emotional, and behavioral functioning of bilingual and bicultural children, including those native to the United States and those who have recently arrived in the country. This diverse group has significant differences both within the group and in comparison with English-speaking children native to the United States. These differences are often found in the domains most influenced by culture and are critical to understanding social and emotional functioning (e.g., languages spoken, acculturation, educational experiences, family structures, access to social support). This makes the social–emotional assessment of these children an extraordinarily complex task. Although these differences are substantial, it is important to remember that they also coexist with significant human commonalities (Achenbach et al., 2008).

In this chapter, we frame the assessment of social, emotional, and behavioral functioning as an assessment of mental health rather than just as social,

http://dx.doi.org/10.1037/14320-008
Assessing Bilingual Children in Context: An Integrated Approach, A. B. Clinton (Editor)

emotional, and behavioral problems. A comprehensive assessment of mental health in lieu of evaluation of psychopathology includes an understanding of strengths, resources, and resilience in addition to symptoms and problems. We address the challenges presented in understanding the social–emotional strengths and needs of bilingual and bicultural children and provide suggestions that reflect best practices in conducting social and emotional assessments of these children.

This chapter pays special attention to school-based practice. This emphasis builds on two important aspects of schools and mental health. First, to the extent that children receive mental health services at all, the majority receive them in schools (Rones & Hoagwood, 2000). Second, school is where children have the most contact with the adults who will notice social, emotional, or behavioral difficulties and provide assistance. This role of schools as places where children in need can be first identified and as places where they are most likely to receive the services they need is especially important for immigrant youth, who often have less access to health care through other resources.

Knowledge of the unique strengths and needs of bilingual, bicultural, and immigrant youth is important in order for practitioners to provide appropriate and responsive services. A large number of children need mental health services and are likely to benefit from a comprehensive assessment of their strengths and needs in order to provide the appropriate supports and services. Research in the United States has suggested that between 12% and 22% of all youth under the age of 18 have a diagnosable mental health disorder (Costello et al., 1996; Kessler et al., 2005; Lavigne et al., 1996; Shaffer et al., 1996; U.S. Department of Health and Human Services, 1999). When those who experience significant psychosocial distress but do not meet the criterion for a formal diagnosis are included, the number of youth who need mental health services is likely far larger (Adelman & Taylor, 2006).

Mental health needs are not evenly distributed across communities. Although there is not strong support for a link between culture and mental health problems, there is strong evidence that poverty influences the prevalence of social, emotional, and behavioral problems (Costello, Keeler, & Angold, 2001; Mclaughlin, Costello, Leblanc, Sampson, & Kessler, 2012). A recent Gallup poll found that the rates of depression among those living in poverty were about twice those of people not living in poverty (Brown, 2012). Those living in poverty also had less access to health care, higher levels of chronic disease, and poorer health habits. The high rates of poverty among bilingual, bicultural, and immigrant families suggest that this group of children is likely to be at a higher risk of mental health problems than children from nonimmigrant families, who are less likely to be poor (Hernandez, Denton, & Macartney, 2009).

ASSESSING THE WHOLE CHILD

Assessment can be defined as the process of gathering information to inform decisions (Salvia, Ysseldyke, & Bolt, 2009). To make informed decisions about immigrant, bicultural, and bilingual children's social and emotional functioning, practitioners must take into account personal resources and an overall sense of well-being in addition to problems and symptoms. Suldo and Shaffer (2008) and others (e.g., Samia, 2011) have argued that psychopathology and wellness make important independent contributions to mental health. This argument is in keeping with evidence that has suggested that symptom severity alone does not account for impairment in people with mental health problems (Winters, Collett, & Myers, 2005) and that strengths and sources of resilience account for outcomes better than deficits or risk factors alone (Garmezy, 1993; Werner & Smith, 1992).

Including strengths and resources as part of the focus of a comprehensive social–emotional assessment has several advantages. Conversations about strengths encourage greater client motivation and participation in the assessment process and subsequent treatment (Epstein et al., 2003). They also encourage practitioners to focus on the enhancement of skills and learning and not just on diminishing symptoms (Donovan & Nickerson, 2007; Epstein et al., 2003). Given this, our approach to the social–emotional assessment of bilingual children focuses on gathering data on sources of resilience and support as well as on symptoms or problems.

This approach is perhaps especially important in working with bilingual, bicultural, and immigrant youth. Among this group, immigrant youth are subject to more developmental risks than nonimmigrant children are (e.g., poverty, poor academic performance related to not having sufficient English language skills, social isolation). Yet, researchers have found that most children in immigrant families have positive outcomes and fewer social and behavioral problems than their nonimmigrant peers. This "immigrant paradox" reminds practitioners that focusing only on risks and symptoms provides an incomplete picture of the lives of these children (Georgiades, Boyle, & Duku, 2007).

We also advocate for an ecological approach to assessment (Gutkin, 2012; Ysseldyke, Lekwa, Klingbeil, & Cormier, 2012). Building on the work of Bronfenbrenner (1979), an *ecological approach* emphasizes the transactional nature of children's environments and focuses our attention on the quality of their relationships or their social relationships rather than solely on individual symptoms or problems. Gutkin (2009) argued that focusing assessment solely on the individual characteristics of an individual child does not provide sufficient useful information to develop effective interventions. This is perhaps even truer for bilingual, bicultural, and immigrant youth who are affected by and cope with multiple complex cultural contexts and social transactions, making the traditional emphasis of assessments on personal characteristics even less useful.

Truly comprehensive assessments must not only include an assessment of strengths and social ecology but must also be comprehensive in the sources and kinds of information used. One approach to understanding what constitutes a comprehensive assessment is the notion of *R.I.O.T.*, or (a) record review/history; (b) interviews; (c) observations; and (d) tests or, more appropriate in the assessment of social and emotional strengths and needs, standardized behavior rating scales (Leung, 1993).

Levitt and Merrell (2009) suggested another rubric for judging the comprehensiveness of social–emotional assessment: the *rule of two*. Like R.I.O.T., the rule of two focuses on the principle that a comprehensive assessment must have multiple elements, but, as Levitt and Merrell (2009) put it, "acknowledges the reality that resources and time are often limited" (p. 19). The rule of two suggests that a comprehensive social–emotional assessment should include information from a minimum of two settings, two informants, and two assessment methods.

In the following sections, we use the rule of two and the framework of R.I.O.T. in our discussion of the assessment of membership and the characteristics of individual children and youth. Exhibit 7.1 illustrates how this would look in a matrix of assessment activities. For bilingual, bicultural, and immigrant youth, each of these approaches to data gathering has strengths and limitations. Some of the important unique influences on the assessment process with bilingual, bicultural, and immigrant youth include the use of interpreters, cultural influences on question asking and answering, and the lack of adequate norms for this group among standardized norm-based instruments.

EXHIBIT 7.1
Matrix for a Comprehensive Social and Emotional Assessment

Informant	Record review/history	Interview	Observation	Test/rating scale
Student				
Teacher				
Parent				
Assessor				
Other				

UNIQUE ISSUES IN THE ASSESSMENT OF BILINGUAL, BICULTURAL, AND IMMIGRANT YOUTH

Use of Interpreters

When interacting with bilingual youth or parents, practitioners sometimes need a translation of written materials but will more often use the services of an interpreter to translate the spoken language used in interviews. Meaningful use of interpreters requires important skills on the parts of the person speaking and the person interpreting. For example, it is important for practitioners being translated to use a minimal number of technical terms, which are often difficult to translate. It is also important that the persons speaking adopt a pace that is often slower than their typical speed or focus on communicating only one thought or idea in each segment to be translated. Finally, the practitioner should learn to speak directly to the person being interviewed and avoid speaking to the interpreter or saying, for example, "Tell him that . . . ." In a similar vein, in meetings or group interviews it is important to avoid cross-talk among the group while the interpreter is speaking to the child or the parent.

It is also important that interpreters be thoroughly trained and prepared for their role (Rhodes, Ochoa, & Ortiz, 2005). Prior to interviews or meetings with children or families, an interpreter should be reminded that clinical interviews require a substantial degree of privacy and confidentiality. Practitioners using interpreters should also stress the need for precise translation when possible and for checking with the assessor regarding any summarizing or needed alterations to phrasing. In addition, it is useful for interpreters to be given time to review all questionnaires, interview guides, or other protocols used in the assessment process (Rhodes et al., 2005); this will help create the conditions for greater integrity in the translation. During a meeting, the practitioner should pay close attention to seating arrangements to allow for effective communication between the clinician, family, child, and the interpreter (Stansfield, 1980).

Cultural Influences on Asking and Answering Questions

In addition to the issue of language and the use of interpreters, there are other cultural influences on the process of gathering information, especially on the process of conducting interviews with children and their parents. Regardless of language or culture, practitioners conducting interviews regarding mental health must recognize that many of the questions they ask a child or family members are sensitive in nature. Establishing a relationship is critical before questions about more delicate subjects (e.g., substance abuse, sexual behaviors or identity, suicidal ideation) can be introduced into the conversation.

Establishing a collaborative relationship with a client who comes from a different cultural background and speaks a different language requires the practitioner to make an effort to understand the cultural experiences, beliefs, and norms of the people they work with. Yet, practitioners also need to adopt an attitude of respectful curiosity or "not knowing" (Goolishian & Anderson, 1992). The *stance of not knowing* is described as follows: "The not knowing position entrails a general attitude or stance in which the therapist's actions communicate an abundant, genuine curiosity" (Goolishian & Anderson, 1992, p. 29). A stance of not knowing is an important counterweight to the assumption that general knowledge of cultural beliefs and practices will itself suffice for effective communication. Although this cultural knowledge can be important in working with bilingual and bicultural youth, it can provide only a limited and sometimes oversimplified view of a client's world. The stance of not knowing allows the practitioner to see the uniqueness of "this" client at a certain moment alongside cultural identification and group affiliation.

Practitioners assessing bilingual children for issues regarding mental health must consider the broader communication style of the person interviewed. Many cultural groups use conversational styles that are notably different from mainstream American styles, and clinicians should attempt to match verbal and/or nonverbal communication styles to the greatest extent possible (Ortiz & Flanagan, 2008; Rhodes et al., 2005). To accomplish this, practitioners must combine the stance of not knowing with general knowledge about differences in communication styles and ways of communicating information. This "learning about" a culture can be facilitated by reading one of the many texts focused on multicultural or cross-cultural counseling (e.g., Atkinson, 2004; McGoldrick, Giordano, & Garcia-Preto, 2005; Pedersen, Draguns, Lonner, & Trimble, 2008) as well as by reading non-academic literature such as memoirs or stories of immigration experiences. It is, of course, useful for practitioners to place themselves in situations where they are exposed to the target culture (e.g., visiting neighborhoods, shopping at stores, or eating at restaurants).

Cultural differences regarding beliefs about mental health and mental illness may also influence the assessment process. Parents who see mental health problems as socially stigmatizing are often more reluctant to discuss these problems with people outside the family. Therefore, it is crucial that the psychologist normalizes the experience of the family and is especially careful to convey compassion and understanding before approaching topics regarding problematic mental health behaviors or symptoms. Opening an interview with questions about strengths and resources may help families to develop the trust necessary to share potentially shameful or embarrassing details with the psychologist. For immigrant families, interviews may also be inhibited by expectations regarding treatment options and the outcomes of an assessment, especially if the family has relocated from an area where children with significant mental or physical disabilities are segregated or institutionalized. If the assessor suspects that a family is not being forthcoming for this reason, it can be helpful to explain in advance the outcomes of an assessment and the range of services that may be available to their family should there be a need. The following case study illustrates the importance of exploring a family's perceptions of treatment options and outcomes.

Case Study: Family Beliefs and Collaboration

Maria is a 14-year-old student who is in the ninth grade.[1] She immigrated to the United States from Mexico with her mother, father, grandmother, and two siblings 9 years ago. In the spring of her eighth-grade year, Maria ran away from home and lived on the street and with friends. According to police reports, Maria was arrested while under the influence of several illegal substances, including methamphetamines, cocaine, and inhalants. As she settled into her classes anew, her teachers were immediately concerned about her behavior. Maria was largely unresponsive and appeared to be "spacing out," spending large periods of time staring at the ceiling or corner of the room. She did not interact with her peers in any way and needed prompts to leave class after the bell rang. She was not completing any in-class work and was unable to answer questions. The psychologist who interviewed Maria found her behavior extremely concerning. She was able at times to answer specific questions about her past, but she would often stop speaking midway through a sentence, unable to continue her line of thought without help. She was not able to describe what was currently being taught in her classes.

Maria's father met with her school team and was interviewed with the assistance of a translator. He described her as high-functioning, noting that she wakes up on her own and does her homework in the afternoon. When her in-school behavior was described to her father, he explained that she needs time to adjust to this new school without her friends. Maria's father completed a rating scale in Spanish, ranking internalizing and externalizing behaviors within the average range.

The next day, Maria's sister Angie came to the school. She explained to the psychologist that she was worried about her sister and was afraid her father had not been honest about how she is functioning at home. According to Angie, Maria needed constant supervision to remember to eat, to dress herself, and where she needs to go. At one point during the week before, Maria tried to get out of a moving car while the family was

---

[1] The details of the case studies have been changed to protect the anonymity of the individuals involved.

driving on the freeway. Angie was worried and explained that her parents were concerned that if the police or school officials understood how she is really doing, they would take her away to a locked facility.

In this case, issues regarding communication and trust between the family and the psychologist played a major role. The family's beliefs regarding what might happen to Maria as a result of the assessment led to an inaccurate portrayal of her functioning in the home. This scenario highlights the importance of trust, rapport, and the psychologist's need to inform a family of the treatment milieu for Maria, because her father's desire to protect his daughter from institutionalization left him not comfortable sharing his concerns about his daughter's well-being with the psychologist. This scenario also demonstrates the importance of gathering multiple types of assessment data from multiple sources. In this case, the psychologist was based in a school and had collected observation and interview data personally and from Maria's teachers. Without those perspectives, a psychologist placing a large emphasis on the data collected from Maria's father might have mistakenly greatly overestimated her current level of functioning.

Selection of Valid and Appropriate Assessment Methods

All clinicians are ethically responsible for the selection of reliable and valid assessment instruments. Unfortunately, the majority of standardized instruments available to measure social, emotional, and behavioral concerns in children (i.e., rating scales, structured interviews) are not available in translated formats (as would be appropriate in direct use with bilingual families) and/or were not designed with the unique strengths and needs of this population in mind. In fact, in comparison with assessments for areas such as cognitive ability or academic achievement, many social or emotional rating scales, especially narrow-band scales (e.g., rating scales specifically for depression, anxiety, or specific diagnoses such as Asperger's syndrome), do not have large standardization samples that include students from a variety of cultural or linguistic backgrounds. Thus, clinicians should always carefully review the manuals of any instruments used in a social–emotional assessment of a bilingual student to seek confirmation that the client's background is represented in the norming or standardization sample.

According to the *Standards for Educational and Psychological Testing*, developed and published by the American Educational Research Association (AERA), the American Psychological Association (APA), and the National Council on Measurement in Education (NCME; 1999), assessment authors should note when items have been screened for appropriateness across multiple cultures, list any minority groups that the instrument has been translated for or used with (including, if applicable, data that demonstrate how scores for a particular group compare with the broad norming sample), and should provide guidelines and cautions for the use of a measure with groups who are not represented in the norming sample. In addition, the *Standards* also describe the process that practitioners should use in evaluating the acceptability of a given instrument, which includes an evaluation of psychometric properties, including those listed earlier regarding minority cultural or linguistic groups, professional judgment, and an evaluation of the alternate assessment options available (AERA, APA, NCME, 1999). Professionals assessing the social and emotional strengths and needs of bilingual students often find themselves relying on professional judgment regarding instrument selection and score interpretation simply because there is such a dearth of reliable and valid instruments to use for these purposes with these youth. In general, in the absence of clear information that a particular rating scale is appropriate to use with a particular bilingual student, clinicians should be cautious when interpreting scores and should seek cross-validation from multiple sources of information.

METHODS OF DATA COLLECTION: OVERVIEW AND UNIQUE CONSIDERATIONS

It is not within the scope of this chapter to comprehensively review all the methods of data collection involved in the assessment of mental health in children and adolescents. Therefore, we briefly introduce the types of data involved in the assessment process, with an emphasis on unique considerations for working with bilingual youth.

Record Reviews

Working from a R.I.O.T. framework (Leung, 1993), assessment begins with an examination of extant records about a child. When conducting social, emotional, or behavioral assessments, assessors must think critically about what types of records may provide useful data. Depending on the referral questions, medical records may provide a useful history, especially if there is a possibility that changes in mood or behavior may be related to medication use or physical conditions. School-based records such as academic documents (e.g., report cards) and discipline records may help establish a timeline for changes in behaviors or functioning. In addition to records that all children would have, bilingual youth may have school-based records that include screening data for language use. For example, bilingual students in California are given the California English Language Development Test annually until they are classified as fully proficient in English (California Department of Education, n.d.).

Interviews

Interviews are a key feature of social, emotional, and behavioral assessments. They can be useful in gathering information from children, parents, teachers, or other significant adults. They can also be unstructured, semistructured, or structured (Merrell, 2008). *Unstructured interviews* are often neither focused nor reliable enough for assessment purposes and their lack of structure can make them unreliable. *Structured interview protocols*, such as the Diagnostic Interview for Children and Adolescents (Reich, Welner, & Herjanic, 1997) or the Schedule for Affective Disorders and Schizophrenia for School-Age Children (Kaufman, Birmaher, Brent, Rao, & Ryan, 1996), are highly scripted and designed more for making specific diagnostic decisions rather than gathering broader information about social support and engagement. *Semistructured interviews* have the advantage of being flexible, allowing practitioners to select questions that address the unique needs of a particular child. Exhibit 7.2 is a sample interview guide.

When conducting interviews with bilingual children or their families, assessors should keep issues regarding interpretation, translation, and cultural differences in communication in mind (as discussed earlier in this chapter). Many structured interviews ask highly personal and/or sensitive questions, and responses should be interpreted in light of the rapport that has been established, comfort with the assessor and translator, and familial beliefs about mental health treatment.

Observations

Direct observations of children in home, school, or clinic settings may provide useful assessment data. Observations can be formal or informal, structured or unstructured, and can vary widely according to the type of information sought. Observational data can be extremely helpful from an ecological perspective because the observer has the chance to view antecedents and consequences to behavior, which may prove useful for intervention planning (Merrell, 2008). The utility of observational data may vary with the nature of the behavior in question, particularly when behaviors are vague, complex, or occur rarely (Mash & Hunsley, 2007). To the greatest extent possible, observations should occur in a child's natural setting (for purposes of validity); however, potential reactivity to observation must always be considered. Consider an observation of familial interactions: The presence of an assessor will always have some impact on behavior, and this impact may be heightened when cultural and/or linguistic differences exist between the assessor and the family.

EXHIBIT 7.2
Child and Adolescent Interview Protocol

Child's name: _____

Interviewer's name: _____

Date of interview: _____

Home/family
1. Whom do you live with? (If there is a noncustodial parent, find out what the visitation schedule is.)
2. Family living outside the home

Health
3. Recent doctor visits?
4. Significant illnesses or injuries?
5. Medication? Now or in past?
6. Vision and hearing?

Education/school
7. Current school? Grade or level?
8. School history, including preschool
9. Favorite classes or subjects?
10. Most difficult classes or subjects?
11. Do you get any extra help with these subjects? Who helps you? How do they help you?
12. Recent grades?
13. Experiences with homework? (How does the student experience homework? Is it difficult, easy, or so forth? About how much homework does the student complete in a day or week? Try to get a percentage.)

Activities and self: Positive qualities, interests, and skills and engagement in productive activities
14. What are some things you like to do or think that you are good at?
15. How do you like to spend your free time? What ways do you have of relaxing and having fun? Hobbies? Sports? Music? Movies?
16. How do you relax and have fun with your family? (Include common interests and activities.)

Coping
17. How do you calm yourself down when upset or angry?
18. How do you handle difficult or stressful situations? Give an example of the last difficult situation you faced and how you handled it.

Social support and role models
19. What are your friends like (ages, gender)? What are some things you like to do together?
20. Who are you closest to in your family?
21. When you get into trouble at home, how do your parents handle it?
22. Who in your life helps you reach your goals or explore your interests?
23. Name some people that you respect or that you see doing things you like or appreciate. What kinds of things do they do?

(*continues*)

EXHIBIT 7.2
Child and Adolescent Interview Protocol   *(Continued)*

Required helpfulness
24. Who counts on you? (Follow up with, "What do you do for them?")
25. Tell me about a time you did something nice for someone else or you helped someone out or you gave him or her something they needed. What types of things do you enjoy doing for others?
26. How do you help out around the house?

Participation in community
27. Do you belong to any clubs, teams, community organizations, or churches (synagogues, temples, etc.)?

Goals and aspirations
28. If things went well for you over the next month, what would be different?
29. How do you see yourself in a year?
30. How about when you are an adult?

Transitions
31. Did you recently change schools or are you planning to change schools?
32. Have you changed houses or are you planning to move soon?
33. Have there been any big changes in your family recently?

"Waking day" interview
34. Think of a regular day for you. Tell me what you do first thing when you get up. What do you do next? And then what? (Have child describe what they do from waking up to going to bed at night.)

Screening for problems
35. Have you been feeling sad or angry lately? (D)
36. Have you lost interest in or stopped enjoying the things that you usually like to do? (D)
37. Have you ever thought your life was not worth living or thought about hurting yourself in some way? (D)
38. How is your appetite? What kinds of things do you like to eat? Have you gained or lost weight lately? (D)
39. How do you sleep? About how much do you sleep each night? (D)
40. Do you often have trouble paying attention to details or keeping your mind on what you are doing? (ADHD)
41. Are you told to sit still a lot? (ADHD)
42. Do you usually get upset and lose your temper if things don't go your way? (ODD)
43. Do you talk back or argue with your parents a lot? Your teachers?
44. Do you worry more than other kids your age? If yes: Do you worry as often as every day or every other day? What do you worry about? (A)

Summary sheet/global impressions
45. Significant strengths.
46. Significant needs or risks.
47. Actions needed to enhance strengths and reduce risk.

Note. A = anxiety; ADHD = attention-deficit/hyperactivity disorder; D = depression; ODD = oppositional defiant disorder.

In general, little research has been conducted regarding the validity of behavioral observation as a form of assessment for culturally and/or linguistically diverse youth (Merrell, 2008). Accordingly, clinicians should use observation data cautiously and always as a portion of a more comprehensive assessment.

Norm-Based Rating Scales

Rating scales are an important and widely used component of social and emotional assessments. They provide summary observations of children on the basis of observations of an individual across time and in different settings. Rating scales can be used for diagnosis and classification or as part of the problem-solving process. Normative data, such as those provided by standard scores, provide useful information about the severity of a problem. Rating scales also can play an important role in developing interventions because they point practitioners to problems or areas of strength that need further investigation and clarification. Many rating scales, including those identified in this section, are available in various versions for different informants. In this way, rating scales are an excellent way to ensure that data are being collected across multiple informants and settings. When possible, practitioners who are not school-based should work with families and schools to collect rating scales from teachers.

Behavior rating scales are often described as falling into two categories—discrete or behavior specific and broad-based or omnibus. A discrete instrument provides information on a particular domain of behavior or a narrow range of behaviors, which are often associated with a specific diagnosis. Such an instrument would include scales specifically designed to assess the signs and symptoms of disorders such as attention-deficit/hyperactivity disorders, anxiety disorders, and autism (Busse, 2005).

Although narrow scales have important uses, we advocate for the use of broad scales such as the Behavioral Assessment System for Children—Second Edition (BASC–2; Reynolds & Kamphaus, 2004) or the Child Behavior Checklist (CBCL; Achenbach, 2001a) because of their ability to yield information beyond narrow diagnostic categories. This additional information can help identify problem areas that coexist with a primary diagnosis (e.g., a depressed child who also aggressively acts out) or help identify areas of strength or intact functioning.

The Youth Self-Report (YSR; Achenbach, 2001c), CBCL for ages 6 to 18 (Achenbach, 2001a), and the Teacher Report Form for ages 6 to 19 (TRF; Achenbach, 2001b) are all parts of the well-researched and widely used Achenbach System of Empirically Based Assessment (ASEBA). These instruments, especially the CBCL and TRF, are among the most well-researched assessment instruments available. Versions of these scales have been translated into more than 70 languages, resulting in an extensive database of cross-cultural literature (Achenbach & Rescorla, 2006). In addition, there have been studies comparing American children with children from Holland (Achenbach, Verhulst, Baron, & Akkerhuis, 1987), Australia (Achenbach, Hensley, Phares, & Grayson, 1990), China (Weine, Phillips, & Achenbach, 1995), and several other countries.

Since its publication in 1992, the BASC has become one of the most widely used tools for assessing behavior and emotions in children, adolescents, and young adults, ranging in age from 2 to 25 years old. The BASC–2 is the recently updated version, providing a set of tools that use a multidimensional approach to gathering information in different domains (behavioral, personality, and developmental), in different ways (rating scales, history-taking, and direct observation), and from different sources (parents, teachers, clinicians, and the children themselves; Reynolds & Kamphaus, 2004). The BASC–2 includes several forms that are available in Spanish. However, the Spanish normative sample is limited in that the majority comes from the West, with only a small sample from other regions of the country (Reynolds & Kamphaus, 2004).

As discussed earlier in this chapter, assessors are ultimately responsible for decisions regarding the validity of rating scales for use with bilingual and bicultural children. In addition to global decisions about the appropriateness of scales as a whole, clinicians may also need to examine individual items and make professional judgments regarding particular responses. For example, broad rating scales such as the BASC–2 and YSR often include items designed to screen for symptoms of broad psychopathology, such as questions about hearing voices or speaking with people who are not real. Youth from diverse cultures may interpret these items differently than would those from mainstream U.S. culture because cultural norms may involve beliefs about ancestors, spirits, and so forth, that may lead a student to respond affirmatively to an item that would mistakenly suggest that a student is experiencing hallucinations. When uncertain about a response to any individual item on a rating scale, practitioners should always follow up with further questions to clarify the intent of the rater. The following case study illustrates the importance of exploring a client's responses to the questions on a rating scale and understanding the cultural factors that may influence how he or she responds.

Case Study: Cultural Context

Keanu is a 10-year-old boy of native Hawaiian and Filipino decent. He lives with his mother and grandmother in a rural area of Hawaii. In the home, the family speaks primarily in Tagalog, the first language of his grandmother, as well as some English. Keanu was brought to the psychologist by his grandmother because he had been having nightmares and trouble sleeping. His teacher was concerned because his grades have declined and he is not as alert or attentive in class as he was at the beginning of the school year.

When Keanu's mother, Ms. Lee, was interviewed, she explained that she recently ended a 4-year relationship with her boyfriend. She shared that her boyfriend was abusive to her and that she believed that Keanu was having a hard time because he was worried about her. Keanu's mother completed several emotional and behavioral rating scales about Keanu's recent behavior. The scores indicated that he was at risk of anxiety and depression.

Keanu and his teacher were also asked to complete behavioral rating scales. The scale completed by his teacher showed a pattern similar to Mrs. Lee's, with elevated scores in the anxiety and depression subscales. When Keanu's responses were analyzed, his scores were in the at-risk range for anxiety and also for abnormal and bizarre behavior. In addition, the score report warned that because of his response pattern, Keanu's scores may not be valid.

On further examination of Keanu's self-ratings, the psychologist noticed that he had marked "yes" for several items that are noteworthy, including questions about speaking to people who are not really there and hearing voices when he is alone. The psychologist followed up in an interview with Keanu about these responses. Keanu explained that he often hears the voice of his grandfather and other ancestors when he is alone at night. According to Keanu, when he is upset, he asks them for help, and they tell him that he is safe and should go back to sleep.

In this case, although the family is bilingual, issues regarding translation, cross-cultural communication, and the establishment of rapport were not of concern. However, had the psychologist failed to take culture into consideration, she might have mistaken Keanu's responses on the rating scales as representative of extremely concerning behaviors.

ASSESSING SOCIAL AND EMOTIONAL STRENGTHS AND NEEDS

An assessment of the social and emotional functioning of bilingual, bicultural, and immigrant youth should explore strengths as well as problems, be ecological in its focus, and be comprehensive. Our sense of comprehensiveness is captured by the acronym R.I.O.T. (Leung, 1993) and Levitt and Merrell's (2009) rule of two. We further conceptualize social and emotional assessment for bilingual youth as having two broad aspects: (a) assessment of membership and (b) assessment of personal characteristics, including strengths and emotional challenges.

Membership

Bicultural and immigrant youth are often caught between cultures and because of this can lack full membership in both their home cultures and the English-speaking world of their schools and the social institutions that surround them. Walzer (1983) described this lack of membership as being in a "condition of infinite danger" (p. 32). Although poverty, stress, social isolation, and the challenge of mastering English all present significant challenges to membership for bilingual, bicultural, and immigrant youth, it is important to acknowledge that these youth have significant strengths. Indeed, it is possible that the process of adapting to multiple languages and cultural contexts is itself a strength, suggesting a cognitive and social flexibility that allows for multiple identities rather than a fixed identity (Trueba, 2002). For these youth, membership in multiple cultures, each with its own forms of communication and habits of relating, is a resource that allows them to adapt flexibly to multiple social contexts.

Understanding the notion of membership is important to understanding the unique strengths of bilingual, bicultural, and immigrant youth and is a valuable aspect of a comprehensive assessment. We recommend that practitioners consider three interconnected aspects of membership when conducting mental health assessments: acculturation, language proficiency, and social resources.

Broadly, *acculturation* refers to the process of adapting one's behaviors, beliefs, attitudes, and values to fit those of a new culture. Examples include the shift toward preferring American foods, adoption of Western medical remedies, the preference of English to the home language, and a shift toward a more individualistic (rather than collectivistic) sense of self. Current models of acculturation view this process as comprising two distinct linear models, with one representing adherence to the new culture (acculturation) and another representing *enculturation*, or adherence to one's culture of origin (e.g., Atkinson, 2004; Kim, 2007). From this perspective, an individual can be bicultural (high adherence to both original and new culture), monocultural (high adherence to either new or old culture), or neither (low adherence to both old and new cultures).

Acculturation and enculturation are not inherently either risk or protective factors but may function as such when considered in relation to the whole picture of a child. For example, a child who becomes highly acculturated may have more access to support at school or to community-based services and may have a stronger sense of connection to his or her peers. In this case, acculturation could be viewed as a protective factor for that child. However, a child who is not acculturated may experience what is referred to as *acculturative stress* (conceptually similar to culture shock), which may serve as a risk factor if the child feels isolated, alienated, or frightened by his or her experiences in a new school. This acculturation stress has been linked to behavior problems in adolescents (Beiser et al., 2010). Yet, disconnection from one's home culture can also be a significant stressor.

For example, acculturation may influence the support children receive from their families. The processes of acculturation and enculturation may occur at different rates for different members of a family (Miller, Yang, Hui, Choi, & Lim, 2011). Immigrant children are thought to acculturate at faster rates than their families because of the immersion that occurs at school as well as because of developmental considerations (e.g., children learn new languages more quickly than adults and children may have been less exposed to the values and beliefs of a home culture if they were young prior to moving). This mismatch of acculturation (or *acculturation gap*) between a child and his or her family can lead to stress in relationships between family members as they struggle with the cultural push and pull within the family system (Villalba, 2007). These acculturation gaps are associated with family conflict, depression, externalizing behavior problems, and lower academic achievement (Telzer, 2010). However, acculturation can be an asset for bilingual, bicultural, and immigrant youth; the ability to move back and forth between cultures and to adapt to the dominant culture without losing one's primary culture is a significant strength and has been linked to greater success and more successful developmental outcomes (Eccles & Gootman, 2002; Luthar & McMahon, 1996). This has been described as *border crossing* (Delgado-Gaitan & Trueba, 1991).

Acculturation and enculturation are tied closely to language use, and we recommend that practitioners address these issues simultaneously. In addition to being a marker for acculturation, language skills are relevant to the assessment process in a number of ways. First, for assessments conducted in English, language proficiency is extremely important in understanding the questions asked in clinical interviews or understanding the questions on a standardized rating scale such as the BASC–2 Self-Report of Personality (BASC–2 SRP; Reynolds & Kamphaus, 2004). Many of the terms and concepts regarding emotional and behavioral health are complex and not easily understood, even by individuals with a conversational level of English language proficiency. For bilingual children and their families, it is especially important that practitioners ascertain the child's pattern of language use and development before proceeding with an assessment.

Given the importance of language and acculturation in how bilingual, bicultural, and immigrant children adapt, it is important to consider this in the assessment of these youth. Several instruments have been developed to measure acculturation levels, both broadly and for specific cultures. Examples include the Multigroup Ethnic Identity Measure (Phinney & Ong, 2007), a six-item broad measure, and the Acculturation Rating Scale for Mexican Americans (Cuellar, Arnold, & Maldanado, 1995), a 30-item measure with subscales for Mexican orientation and Anglo orientation. One of the more interesting tools used to assess language is the Bilingual Verbal Ability Tests (BVAT; Muñoz-Sandoval, Cummins, Alvarado, & Ruef, 2005). The BVAT yields English Language Proficiency and Bilingual Verbal Ability scores. Bilingual verbal ability represents the combined cognitive–academic language abilities (English and the person's native language) possessed by bilingual persons. In addition to standardized measures of acculturation and language, similar information can also be gathered using semistructured interviews. Examples of questions that address language development and preference can be found in Exhibit 7.3.

The second aspect of membership, social support and engagement, involves assessment of protective factors, including the presence of caring relationships, involvement in positive activities in the community, and access to opportunities for participation and contribution. These protective factors form the basis for positive developmental outcomes and the ability to

EXHIBIT 7.3
Questions About Language and Culture

1. What language did the client learn first?
2. What language does the client use when he or she speaks to
   • parents?
   • siblings?
   • others in household?
   • adults in the neighborhood?
   • peers in the neighborhood?
   • adults at school?
3. What language does the client prefer when
   • listening to music?
   • watching TV?
   • reading at home?
4. Client's educational experiences:
   • Years of education in home language
   • Years of bilingual education
   • Years of English only education
5. Information about parents:
   • Time in United States
   • Parents' occupations
   • Parents' level of education
6. What language does the client believe he or she speaks best?

bounce back from adversity (Benard, 2004). This information can be gathered by semistructured interviews, norm-based standardized rating scales, and visual models such as Ecomaps (Compton & Galaway, 1989; Nastasi, 1999; Rickert & Rettig, 2006).

Ecomaps are visual representations of relationships with significant others (Nastasi, Moore, & Varjas, 2004). Children are instructed to identify persons who are important to them and draw each of these persons in relation to themselves. Each relationship is then identified as supportive, stressful, or ambivalent using different drawn lines (Nastasi et al., 2004). Ecomaps have the advantage of providing useful information about how children perceive their significant relationships from an emic or insider's perspective. Ecomaps have also been used extensively in research in other cultures (Nastasi et al., 2007; Nastasi, Jayasena, Summerville, & Borja, 2011).

In interviewing children or parents about social support and engagement, practitioners must find a balance between the generalizations we develop from studies of groups and the stance of respectful curiosity or not knowing, which allows us to treat the person in front of us as a universe of one. Questions can focus on activities that the person engages in; membership in clubs, churches, or other community groups; friendships; and incidents of *required helpfulness*, when the person has an opportunity to take care of someone or give back to the family or community. Examples of these and other questions related to social support and engagement can be found in Exhibit 7.3.

Rating scales such as the BASC–2 SRP, Parent Rating Scale, and Teacher Rating Scale (Reynolds & Kamphaus, 2004) and the CBCL for ages 6 to 18, YSR, and the TRF for ages 6 to 19 (Achenbach, 2001a, 2001b, 2001c) provide valuable information about a child's social functioning. For example, the BASC scales contain subscales that address areas such as social skills, leadership, relations with parents, interpersonal relations, and social stress (Reynolds & Kamphaus, 2004). In addition, the instruments that are part of the ASEBA are strongly associated with accurately identifying psychopathology (Merrell, 2008). They also have competence items grouped into three scales: Activities, Social, and School (Achenbach, 2001a, 2001b, 2001c).

Assessment of Personal Characteristics

In addition to assessing membership (acculturation, enculturation, language use and development, and social support), it is also important to evaluate the personal characteristics of the child. As we noted earlier, we believe that this aspect of the assessment process must address strengths and resources as well as problems. Like the construct of membership, personal characteristics can be assessed through semistructured interviews and norm-based standardized rating scales. As discussed earlier in the chapter, we generally recommend broad spectrum rating scales such as the BASC and ASEBA families of instruments because they allow practitioners to gather information beyond a specific diagnostic category, including information about strengths, resources, and competences. Both the BASC–2 and the ASEBA scales provide extensive information about internalizing and externalizing problems. The BASC–2 also provides extensive information about personal competencies or adaptive behaviors and includes scales that measure constructs such as self-esteem, adaptability, study skills, and locus of control.

Semistructured interviews of children or parents about personal characteristics should not only focus on common problems such as depression, anxiety, poor attention or concentration, and oppositional behavior but should also include information about four categories of personal strengths that have been found to have importance across ethnicity and culture (Eccles & Gootman, 2002; Ungar, 2008; Werner & Smith, 1992): (a) social competence, (b) problem solving, (c) autonomy, and (d) sense of purpose (Benard, 2004). Interviews that focus on these domains often include questions about how children solve problems and cope and questions about goals and aspirations. Examples of these and other questions related to personal characteristics can be found in Exhibit 7.3.

CONCLUSION

The assessment of the social, emotional, and behavioral strengths and needs of bilingual youth is a complex task. Clinicians must broaden their traditional approaches to assessment, accept the limitations of formal instruments, and take an ecological approach that takes the child's unique situations into account. Particular care should be taken when using interpreters or translation because the content covered in a social–emotional assessment can be extremely sensitive for youth and families. Above all else, we urge clinicians to focus on the social and emotional strengths that exist within all youth. When assessments are conducted with this in mind, the results can be applied to identify strategies, steps, resources, and other aspects of solutions, rather than simply stating problems.

REFERENCES

Achenbach, T. M. (2001a). *Child Behavior Checklist for ages 6–18*. Burlington, VT: Department of Psychiatry, University of Vermont.

Achenbach, T. M. (2001b). *Teachers' Report Form for ages 6–18*. Burlington, VT: Department of Psychiatry, University of Vermont.

Achenbach, T. M. (2001c). *Youth Self-Report for ages 6–18*. Burlington, VT: Department of Psychiatry, University of Vermont.

Achenbach, T. M., Becker, A., Döpfner, M., Heiervang, E., Roessner, V., Steinhausen, H. C., & Rothenberger, A. (2008). Multicultural assessment of child and adolescent psychopathology with ASEBA and SDQ instruments: Research findings, applications, and future directions. *Journal of Child Psychology and Psychiatry, 49*, 251–275. doi:10.1111/j.1469-7610.2007.01867.x

Achenbach, T. M., Hensley, V. R., Phares, T. V., & Grayson, D. D. (1990). Problems and competencies reported by parents of Australian and American children. *Child Psychology & Psychiatry & Allied Disciplines, 31*, 265–286. doi:10.1111/j.1469-7610.1990.tb01566.x

Achenbach, T. M., & Rescorla, L. A. (2006). *Multicultural understanding of child and adolescent psychopathology: Implications for mental health assessment*. New York, NY: Guilford Press.

Achenbach, T. M., Verhulst, F. C., Baron, G., & Akkerhuis, G. W. (1987). Epidemiological comparisons of American and Dutch Children: I. Behavioral/emotional problems and competencies reported by parents for ages 4 to 16. *Journal of the American Academy of Child & Adolescent Psychiatry, 26*, 317–325. doi:10.1097/00004583-198705000-00006

Adelman, H. S., & Taylor, L. (2006). Mental health in schools and public health. *Public Health Reports, 121*, 294–298.

American Educational Research Association, American Psychological Association, National Council on Measurement in Education. (1999). *Standards for educational and psychological testing*. Washington, DC: Author.

Atkinson, D. (2004). *Counseling American minorities* (6th ed.). New York, NY: McGraw-Hill.

Beiser, M., Hamilton, H., Rumens, J., Oxman-Martinez, J., Ogilvie, L., Humphrey, C., & Armstrong, R. (2010). Predictors of emotional problems and physical aggression among children of Hong Kong Chinese, Mainland Chinese, and Filipino immigrants to Canada. *Social Psychiatry and Psychiatric Epidemiology, 45*, 1011–1021. doi:10.1007/s00127-009-0140-3

Benard, B. (2004). *Resiliency: What we have learned*. Oakland, CA: WestEd.

Bronfenbrenner, U. (1979). *The ecology of human development*. Cambridge, MA: Harvard University Press.

Brown, A. (2012). *With poverty comes depression, more than other illnesses*. Retrieved from http://www.gallup.com/poll/158417/poverty-comes-depression-illness.aspx

Busse, R. T. (2005). Rating scale applications within the problem-solving model. In R. Brown (Ed.), *Assessment for intervention: A problem-solving approach* (pp. 200–218). New York, NY: Guilford Press.

California Department of Education. (n.d.). *California English Language Development Test—CalEdFacts*. Retrieved from http://www.cde.ca.gov/ta/tg/el/cefceldt.asp

Compton, B. R., & Galaway, B. (1989). *Social work processes* (4th ed.). Belmont, CA: Wadsworth.

Costello, E., Keeler, G. P., & Angold, A. (2001). Poverty, race/ethnicity, and psychiatric disorder. *American Journal of Public Health, 91,* 1494–1498. doi.org/10.2105/AJPH.91.9.1494

Costello, E. J., Angold, A., Burns, B. J., Stangl, D. K., Tweed, D. L., Erkanli, A., & Worthman, C. M. (1996). The Great Smoky Mountains Study of Youth: Goals, design, methods, and the prevalence of DSM–III–R disorders. *Archives of General Psychiatry, 53,* 1129–1136. doi.org/10.1001/archpsyc.1996.0183012 0067012

Cuellar, I., Arnold, B., & Maldanado, R. (1995). Acculturation rating scale for Mexican Americans–II: A revision of the original ARSMA. *Hispanic Journal of Behavioral Sciences, 17,* 275–304. doi:10.1177/07399863950173001

Delgado-Gaitan, C., & Trueba, H. T. (1991). *Crossing cultural borders: Education for immigrant families in America.* New York, NY: Falmer Press.

Donovan, S., & Nickerson, A. (2007). Strength-based versus traditional social–emotional reports: Impact on multidisciplinary team members' perceptions. *Behavioral Disorders, 32,* 228–237.

Eccles, J., & Gootman, J. (2002). *Community programs to promote youth development.* Washington, DC: National Academy Press.

Epstein, M. H., Harniss, M. K., Robbins, V., Wheeler, L., Cyrulik, S., Kriz, M., & Nelson, R. (2003). Strength-based approaches to assessment in schools. In M. D. Weist, S. W. Evans, & N. A. Lever (Eds.), *Handbook of school mental health: Advancing practice and research* (pp. 285–299). New York, NY: Kluwer Academic/Plenum.

Garmezy, N. (1993). Children in poverty: Resilience despite risk. *Psychiatry: Interpersonal and Biological Processes, 56,* 127–136.

Georgiades, K., Boyle, M. H., & Duku, E. (2007). Contextual influences on children's mental health and school performance: The moderating effects of family immigrant status. *Child Development, 78,* 1572–1591. doi.org/10.1111/j.1467-8624.2007.01084.x

Goolishian, H. A., & Anderson, H. (1992). Strategy and intervention versus nonintervention: A matter of theory? *Journal of Marital and Family Therapy, 18*(1), 5–15.

Gutkin, T. B. (2009). Ecological school psychology: A personal opinion and a plea for change. In T. B. Gutkin & C. R. Reynolds (Eds.), *The handbook of school psychology* (4th ed., pp. 463–496). New York, NY: Wiley.

Gutkin, T. B. (2012). Ecological psychology: Replacing the medical model paradigm for school-based psychological and psychoeducational services. *Journal of Educational & Psychological Consultation, 22*(1–2), 1–20. doi.org/10.1080/104 74412.2011.649652

Hernandez, D., Denton, N.A., & Macartney, S. (2009). *Children in immigrant families—The U.S. and 50 states: Economic need beyond the official poverty measure*. Retrieved from http://mumford.albany.edu/children/img/Research_brief_2.pdf

Kaufman, J., Birmaher, B., Brent, D., Rao, U., & Ryan, N. (1996). *The schedule for affective disorders and schizophrenia for school-age children.* Pittsburgh, PA: University of Pittsburgh Medical Center.

Kessler, R. C., Berglund, P., Demler, O., Jin, R., Merikangas, K. R., & Walters, E. E. (2005). Lifetime prevalence and age-of-onset distributions of DSM–IV disorders in the National Comorbidity Survey replication. *Archives of General Psychiatry, 62,* 593–602. doi.org/10.1001/archpsyc.62.6.593

Kim, B. (2007). Adherence to Asian and European American cultural values and attitudes toward seeking professional psychological help among Asian American college students. *Journal of Counseling Psychology, 54,* 474–480. doi.org/10.1037/0022-0167.54.4.474

Lavigne, J. V., Gibbons, R. D., Christoffel, K. K., Arend, R., Rosenbaum, D., Binns, H., & Dawson, N., . . . Issacs, C. (1996). Prevalence rates and correlates of psychiatric disorders among preschool children. *Journal of the American Academy of Child and Adolescent Psychiatry, 35,* 204–214. doi.org/10.1097/00004583-199602000-00014

Leung, B. (1993). Back to basics: Assessment is a R.I.O.T.! *NASP Communiqué, 22*(3), 1–6.

Levitt, V., & Merrell, K. (2009). Linking assessment to intervention for internalizing problems of children and adolescents. *School Psychology Forum, 3*(1), 13–26.

Luthar, S., & McMahon, T. (1996). Peer reputation among inner city adolescents: Structure and correlates. *Journal of Research on Adolescence, 6,* 581–603.

Mash, E., & Hunsley, J. (2007). Assessment of child and family disturbance. In E. Mash & R. Barkely (Eds.), *Assessment of childhood disorders* (4th ed., pp. 3–50). New York, NY: Guilford Press.

McGoldrick, M., Giordano, J., & Garcia-Preto, N. (Eds.). (2005). *Ethnicity and family therapy* (3rd ed.). New York, NY: Guilford Press.

Mclaughlin, K. A., Costello, E., Leblanc, W., Sampson, N. A., & Kessler, R. C. (2012). Socioeconomic status and adolescent mental disorders. *American Journal of Public Health, 102,* 1742–1750. doi:10.2105/AJPH.2011.300477

Merrell, K. (2008). *Behavioral, social, and emotional assessment of children and adolescents* (3rd ed.). New York, NY: Erlbaum.

Miller, M. J., Yang, M., Hui, K., Choi, N.-Y., & Lim, R. H. (2011). Acculturation, enculturation, and Asian American college students' mental health and attitudes toward seeking professional psychological help. *Journal of Counseling Psychology, 58,* 346–357. doi:10.1037/a0023636

Muñoz-Sandoval, A. F., Cummins, J., Alvarado, C. G., & Ruef, M. L. (2005). *Bilingual Verbal Ability Tests.* Itasca, IL: Riverside.

Nastasi, B. K. (1999). Audiovisual methods in ethnography. In J. J. Schensul & M. D. LeCompte (Eds.), *Enhanced ethnographic techniques: Audiovisual techniques, focused group interviews, and elicitation techniques—Ethnographer's toolkit, Book 3* (pp. 1–50). Walnut Creek, CA: AltaMira Press.

Nastasi, B. K., Hitchcock, J. H., Burkholder, G., Varjas, K., Sarkar, S., & Jayasena, A. (2007). Assessing adolescents' understanding of and reactions to stress in different cultures: Results of a mixed-methods approach. *School Psychology International, 28,* 163–178. doi:10.1177/0143034307078092

Nastasi, B. K., Jayasena, A., Summerville, M., & Borja, A. (2011). Facilitating long-term recovery from natural disasters: Psychosocial programming in tsunami-affected schools of Sri Lanka. *School Psychology International, 32,* 512–532. doi:10.1177/0143034311402923

Nastasi, B. K., Moore, R. B., & Varjas, K. M. (2004). *School-based mental health services: Creating comprehensive and culturally specific programs.* Washington, DC: American Psychological Association.

Ortiz, S., & Flanagan, D. (2008). Best practices in working with culturally diverse children and families. In A. Thomas & J. Grimes (Eds.), *Best practices in school psychology V* (pp. 337–351). Bethesda, MD: NASP.

Pedersen, P., Draguns, J., Lonner, W., & Trimble, J. (2008). *Counseling across cultures* (6th ed.). Thousand Oaks, CA: Sage.

Phinney, J., & Ong, A. (2007). Conceptualization and measurement of ethnic identity: Current status and future directions. *Journal of Counseling Psychology, 54,* 271–281. doi:10.1037/0022-0167.54.3.271

Reich, W., Leacock, N., & Shanfeld, K. (1997). *DICA–IV Diagnostic Interview for Children and Adolescents–IV* [Computer software]. Toronto, Canada: Multi-Health Systems.

Reynolds, C. R., & Kamphaus, R. W. (2004). *Behavior Assessment System for Children manual* (2nd ed.). Circle Pines, MN: AGS.

Rhodes, R., Ochoa, S. H., & Ortiz, S. (2005). *Assessing culturally and linguistically diverse students.* New York, NY: Guilford Press.

Rickert, D., & Rettig, K. (2006). Family Support Ecomaps. *Journal of Divorce & Remarriage, 46,* 1–2, 85–106. doi:10.1300/J087v46n01_05

Rones, M., & Hoagwood, K. (2000). School-based mental health services: A research review. *Clinical Child and family Psychology Review, 3,* 223–241.

Salvia, J., Ysseldyke, J., & Bolt, S. (2009). *Assessment* (11th ed.). Boston, MA: Houghton Mifflin.

Samia, L. M. (2011). *Screening for internalizing problems in middle school students utilizing a positive indicator of mental health* (Unpublished doctoral dissertation). Chapman University, Orange, CA.

Shaffer, D., Fisher, P., Dulcan, M. K., Davies, M., Piacentini, J., Schwab-Stone, M. E., . . . Regier, D. A. (1996). The NIMH Diagnostic Interview Schedule for Children Version 2.3 (DISC-2.3): Description, acceptability, prevalence rates, and performance in the MECA Study. *Journal of the American Academy of Child and Adolescent Psychiatry, 35,* 865–877. doi.org/10.1097/00004583-199607000-00012

Stansfield, M. (1980). Psychological issues in mental health interpreting. In F. Caccamise, J. Standgarone, & M. Mitchell-Caccmise (Eds.), *Century of deaf awareness* (pp. 102–114). Silver Spring: MD: Registry of Interpreters for the Deaf.

Suldo, S. M., & Shaffer, E. J. (2008). Looking beyond psychopathology: The dual-factor model of mental health in youth. *School Psychology Review, 37*, 52–68.

Telzer, E. H. (2010). Expanding the acculturation gap–distress model: An integrative review of research. *Human Development, 53*, 313–340. doi:10.1159/000322476

Trueba, E. (2002). Multiple ethnic, racial, and cultural identities in action: From marginality to a new cultural capital in modern society. *Journal of Latinos and Education, 1*(1), 7–28. doi:10.1207/S1532771XJLE0101_2

Ungar, M. (2008). Resilience across cultures. *British Journal of Social Work, 38*, 218–235. doi:10.1093/bjsw/bcl343

U. S. Department of Health and Human Services. (1999). *Mental health: A report of the Surgeon General*. Rockville, MD: Author.

Villalba, J. A. Jr. (2007). Culture-specific aspects to consider when counseling Latino/a children and adolescents. *Journal of Multicultural Counseling and Development, 35*, 15–25. doi:10.1002/j.2161-1912.2007.tb00046.x

Walter, M. (1983). *Spheres of justice: A defense of pluralism and equality*. New York: Basic Books.

Weine, A. M., Phillips, J. S., & Achenbach, T. (1995). Behavioral and emotional problems among Chinese and American children: Parent and teacher reports for ages 6 to 13. *Journal of Abnormal Child Psychology, 23*, 619–639. doi:10.1007/BF01447666

Werner, E. E., & Smith, R. S. (1992). *Overcoming the odds: High-risk children from birth to adulthood*. Ithaca, NY: Cornell University Press.

Winters, N. C., Collett, B. R., & Myers, K. (2005). Ten-year review of rating scales, VII: Scales assessing functional impairment. *Journal of the American Academy of Child & Adolescent Psychiatry, 44*, 309–338. doi:10.1097/01.chi.0000153230.57344.cd

Ysseldyke, J., Lekwa, A., Klingbeil, D., & Cormier, D. (2012). Assessment of ecological factors as an integral part of academic and mental health assessment. *Journal of Educational & Psychological Consultation, 22*, 21–43. doi:10.1080/10474412.2011.649641

III

A NEW VISION:
INTEGRATING CONCEPTS
IN BILINGUAL ASSESSMENT

8

ACCULTURATION AND SOCIOCOGNITIVE FACTORS

PATRICIO A. ROMERO AND JENNIFER BRANSCOME

Many challenges await a child immigrating to the United States. Integrating into American culture is one of those many challenges. This multifaceted process involves many factors, including language acquisition, immigrant status, and socioeconomic level, and can take many years to complete. Understanding issues surrounding integration into a new society can allow psychologists to adequately assist culturally and linguistically diverse (CLD) children should problems arise within the school system, the family system, or with peers.

In this chapter, we discuss several of the factors a CLD child faces when integrating into his or her new culture. The primary focus of this chapter is *sociocognitive factors* (e.g., educational attainment) related to acculturation, as well as the process of acculturation itself (i.e., phases and levels). To illustrate the various phases of acculturation and related factors, we present a case study featuring Nancy, a teenager who immigrated to the United States

http://dx.doi.org/10.1037/14320-009
Assessing Bilingual Children in Context: An Integrated Approach, A. B. Clinton (Editor)

immediately following the 2010 earthquake in Haiti. Selected tools used in the assessment of acculturation are discussed as well as interventions and resources for working with CLD children. Finally, a brief assessment checklist is provided for the practitioner.

SOCIOCOGNITIVE FACTORS

Language

Researchers have estimated that by 2030, 40% of school age children will be English learners (Thomas & Collier, 2000). These numbers highlight the importance of understanding issues surrounding the acquisition of a new language as part of the acculturation process. Research has suggested that children who are highly proficient in their primary language (L1) are more likely to acculturate successfully into their adopted culture. For instance, if a child demonstrates a high level of *cognitive and academic language proficiency* (CALP), or "academic" language, in their L1, empirical evidence indicates that he or she will be able to more quickly and efficiently attain CALP in their second (L2) or third, or fourth language (Cummins, 1976). This allows for a more successful academic career from kindergarten through college. Those who have not attained a moderate to high level of CALP in their L1 tend to have more difficulty in attaining CALP in their L2, which could lead to poorer academic outcomes across grade levels. In addition, if a CLD individual has adequate *basic interpersonal communication skills* (BICS; i.e., "social" language) within L2, he or she has a reasonably good chance to build a solid social network with peers and teachers within the new culture. Social networks formed within a CLD individual's new culture are integral to the acculturation process. Therefore, the BICS and CALP skills a CLD child possesses can help or hinder him or her significantly during the participation phase of acculturation (discussed later in more detail) in which a CLD child is actively exploring his or her new environment.

Other areas of concern related to language and acculturation include corrective feedback and the presence and degree of an accent. *Corrective feedback* includes either oral or written information regarding the accuracy of language use in terms of vocabulary, verb conjugation, and pronunciation, for example (Storch, 2010; Van Beuningen, 2010). Although the usefulness of corrective feedback is debated (Havranek, 2002; Storch, 2010), research has suggested that appropriate, timely, repetitive, accurate, and constructive instruction both with BICS and CALP is a significant positive predictor in the acquisition of L2 (Havranek, 2002; Van Beuningen, 2010).

In addition to the L2 corrective feedback a child receives in his or her new school and community cultures, a child may (or may not) receive similar corrective feedback from his or her parents or caregivers. Parents with higher levels of proficiency in L2 are able to provide appropriate corrective oral feedback. Research has suggested, however, that parental proficiency in L2 is not integral to a child's successful acquisition of L2 (Kenny, 1996; Schwartz, 2012; Schwartz, Kozminsky, & Leikin, 2009). Instead, studies have suggested that a parent's level of educational attainment preimmigration and their post-immigration socioeconomic status (SES) play a larger role in a child's success-ful mastery of L2 than parents' L2 language proficiency (Schwartz et al., 2009).

Another area that may affect the acculturation process is the presence and degree of a child's accent when speaking both L1 and L2. Studies have suggested that perception of language fluency is affected by speaker charac-teristics, such as accentedness (Kang, Rubin, & Pickering, 2010; Wu, 2010). *Accentedness* includes speech variables that affect the pronunciation of words, including vowel duration, intonation, speech rate, and pause. Native speakers may believe a CLD individual's accent indicates a lack of sufficient language proficiency in their L2 and suggests possible signs of learning disabilities or speech impairments. When considering the accent of a nonnative speaker of a language, it is important to consider the time of acquisition of a language, time of entry into the second culture, and the particulars of the L2 (e.g., phonetic structure). For instance, there are no words in the Spanish lan-guage that have *th* as a prefix. Therefore, native Spanish speakers often have significant difficulty saying words in the English beginning with *th*. This in turn affects the production of speech (i.e., it produces an accent), rather than being an indicator of an underlying dysfunction (e.g., learning disability).

Education Attainment and Acculturation

Research on immigrants who arrive in their new culture with an advanced level of educational attainment has been mixed in terms of educational and professional outcomes (Duleep & Dowhan, 2008; Sakamoto & Xie, 2006). Some studies have suggested that level of educational attainment at the time of immigration affects a person's ability to secure employment commensurate with his or her level of education. Those with higher levels of education at the time of immigration are believed to obtain employment more easily and command higher salaries relative to those who immigrate with a lower level of education. However, these findings are not consistently observed (Duleep & Dowhan, 2008; Schwartz et al., 2009). Other variables, such as certifica-tion, language skills, and the labor market, undoubtedly affect the relation-ship between job attainment and preimmigration educational attainment (Duleep & Dowhan, 2008).

In addition, there is potential for a "negative side" to having a higher education: It may be detrimental to the acculturation of a CLD child (Kaplan & Marks, 1990). One potential issue may be that the CLD individual risks rejection from the majority culture because he or she excels. A second issue, depending on culture of origin, is "model minority" status (Wong, Lai, Nagasawa, & Lin, 1998). Those in the so-called model minority typically are expected to be high-achieving, behaviorally compliant students (Wong et al., 1998). However, this designation may lead a CLD child to risk rejection in several areas depending on his or her conformity (or nonconformity) to and acceptance of the stereotypical expectations of the model minority. These risks may include lower achievement status and dysfunctional mental health outcomes (Gupta, Szymanski, & Leong, 2011).

Although CLD children may experience deleterious effects as a result of possessing a high level of educational achievement, Berry (1997) reported that obtaining an education is associated with positive adaptations and acculturation. For example, higher education is predictive of lower stress (Beiser et al., 1988; Jayasuriya, Sang, & Fielding, 1992). Berry (1997) proposed several reasons for these positive cultural adaptations. First, when a CLD child participates in formal education, he or she is learning several skills other than the information provided in the classroom or textbooks. In the formal educational setting, both the CLD and native-language-speaking child will learn life skills such as reasoning, analysis, and problem solving from teachers and peers. Second, the educational setting is often correlated with access to other resources, such as income, higher SES, and access to support networks, all of which are themselves protective factors (Berry, 1997). Third, education allows many immigrants to gain valuable information about their new culture. Within the educational setting, new members of a culture can learn about the customs, language, and norms of the new society.

Socioeconomic Status

SES can be a protective factor for CLD children, similar to that of educational attainment. Often, however, the SES of the immigrant family may change drastically once they arrive in the new culture. Many factors may contribute to this change in SES, including access to employment, recognition of academic credentials, and loss of status. These factors lead to fewer resources, which may limit the mobility and occupational attainment of the immigrant family (Aycan & Berry, 1996). It has often been stated that the "departure status" of many immigrant families is frequently higher than the family's "entry status" (Duleep & Dowhan, 2008). Credentials, such as educational and work experience, may be devalued on arrival (Cumming, Lee, & Oreopoulos, 1989; Duleep & Dowhan, 2008). This potential difference in status and occupational attainment may lead to more serious, long-lasting concerns such as mental health issues and poverty.

Immigration Status

Many kinds of cultural groups exist in plural societies. This variety is primarily due to three factors: voluntariness, mobility, and permanence. First, some groups enter into the acculturation process voluntarily (i.e., immigrants), whereas others experience acculturation without either deliberately or willingly seeking it out (i.e., refugees, indigenous peoples). Second, groups may have contact with the new culture because they have migrated to a new location (i.e., immigrants and refugees), whereas others have had contact with the new culture because it came to them (i.e., indigenous peoples and "national minorities"). Third, among those who have immigrated, some are relatively permanently settled into the process (e.g., immigrants), whereas for others the situation is a temporary one (e.g., sojourners, such as international students and guest workers, or asylum seekers who may eventually be deported).

Cultural Identity

One issue closely tied to the acculturation of a CLD child is that of cultural identity. A person's cultural identity shapes his or her viewpoints, thoughts, and behaviors. *Cultural identity* can be viewed as the perception a person has of himself or herself as a "cultural being" (Baruth & Manning, 2012), with all attendant aspects of that conceptualization, such as values, beliefs, and traditions. A person's cultural identity defines him or her, at both the conscious and unconscious level, as an individual and as a member of a larger cultural group. Finally, a person's cultural identity plays a role in shaping a person's worldview, the cognitive structure around which he or she shapes his or her opinions, attitudes, beliefs, thoughts, and behaviors. Therefore, it is important to have an understanding of a CLD child's cultural identity as he or she negotiates the balance between his or her culture of origin and the new culture, because it will affect his or her level of acculturation, depending on the strength and investment in that identity (Berry, Phinney, Sam, & Vedder, 2006).

Acculturative stress, or *culture shock,* occurs when a person is exposed to a new culture and experiences significant stress and anxiety as a result. This anxiety results from the acculturation process and may lead to poor mental and physical health as well as identity confusion (Berry, Kim, Minde, & Mok, 1987). A CLD child experiencing acculturative stress may appear to be performing well in school and completing his or her daily life activities. However, this child may also experience symptoms of depression or lethargy. This state can persist and develop to crisis proportions, with the student manifesting a number of symptoms similar to a severe psychological disorder, such as major depressive disorder. The CLD child who is confronted with a sense of meaninglessness may be in what is considered a "shock phase" (Berry et al., 1987). Indeed, the ability to function within the customs and expectations of the new environment may prompt an awareness of a full separation from the home culture. This issue should be one to consider carefully when working with a CLD child. Acculturative stress may affect numerous aspects of the child's life, including educational achievement, mental health functioning, and successful acculturation to the new culture.

ACCULTURATION

Acculturation can be a complex process for immigrants adjusting to a new culture. Much has been published regarding the process of acculturation in general as well as in specific populations (see Berry, 2005). Acculturation is generally considered to be a continual process that progresses as immigrants are exposed to the majority of a culture (Pazos & Nadkarni, 2010). During the acculturation process, changes can be expected in many areas, including a person's language, values, and customs. Language is considered to be one of the more important factors in a person's degree of acculturation (Pazos & Nadkarni, 2010), although L2 acquisition should not be automatically equated with acculturation into a new culture.

Perhaps the most widely accepted theory of acculturation has been Berry's (1997, 2005) acculturation framework. Berry's (2005) framework is based on the definition of *acculturation* as "the dual process of cultural and psychological change that takes place as a result of contact between two or more cultural groups and their individual members" (p. 298). At the group level, Berry (2005) indicated that acculturation includes changes in social structures and institutions as well as in cultural practices. At the individual level, Berry (2005) stated that acculturation involves individual changes in a person's behavioral repertoire. From this perspective, cultural change implies molding key components of culture such as values, beliefs, expectations, norms, and roles as well as adjustments in cultural practices and related psychological functioning. These changes can take years, sometimes generations and sometimes centuries, to be fully implemented.

The *acculturation matrix* (AM; C. Collier, Brice, & Oades-Sese, 2007) defines potential responses that primary and secondary students may have to the acculturation process (Pazos & Nadkarni, 2010). The AM applies to the culture of the school system in particular. The four elements of the AM are assimilation, integration, deculturation or marginalization, and rejection. The premise behind the AM is that L2 acquisition can occur separately from acculturation. Within the AM, *assimilation* refers to the replacement of a child's heritage of origin by his or her new culture or language. *Integration*, however, involves the blending of the heritage of origin with the new culture or language. *Deculturation* or *marginalization* is problematic in that a child accepts neither the heritage of origin nor the new culture. The final category of the AM is *rejection*. In this area, a child will either willingly reject his or her heritage of origin or the new culture. The process of acculturation, whether a part of L2 acquisition or not, can result in acculturative stress. Acculturative stress refers to emotional and behavioral consequences of moving from one's culture of origin to a new culture. This could involve feelings of anxiety, loss of perception of control, distractibility, and other general stress responses (Pazos & Nadkarni, 2010).

It is hypothesized that individuals experience four phases of acculturation as their contact with the majority group in their new culture increases. Although the AM provides a helpful rubric for the psychologist working with the CLD child, it is important to keep in mind that Brown's (1987) theory of acculturation is predicated on the assumption that an individual possesses the independence to choose how he or she wishes to acculturate. This independence of choice, however, is not applicable in all cases (Berry, 1976). At times, immigrants will be able to choose which adaptation—the end point of acculturation—strategy they will undergo. However, there are times these decisions are out of the immigrant's control. The more control in adaptation (e.g., higher language proficiency, higher SES, more family support, higher educational attainment), the more likely an individual is to experience less acculturative stress. Also, the amount of acculturative stress that an individual has experienced will also help him or her in deciding which adaptive strategy to choose. For example, if individuals perceive that a society has isolated them and made them unwelcome, those individuals may choose to separate themselves from the culture. However, if a person perceives that he or she has been welcomed and that his or her culture is valued and appreciated, that person may be more willing to integrate into the new country's culture.

Stages of Acculturation

According to Brown (1987), CLD children undergo four successive stages of acculturation as they enter school and society: the honeymoon stage, the observation stage, the increasing participation stage, and the mental isolation stage. The first stage of acculturation, the *honeymoon stage*, is considered a preliminary stage in which the initial awareness of the future and the possibility of moving to a new environment is recognized. During this stage, individuals typically report feelings of euphoria and excitement as the transition is made to the new culture, which may include unrealistic expectations.

A qualitative study by Mateu-Gelabert (2002) provides a sense of the honeymoon phase of acculturation. The author interviewed several adults from the Dominican Republic, as well as new immigrants to New York City. Several participants in the study reported fantastical expectations for their lives in the United States, such as "money growing on trees," thus explaining some of the appeal that the United States may have for residents of the Dominican Republic. Unrealistic expectations tend to be especially true for individuals who live in poverty. Another participant in the same study by Mateu-Gelabert related how her relatives residing in the United States described the country: "It's like God lives here. Like the last Coke in the desert. All you see are beautiful people with money" (p. 12). Stories such as these may well contribute to the level of excitement in preparing to move to the United States or having recently arrived during the initial stages of acculturation.

Throughout this chapter, we use the story of "Nancy" to illustrate the acculturation process. In the following portion of Nancy's story, she demonstrates behaviors particular to the honeymoon phase of acculturation.

Case Study: Honeymoon Stage

On January 12, 2010, a catastrophic 7.0 magnitude earthquake devastated the island nation of Haiti, killing over 300,000 individuals and leaving over 1,000,000 others homeless. As a result, many of those who were left without a home were forced to exit the country, leaving behind their friends, family, and the lives they had worked so hard to create. One of these individuals was a young girl named Nancy, [1] who lost her father in the earthquake. She, along with her mother and brother, entered the United States and sought refuge at the home of her aunt, who lived in a major urban city. Despite being forced to deal with such adversity at a young age, Nancy was hopeful that she could make the best of the situation and looked forward to attending a new school and meeting new people. Nancy is a bright young woman. In Haiti, she attended a private school, where she was one of the top students in her class. She also speaks four languages: English, Spanish, French, and Creole. Because of her history of success in academics, Nancy looked forward to continuing her education in the United States. Her excitement and eagerness to begin a new life in the United States is a clear indicator that Nancy was beginning the acculturation process and entering the honeymoon stage.

On her first day of school, Nancy, accompanied by her mother and aunt, met with the school guidance counselor and school psychologist to discuss her transition to the United States and the challenges she would face as she started school. The first obstacle they encountered was

---

[1]The details of the case studies have been changed to protect the anonymity of the individuals involved.

determining the grade that was appropriate for Nancy. Since Nancy's previous school was left in ruins by the earthquake, her new school had difficulty obtaining her academic records. Fortunately, the guidance counselor knew of a database that housed the records of international students. With this information, the officials determined that Nancy should be placed in the 11th grade. From there, it was determined that Nancy would benefit from regularly scheduled counseling sessions to help her cope with the hardships she had experienced and to help her fully adjust to her new school. Nancy's initial adjustment to her life went well. Her teachers reported that she made the transition seamlessly and demonstrated a high level of proficiency with the English language. She also showed familiarity with much of the material being presented in her classes while also exhibiting an impressive amount of knowledge regarding American culture.

Perhaps the biggest obstacle for Nancy came early in her acculturation process. In her first session with the school psychologist, Nancy explained that a recent visit to the doctor revealed that her mother had Stage IV breast cancer. Tragically, within a month of receiving this news, Nancy's mother passed away. Because Nancy had little contact with her aunt prior to immigrating to the United States, she briefly contemplated returning to Haiti and living with other family members. However, after much consideration, Nancy chose to fulfill her mother's wish that she remain in the United States and obtain an education. Again, despite the many hardships that she was forced to cope with, Nancy continued to excel in school.

The *observation stage*, the second stage of acculturation, is that in which an individual is first exposed to the new culture. Contact with the new culture may cause mixed emotions for the CLD child. During this stage, CLD children are typically characterized as passive, yet alert, observers and listeners. In this stage, children often demonstrate what is described as a "silent" speaking phase, where verbal output drops dramatically (Krupa-Kwiatkowski, 1998). During this phase, the child investigates the newly acquired culture and attempts to speak and act like others in the new environment. The child begins to realize the apparent differences between their "home" culture and the newly acquired culture. This knowledge may lead to what has been termed the *disenchantment stage of acculturation*. This stage occurs as the newcomer encounters problems with being accepted by his or her peers in the newly acquired environment and problems with participating in the new environment. On first immigrating, the problems encountered by the CLD child will be focused on obtaining basic needs such as food, shelter, and clothing. Once these needs are met, however, the problems become more complex and social in nature, such as misunderstandings related to language, customs, and mannerisms. When a CLD child determines that it is no longer possible to maintain a passive approach to the mainstream culture, this second (observation) stage is over.

Case Study: Observation Stage and Disenchantment Stage

> During her counseling sessions, Nancy experienced difficulty with discussing her feelings about the death of her parents, which made it difficult to help her progress through the stages of grief effectively. Rather than encouraging her to deal with feelings she was not ready to explore, the school psychologist encouraged Nancy to focus more on her life at her current school and the problems she was experiencing there. Nancy discussed several aspects of her new life in the United States that were markedly different from her life in Haiti. She described her new peers as immature and materialistic, which she saw as a barrier to developing relationships with them. It also appeared that she had not yet begun to understand the unique sense of humor possessed by these students; neither had she fully grasped the subtle nuances of the English language. Her recognition of the differences between her old and new culture illustrated that she had progressed from the honeymoon phase of acculturation to the second phase, the observation stage. Her misunderstanding of her peers' language and humor provides an example of disenchantment.

The third stage of acculturation is called the *increasing participation stage*. During this stage, the child willingly (or perhaps not so willingly) takes on an active role in the new environment, which has been reported to increase the level of frustration among a subgroup of individuals going through the acculturation process (C. Collier et al., 2007). Conversely, there are many individuals who undergo acceptance of the cultural differences and attempt to make sense of them. This increased degree of participation can lead to a number of accomplishments, ultimately resulting in a high level of self-esteem, satisfaction, and self-confidence.

Alternatively, with greater participation in the new environments, the child's "new" culture and his or her culture of origin may begin to clash, thus resulting in a resistance to adapting to the new environment. The disenchantment common at the end of the observation phase often leads to a sense of isolation during the increasing participation phase. This is sometimes referred to as the *mental isolation stage of acculturation*. At this stage, newcomers experience a kind of homesickness. They miss their "home" culture and feel more like an outsider in the new culture. They may limit or avoid all contact with the new culture. They may spend more or all of their time with their own culture or language group. This process of gradual adaptation, fascination, disenchantment, and mental isolation may continue in a repeating cycle for some time without full adjustment. This is especially true for students or young people whose families are moving them in and out of school situations—for example, migrant and seasonal agricultural workers.

Nancy's story concludes below and demonstrates the final stage of acculturation, increased participation.

Case Study: Increased Participation Stage

To ensure that Nancy's transition was as smooth as possible, the school psychologist began looking for ways to incorporate elements of her Haitian culture into the counseling sessions. For example, Nancy introduced the school psychologist to her favorite Haitian musician, and the two of them listened to a few of her favorite songs. This helped Nancy to develop a strong therapeutic relationship with the psychologist, which facilitated Nancy's progression to the next phase of acculturation: the increased participation stage. In school, Nancy quickly rose to the top of her class academically while beginning to form friendships with several of her peers. She started to get involved in various extracurricular activities in the community, such as volunteering at a local soup kitchen and eating lunch with elderly people once a week. She went on to graduate with honors and enrolled in a 4-year university program in which she chose to major in physical therapy.

Nancy was a student who impressed and inspired the entire school community. During her first semester of college, she returned to her high school to visit and inform the staff of her progress. She was still performing admirably in her studies and stated that, on completing her degree, she would like to return to Haiti to provide much-needed services to those who were still trying to recuperate from the earthquake. She expressed her gratitude to the school psychologist for his help in introducing her to the American way of life, while also acknowledging that she now had a much better understanding of the unique aspects of the American language and culture. In addition, Nancy informed the staff that she had obtained the services of another psychologist to finally help her to cope with the loss of her parents. She concluded her meeting with the school psychologist by recognizing the patience he took with her as she progressed through the stages of acculturation and acknowledging that she would not have been able to succeed as she did without his guidance.

For a child with a more flexible temperament, these states of the acculturation cycle may mean a series of small adjustments, or problems to be overcome, one by one. Others, however, may experience the acculturation process as a series of highs and lows as they face barriers in communication and interaction and discover significant differences in values and perceptions between their two cultures. For the children who are more successful during the acculturation process, the path of increasing participation constitutes an acceptance of, and tentative involvement with, external manifestations of the new culture. The child begins to develop a greater tolerance and ability to cope with the external cultural patterns of the environment, which become internalized and part of the child's schema. Eventually, the child acquires alternative ways of learning, behaving, feeling, and responding to others, all of which are equally valid.

For some students and their families, there may be an additional phase of acculturation, usually referred to as the *reentry phase*. This stage of acculturation may occur if the CLD child, his or her family, or both return to their place of origin. This occurrence is common with the families of international students attending American schools and with migrant workers and parents who reside in the United States for educational or work experiences. The acculturation cycle may be repeated as these CLD children depart and reenter the new culture.

Adaptation is the endpoint of the acculturation experience, the point at which the sense of being foreign to the new culture no longer exists. Adaptation is a multifaceted process, akin to the overarching acculturation process. It is possible to have both healthy and unhealthy adaptation outcomes. Berry (2005) described four categories of adaptation: assimilation, separation, marginalization, or integration. *Assimilation* involves taking in all of the new culture's values and beliefs and abandoning those of the culture of origin. *Separation* involves maintaining the culture of origin and rejecting the new culture. Those who separate may experience high levels of acculturative stress and lower self-esteem (Berry, 2005). *Marginalization* involves rejecting the culture of the host country as well as the culture of origin. Those who choose this strategy typically have high levels of acculturative stress and experience feelings of alienation and loss of identity. The final category of adaptation is the one that is most often chosen: *integration*. In this category, the CLD child maintains his or her culture of origin while simultaneously integrating his or her adopted culture. This stage may be conceptualized as a merging of the two cultures. Those who integrate typically experience the lowest level of acculturative stress than in any of the other categories of adaptation (Kosic, 2002).

ASSESSMENT OF ACCULTURATION

Identification and referral of CLD individuals for special education programs is currently one of the most controversial issues in public education in the United States (cf. Abedi, 2006; Coutinho & Oswald, 2006). To make informed decisions, professionals involved in the process of referral and placement must have knowledge and understanding of educational exceptionalities as well as cultural and linguistic characteristics of native and immigrant children. The interactive effects of these characteristics on the child experiencing cultural and/or linguistic adaptation and acculturation must be taken into account in the referral and placement decision process. Without this knowledge, education personnel cannot make appropriate identification, referral, and service decisions for the CLD child (V. P. Collier, 1987).

Kim and Abreu (2001) reviewed 33 acculturation assessment instruments compiled from the online database PsycINFO (http://www.apa.org/pubs/databases/psycinfo/index.aspx). Of these 33 instruments, the majority (23) were developed for use with Hispanic populations (e.g., "general" Hispanics, Mexican Americans, Puerto Rican Americans, and Cuban Americans). Two were designed for use with African Americans, three with Asian Americans, one with Native Americans, one with Hawaiians, and one with all ethnic minority groups. The authors found that some positive aspects of these assessments were their acceptable levels of reliability and internal consistency and the inclusion of items designed to evaluate specific dimensions of behavioral acculturation (language use, choice of friendship, and food preferences). A negative aspect was that nearly three quarters of the instruments had no evidence of test–retest reliability.

Taras (2008) also provided a review of acculturation instruments. Taras's review assessed 59 assessments published between 1947 and 2004. For each instrument, Taras reported psychometric properties (when available), descriptions of the areas assessed, the populations for which the instruments were developed, and in some cases, the complete instrument itself. As with Kim and Abreu's (2001) review, Taras's review of instruments revealed an absence of key psychometric properties for many instruments. In addition, the instruments varied widely in subject matter (e.g., the four stages of acculturation, customs and beliefs, cultural identity, family practices, health beliefs and practices), although all of the scales purported to measure acculturation. Taras's analysis of acculturation instruments illustrated the difficulty practitioners may face when trying to adequately and accurately assess acculturation in CLD children.

One instrument of particular interest is the Acculturation Quick Screen (AQS; C. Collier, 1998). Of the many acculturation instruments available, the AQS is one of the most commonly used measures, particularly within the school system (cf. García-Vásquez, 1995; Washoe County School District, 2009; Watson, Rinaldi, Navarrete, Bianco, & Samson, 2007). The AQS is a brief measure designed to assess the level and rate of acculturation within the public school system (Martines, 2008). The AQS appears to have several benefits. One is that the administration of the instrument is not limited to school psychologists; the AQS can be administered in the classroom setting by a variety of qualified examiners (e.g., teachers). An additional advantage is that a baseline level of acculturation can be established from which future gains in acculturation can be compared.

On the AQS, acculturation levels are described as follows: (a) significantly less acculturated, (b) less acculturated, (c) in transition, (d) more acculturated, and (e) significantly more acculturated (C. Collier et al., 2007). It is expected that the rate of acculturation for most students will increase anywhere between 10% and 12% each year (C. Collier, 2011). An additional benefit of the AQS is that it can be used to monitor a student's acculturation progress throughout the school year and beyond. On the basis of a child's level of acculturation, appropriate strategies can be developed to address acculturation-related issues a child may be experiencing. Teaching and assessment strategies may also be informed by knowledge of a CLD child's level of acculturation. Another advantage of the AQS is that it was not designed for students of a particular ethnicity, which allows for use and meaningful comparison across groups.

Although it would be outside the range of this chapter to provide a comprehensive list of acculturation instruments, the following list provides a sample of the wide range of measures available to the practitioner. In addition, Appendix 8.1 provides a brief acculturation checklist.

- Acculturation and Biculturalism Scale (Triandis et al., 1982)
- Acculturation Quick Screen (C. Collier, 1998)
- Acculturation Rating Scale for Mexican Americans (Cuellar, Harris, & Jasso, 1980)
- African American Acculturation Scale (Landrine & Klonoff, 1995)
- Behavioral Acculturation Scale (Szapocznik, Scopetta, Kurtines, & Aranalde, 1978)
- Benet-Martinez Acculturation Scale (Taras, 2008)
- Bicultural/Multicultural Experience Inventory (Ramirez, 1984)
- Chicano Adolescent Acculturation Scale (Olmedo, Martinez, & Martinez, 1978)
- Children's Acculturation Scale (Franco, 1983)
- Children's Hispanic Background Scale (Martinez, Norman, & Delaney, 1984)
- The East Asian Acculturation Measure (Barry, 2001)
- Language-Based Acculturation Scale for Mexican Americans (Deyo, Diehl, Hazuda, & Stern, 1985)
- Multicultural Acculturation Scale (Wong-Rieger & Quintana, 1987)
- NaMea Hawai'i Scale (Rezentes, 1993)
- Navajo Acculturation Scale (Boyce & Boyce, 1983)
- Padilla Acculturation Scale (Padilla, 1980)

- The Psychological Acculturation Scale (Tropp, Erkut, Coll, Alarcon, & Garcia, 1999)
- The Rosebud Personal Opinion Survey (Hoffmann, Dana, & Bolton, 1985)
- Scale to Assess African American Acculturation (Snowden & Hines, 1999)
- The Suinn-Lew Asian Self-Identity Acculturation (Suinn, Rickard-Figueroa, Lew, & Vigil, 1987)
- Value Acculturation Scale (Szapocznik, Scopetta, Kurtines, & Aranalde, 1978)

CULTURALLY COMPETENT INTERVENTION AND COUNSELING

There are many factors involved in providing culturally competent interventions to children who are undergoing the acculturation process. First, psychologists must be aware of the positive and negative influences of sociocognitive factors such as language proficiency, SES, and educational attainment within the individual. The psychologist must further understand that outcomes differ from case to case. Moreover, psychologists must build an awareness of the culture and customs of the individual for whom they are providing interventions. In addition, the psychologist should engage in self-reflection so as to increase personal awareness of assumptions made about other groups or cultures and to help recognize how they must be adjusted to the counseling process (Guerrero & Leung, 2008).

With regard to individual counseling, three variables may interact in such a way as to seriously hinder counseling with ethnic minority groups (Sue & Sue, 1999): (a) culture-bound values, (b) class-bound values, and (c) language variables. Sue and Sue (1999) indicated that *culture-bound values* rely too heavily on the individual, when there should be an emphasis on the family and community. A focus on the individual is contradictory to many individuals with a collectivist background. *Class-bound values* are those that arise when psychologists have to adhere to a strict schedule with the individual and develop long-term goals for the counseling sessions. Many newly immigrated individuals may seek counseling expecting an immediate resolution to their problems and may not foresee the benefits of the intervention if it takes a significant amount of time. Third is the *language variable* in counseling. Typically, counseling sessions are conducted in English and require a large amount of verbalization. These three generic characteristics are contrasted with value systems of various ethnic groups. Religion, nationality, family, beliefs, and customs are all variables necessary to be considered when working with an increasingly diverse population. In addition, people from diverse sociocultural backgrounds, because of their different values and beliefs, tend to define health and illness differently. Misunderstandings that arise from cultural variations in verbal and nonverbal communication may lead to alienation and an inability to develop trust and rapport.

When working with students of different ethnicities, gender, ages, and backgrounds, one must be mindful of culturally appropriate interventions and strategies during communication. For instance, there are many different communication styles that can be used to assure successful outcomes. There are many verbal and nonverbal gestures, such as body language and facial expressions, which help the professional understand clinically the issues of the individual. As professionals, it is important to understand what is culturally appropriate when reciprocating communication. In addition, psychologists need to be mindful to not offend clients by engaging in behaviors that are disrespectful to their culture or insensitive to their traditions and beliefs (Sue & Sue, 1999). Psychologists are constantly in communication with clients and their families. The key to all successful sessions is clear and precise communication. There are many different types of communication that can be used to convey feelings, emotions, or thoughts. To understand how to deliver and receive such imperative communication styles, one must use cultural understanding throughout one's clinical practice (Sue & Sue, 1999).

CONCLUSION

A CLD child immigrating to a new culture faces many issues, particularly language acquisition, potential status shifts due to socioeconomic factors or immigration conditions, and acculturation. Although the process of acculturation can be a difficult one for a child whose family has recently immigrated to the United States, it is not necessary that it be a negative one. If provided with the fundamental knowledge required to address the needs of the CLD child, psychologists may effectively address many of the potential issues a CLD child faces. With proper educational, familial, and societal support, CLD children have the potential to successfully adapt to their new culture and experience significant success.

APPENDIX 8.1 BRIEF ACCULTURATION CHECKLIST

Language

- What is the student's L1? _____
- What is the student's L2? _____
- What is the student's L3? _____
- What is the primary language spoken at home? _____
- CALP ratings (if known):
  - Oral expression _____
  - Oral comprehension _____
  - Writing skills _____
  - Reading skills _____
- If no CALP ratings are known, what is the estimated proficiency (beginning, intermediate, or advanced?) in each area?
  - Oral expression _____
  - Oral comprehension _____
  - Writing skills _____
  - Reading skills_____

Education

- At what age or grade did the student begin attending a U.S. school? _____
- Were there significant interruptions in attendance (e.g., returning to country of origin for weeks, months, or years)? _____
  _____
  - If so, how long was the child not in school in the United States? _____
  - Did he or she attend school in his or her country of origin? _____
- Did the student attend school in the country of origin? _____
  - If so, for how long? _____
  - Were there disruptions in attendance? _____
  - If so, for how long? _____
- Is the student currently receiving English language learner services? _____
  - If so, what services? _____

Note. CALP = cognitive and academic language proficiency; L1 = primary language; L2 = secondary language; L3 = tertiary language.

Family

- How long ago did the family or the student immigrate to the United States? _____
- Was the move voluntary? _____
- Are one or more caregivers or parents employed? _____
- What is the highest level of educational attainment of the mother? _____
- What is the highest level of educational attainment of the father? _____

Acculturation

Assessment of level of acculturation (e.g., integrated, assimilated) is typically conducted through structured questionnaires or self-report inventories. Some areas that are typically assessed are

- Language use:
  - What language does the student think in? _____
  - Use with friends? _____
  - Use with family? _____
  - Use at home? _____
  - Feel most comfortable speaking? _____
- Music and entertainment:
  - What types of entertainment are of interest? _____
  - Is it primarily American? _____
  - Is it primarily from the country of origin? _____
  - Is it a mixture of both? _____
- Food preference:
  - What types of food does the student eat and/or prefer? _____
  - Primarily American? _____
  - Primarily from the country of origin? _____
  - Is it a mixture of both? _____
- Socialization:
  - With whom does the student socialize most? _____
  - Are friends mostly from the culture of origin? _____
  - Are friends mostly American? _____
  - Is it a mixture of both? _____
- Cultural identity:
  - With what culture does the student identify most? _____
  - Does the student feel comfortable only in the culture of origin? _____

- Does the student feel comfortable only in American culture? _____
- Does the student feel a part of both the culture of origin and American culture? _____

REFERENCES

Abedi, J. (2006). Psychometric issues in the ELL assessment and special education eligibility. *Teachers College Record, 108,* 2282–2303. doi:10.1111/j.1467-9620.2006.00782.x

Aycan, Z., & Berry, J. W. (1996). Impact of employment-related experiences on immigrants' psychological well-being and adaptation to Canada. *Canadian Journal of Behavioural Science/Revue Canadienne des Sciences du Comportement, 28,* 240–251. doi:10.1037/0008-400X.28.3.240

Barry, D. T. (2001). Development of a new scale for measuring acculturation: The East Asian Acculturation Measure (EAAM). *Journal of Immigrant Health, 3,* 193–197. doi:10.1023/A:1012227611547

Baruth, L. G., & Manning, M. L. (2012). *Multicultural counseling and psychotherapy: A lifespan approach.* Boston, MA: Pearson.

Beiser, M., Wood, M., Barwick, C., Berry, J. W., deCosta, G., Milne, W., . . . Vela, E. (1988). *After the door has been opened: Mental health issues affecting immigrants and refugees in Canada.* Ottawa, Canada: Ministries of Multiculturalism and Citizenship, and Health and Welfare.

Berry, J. W. (1976). *Human ecology and cognitive style: Comparative studies in cultural and psychological adaptation.* New York, NY: Sage/Halsted.

Berry, J. W. (1997). Immigration, acculturation and adaptation. *Applied Psychology, 46,* 5–34.

Berry, J. W. (2005). Acculturation: Living successfully in two cultures. *International Journal of Intercultural Relations, 29,* 697–712. doi:10.1016/j.ijintrel.2005.07.013

Berry, J. W., Kim, U., Minde, T., & Mok, D. (1987). Comparative studies of acculturative stress. *The International Migration Review, 21,* 491–511. doi:10.2307/2546607

Berry, J. W., Phinney, J. S., Sam, D. L., & Vedder, P. (2006). Immigrant youth: Acculturation, identity, and adaptation. *Applied Psychology, 55,* 303–332. doi:10.1111/j.1464-0597.2006.00256.x

Boyce, W. T., & Boyce, J. C. (1983). Acculturation and changes in health among Navajo boarding school students. *Social Science & Medicine, 17,* 219–226. doi:10.1016/0277-9536(83)90119-3

Brown, H. D. (1987). *Principles of language learning and teaching.* Upper Saddle River, NJ: Prentice Hall.

Collier, C. (1998, February). *Acculturation: Implications for assessment, instruction, and intervention.* Paper presented at the meeting of the National Association for Bilingual Education, Dallas, TX.

Collier, C. (2011). *AQS scoring form.* Retrieved from http://crosscultured.com/documents/2011%20Updates/AQSIII%202011%20Scoring%20Form%20sample.pdf

Collier, C., Brice, A. E., & Oades-Sese, G. V. (2007). Assessment of acculturation. In G. B. Esquivel, N. Lopez, & S. Nahari (Eds.), *Handbook of multicultural school psychology: An interdisciplinary perspective*. Mahwah, NJ: Erlbaum.

Collier, V. P. (1987). Age and rate of acquisition of second language for academic purposes. *TESOL Quarterly, 21,* 617–641. doi:10.2307/3586986

Coutinho, M. J., & Oswald, D. (2006). *Disproportionate representation of culturally and linguistically diverse students in special education: Measuring the problem.* Retrieved from http://www.nccrest.org/Briefs/students_in_SPED_Brief.pdf

Cuellar, I., Harris, L. C., & Jasso, R. (1980). An acculturation scale for Mexican–American normal and clinical populations. *Hispanic Journal of Behavioral Sciences, 2,* 199–217.

Cumming, P., Lee, E., & Oreopoulos, D. G. (1989). *Access: Task force on access to professions and trades in Ontario.* Toronto, Ontario, Canada: Ontario Ministry of Citizenship.

Cummins, J. (1976). Cognitive/academic language proficiency, linguistic interdependence, the optimum age question and some other matters. *Working Papers on Bilingualism, 19,* 121–129.

Deyo, R. A., Diehl, A. K., Hazuda, H., & Stern, M. P. (1985). A simple language-based acculturation scale for Mexican Americans: Validation and application to health care research. *American Journal of Public Health, 75*(1), 51–55. doi:10.2105/AJPH.75.1.51

Duleep, H. O., & Dowhan, D. J. (2008). Research on immigrant earnings. *Social Security Bulletin, 68*(1), 31–50.

Franco, J. N. (1983). An acculturation scale for Mexican–American children. *The Journal of General Psychology, 108,* 175–181. doi:10.1080/00221309.1983.9711491

García-Vásquez, E. (1995). Acculturation and academic: Effects of acculturation on reading achievement among Mexican–American students. *Bilingual Research Journal, 19,* 305–315. doi:10.1080/15235882.1995.10668607

Guerrero, C., & Leung, B. (2008). Communicating effectively with culturally and linguistically diverse families. *Communiqué, 36,* 1–8.

Gupta, A., Szymanski, D. M., & Leong, F. T. L. (2011). The "model minority myth": Internalized racialism of positive stereotypes as correlates of psychological distress, and attitudes toward help-seeking. *Asian American Journal of Psychology, 2,* 101–114. doi:10.1037/a0024183

Havranek, G. (2002). When is corrective feedback most likely to succeed? *International Journal of Educational Research, 37,* 255–270. doi:10.1016/S0883-0355(03)00004-1

Hoffmann, T., Dana, R. H., & Bolton, B. (1985). Measured acculturation and MMPI–168 performance of Native American adults. *Journal of Cross-Cultural Psychology, 16,* 243–256. doi:10.1177/0022002185016002007

Jayasuriya, L., Sang, D., & Fielding, A. (1992). *Ethnicity, immigration, and mental illness: A critical review of Australian research.* Canberra: Australian Government Publishing Services.

Kang, O., Rubin, D., & Pickering, L. (2010). Suprasegmental measures of accentedness and judgments of language learner proficiency in oral English. *Modern Language Journal, 94*, 554–566. doi:10.1111/j.1540-4781.2010.01091.x

Kaplan, M. S., & Marks, G. (1990). Adverse effects of acculturation: Psychological distress among Mexican American young adults. *Social Science & Medicine, 31*, 1313–1319. doi:10.1016/0277-9536(90)90070-9

Kenny, K. D. (1996). *Language loss and the crisis of cognition: Between socio- and psycholinguistics.* Berlin, Germany: Mouton de Gruyter. doi:10.1515/9783110812374

Kim, B. S. K., & Abreu, J. M. (2001). Acculturation measurement: Theory, current instruments, and future directions. In J. G. Ponterotto, M. J. Casar, L. A. Suzuki, & C. M. Alexander (Eds.), *Handbook of multicultural counseling* (2nd ed., pp. 394–424). Thousand Oaks, CA: Sage.

Kosic, A. (2002). Acculturation attitudes, need for cognitive closure, and adaptation of immigrants. *The Journal of Social Psychology, 142*, 179–201. doi:10.1080/00224540209603894

Krupa-Kwiatkowski, M. (1998). "You shouldn't have brought me here!" Interaction strategies in the silent period of an inner-direct second language learner. *Research on Language and Social Interaction, 31*, 133–175. doi:10.1207/s15327973rlsi3102_1

Landrine, H., & Klonoff, E. A. (1995). The African American Acculturation Scale: Development, reliability, and validity. *The Journal of Black Psychology, 20*, 104–127. doi:10.1177/00957984940202002

Martines, D. (2008). *Multicultural school psychology competencies: A practical guide.* Thousand Oaks, CA: Sage.

Martinez, R., Norman, R. D., & Delaney, H. D. (1984). A children's Hispanic background scale. *Hispanic Journal of Behavioral Sciences, 6*, 103–112. doi:10.1177/07399863840062001

Mateu-Gelabert, P. (2002). *Dreams, gangs, and guns: The interplay between adolescent violence and immigration in a New York City neighborhood.* New York, NY: Vera Institute of Justice.

Olmedo, E. L., Martinez, J. L., Jr., & Martinez, S. R. (1978). Measure of acculturation for Chicano adolescents. *Psychological Reports, 42*, 159–170. doi:10.2466/pr0.1978.42.1.159

Padilla, A. M. (1980). The role of cultural awareness and ethnic loyalty in acculturation. In A. M. Padilla (Ed.), *Acculturation: Theory, models and some new findings* (pp. 47–84). Boulder, CO: Westview.

Pazos, H., & Nadkarni, L. I. (2010). Competency with linguistically diverse populations. In J. A. E. Cornish, B. A. Schreier, L. Nadkarni, L. Henderson Metzger, & E. Rodolfo (Eds.), *Handbook of multicultural counseling competencies* (pp. 153–194). Hoboken, NJ: Wiley.

Ramirez, M. (1984). Multicultural/Multiracial Experience Inventory. In M. Ramirez (Ed.), *Multicultural/multiracial psychology* (pp. 245–254). Northvale, NJ: Jason Aronson.

Rezentes, W. C. (1993). Na Mea Hawai'i: A Hawaiian acculturation scale. *Psychological Reports*, *73*, 383–393. doi:10.2466/pr0.1993.73.2.383

Sakamoto, A., & Xie, Y. (2006). The socioeconomic attainment of Asian Americans. In P. G. Min (Ed.), *Asian–Americans. Contemporary trends and issues* (pp. 54–79). Thousand Oaks, CA: Pine Forge. doi:10.4135/9781452233802.n4

Schwartz, M. (2012). Second generation immigrants: A socio-linguistic approach of linguistic development within the framework of family language policy. In M. Leiken, M. Schwartz, & Y. Tobin (Eds.), *Current issues in bilingualism: Cognitive and socio-linguistic perspectives* (pp. 119–136). Dordrecht, Holland: Springer Science + Business Media.

Schwartz, M., Kozminsky, E., & Leikin, M. (2009). Socio-linguistic factors in second language lexical knowledge: The case of second-generation children of Russian–Jewish immigrants in Israel. *Language, Culture and Curriculum*, *22*(1), 15–28. doi:10.1080/07908310802504119

Snowden, L. R., & Hines, A. M. (1999). A scale to assess African American acculturation. *The Journal of Black Psychology*, *25*, 36–47. doi:10.1177/0095798499025001003

Storch, N. (2010). Critical feedback on written corrective feedback research. *International Journal of English Studies*, *10*(2), 29–46.

Sue, D. W., & Sue, D. (1999). *Counseling the culturally different: Theory and practice*. New York, NY: Wiley.

Suinn, R. M., Rickard-Figueroa, K., Lew, S., & Vigil, P. (1987). The Suinn-Lew Asian Self Identity Acculturation Scale: An initial report. *Educational and Psychological Measurement*, *47*, 401–407. doi:10.1177/0013164487472012

Szapocznik, J., Scopetta, M. A., Kurtines, W., & Aranalde, M. A. (1978). Behavioral Acculturation Scale and Value Acculturation Scale. *International Journal of Psychology*, *12*, 113–130.

Taras, V. (2008). *Instruments for measuring acculturation*. Retrieved from http://ucalgary.ca/~taras/_private/Acculturation_Survey_Catalogue.pdf

Thomas, W. P., & Collier, V. P. (2000). Accelerated schooling for all students: Research findings on education in multilingual communities. In P. Gibbon (Ed.), *Intercultural education in European classrooms* (pp. 15–36). Stoke-on-Trent, England: Trentham Books.

Triandis, H. C., Kashima, Y., Hui, H., Lisansky, J., & Marin, G. (1982). Acculturation and biculturalism indices among relatively acculturated Hispanic young adults. *Interamerican Journal of Psychology*, *16*, 140–149.

Tropp, L. R., Erkut, S., Coll, C. G., Alarcón, O., & García, H. A. V. (1999). Psychological acculturation: Development of a new measure for Puerto Ricans on the U.S. mainland. *Educational and Psychological Measurement*, *59*, 351–367. doi:10.1177/00131649921969794

Van Beuningen, C. (2010). Corrective feedback in L2 writing: Theoretical perspectives, empirical insights, and future directions. *International Journal of English Studies*, *10*(2), 1–27.

Washoe County School District. (2009). *Response to intervention for English language learners. Secondary.* Retrieved from http://www.washoe.k12.nv.us/rti/secondary_ell.pdf

Watson, S. M. R., Rinaldi, C., Navarrete, L., Bianco, M., & Samson, J. (2007). *Info sheet about diverse learners.* Retrieved from https://www.cldinternational.org/InfoSheets/Diverse.asp

Wong, P., Lai, C. F., Nagasawa, R., & Lin, T. (1998). Asian Americans as a model minority: Self-perceptions and perceptions by other racial groups. *Sociological Perspectives, 41*(1), 95–118. doi:10.2307/1389355

Wong-Rieger, D., & Quintana, D. (1987). Comparative acculturation of Southeast Asian and Hispanic immigrants and sojourners. *Journal of Cross-Cultural Psychology, 18,* 345–362. doi:10.1177/0022002187018003005

Wu, C.-H. (2010). *The evaluation of second language fluency and foreign accent* (Doctoral dissertation). Retrieved from https://www.ideals.illinois.edu/bitstream/handle/2142/24027/Wu_Chen-huei.pdf?sequence=1

9

ASSESSING BILINGUAL STUDENTS' WRITING

JILL FITZGERALD, CAROL B. OLSON, SANDRA G. GARCIA,
AND ROBIN C. SCARCELLA

Marisela Gonzalez (a pseudonym) is a 12-year-old student attending sixth grade[1] in a large urban middle school in Santa Ana, California, where 98% of the students are Chicano/Latino and 88% are designated as English learners. An immigrant from Mexico, Marisela arrived in the United States at the age of 6, and after being enrolled in English language development for bilingual learners earlier in elementary school, was transitioned into mainstream English language arts. Marisela speaks Spanish at home, and she is quite fluent in conversational English due to her many years of exposure to English in school. However, she is still struggling to acquire academic English, and her writing reflects her struggle.

On one occasion, to assess the writing ability of Marisela and her classmates, her teacher, Ms. Maria Gómez-Greenberg, read an article to the students about an earthquake in Haiti titled, "Sometimes the Earth Is Cruel,"

---

[1]The details of the case studies have been changed to protect the anonymity of the individuals involved.

http://dx.doi.org/10.1037/14320-010
Assessing Bilingual Children in Context: An Integrated Approach, A. B. Clinton (Editor)

by award-winning journalist Leonard Pitts (2010). She asked the students to follow along silently as she read aloud. After clarifying the meaning of difficult vocabulary words and discussing the article, she gave them 50 minutes to write an analytical essay about the author's theme in the text and also to discuss how he used both literal and figurative language to convey his meaning. Marisela wrote the following:

> In this story there was alot of people that sufferd. People died and sufferd from all the earthquakes. Also, littel boys and girls parents died. People had to reboit their houses when they Gought destroyed. Alot of people sufferd because every year there was an earthquake. It only happen to hati that why people were tired of it. After the arthquack happened people were very bore. It was very bad alot people died over 100,000 people died this last earthquack. Sometimes when it raind it will not stop for days. Sometimes the earth was cruel, but they had no choice but to exept it. That is how much the sufferd. When people died the dig there selfes they weep and mourn we recover and memoriaize the dead. People also got very sick and neded medisen. People use to pray that begins, "There, but for the grace of good . . .". People did everything they can. People use to write relief checks, donate blood, volunteer material and time and to fear. That what people did to help people that were very sick. Thats why we should be happy to be safe. This story is a good example. so people can see what will happen if that was us. Also, people can help and doneate stuff like close, shoes, meony, old stuff, to us. I think we should do that to help our people that are very sick. alot of people died of bing hongry because the earth quake distroyed there homes and there food.

In this chapter, we address central issues involved in thinking about writing assessment when students such as Marisela write in a second language. We consider prior theory and research that supports our stance on bilingual writing assessment, and we propose a set of guidelines for considering composing and composition assessment for bilingual students. Throughout our chapter, we illustrate selected points by periodically returning to Marisela's composition and her teacher's assessment of her writing.

Writing assessment is a complicated issue to address even for monolingual students. When bilingualism is involved, it is even more complicated because, as other authors of this volume attest, cultural and situational attachments are threaded with language use in myriad ways (cf. Garcia & Pearson, 1991). One of our first tasks is to consider how much complexity we might address in a single chapter. To center our work, we begin by considering how the term *bilingual writing* can be used to refer to different situations. For the purposes of our chapter, we use this term to refer to the composing processes used by, and compositions produced by, individuals who are (a) learning to compose in a new language while continuing to learn to compose in their native language, (b) learning to compose in a new language with no continuing instruction in native language, and/or (c) mature bilingual individuals proficient in composing in two or more languages. Some issues and considerations weave through all three bilingual situations, but each bilingual situation also poses unique issues and considerations.

In this chapter, although the issues and framework we present are applicable to all three bilingual situations, we focus primarily on writing assessment in the second language. We mainly have in mind situations in which immigrant students are immersed in a new language in their everyday environment and their native language is used primarily in their homes. Because our own experiences are embedded in the context of the United States where immigrant students are learning English, our examples come from that situation. We caution, however, that it is important to keep in mind that the cultural and sociopolitical considerations of other contexts, such as learning a second language through studying a subject (e.g., native Korean students learning English through English classes in their homeland), can affect how writing is taught, appreciated, and assessed.

The need to better understand bilingual writing assessment—how to accomplish it, how to interpret results, and how to use it to improve instruction—is great. Few international data are available to inform school-age children's performance when writing in a second language, whether it occurs in English-as-a-foreign-language school-subject settings or in immigrant immersion in countries where the language is different from the mother tongue. However, the most recent National Assessment of Educational Progress (National Assessment of Educational Progress, National Center for Education Statistics, National Assessment Governing Board, Institute of Education Sciences, U.S. Department of Education, 2011a, 2011b; U.S. Department of Education, Institute of Education Sciences, National Center for Education Statistics, 2012) in the United States revealed a significant gap between the computer-based English writing of eighth-grade English learners and their monolingual peers, with English learners averaging a score of 108 versus their monolingual counterparts' mean score of 152 (scale range is 0 to 300, $M = 150$, $SD = 35$). Of eighth-grade English language learners, 65% performed below the basic level and 29% performed below the proficient level. At the 12th grade, the gap was wider: 96 versus 152, with 80% of English learners performing below the basic level and 99% scoring below the proficient level. Such status reports coupled with the growing number of second language learners worldwide suggest that serious attention to bilingual writing assessment is needed.

In the following sections, we convey the need for research and theory on bilingual writing and explain the outlook on composing and development of writing over time that has influenced our thinking. We then propose a set of guidelines for considering composing and composition assessment for bilingual students.

NEED FOR RESEARCH AND THEORY ON BILINGUAL WRITING AND THE ORIGINS OF OUR STANCE ON BILINGUAL WRITING ASSESSMENT

Understanding of bilingual writing assessment must be based on a sound research-based theory of how bilingual writing develops over time—in our case, to be more specific, how second language writing develops over time. Unfortunately, to our knowledge, little formal or comprehensive theory specific to the bilingual, or even second language, writing case exists. Although hazards exist in the blanket application of monolingual writing theory to bilingual writing situations, we suggest that as a start, at least some of what is known about monolingual composing and its development might serve as a springboard for considering issues involved in bilingual writing assessment.

Composing Processes

How we conceptualize composing and composition should affect how we conceptualize their assessment when individuals are writing in a second language. In this part of the chapter, we focus on an epistemological outlook on composing processes as opposed to composition products—processes that likely adhere for bilingual individuals writing in a second language. A key tenet of our outlook is that composing processes are both social and cognitive. Figure 9.1 depicts a rough amalgamation of composing processes that are embedded in a transactional setting in which authors deploy a complex of strategies and mechanisms. Of course, students who are composing in a second language bring to bear social and cognitive processes from previously learned languages and the new language they are learning, and cross-linguistic interactions may occur as well. It is precisely that set of interactions that we need to explicate more fully in the future if we are to round out a sound theory of composing in a second language.

Social Processes

The two-way arrows in Figure 9.1 represent social understandings used by authors who work to connect with imagined readers. Forerunners of the view that social processes undergird composing include Young, Becker, and Pike's new rhetoric dating from 1970, the work of Bahktin (1981), Bizzel (1982), Bruffee (1986), and to a limited extent, the social constructionism

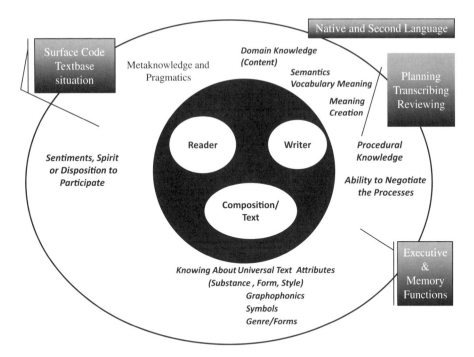

Figure 9.1. Composing as transaction. A rough amalgamation of composing processes that are embedded in a transactional setting in which authors deploy a complex of strategies and mechanisms. From "Struggling Writers: Constructing Their Instruction: What and How," by J. Fitzgerald, 2013, *Annals of Dyslexia,* 63, p. 81. Copyright 2011 by Springer. Adapted with permission.

of Bartholomae (1985). In describing composition as negotiation of meaning between author and reader, Nystrand (1989) wrote, "Written communication is a fiduciary act for both writers and readers in which they continuously seek to orient themselves to a projected state of convergence between them" (p. 75). Authors are social actors who write to "engage in social dialogues with other people, using certain genres to enact certain relationships" (Dyson, 1992, p. 41). The social processes at play in constructing meaning in a second language deserve assessment attention (T. McNamara, 2001).

Social habits and learned understandings that are different across cultures may contribute to special challenges when students write in a second language (Gonzalez, Moll, & Amanti, 2005; Trumbull & Farr, 2005). Genre or rhetorical structure differences may exist across cultures, and students' knowledge of vocabulary, morphology, and syntax can also be bound by culture. Student sociolinguistic experiences in a particular culture are often stored as automatic responses and understandings that may transfer in a facilitative or inhibitory way to second language writing. As an example, how narratives are structured for specific situations and particular audiences with particular goals, and even the frequency with which narratives occur, varies across cultural settings. A classic case in the literature is that native Pacific Islanders tend to tell stories through communal interruption, with one speaker interrupting to elaborate on another speaker's point, gradually building a story together (Tharp, 1982). Pacific Islander children intuitively learn the story structure they hear in their homes. When learning another language, such as English, in which narratives are structured according to a European folktale tradition, writing the new story structure can be perplexing.

An additional example is that some second language writers might avoid directness and avoid writing thesis statements with strong claims because doing so is considered rude in the homeland culture. In some cultures, providing a lot of detailed embellishment of an idea is essential. However, in the United States, for academic writing, directness, strong theses, and sufficient but minimal detail are more commonly expected. As well, some individuals, such as recent immigrants to the United States, would not have sufficient subject matter knowledge for topics that are clearly geographically and socio-culturally linked, such as Thanksgiving or the Fourth of July.

Cognitive Processes

Figure 9.1 shows four categories of cognitive processes and one emotional–cognitive category represented in the outer circle. The four sets of cognitive processes are the following: (a) Writers use metaknowledge and pragmatics (e.g., Langer, 1986), such as knowing about the functions and purposes of composing, knowing that authors interact with readers, monitoring one's own meaning making, and monitoring word production strategies; (b) domain knowledge, often called *world knowledge* or *prior knowledge*, is another cognitive factor that comes into play; (c) procedural and conditional knowledge (Langer, 1986) are constantly involved—that is, knowing how to access, use, and generate knowledge, as well as integrating processes and knowing when to activate and use knowledge for a particular composing occasion (Kellogg, 1994); and (d) writers also need knowledge about universally desirable characteristics of the written composition, such as orthographics, sentence syntactical rules (Kellogg, 1994), and syntax of larger chunks of text—organization and genre (Shanahan, 1984). Finally, a set of emotional–cognitive factors includes sentiments about composing and the spirit or disposition to compose.

Moreover, during composing, writers must act on three mental levels. They must think about the explicit ideas and subject matter they want to write about, often called the *situation model* (D. S. McNamara & Kintsch, 1996). In narratives, the situation model includes characters, actions, events, processes, characters' thoughts and emotions, and more. In informational text, it involves the substance of the matter being discussed, such as components of a system and their relationships, properties of the components, and more (Graesser, McNamara, & Kulikowich, 2011). The bilingual writer also needs to put the ideas and subject matter from the situation base into specific propositions, or meaningful thoughts, still free of print, often called the *textbase* (D. S. McNamara & Kintsch, 1996). Then the author also must set the situation model and corresponding textbase into actual print, called the *surface code representation* (D. S. McNamara & Kintsch, 1996). Finally, all of the trileveled mental activity occurs throughout planning, text generation, and reviewing (Hayes, 2006).

Central processing factors involved in written composition include working memory, short- and long-term memory, self-regulation, and executive control of multiple processes. Self-regulation refers to occasions when individuals manage their own mental mechanisms such as during planning and revising (Graham & Harris, 2000). The central executive function in working memory is a monitor or system for devoting attention (Baddeley, 2001). It oversees storage components, a fluid component and a crystallized one, and interactions among them.

Finally, neurological factors are involved in composing. For example, neurological and psychological research evidence has also pointed to syntactical and lexical features in written composition as potential proxies for the centrality of working memory in composing (Vanderberg & Swanson, 2007). Neurological studies have supported the contention that word generation fluency is involved in regions of the brain thought to be associated with working memory (Wagner, Paré-Blagoev, Clark, & Poldrack, 2001). Spelling in written compositions has also been shown to strongly reflect working memory (Crosson et al., 1999), and different functional magnetic resonance imaging patterns have been observed on writing tasks for better as compared with poorer writers. For instance, when writing newly taught letters, poorer writers activate more brain regions than better writers (Richards et al., 2011). When writing familiar letters, better and poorer writers also show different brain activation in the left fusiform gyrus, a region associated with orthographic coding (Richards et al., 2011). As well, in the left inferior frontal gyrus brain region associated with working memory, connectivity normalized after children received 3 weeks of special instruction in spelling (Richards & Berninger, 2008).

To our knowledge, neurological evidence of any type about bilingual individuals' composing is less common than for monolinguals. However, the generally supported contention that language is primarily localized in the left hemisphere for monolingual right-handed individuals may not hold true for bilingual individuals. Recent research has found that hemispheric localization for language depends on bilingual status and age of acquisition of a second language (Peng & Wang, 2011). Bilateral hemispheric involvement for both languages has been revealed during reading tasks for individuals who acquired both languages by age 6, and left hemispheric dominance occurred for bilingual individuals who acquired the second language after age 6. The different hemispheric involvement during reading for bilingual individuals as compared with monolinguals could lead to conjecture that selected neurological bases that come into play for certain bilingual individuals during composing may differ from those that occur during monolingual composing.

Development of Writing Ability Over Time

With few exceptions, only recently has attention been paid to how individuals' composing and composition develop over time. Also, for the most part, writing development has been studied within limited age spans, rather than over a long period such as from preschool through early adulthood (Alamargot & Fayol, 2009; cf. Graham & Harris, 2011). In this section, we portray two ways of thinking about how writing ability develops over time. The first way is a model of critical factors involved in writing ability development described by Kellogg (2008). For the second way, we describe six phases of development as they are grounded in the four cognitive categories involved in composing, as depicted in Figure 9.1. The two ways of thinking about writing development are not mutually exclusive. Both outlooks are incomplete with regard to bilingual writing in that they do not specifically address ways in which bilingualism affects such development. However, they provide a sense of current views on writing development in general and are useful as a start for considering bilingual writing development and its assessment.

Kellogg's Developmental Model of Writing

Kellogg's (2008) developmental model of writing skill expanded on the earlier work of Bereiter and Scardamalia (1987). Kellogg proposed that mental microprocess changes, including development of working memory, drive an individual's progression across the life span through three macrostages of writing skill development. In Kellogg's outlook on writing development, working memory has a central role. Over time, automaticity in phonological loop, automaticity in visual–spatial-sketchpad processing, and working memory storage capacity permit greater attention to executive functioning and self-control over composing processes (Kellogg, 1996; Vanderberg & Swanson, 2007). *Phonological-loop* references memory traces for sounds and articulatory rehearsal that revive the memory traces. *The visual–spatial sketchpad* temporarily holds information about what is seen. The central activity across the developmental phases is to represent and coordinate in the mind the author's ideas, the text words, and the imagined reader's interpretation.

The first phase is *knowledge telling,* in which an individual's facility with text and imagined reader representations is limited. For example, for younger children, lower level linguistic aspects of composing consume considerable working memory resources, and little capacity remains to devote to other issues, such as potential reader engagement (e.g., McCutchen, 1996). Marisela's essay in the opening of our chapter reflects her knowledge-telling stance. Instead of addressing the prompt, she simply summarized the events described in Leonard Pitt's (2010) article.

The second phase is *knowledge transforming,* in which text representation becomes more detailed and an individual can interact more stably with written text representations. For instance, typically developing older children and adolescents with larger working memory spans use revision processes that include macrostructure representations of text, versus those with smaller working memory spans who tend to use narrower forms of revision. Older students' compositions contain a higher proportion of words that are nouns, which in turn has been considered to reflect the older students' increased visual–spatial sketchpad capacity in working memory (Hudson, 2009). Furthermore, word diversity in compositions has been shown to be positively related to age and judgments of quality of composition (Chipere, Malvern, Richards, & Durán, 2001). As well, individual differences in working memory are more predictive of junior high students' composition quality as compared with that of intermediate-level students, and that of intermediate-level students compared with that of primary grade students (Berninger, Fuller, & Whitaker, 1996).

The third phase is *knowledge crafting,* an advanced stage that characterizes mature writers, including professional writers, who have great facility in the mental representations necessary to the writer–composition–reader transaction and who are especially facile in writing to the imagined reader.

Six Phases of Cognitive Development Over Time: Different Cognitions Are More or Less Crucial at Different Phases of an Individual's Writing Development

Another way to think about development of writing over long periods is to consider how the four main cognitive categories develop over time—the categories shown in the outer circle in Figure 9.1—that is, metaknowledge and pragmatics, domain knowledge, procedural knowledge, and knowledge of universal text attributes. In the following section, we depict six phases of writing development, drawing heavily from the earlier work of Shanahan and Lomax (1986, 1988), Chall (1996), and especially Fitzgerald and Shanahan (2000): literacy roots, initial literacy, confirmation and fluency, writing for learning the new, and taking multiple stances, and deeper analysis and synthesis. We emphasize that the four cognitive categories are at play during composing all the time throughout various developmental progressions. However, our key point in the following exposition is that certain cognitive categories play critical roles at particular developmental levels more than at other developmental levels. Notice that across the six phases, different cognitive categories are highlighted as crucial. When educators understand that different cognitive factors are highlighted at different developmental phases, they can use that knowledge during assessment and instruction to discern students' level of development and move students from one phase to another. We return to this point in a later section on guidelines for writing assessment (see the subsection "Diagnostic Assessment" in Guideline 3 and also Guideline 6, "Value Students' Developmental Level While Writing in the Second Language").

Phase 1: Literacy Roots. Literacy roots, one of the most essential cognitive categories in the earliest phase of learning to compose, is the beginning of learning about universal text attributes. In literacy roots, children start to gain an understanding about the way compositions "look"—for example, that words move left to right on the page, that words are bounded by white space, that ideas are often marked by capitals for the first word in a sentence and a punctuation mark at the end, and that letters look different on the page than stories do. Students learn that they can put pencil to paper to represent thoughts. Scribbling and drawing mark the first efforts and signal students' learning that marks on a page represent an author's intent to convey or create something. In essence, learning about symbols and simple genre issues in primitive ways takes precedence. As children move toward the next phase, they begin to learn about *graphophonics* and *orthographics*, the particular language's sounds, letters, and words. They begin to learn the nature of words in the language, that some words sound the same at their ends or beginnings, that they can be broken into parts, and that the parts can be put together.

Phase 2: Initial Literacy. In the second phase, *initial literacy*, knowledge of universal text attributes continues to grow, with graphophonics and orthographics now taking center stage. During this period, for instance, writers learn that words have certain letters that represent sounds and that some words have certain "looks"—for instance, a silent *e* at the end of a word makes a difference in how a word sounds (e.g., Gentry & Gillet, 1993).

Phase 3: Confirmation and Fluency. During the *confirmation and fluency* phase, consolidation of lower level, previously learned strategies and understandings occurs, such that lower level linguistic abilities, such as spelling simple words, become more automatic, and more attention is released for the cognitions in the procedural knowledge category to take center stage. As strategies for writing words and sentences become more integrated, automatic, and fluent, students are better able to write longer words and sentences with more complex sentence.

Phase 4: Writing for Learning the New. In the fourth phase, *writing for learning the new*, there is a dramatic turn from the word- and sound-level work of linking thoughts to speech to print and toward higher level linguistic factors, such as learning more about rhetorical structures and genres (in the cognitive category, universal text attributes). The cognitive category of procedural knowledge becomes increasingly important for knowing how to elaborate ideas, plan, transcribe, and revise.

Phases 5 and 6: Taking Multiple Stances and Deeper Analysis and Synthesis. As students move into the fifth and sixth phases, *taking multiple stances* and *deeper analysis and synthesis*, respectively, there is increased emphasis on the metaknowledge cognitive category as students learn how to analyze and critique their own writing while seeing it from the reader's point of view. They are better able to know how to write according to the expectations of readers. Domain knowledge becomes increasingly critical because it provides the child with substantive knowledge to write about. Vocabulary expansion, especially having a diverse vocabulary, is particularly important for representing a student's domain knowledge in compositions and undergirding the growth of author's voice.

Compositions as Windows Into Composing Processes

Especially important for bilingual writing assessment, composition characteristics can be viewed as windows into authors' cognitive processes (Vanderberg & Swanson, 2007). Selected features of compositions have long been viewed as proxies, approximations, or correlates of underlying mental processes (cf. Attali & Burstein, 2006). Syntactic complexity and orthographic correctness in a composition are examples of composition characteristics thought to reflect working memory phonological-loop capacity and efficiency (cf. Kellogg, 2008). Examples of composition representations of authors' mental visual–spatial sketchpad capacity are word choice, such as the extent of word diversity as measured by type-token ratio and lexical density, and sophistication, whether a word carries broad, deep, nuanced, and/or associated meanings (cf. Hudson, 2009; Kellogg, 2008). In the following sections, we highlight various ways in which composition characteristics can be used during bilingual writing assessment.

GUIDELINES FOR ASSESSING WRITING
WITH BILINGUAL STUDENTS

We propose a preliminary set of guidelines for practitioners for making decisions about bilingual students' writing. We present the guidelines tentatively because there is a great need for more research and theory development around composing when writing in a second language. The guidelines are organized in Appendix 9.1 as a checklist for educator use.

Assessment guidelines can be useful to educators and others who assess bilingual students' writing because they imply the need for educators to understand how composing develops for bilingual individuals. Although a battery of tests could be implemented for bilingual writing assessment, educators who work from an informed knowledge base about composing and bilingual writing development can better interpret students' writing status, have a basis for setting goals for students' learning, and know which composing abilities to emphasize next in instruction so that students will make the greatest progress. Implicit in the establishment and use of guidelines is the assumption that writing assessment is an ongoing activity.

Guideline 1: Be Aware of One's Own Lenses as We Assess Bilingual Students' Writing

Teachers and educational specialists see bilingual students' composing processes and compositions through the lens of their own backgrounds and experiences. When assessing bilingual students' writing, personal lenses may result in overlooking or distorting important information. As we examine bilingual students' second language writing, it is especially important to be aware of how monolingual lenses or backgrounds in writing instruction might warp what we see.

For example, Marisela's teacher, Ms. Gómez-Greenberg, is a second language learner herself. Having immigrated to the United States from Colombia when she was 13, she has a special empathy for her students' struggles with academic English. Also, as a native Spanish speaker, she can take advantage of her knowledge of *cognates*, or words that look similar in Spanish and English, as well as her own earlier challenges in learning English, to help her students understand the meaning of many English words. However, she received little instruction in how to write academic essays in English herself. Ms. Goméz-Greenberg has had limited preparation in how to teach her students to master the formal register of English and genre conventions of the interpretive text-based essay that is so often the gateway to postsecondary success. As a consequence, she does not always know how best to address the challenges presented in her students' essays. Fortunately, Ms. Gómez-Greenberg volunteered to participate in her district's 2-year professional development program to enhance her already strong cultural lens as well as her abilities as a writing specialist.

Guideline 2: Be Aware That Writing Assessment Is a Sensitive Matter for Bilingual Students

An individual's identity is integrated into his or her language use (Gee, 2000). When we assess language in compositions, we touch on more than an essay because we are given a sense of a person's identity (T. McNamara, 2001). For students who are becoming bilingual and learning to write in a second language, we want to provide encouragement in this complex process of personal and academic development. For example, when Ms. Gómez-Greenberg evaluated Marisela's essay, she did not use a red pen to mark the paper. She wanted to boost Marisela's confidence, to help her to feel good about herself as an emerging writer, so she took care to open her comments to Marisela with a "glow" (a positive comment) and to close with an encouraging word. Ms. Goméz-Greenberg further communicated to Marisela a sense of certainty that her student would improve her writing during a second draft of the essay. Notice her language in the opening and ending of her response letter to Marisela:

> [Opening.] You did a great job explaining your reaction to the article. Your sympathy for the Haitian people is heartfelt.

> [Closing.] When you revise, remember to talk about what the theme of the article is. Why is Leonard Pitts writing this article? What is he telling the reader? Remember that the theme is the author's message or main idea. In your next draft, break down your paper into three parts: an introduction, a main body (which may consist of several paragraphs), and a conclusion. Be sure to discuss the language the author uses to discuss the earthquake and its impact on the Haitian people. Do you remember when we studied personification? Look for that. I have circled several misspelled words on your paper that I want you to correct. If you spell a lot as two words, you'll already have fixed a lot of the errors in your paper. . . . Good luck on your next draft.

Guideline 3: Consider the Specific Purpose for Assessment at the Moment of Assessment

There can be many purposes for bilingual writing assessments. Two primary types of bilingual assessment are summative/comparative and diagnostic assessment, and the two tend to be linked to another important dimension: whether one is assessing the writer's composing processes or the writer's composition products.

Summative/Comparative Assessment

The purpose of *summative/comparative assessment* is to make a global statement about a student's overall writing achievement status at a single point and often to consider it in comparison with some group or groups (Romberg, 2008; cf. Gardner, 2012). As well, summative assessment is often used to consider where a student's writing achievement is in relation to long-range development (cf. Gardner, 2012). Summative assessment typically focuses on students' written products, or writing performance, without attending to the composing processes that go into the final product.

Ms. Gómez-Greenberg provided summative assessment for Marisela's essay. She took careful notes about how fluent the essay writing was, its overall quality, how sophisticated the ideas were, Marisela's knowledge and command of essay structure, and her control of mechanics. She rated the essay 2 on a 6-point scale.

Summative/comparative assessment is often accomplished with a standardized test, and typically, English learners are included in large-scale assessments. For instance, in the United States, the National Assessment of Educational Progress (National Assessment of Educational Progress, National Center for Education Statistics, National Assessment Governing Board, Institute of Education Sciences, U.S. Department of Education, 2011a, 2011b) uses a standardized test to gauge students' English writing achievement at given points and to compare the writing achievement status of subgroups of students, such as English learners versus monolingual English students. Although critics of the practice abound (e.g., Garcia & Pearson, 1991; Mountford, 1999; Roever & McNamara, 2006), school district personnel in the United States sometimes require that English learners take the same standardized English tests that native English speakers take.

A common standardized writing assessment used in the United States is the Test of Written Language 4 (Hammill & Larsen, 2009), which measures 9- to 17-year-olds' conventional linguistic and conceptual aspects of English writing, such as vocabulary, spelling, and sentence combining. Another commonly used standardized measure of writing is the Test of Early Written Language (Hresko, Herron, Peak, & Hicks, 2012), which measures 4- to 11-year-olds' understanding of English language and mechanics as well as ability to create a story from a picture. Finally, the Oral and Written Language Scales (Carrow-Woolfolk, 2011), for 5- to 21-year-olds, measures multiple linguistic levels of written English language (lexical, syntactic, pragmatic, and supralinguistic).

Although standardized scores may provide information about a bilingual student's writing in relation to monolingual peers' writing, it is also extremely important to recognize the limitations of using such standardized assessments with bilingual students. Comparing second language learners' composing and/or compositions with monolingual speakers' composing and/or compositions must be contextualized in relation to the bilingual learner's length of time in the country and/or length of English study time and more.

Even when second language learners are included in the norming sample for standardized tests, common psychometric standards for sample size are often not met (McCauley & Swisher, 1984). There is some minimal psychometric evidence that when nonadjudicated scores are used for large-scale writing assessment developed primarily for monolingual native speakers, English writing score error estimates for English learners were greater than for their counterpart monolingual students (Huang, 2012), raising the question of biased assessment. Finally, some standardized test authors allow for accommodations for second language learners, but a recent meta-analysis of the most common types of accommodations for a variety of tests used with English learners in the United States revealed that most accommodations do not pose a significant benefit to the student (Kieffer, Lesaux, Rivera, & Francis, 2009). Of seven accommodations studied (e.g., giving a dictionary, allowing extra time), only one—providing English dictionaries or glossaries—had a statistically significant effect on English learners' performance in mathematics or science assessments. In short, caution and caveats are in order when interpreting second language learners' writing status when using standardized tests that were created for monolinguals.

Diagnostic Assessment

The main purpose of *diagnostic assessment* is to consider not just the overall quality of a student's composition but also what the composition reveals about the author's strengths and challenges in relation to concurrent goals for the student's learning about composing. For diagnostic assessment, compositions are viewed as windows into authors' thinking. The educator examines how composition characteristics reflect a student's knowledge about composing. The informed writing educator has a sound understanding of composing processes and their developmental progression. In the case of bilingual composing, without a formal theoretical and research-based understanding of bilingual or second language composing, it is likely that writing educators need to fall back, at least in part, on what is known about monolingual composing as was summarized in the opening to this chapter.

We emphasize diagnostic assessment because it likely has more potential for affecting everyday instruction than summative assessment. Diagnostic assessment is important for helping students to make progress in writing in a new language (De Ramírez & Shapiro, 2006; García, 1991). It can be done purposefully at a given time or during daily instruction at any time a student has written a composition, including drafts of a composition and with any type of writing—argumentative, persuasive, descriptive, narrative, and so on. When accomplished with everyday writing, it is authentic and curriculum-based in nature, meaning it is situated in daily classroom kinds of writing. Another positive feature of diagnostic assessment is that it generally includes multiple indices of student development, with different foci and different ways of helping a teacher or parent to get a more robust understanding of a student's knowledge about composing (Garcia & Pearson, 1991; LaCelle-Peterson & Rivera, 1994).

In Exhibit 9.1, we extract from Figure 9.1 some of the most critical features of compositions to consider in relation to understanding bilingual students' thinking during composing in a second language. Though it is not a comprehensive list, it offers a way to consider whether students' compositions reflect various processes. From Marisela's composition at the opening of this chapter, here are a few examples of how educators might use the writing sample to garner some important diagnostic information about Marisela's thinking. First, learning how to write organizational structures for key genre is an important cognitive ability (in Exhibit 9.1, see the third entry under "Knowledge of Universal Text Attributes"). When Ms. Gómez-Greenberg read Marisela's essay, she realized Marisela had little understanding of how to structure a formal essay. For example, her essay lacked a lead-in sentence, a thesis statement, and supporting details. Instead, Marisela joined her ideas into one long paragraph. As a result of her diagnostic assessment, Ms. Gómez-Greenberg decided to teach Marisela about key features of the organizational structure of an academic essay. She taught her to write a formal introduction with a *hook,* or an attention-getting opening, taught her about *TAG* (title, author, genre), helped her to understand what a thesis is, showed her that a well-organized academic essay has a main body with evidence that might include quotations from the text, and explained that there should be a compelling conclusion.

EXHIBIT 9.1
Key Composing Processes to Assess for Second Language Writers

	Does the composition reflect that the author . . .
Social processes	Makes an effort to connect with intended audience?
Cognitive processes	Understands the need to write for an audience?
Metaknowledge/pragmatics	Understands the need to monitor the sensibility of what is written?
Domain knowledge	Has background knowledge sufficient to the composing task?
Procedural knowledge	Knows and uses planning, revision, and other strategies?
Knowledge of universal text attributes	Has mastered at a developmentally appropriate level the mechanics of the language used in writing?
	Has mastered at a developmentally appropriate level the sentence-level grammatical rues in the language of writing?
	Has mastered at a developmentally appropriate level the organizational structures for key genre?
	Shows evidence of native language facilitation or interference?
Emotional/motivational intention	Is sufficiently motivated to complete the composing task?

As another example, Marisela's composition reflected a need to expand her writing for a particular audience, or her *metaknowledge* (see the cognitive category "Metaknowledge/Pragmatics" in Exhibit 9.1). Marisela used conversational English to write her essay. In formal essays, a different register of English is expected by the reader. For example, instead of "doneate stuff like close [sic]," we might say, "donate articles of clothing."

As a third example, Ms. Gómez-Greenberg realized she needed to develop a plan for how to tackle Marisela's numerous spelling errors (see the first entry in Exhibit 9.1 under "Knowledge of Universal Text Attributes"). Ms. Gómez-Greenberg chose one spelling pattern in particular—the understanding that past tense spelling often requires an *e* before a *d*—and she taught a mini-lesson to Marisela and others in the class who displayed the same lack of orthographic knowledge.

Guideline 4: Use Writing Assessment to Build Students' Motivation to Write

For many new language learners, especially for new arrivals to foreign lands, such as immigrants or refugees, feelings of isolation can be intense (Bhugra, 2004). As other authors in this volume attest, one's new language sounds strange, and cultural differences loom large; thus, students can feel they are outsiders in the new classroom setting. Sometimes, learning to express oneself in writing can be one way out of isolation. When educators consider such factors in relation to how they assess bilingual students' composing and their compositions, they hold a key to bolstering students' motivations to continue to write. Guidelines 5 and 6 are specific examples that can help to build student motivation through assessment.

Guideline 5: Focus on the "Big Things" First

Placing construction of meaning above all else in assessment is an important guideline; it is also one that can help promote students' motivation to write. When we value the content of what is being conveyed and reaching the audience over lower-level features such as correct grammar or correct spelling, we empower students' voices. It is not that lower linguistic matters are unimportant. Rather, assessment of ideas, meaning, word choice, emotion, and voice are primary. Assessment of linguistic features such as sentence syntax and spelling are secondary. When bilingual students understand that we mainly want them to think of composing and composition as expressions of inner thoughts and knowledge and to think of composing as a means of reaching out to another person, they write more freely. In such a way, emphasizing the best way to construct an essay to convey meaning can be motivating, which in turn leads to students wanting to write more and further improve their writing.

When Ms. Gómez-Greenberg wrote her response to Marisela's essay, she did not overwhelm her by pointing out all of the problems or challenges in the piece. Instead, she thought about the most important "big" issue—ensuring the big idea, the "theme," would come across well. Her opening suggestion in her response to Marisela was to think about the theme. To prompt Marisela, she asked two questions: "Why is Leonard Pitts writing this article?" and "What is he telling the reader?" She also reminded Marisela of the definition of "theme": "the author's message or main idea." Ms. Gómez-Greenberg also talked about another "big idea": text structure, and she followed her emphasis on theme with explicit instructions about how Marisela might organize her essay in a next draft. She left the "smaller" issue of spelling to last in her response, and even there, she suggested that Marisela focus on one type of misspelling in particular.

Guideline 6: Value Students' Developmental Level While Writing in the Second Language

The goal of bilingual writing assessment should be to move the bilingual student through a series of developmental progressions toward mastery. Although we do not have sufficient research on the issue of how bilingual individuals at different ages acquire the ability to write in a new language or how they move through developmental phases, when we assess their composing and compositions, we can be alert to the individual's current developmental level. Understanding current outlooks on how writing develops over time can aid educators to determine bilingual students' current levels of composing. As well, such understanding can help educators know what to emphasize, given a student's particular developmental phase.

All features of writing in the new language cannot advance simultaneously. We can set incremental goals for students when we praise what a student is doing well in relation to the specific developmental level the student's writing reflects. We can deemphasize composing processes and features of compositions that are out of reach but emphasize the ones that are within reach. Understanding the importance of different critical features at various progressions for typically developing monolingual writers could help educators to consider which stage individual second language writers are in.

It is also important for educators to understand that second language writers could progress through some or all the phases more or less rapidly than monolingual speakers. For instance, few native English-speaking adolescents have difficulty learning modal auxiliaries (e.g., *might be*, *can do*), articles (*the*, *a*), and causative structures (e.g., *he made me do it*), but many adolescent second language English learners do have significant difficulty learning such aspects of English. Still, examining second language writers' compositions and considering the phases of development could help educators think about what to emphasize in instruction to support students to the next stage.

Attention to daily informal assessments can provide clues to students' developmental phases, and they can be helpful in tracking students' progress through developmental phases over time. As an example, teachers can keep error logs, such as an error log for spelling, to look for patterns of errors that can inform students' cognitive development. Students who regularly use correct letters for initial sounds in words but commonly omit the (silent) letter *e* from ends of words, have not yet learned that how a word looks affects the sounds that some letters make in the word. Students who make such errors are likely to be anchored in Phase 2, the initial literacy phase, in the developmental progression we presented earlier. Educators who understand the phases of development can then realize that instructional focus on specific basic spelling patterns will help to move the students toward the next phase, confirmation and fluency.

As another example, when teachers realize that students are in a more advanced phase of bilingual writing, they can assess students' ability to elaborate ideas. For students who are anchored in Phase 4, writing for learning the new, over the course of 2 or 3 weeks educators might specifically focus on assessment of students' ability to extend and support major points in their compositions. A teacher could underline in blue major points in two or three compositions and circle in green supporting elaboration. For bilingual students who are not elaborating, the teacher could then offer a mini-lesson in how to extend and support ideas. The educator's diagnostic assessment in this case can lead the teacher to support bilingual writers' progression to the next phases of composing.

Marisela's essay is just one of many that Ms. Gómez-Greenberg saw on a weekly basis. Consistencies across essays written by Marisela at about the same time as the Haitian earthquake essay affirmed the teacher's judgment that Marisela's current developmental writing level was at the knowledge-telling stage and perhaps at the cusp of a Phase 2 (initial literacy) to Phase 3 (confirmation and fluency) progression. She is still grappling with graphophonics and orthographics, but she is also ready to dive into consolidating strategies and learning more about rhetorical structures. From the examples presented, it appears that Ms. Gómez-Greenberg provided important guidance in stretching Marisela's composing knowledge to lead her into a new progression.

CONCLUSION

After Ms. Gómez-Greenberg gave her response letter to Marisela and spent time in a mini-lesson or two, Marisela revised her essay. Here is her introduction to that essay:

> Watching the news, I heard that a horrific earthquake hit haiti. The earth is cruel article was written by Leonard Pitts. The story is about a terrible earthquake that happened in haiti. This earthquake was really horrible it destroyed lots of houses and killed many people. My theme is never give up and always try your best to survive.

Although some issues linger, Marisela's introduction was much improved. When, like Ms. Gómez-Greenberg, teachers consider central issues involved in bilingual writing assessment, they will successfully formulate instruction to promote growth in bilingual students' writing skill if they consider prior composing theory and research and are guided by a set of principles for assessment.

APPENDIX 9.1: CHECKLIST FOR ASSESSING BILINGUAL WRITERS

Be aware of our lenses.	☐
Be aware that writing assessment is a sensitive matter.	☐
Consider the purpose of assessment: Summative versus diagnostic.	☐
Consider how writing assessment can be used to motivate.	☐
Focus on the "big things" first.	☐
Value students' developmental level.	☐

REFERENCES

Alamargot, D., & Fayol, M. (2009). Modeling the development of written composition. In R. Beard, D. Myhill, J. Riley, & M. Nystrand (Eds.), *The SAGE handbook of writing development* (pp. 23–47). Los Angeles, CA: SAGE. doi:10.4135/9780857021069.n3

Attali, Y., & Burstein, J. (2006). Automated essay scoring with E-rater V. 2.0. *The Journal of Technology, Learning and Assessment, 4*(3), 13–18.

Baddeley, A. D. (2001). Is working memory still working? *American Psychologist, 56,* 851–864. doi:10.1037/0003-066X.56.11.851

Bahktin, M. M. (1981). *The dialogic imagination.* Austin: University of Texas Press.

Bartholomae, D. (1985). Inventing the university. In M. Rose (Ed.), *When a writer can't write* (pp. 134–165). New York, NY: Guilford Press.

Bereiter, C., & Scardamalia, M. (1987). *The psychology of written composition.* Hillsdale, NJ: Erlbaum.

Berninger, V., Fuller, F., & Whitaker, D. (1996). A process approach to writing development across the life span. *Educational Psychology Review, 8,* 193–218. doi:10.1007/BF01464073

Bhugra, D. (2004). Migration, distress and cultural identity. *British Medical Bulletin, 69,* 129–141. doi:10.1093/bmb/ldh007

Bizzel, P. (1982). Cognition, convention, and certainty: What we need to know about writing. *PRE/TEXT, 3,* 213–243.

Bruffee, K. A. (1986). Social construction, language, and the authority of knowledge: A bibliographical essay. *College English, 48,* 773–790. doi:10.2307/376723

Carrow-Woolfolk, E. (2011). *Oral and Written Language Scale II.* Torrance, CA: Western Psychological Services.

Chall, J. S. (1996). *Stages of reading development.* Fort Worth, TX: Harcourt Brace.

Chipere, N., Malvern, D. D., Richards, B. J., & Durán, P. (2001). *Using a corpus of school children's writing to investigate the development of lexical diversity.* Retrieved from http://ucrel.lancs.ac.uk/publications/CL2003/CL2001%20conference/papers/chipere.pdf

Crosson, B., Rao, S. M., Woodley, S. J., Rosen, A. C., Hammeke, T. A., Bobholz, J. A., . . . Stein, E. A. (1999). Mapping of semantic, phonological, and orthographic verbal working memory in normal adults with functional magnetic resonance imaging. *Neuropsychology, 13,* 171–187. doi:10.1037/0894-4105.13.2.171

De Ramírez, R. D., & Shapiro, E. S. (2006). Curriculum-based measurement and the evaluation of reading skills of Spanish-speaking English language learners in bilingual education classrooms. *School Psychology Review, 35,* 356–369.

Dyson, A. H. (1992). The case of the singing scientist: A performance perspective on the "stages" of school literacy. *Written Communication, 9*, 3–47. doi:10.1177/0741088392009001001

Fitzgerald, J. (2013). Struggling writers: Constructing their instruction: What and How. *Annals of Dyslexia, 63*, 80–95.

Fitzgerald, J., & Shanahan, T. (2000). Reading and writing relationships and their development. *Educational Psychologist, 35*, 39–50. doi:10.1207/S15326985 EP3501_5

García, G. E. (1991). Factors influencing the English reading test performance of Spanish-speaking Hispanic children. *Reading Research Quarterly, 26*, 371–392. doi:10.2307/747894

Garcia, G. E., & Pearson, P. D. (1991). The role of assessment in a diverse society. In E. H. Hiebert (Ed.), *Literacy for a diverse society: Perspectives, practices, and policies.* (pp. 253–278). New York, NY: Teachers College Press.

Gardner, J. (2012). Quality assessment practice. In J. Gardner (Ed.), *Assessment and learning* (2nd ed., pp. 103–122). Thousand Oaks, CA: Sage. doi:10.4135/9781446250808.n7

Gee, J. (2000). Identity as an analytic lens for research in education. *Review of Research in Education, 25*, 99–125.

Gentry, J. R., & Gillet, J. W. (1993). *Teaching kids to spell.* Portsmouth, NH: Heinemann.

Gonzalez, M., Moll, L. C., & Amanti, C. (2005). *Funds of knowledge: Theorizing practices in households and classrooms.* Mahwah, NJ: Erlbaum.

Graesser, A., McNamara, D. S., & Kulikowich, J. M. (2011). Coh-Metrix: Providing multilevel analyses of text characteristics. *Educational Researcher, 40*, 223–234. doi:10.3102/0013189X11413260

Graham, S., & Harris, K. (2000). The role of self-regulation and transcription skills in writing and writing development. *Educational Psychologist, 35*, 3–12. doi:10.1207/S15326985EP3501_2

Graham, S., & Harris, K. (2011). Writing difficulties. In A. McGill-Franzen & R. L. Allington (Eds.), *Handbook of reading disability research* (pp. 232–241). New York, NY: Routledge.

Hammill, D. D., & Larsen, S. C. (2009). *Test of Written Language 4.* Torrance, CA: Western Psychological Services.

Hayes, J. R. (2006). New directions in writing theory. In C. A. MacArthur, S. Graham, & J. Fitzgerald (Eds.), *Handbook of writing research* (pp. 28–40). New York, NY: Guilford Press.

Hresko, W. P., Herron, S. R., Peak, P. K., & Hicks, D. L. (2012). *Test of Early Written Language-3.* Torrance, CA: Western Psychological Services.

Huang, J. (2012). Using generalizability theory to examine the accuracy and validity of large-scale ESL writing assessment. *Assessing Writing, 17*, 123–139. doi:10.1016/j.asw.2011.12.003

Hudson, R. (2009). Measuring maturity. In R. Beard, D. Myhill, J. Riley, & M. Nystrand (Eds.), *The SAGE handbook of writing development* (pp. 349–362). London, England: SAGE. doi:10.4135/9780857021069.n24

Kellogg, R. (1994). *The psychology of writing.* New York, NY: Oxford University Press.

Kellogg, R. T. (1996). A model of working memory in writing. In M. C. Levy & S. Randall (Eds.), *The science of writing: Theories, methods, individual differences, and applications* (pp. 57–72). Mahwah, NJ: Erlbaum.

Kellogg, R. T. (2008). Training writing skills: A cognitive developmental perspective. *Journal of Writing Research, 1,* 1–26.

Kieffer, M. J., Lesaux, N. K., Rivera, M., & Francis, D. J. (2009). Accommodations for English language learners taking large-scale assessments: A meta-analysis on effectiveness and validity. *Review of Educational Research, 79,* 1168–1201. doi:10.3102/0034654309332490

LaCelle-Peterson, M. W, & Rivera, C. (1994). Is it real for all kids? A framework for equitable assessment policies for English language learners. *Harvard Educational Review, 64,* 55–75.

Langer, J. A. (1986). *Children reading and writing: Structures and strategies.* Norwood, NJ: Ablex.

McCauley, R. J., & Swisher, L. (1984). Psychometric review of language and articulation tests for preschool children. *The Journal of Speech and Hearing Disorders, 49,* 34–42.

McCutchen, D. (1996). A capacity theory of writing: Working memory in composition. *Educational Psychology Review, 8,* 299–325. doi:10.1007/BF01464076

McNamara, D. S., & Kintsch, W. (1996). Learning from text: Effects of prior knowledge and text coherence. *Discourse Processes, 22,* 247–288. doi:10.1080/01638539609544975

McNamara, T. (2001). Language assessment as social practice: Challenges for research. *Language Testing, 18,* 333–349.

Mountford, R. (1999). Let them experiment: Accommodating diverse discourse practices in large-scale writing assessment. In C. R. Cooper & L. Odell (Eds.), *Evaluating writing: The role of teachers' knowledge about text, learning, and culture* (pp. 366–396). Urbana, IL: National Council of Teachers of English.

National Assessment of Educational Progress, National Center for Education Statistics, National Assessment Governing Board, Institute of Education Sciences, U.S. Department of Education. (2011a). *The nation's report card. Writing 2011: Grade 8 national results.* Retrieved from http://nationsreportcard.gov/writing_2011/g8_national.asp?tab_id=tab2&subtab_id=Tab_9#chart

National Assessment of Educational Progress, National Center for Education Statistics, National Assessment Governing Board, Institute of Education Sciences, U.S. Department of Education. (2011b). *The nation's report card. Writing 2011: Grade 12 national results.* Retrieved from http://nationsreportcard.gov/writing_2011/g12_national.asp?tab_id=tab2&subtab_id=Tab_8#chart

Nystrand, M. (1989). A social-interactive model of writing. *Written Communication*, 6, 66–85. doi:10.1177/0741088389006001005

Peng, G., & Wang, S.-Y. W. (2011). Hemisphere lateralization is influenced by bilingual status and composition of words. *Neuropsychologia, 49*, 1981–1986. doi:10.1016/j.neuropsychologia.2011.03.027

Pitts, L. (2010, January 14). Sometimes the earth is cruel. *The Dallas Morning News*. Retrieved from http://www.dallasnews.com/opinion/latest-columns/20100114-Leonard-Pitts-Sometimes-the-9424.ece

Richards, T. L., & Berninger, V. (2008). Abnormal fMRI connectivity in children with dyslexia during a phoneme task: Before but not after treatment. *Journal of Neurolinguistics, 21*, 294–304. doi:10.1016/j.jneuroling.2007.07.002

Richards, T. L., Berninger, V. W., Stock, P., Altemeier, L., Trivedi, P., & Maravilla, K. R. (2011). Differences between good and poor child writers on FMRI contrasts for writing newly taught and highly practiced letter forms. *Reading and Writing, 24*, 493–516. doi:10.1007/s11145-009-9217-3

Roever, C., & McNamara, T. (2006). Language testing: The social dimension. *International Journal of Applied Linguistics, 16*, 242–258. doi:10.1111/j.1473-4192.2006.00117.x

Romberg, T. A. (2008). *The impact of reform instruction on student mathematics achievement?: An example of a summative evaluation of a standards-based curriculum*. New York, NY: Routledge.

Shanahan, T. (1984). Nature of the reading–writing relation: An exploratory multivariate analysis. *Journal of Educational Psychology, 76*, 466–477. doi:10.1037/0022-0663.76.3.466

Shanahan, T., & Lomax, R. G. (1986). An analysis and comparison of theoretical models of the reading–writing relationship. *Journal of Educational Psychology, 78*, 116–123. doi:10.1037/0022-0663.78.2.116

Shanahan, T., & Lomax, R. G. (1988). A developmental comparison of three theoretical models of the reading–writing relationship. *Research in the Teaching of English, 22*, 196–212.

Tharp, R. G. (1982). The effective instruction of comprehension: Results and description of the Kamehameha Early Education Program. *Reading Research Quarterly, 17*, 503–527. doi:10.2307/747568

Trumbull, E., & Farr, B. (2005). *Language and learning: What teachers need to know*. Norwood, MA: Christopher-Gordon.

U.S. Department of Education, Institute of Education Sciences, National Center for Education Statistics. (2012). *The nation's report card: Writing 2011*. Retrieved from http://nces.ed.gov/pubsearch/pubsinfo.asp?pubid=2012470

Vanderberg, R., & Swanson, H. L. (2007). Components of working memory are important to the writing process? *Reading and Writing, 20*, 721–752. doi:10.1007/s11145-006-9046-6

Wagner, A. D., Paré-Blagoev, E. J., Clark, J., & Poldrack, R. A. (2001). Recovering meaning: Left prefrontal cortex guides controlled semantic retrieval. *Neuron, 31*, 329–338. doi:10.1016/S0896-6273(01)00359-2

Young, R. E., Becker, A., & Pike, K. L. (1970). *Rhetoric: Discovery and change.* New York, NY: Harcourt, Brace & World.

10

IMPLICATIONS OF BILINGUALISM FOR READING ASSESSMENT

SHAROLYN D. POLLARD-DURODOLA, ELSA CÁRDENAS-HAGAN, AND FUHUI TONG

The children who are most likely to experience difficulties in learning to read are those who enter school unable to attend to the sounds of language, have limited letter and sound knowledge, and demonstrate low verbal abilities (National Early Literacy Panel, 2009). Deficits in these abilities place children entering school with low English proficiency at special risk (Snow, Burns, & Griffin, 1998). Figures from the National Center for Education Statistics paint a dismal picture of the reading proficiency of students who speak a language other than English in the home, with 30% of English learner (EL) fourth graders and 29% of EL eighth graders reading at or above basic reading competencies in comparison with 70% of non-EL fourth graders and 77% of non-EL eighth graders in the United States (U.S. Department of Education, Institute of Education Sciences, National Center for Education Statistics, 2011).

http://dx.doi.org/10.1037/14320-011
Assessing Bilingual Children in Context: An Integrated Approach, A. B. Clinton (Editor)

It is reasonable to assume that ELs who are at risk of reading disabilities (RDs) have similar or lower performance profiles than ELs without RDs. Research has suggested that a significant percentage of ELs are at risk of reading difficulties and that the gap between them and their native English-speaking peers will widen without early identification of reading deficits and a plan for intensive intervention (Gunn, Biglan, Smolkowski, & Ary, 2000; McCardle, Mele-McCarthy, & Leos, 2005; Siegel, 2011; Vaughn, Mathes, Linan-Thompson, & Francis, 2005).

Assessing RDs in children who speak another language in the home while acquiring English and/or native language literacy in the school is complex, partially because of sociohistorical, experiential (e.g., sustained poverty, immigration), and school-level (e.g., native language and literacy ability, mismatch between dialect and school language) factors that can contribute to ELs' underachievement in reading (Francis, Rivera, Lesaux, Kieffer, & Rivera, 2006; Limbos & Geva, 2001; Waxman, Padrón, & García, 2007). As a result, practitioners struggle to distinguish between ELs who are developing normally with basic weaknesses in their reading or language abilities and students who are experiencing reading failure (Geva, 2000). Compounding this issue is an all too common wait-and-see approach in schools, which delays identification and referral of ELs for special instructional services until the fourth or fifth grade (Gorman, 2009; Limbos & Geva, 2001; Samson & Lesaux, 2009), controversial standardized assessment measures that do not clearly indicate whether low test scores of ELs are an indication of low reading achievement or language difficulties and differences (Chiappe, Siegel, & Gottardo, 2002; Gersten & Baker, 2003), and misconceptions about RDs in ELs (Geva, 2000).

A comprehensive approach to the identification and assessment of RDs in EL students may well depend on the use of multiple data sources, both formal and informal, that not only document areas of reading deficits but also describe contextual factors that may contribute to reading risk, such as language spoken in the home, age of primary and secondary language acquisition, parental educational background, former schooling in another country, native language reading development, and primary and secondary language similarities and differences. The goal of this chapter is, therefore, twofold. The primary goal is to examine current research related to the evaluation of disabled reading processes in children who are acquiring biliteracy, with recommendations for using a comprehensive assessment approach. A secondary, but equally important, goal is to draw attention to the role of language orthography in normative biliteracy development and how language similarities and differences may contribute to reading risk; this should, therefore, should be considered when evaluating children who struggle to read in multiple languages. We begin by taking a look at the influence of orthography in biliteracy development.

THE ROLE OF ORTHOGRAPHY IN
READING ACQUISITION AND RISK

Current research has shown both differences and similarities in the process of reading acquisition across languages (Gorman, 2009). Although vocabulary, fluency, and reading comprehension appear to be important for learning to read in any language, different orthographic or writing systems (e.g., logographic, alphabetic) determine the importance of phonological awareness in learning to read. When learning to read, "the reader must develop an awareness of the linguistic unit the writing system is representing" (Mann, 2003, p. 214). That is, an individual learning to read in an alphabetic language, such as English (e.g., a writing system in which graphemes correspond to phonemes), must attend to phonemes or the smallest unit of sound in a spoken language, whereas a student learning to read a syllabary in a logographic writing system, such as Chinese (e.g., a complex symbol corresponds not to a single sound, but to a portion of a word, potentially often with meaning), attends to syllables, which are also morphemes.

A review of normative reading development in alphabetic versus logographic languages provides evidence of the influence of a language's writing system on EL reading acquisition and possible conditions contributing to reading difficulties and the complexities of assessment. For example, research has shown that children learn to read both Spanish and English, two alphabetic languages, by developing phonological awareness, learning sound–symbol relationships, and phonologically recoding a word several times until they can remember the word's orthographic representation (González, González, Monzó, & Hernandez-Valle, 2000; Juel & Minden-Cupp, 2000). Reading in Spanish and English is dependent on the orthography of each language, which dictates how consistently or inconsistently the alphabetic principle (e.g., correspondence between graphemes and phonemes) can be applied and which linguistic units (e.g., sound units in a spoken language), such as words, syllables, onsets, rimes, and phonemes, are used to decode words (Juel & Minden-Cupp, 2000). Because of the phonetic and orthographic characteristics of alphabetic languages such as English and Spanish, reading acquisition is dependent on converting letters into sounds; less skilled students who are learning to read have difficulties because they have not mastered the alphabetic principle, or the sound–symbol relationships required for reading (Paulesu et al., 2001).

In contrast to alphabetic orthographies that are based on phonology, logographic writing systems are those in which the graphemes (i.e., the smallest written unit of the language) represent syllables (Wang, Cheng, & Chen, 2006). The best-known cases are Chinese and its derivative script, Japanese *kanji* (Koyama, Kakigi, Hoshiyama, & Kitamura, 1998). The Chinese typology follows a morphosyllabic principle for meaning representation in which a character, the smallest unit of Chinese orthography, functions as a visual–spatial symbol of meaning or a lexical morpheme (Cho & Tong, 2012; Guan, Liu, Chan, Ye, & Perfetti, 2011). For example, the simple character 口 corresponds to the syllable /kou3/ and represents the meaning of *mouth* because it resembles the shape of a mouth. In a strict sense, however, the Chinese language is not purely logographic because 80% to 90% of the characters are compounds composed of a radical (i.e., semantic) element implying meaning and a phonetic element to assist pronunciation (McDougall, Brunswick, & de Mornay Davies, 2010). To continue with the previous example, the character 口 can function as a semantic radical that appears in the characters (e.g., 吻 /wen3/ [*kiss*], 喝 /he1/ [*drink*], 吃 /chi1/ [*eat*]) that all relate to the meaning *mouth*. Therefore, contrary to shallow and transparent orthographic systems (e.g., consistent grapheme–phoneme correspondence as in Spanish), Chinese scripts are often considered highly opaque with incoherent and inconsistent grapheme–phoneme correspondence (Cheung, McBride-Chang, & Chow, 2006). Universally, ELs learning to read in opaque orthographies—Chinese as well as English—may experience decoding difficulties due to the inconsistent letter–sound mappings in the language.

A growing body of research has confirmed that reading acquisition in logographic languages is dependent on *morphological awareness*, or knowledge of the smallest components of meaning in a word, such as units that indicate past tense or plural, and this significantly contributes to reading success and impairment in Chinese among Chinese–English bilingual individuals (Pasquarella, Chen, Lam, Luo, & Ramirez, 2011; Wang et al., 2006). This script dependency is largely absent in English and other alphabetic languages that are more dependent on phonology (Shu, McBride-Chang, Wu, & Liu, 2006).

Neuroscience and Orthographic Processing

Neuroscientists who explore noninvasive neuroimages (e.g., functional magnetic resonance imaging [fMRI]; Kuhl, 2011) of brain activities engaged in the reading process of ELs concur that brain activation patterns reflect the influence of orthography in reading acquisition and risk (Berens, Kovelman, Dublins, Shalinsky, & Petitto, 2009; Norton, Kovelman, & Petitto, 2007; Tan et al., 2003). For example, fMRI images of Spanish word reading suggest greater use of the right superior temporal gyrus region of the brain during pseudo-word reading, reflecting more regular grapheme–phoneme decoding strategies that are characteristic of reading in a transparent orthography (Norton et al., 2007). Berens and colleagues (2009) also confirmed greater use of the right superior temporal sulcus region when bilingual children (Spanish–

English) read pseudowords, indicating the use of decoding strategies associated with reading in a transparent orthography.

An fMRI study by You and colleagues (2011) compared the neural correlates of phonological and orthographic processing in English between Chinese-speaking ELs with and without English reading impairment on letter rhyming and letter same/different tasks. Findings indicated reduced activation in the left parietotemporal region during phonological tasks and the left lingual/calcarine cortex during orthographic tasks among impaired English readers compared with the matched sample who were typically learning to read in English. These patterns are consistent with those identified among native English impaired readers who lack both phonological and orthographic skills for accurate word spelling in English, a deep orthography (e.g., Hoeft et al., 2007; Temple et al., 2001). Results of other neuroimaging studies of reading impaired ELs (e.g., Temple et al., 2001) with Chinese as the primary language (e.g., Siok, Perfetti, Jin, & Tan, 2004) also suggest the importance of phonological processing as a robust indicator of English reading disorders across orthographies in one's native language, corroborating findings from behavioral psycholinguistic research (e.g., Lesaux, Rupp, & Siegel, 2007; Lesaux & Siegel, 2003).

In addition to providing a deeper understanding of the role of language orthography in reading acquisition, emerging neuroimaging studies of normative reading development have also suggested that the age of a child's first bilingual language exposure may predict how "strong a reader a bilingual child can and will become in each of their two languages" (Petitto, 2009, p. 192; see also Hernandez & Li, 2007; Kovelman, Baker, & Petitto, 2008). For example, a neuroimaging study (Petitto, 2009) found that Spanish–English bilingual children who were learning to read in a 50/50 bilingual model and who were exposed to both languages prior to the age of 3 demonstrated normative reading abilities similar to those of monolinguals and had better dual language reading performance than students who were exposed to a second language later, in the second and third grades. In a similar investigation, Kovelman and colleagues (2008) found that children with early English exposure demonstrated higher comprehension abilities and suggested that immigrant children, who may experience later exposure to English, may be prone to reading deficits due to the "age effect" (p. 216).

Script-Dependent Hypothesis

ELs who are exposed later to a second language (L2) may demonstrate lower second language reading abilities because they are still in the process of learning a new language but are not reading disabled. The following case scenario of Maria illustrates how later exposure to a second language may provide an important context for assessing reading difficulties.

Case Studies: Spanish Native English Learner Students

Ten-year-old Maria[1] arrived in the United States from Mexico and was placed in a bilingual education classroom in a school district that advocates an early-exit transitional model where students initially receive Spanish reading instruction and then transition to all-English literacy instruction by the third grade. In Mexico, Maria was instructed in Spanish, did not study the English language, and did not exhibit Spanish reading difficulties, as revealed by parental conversations with her teacher in the United States.

When evaluated in English and Spanish, Maria's basic decoding skills, oral language, and listening and reading comprehension skills in English were below average, whereas parallel Spanish skills were within normal limits. This evidence suggests that Maria does not demonstrate a reading disorder. She did not study English prior to her arrival to the United States and, therefore, is developing her English language and literacy skills and needs more instruction in English reading skills. However, the assessment conclusions for this case cannot be generalized to all EL students who are exposed later to a second language and are experiencing L2 reading difficulties, because they are still developing L2 literacy and oral language.

In contrast, consider the case of Cesar, a student who was instructed in Spanish in Mexico City and who also did not have the opportunity to study English as a foreign language until his arrival in the United States at the age of 9.

Cesar was enrolled in a school along the Texas–Mexico border in a general education English classroom because the school did not offer a bilingual education program. Although no formal documentation of Cesar's reading abilities was provided from Mexico, teacher conversations with the family revealed that Cesar was experiencing difficulty with language, literacy, and basic learning skills (e.g., math) in Mexico before his arrival in the United States.

As Cesar struggled in school to acquire English reading skills, he was evaluated with both English and Spanish assessments, which revealed severely impaired oral language and listening comprehension skills in both languages. Specifically, his basic Spanish and English reading skills were in the below-average range with reading comprehension skills in both languages diagnosed as severely impaired.

---

[1]The details of the case studies have been changed to protect the anonymity of the individuals involved.

Cesar demonstrated a language disorder; he had great difficulty understanding and expressing himself in Spanish, his native language, and in English. His language skills negatively affected his reading comprehension skills, and he received speech–language therapy to improve his vocabulary skills and oral expression. Although he can now decode and read in English after 1 year of formal instruction, he continues to require supplemental instruction to further develop reading accuracy, fluency, and comprehension.

Unlike Maria, the cause of Cesar's L2 reading difficulties is more appropriately attributed to his weak oral language abilities and not to normative L2 language and literacy development. This case suggests that L2 reading acquisition may be influenced by one's native language proficiency and competence (Bialystok, 2006; Durgunoğlu, 2002). Mathes, Pollard-Durodola, Cárdenas-Hagan, Linan-Thompson, and Vaughn (2007) confirmed the importance of oral language abilities on the acquisition of second language literacy, whereas Durgunoğlu (2002) postulated that low levels of native language proficiency can retard the transfer of metalinguistic skills such as knowledge of the syntactic structure of language, the phonological units (e.g., syllables, phonemes), spelling, and word recognition, which can affect reading acquisition.

The *script-dependent hypothesis*, a theory of cross-linguistic transfer that contributes to our understanding of L2 literacy acquisition, also contributes to our understanding of Cesar's complex reading difficulties by implying that a student who experiences reading difficulties in the primary language may experience similar difficulties when learning to read in a second language, particularly when both languages share some grapheme–phoneme similarities (Gorman, 2009). Furthermore, if the orthographies are dissimilar, the script-dependent theory postulates that reading deficits may be manifested in one language but not in the other (Gorman, 2009).

Another example of how this theory of transfer plays out in the experience of second language reading is illustrated by an investigation of EL children's reading abilities based on the influence of their first language. In this study, ELs were from diverse linguistic backgrounds, including Chinese, Slavic, and Romance languages (e.g., French, Italian, Spanish). Children in the study who spoke alphabetic languages that were predictable in letter–sound correspondence had an advantage in learning the irregular alphabetic code of the English language (Siegel, 2011). In contrast, children whose first language was Chinese, a nonalphabetic language that cannot be decoded in the same way as an alphabetic language, experienced difficulties in English decoding tasks.

In sum, the assessment of reading difficulties in ELs may be influenced by the development of biliteracy across similar and/or different orthographic systems, the age at which students learn to read in an acquired language, and native oral language along with reading abilities and deficiencies. (Bialystok, 2006; Gorman, 2009; Lindgren, DeRenzi, & Richman, 1985; Siegel, 2011). Nevertheless, recent investigations have suggested that there are also universal cognitive and linguistic factors, such as phonological processing, working memory, orthographic knowledge, and speed of lexical access, that contribute to the acquisition of reading abilities in both monolingual English speakers and EL students (Durgunoğlu, Nagy, & Hancin-Bhatt, 1993; Geva, 2000; Geva & Siegel, 2000). Two of the best indicators of early reading difficulty for both non-EL and EL students are deficits in phonological processing and rapid naming (Limbos & Geva, 2001; Paulesu et al., 2001). Specifically, phonological processing is predictive of word reading skills within and across languages (Geva, 2000).

The following section discusses and summarizes research related to the evaluation process of children who are acquiring biliteracy, and provides recommendations for a comprehensive assessment process that attends to contextual factors that contribute to the conditions for reading risk.

A COMPREHENSIVE APPROACH TO READING ASSESSMENT

Traditionally, identification of RDs has relied on standardized measures revealing a severe discrepancy between aptitude or intellectual ability and reading skill (Gersten & Baker, 2003; Gorman, 2009; Individuals With Disabilities Education Improvement Act, 2004). The reliability and validity of this method have been criticized (Fletcher, Lyon, Fuchs, & Barnes, 2007; Francis et al., 2005), and recommendations have been suggested for alternative approaches that are more comprehensive in nature and that allow opportunities to evaluate students' instructional needs and their responses to those interventions (Wilkinson, Ortiz, Robertson, & Kushner, 2006). In the context of EL assessment practices, a more comprehensive process would integrate both formal and informal data sources, such as home and school environments, and take into consideration native and second language proficiency (see American Educational Research Association [AERA], American Psychological Association [APA], National Council on Measurement in Education [NCME], 1999). The benefits of formal and informal data sources are discussed next.

Formal Data Sources

Research has reported on some formal assessments—standardized and curriculum-based measures (CBMs)—that are frequently used to identify young EL children who are at risk of reading failure. An example of a standardized measure is the Woodcock Language Proficiency Battery–Revised (WLPB-R; Woodcock, 1991; Woodcock & Muñoz-Sandoval, 1995), a standardized language proficiency instrument assessing broad language proficiency in oral language, reading, and written language. An advantage in using the WLPB-R is that it provides a snapshot of a student's native language and reading abilities (e.g., Spanish) in addition to measuring English language and reading knowledge.

Both parallel English and Spanish forms of the WLPB-R were used in the initial screening for at-risk students by Vaughn and colleagues in their English and Spanish Tier 2 reading interventions (see Mathes et al., 2007; Vaughn, Linan-Thompson, et al., 2006, Vaughn, Mathes, et al., 2006). In these studies, eligible first-grade Spanish-speaking students who were learning to read in Spanish or English and who scored below the 25th percentile on the letter–word identification subset in Spanish (Spanish intervention) or in both English and Spanish (English intervention) were identified as experiencing reading difficulties. These students were selected for an intensive 50-minute daily reading intervention to build both literacy and oral language skills.

One criticism of the use of standardized assessments when evaluating reading difficulties in EL students is that it is unclear whether screening batteries developed with monolingual English speakers are appropriate for children whose native language is not English (Chiappe, Siegel, & Wade-Woolley, 2002). Some experts have suggested that such assessments may be inappropriate for ELs because of (a) assessment bias, or the degree to which students have not been exposed to or have not acculturated to the dominant cultural context and norms that are reflected in the assessment (Ortiz & Ochoa, 2005); (b) interpretation of standardized test results using norms for outcome comparisons that may be invalid for individuals from diverse linguistic and cultural backgrounds; (c) language demands that exceed the student's language proficiency (AERA, APA, NCME, 1999; Flanagan, Ortiz, & Alfonso, 2007); and (d) the misinterpretation of students' English oral proficiency on intelligence tests as an indicator of a learning disability or an intelligence deficit (Klingner, Artiles, & Barletta, 2006). For EL students, standardized content-related measures become assessments of both content and language abilities (Abedi, 2006).

Furthermore, it may not be valid to measure EL abilities only in the native or acquired language because, although bilingual individuals may become proficient or dominant in the native or acquired language, they do not cease being bilingual (Flanagan et al., 2007). Screening batteries of reading risk in the native and acquired language are clearly important because assessments should reflect the language dominance of the student, with decisions to test bilingually made on an individual basis (National Association of Bilingual Education & ILIAD Project, 2002). However, research has documented a disregard for students' native language in the assessment process over the last 20 years (Klingner et al., 2006), with little attention paid to addressing possible reading discrepancies in both the primary and secondary language (Ochoa, González, Galarza, & Guillemard, 1996; Ochoa, Rivera, & Powell, 1997).

In contrast to standardized measures, CBMs provide an assessment of the core content (e.g., reading, math) that is taught in a school's curriculum and can be administered frequently to inform instructional decisions, monitor overall student progress (Bentz & Pavri, 2000), and identify specific skill deficits (Shapiro, 2011). The psychometric properties are sensitive to small shifts in growth, and it can be used to establish instructional goals for students in both mainstream and remedial settings (Sandberg & Reschly, 2011).

An example of a CBM to guide assessment decisions is the Dynamic Indicators of Basic Early Literacy Skills (DIBELS; Good & Kaminski, 2002). DIBELS includes short (1-minute) fluency measures designed to assess five areas of early reading skills: phonemic awareness, alphabetic principle and phonics, accurate and fluent reading, vocabulary, and comprehension. It can be administered three times a year (fall, winter, and spring) to identify students who may be at risk of reading difficulties and can be used to monitor at-risk students while they receive additional, targeted instruction (Baker et al., 2008; Gunn et al., 2000). DIBELS allows evaluation of native language skills in Spanish using the *Indicadores Dinámicos del Éxito en la Lectura* (Good, Bank, & Watson, 2003) in addition to English literacy acquisition.

Nine studies from 1995 to 2007 have examined the use of reading CBMs with EL students (see the review of Sandberg & Reschly, 2011). In these studies, investigators reported varied findings that included the following: (a) reading-related CBMs could be reliably used across language groups (Baker & Good, 1995), and (b) there was a correlation between standardized English reading measures and reading CBMs for at-risk ELs (Ives Wiley & Deno, 2005) and for those from multilingual classrooms (Graves, Plasencia-Peinado, Deno, & Johnson, 2005). In addition to these studies, reading interventions with at-risk EL students have successfully used reading CBMs to monitor progress and to identify students who are at risk of reading difficulties (Linan-Thompson & Hickman-Davis, 2002; Vaughn, Mathes, et al., 2006).

Informal Data Sources

Collective evidence has suggested that reliance on standardized assessments alone is not sufficient to guide placement and intervention decisions for ELs who are developing biliteracy skills (Cummins, 1986; Wilkinson et al., 2006). Multiple data sources provide a more comprehensive guide in identification and assessment decisions. Contextual data or background variables that may contribute to the development of reading difficulties should be included among these sources. Informal sources of contextual data may include, but are not limited to, parent interviews, knowledge of the student's culture, classroom observations of reading behaviors, family background and level of literacy, the language spoken in the home, the age of second language exposure, formal primary language learning and school environments, orthographic discontinuities across the native and acquired second language, and disruptions in formal schooling.

Although such information is crucial in the EL assessment process, there is evidence from a survey of 859 school psychologists with experience in assessing bilingual speakers of 85 distinct languages and limited English-proficient students indicating that assessment practices often do not take into account informal data such as the student's primary language use, the number of years of second language (English) instruction, and parental input so as to better understand cultural norms that affect learning (Klingner et al., 2006; Limbos & Geva, 2001; Ochoa et al., 1996, 1997). In addition to disregarding these important background variables, Cummins (1986) suggested that EL assessment practices traditionally have not examined deficits in school practices that result in instructional inconsistencies that exacerbate skill gaps in EL students.

Next, we describe two case studies of EL students that illustrate how multiple languages, family, school/instructional and other contextual factors may contribute to the development of reading deficits in EL students and should, therefore, be considered in the assessment process. In each of these scenarios, multiple sources of data (e.g., family background and literacy, formal L1 schooling, inconsistent literacy instruction) provide a more comprehensive summary of students' reading abilities.

Case Study: Chinese Native English Learner Student

Lin was born in a rural area in China. Before immigrating with her family to the United States at the age of 8, she received formal schooling exclusively in Chinese for 3 years. Because of the poor economic situation in her hometown, there was only one teacher in the entire school, and the reading curriculum was inconsistent without systematic instruction in Chinese orthographic knowledge and skills.

On her arrival in California, Lin was immediately identified as having limited English proficiency and as being socioeconomically disadvantaged, and she was placed in a third-grade ESL (English as a second language) class. Lin's family soon moved to another state because of economic difficulties, and Lin was again placed in an ESL program. After Lin had been in her second school for 18 months, her ESL teacher observed that she was not interested in class, expressed an intention to drop out of school to assist her family, struggled to keep up with the pace of the class, and was a slow reader who became confused if not tracking the reading process with her finger. She performed well on spelling tests when she knew the words in advance but demonstrated poor performance in non-word spelling and reading (i.e., pseudowords). Lin also struggled to express herself verbally in English.

It is evident that Lin initially received a poor foundation in Chinese reading instruction in her native country followed by interruptions in her English literacy instruction due to changes in school enrollment and relocation. Also, she was a relatively recent arrival to the United States with limited exposure to English in China.

Conversations and interviews with the parents would reveal their English proficiency and literacy abilities and whether there are opportunities for English acquisition in the home. Data on family background and the formal education of the student (e.g., age at exposure to English instruction), in addition to an assessment (formal and informal) of the student's reading ability (e.g., weak knowledge of the alphabetic principle, which impairs decoding and fluency building) could be compiled to better understand that Lin is not experiencing an RD but is still in the process of learning the English language while acquiring English literacy instruction. Using the matrix in Appendix 10.1 would provide a more comprehensive evaluation of Lin's reading and oral language skills in both the primary language and English.

Case Study: English Learner Teacher

Three months into the academic year, Mr. Sanchez created a Saturday school to provide a 1-hour literacy intervention for those Spanish-speaking first graders who were struggling to read in mainstreamed English-only classes. Specifically, after 1 year of kindergarten and 4 months in first grade, these children exhibited limited knowledge of the alphabetic principle and could not decode words in a decodable text. Mr. Sanchez noted that the core reading program moved briskly with instructional sequences that introduced a new English letter and sound every 1 or 2 days. Children, however, could not master the information quickly and required additional opportunities to develop skill knowledge (e.g., isolating and blending sounds) in the Saturday school. However, in June, the principal of the school decided that next year, in second grade, the Spanish-speaking children with low English proficiency would receive all literacy instruction in Spanish. Mr. Sanchez and the other first grade teachers worried that children in the Saturday school who were weak in their English reading ability would now be required to learn to read on grade level in both the primary and secondary language.

Although the contextual factors summarized in Exhibit 10.1 would provide a more comprehensive understanding of these struggling readers' difficulties, it would also clearly highlight the discrepancies in their formal school practices that have placed them at risk.

Complexities of Second Language Assessment

Current research has implied that assessment and identification of reading difficulties in EL students is further complicated by tendencies to under- or overrepresent students in special education settings because of misconceptions about second language development (Chamberlain, 2006; Warger & Burnette, 2000). For example, in their examination of predictors of special education placement in elementary EL students, Samson and Lesaux (2009) found that the probability of being identified for special education for an RD was less likely for young ELs than for native English speakers in kindergarten and first grade. However, the opposite pattern was identified in third grade. Their findings suggest that underrepresentation in early grades and overrepresentation in higher grades signals differential treatment by teachers on the basis of language status. To be more specific, teachers assume that young ELs' difficulties stem from a lack of English proficiency, and they tend to wait until students have developed sufficient English competency before referring them for special education evaluation.

However, evidence suggests that EL reading difficulties can be identified early or while the child is acquiring literacy in his or her primary and/or acquired (English) language (Chiappe, Siegel, & Wade-Woolley, 2002; Geva, 2000; Lesaux, Lipka, & Siegel, 2006; Siegel, 2011; see also Vaughn, Linan-Thompson, et al., 2005, 2006; Vaughn, Mathes, et al., 2005, 2006). For example, findings from intervention studies (Vaughn, Linan-Thompson, et al., 2005, 2006; Vaughn, Mathes, et al., 2005, 2006) have indicated that first-grade Spanish-speaking EL students experienced reading deficits in L1 (Spanish-only instruction) or L2 (English-only instruction) at the beginning of the year, as evidenced on the letter–word identification subtest from the WLPB in English and Spanish. To be more specific, they could not identify more than four letters of the alphabet, and they were unable to read more than one word from a list of simple two- to four-letter words in English (e.g., *in, as, it, man, dog*) and Spanish (e.g., *el, las, un, por, alto*).

Furthermore, L2 oral language proficiency does not adequately predict L2 reading ability (Geva, 2000). For example, in a longitudinal study of children at risk of dyslexia in British Columbia, researchers found that in as early as kindergarten, 25% of non-EL and 50% of EL students were at risk of RDs while learning to read in English, based on a battery of tests that included English phonological awareness, letter naming, syntactic awareness, picture-naming speed, and sentence-repetition tasks (Chiappe, Siegel, & Wade-Woolley, 2002; Lesaux et al., 2006; Siegel, 2011). Clearly, postponing assessment and delaying intervention until after the development of English language proficiency is not advantageous for such students whose educational needs would be overlooked when they are already at risk of reading difficulties.

Another investigation (Geva, 2000) indicated that L2 oral language proficiency does not adequately predict L2 reading ability. In this study, investigators documented that children whose oral language and listening comprehension skills were high in English experienced difficulty in phonemic segmentation, reading comprehension, rapid letter naming, and pseudoword reading in English. This profile of reading failure was found in a small percentage of native English speakers and Punjabi and Cantonese EL children, suggesting that research does not support the belief that second language oral proficiency is a good predictor of second language reading development and ability.

In real classroom settings, however, because of their limited knowledge about the development of second language literacy, teachers may demonstrate bias in their assessment and identification of reading deficits (Limbos & Geva, 2001). An investigation of the assessment practices of 51 first-grade teachers with 1 to 27 years of experience teaching EL children revealed that evaluation errors of EL student reading ability could be attributed partially to an overreliance on indicators of second language proficiency. Limbos and Geva (2001) suggested that although teacher nominations play a decisive role in the early identification of children's reading difficulties, dependence on teacher nominations alone might overlook students who would benefit from early intervention and literacy support.

The identification of RDs in ELs is further exacerbated by the lack of assessments that differentiate between L2 acquisition developmental issues and learning disabilities. Sánchez, Parker, Akbayin, and McTigue (2010) found that one of the challenges that contributed to the disproportionate number of ELs identified for learning disabilities is the lack of access to assessments that differentiate between L2 developmental issues and learning disabilities. Data from semistructured interviews with New York State School District administrators and school personnel indicated that it is difficult to find valid assessments in languages other than English and that, even when assessment tools are in Spanish (the L1 for the majority of ELs in the United States), they are normed for Spanish-speaking students in the United States. These students differ from new immigrants and those with interrupted primary language schooling, a factor highly associated with RDs.

CONCLUSION

Clearly, the process of assessing and identifying RDs in children acquiring biliteracy is sometimes inaccurate, resulting in tendencies to over or under identify ELs for critical instructional support (McCardle et al., 2005). The process is further hampered by limited knowledge of the "normal linguistic and acculturation processes" experienced by this population of children (Geva, 2000, p. 14), resulting in an uncertainty about when to assess a student's abilities—early versus later. Although orthographic consistency and phonological complexity provide insight into the way reading difficulties may be manifested across languages, with implications for assessment, the real-life vignettes of Maria, Lin, and Mr. Sanchez suggest that not all EL children who struggle to read have a reading or learning disability and that more effective methods are needed that can pinpoint those cultural, social, and instructional factors that may prevent children from acquiring adequate reading skills (McCardle et al., 2005).

APPENDIX 10.1: CHECKLIST OF DATA SOURCES
TO ASSESS READING RISK

Data sources

Domain I: Family background	Yes	No
1. Parent(s) demonstrates the ability to read and or write. Anecdotal notes:		
2. Parent(s) received formal education in the United States or in another country. Anecdotal notes:		
3. Parent(s) speaks and writes English fluently. Anecdotal notes:		
4. Parent(s) speaks and writes fluently in a language other than English. Anecdotal notes:		
5. Family recently immigrated to the United States (less than 1 year). Anecdotal notes:		
6. Family has moved frequently with changes in school enrollment. Anecdotal notes:		

Domain II: Formal education of the student	Yes	No
1. Student received formal literacy instruction in a language other than English. Anecdotal notes: Language(s): Number of years studied:		
2. Student received formal literacy instruction in English. Anecdotal notes: Age when first exposed to English instruction: Number of years studied:		
3. Student exhibits oral English language proficiency. Anecdotal notes:		
4. Student exhibits written English language proficiency. Anecdotal notes:		
5. Student's English oral language proficiency is parallel to his/her English written language proficiency. Anecdotal notes:		
6. Student learned to read in a native language that is phonetically regular. Anecdotal notes:		

	Yes	No
7. Student learned to read in a native language that is phonetically irregular. Anecdotal notes:		
8. Student has been enrolled in multiple bilingual education models or has received literacy instruction through multiple curricula. Anecdotal notes:		
Domain III: Reading assessment	Yes	No
1. Student's reading abilities have been evaluated in his/her primary language. Anecdotal notes:		
2. Student's reading abilities have been assessed in English. Anecdotal notes:		
3. Assessment tools reflect knowledge or vocabulary that is culturally familiar to the student. Anecdotal notes:		

REFERENCES

Abedi, J. (2006). Psychometric issues in the ELL assessment and special education eligibililty. *Teachers College Record, 108*, 2282–2303. doi:10.1111/j.1467-9620.2006.00782.x

American Educational Research Association, American Psychological Association, & National Council on Measurement in Education. (1999). *Standards for educational and psychological testing*. Washington, DC: American Educational Research Association.

Baker, S. K., & Good, R. (1995). Curriculum-based measurement of English reading with bilingual Hispanic students: A validation study with second-grade students. *School Psychology Review, 24*, 561–578.

Baker, S. K., Smolkowski, K., Katz, R., Fien, H., Seeley, J. R., Kame'enui, E. J., & Beck, C. T. (2008). Reading fluency as a predictor of reading proficiency in low-performing, high-poverty schools. *School Psychology Review, 37*, 18–37.

Bentz, J., & Pavri, S. (2000). Curriculum-based measurement in assessing bilingual students: A promising new direction. *Assessment for Effective Intervention, 25*, 229–248. doi:10.1177/073724770002500303

Berens, M. S., Kovelman, I., Dubins, M., Shalinksky, M. H., & Petitto, L. A. (2009, March). *Shedding new light on reading in bilingual and monolingual children*. Poster presented at the meeting of the Cognitive Neuroscience Society, San Francisco, CA.

Bialystok, E. (2006). Second-language acquisition and bilingualism at an early age and the impact on early cognitive development. In R. E. Tremblay, R. G. Barr, & R. D. Peters (Eds.), *Encyclopedia on early childhood development* (pp. 1–4). Montreal, Canada: Centre of Excellence for Early Childhood Development.

Chamberlain, S. P. (2006). Alfredo Artiles and Beth Harry: Issues of overrepresentation and educational equity for culturally and linguistically diverse students. Interview. *Intervention in School and Clinic, 41*, 228–232. doi:10.1177/10534512060410040501

Cheung, H., McBride-Chang, C., & Chow, B. W. Y. (2006). Reading Chinese. In R. M. Joshi & P. G. Aaron (Eds.), *Handbook of orthography and literacy* (pp. 421–438). Mahwah, NJ: Erlbaum.

Chiappe, P., Siegel, L. S., & Gottardo, A. (2002). Reading-related skills of kindergartners from diverse linguistic backgrounds. *Applied Psycholinguistics, 23*, 95–116. doi:10.1017/S014271640200005X

Chiappe, P., Siegel, L. S., & Wade-Woolley, L. (2002). Linguistic diversity and the development of reading skills: A longitudinal study. *Scientific Studies of Reading, 6*, 369–400. doi:10.1207/S1532799XSSR0604_04

Cho, E., & Tong, F. (2012, April). *Cross language morphological transfer from Korean to English and Chinese*. Paper presented at the annual meeting of American Educational Research Association, Vancouver, British Columbia, Canada.

Cummins, J. (1986). Psychological assessment of minority students: Out of context, out of focus, out of control? *Journal of Reading, Writing, & Learning Disabilities International, 2*, 9–19. doi:10.1080/0748763860020103

Durgunoğlu, A. (2002). Cross-linguistic transfer in literacy development and implications for language learners. *Annals of Dyslexia, 52*, 189–204.

Durgunoğlu, A. Y., Nagy, W. E., & Hancin-Bhatt, B. J. (1993). Cross-language transfer of phonological awareness. *Journal of Educational Psychology, 85*, 453–465. doi:10.1037/0022-0663.85.3.453

Flanagan, D. P., Ortiz, S. O., & Alfonso, V. C. (2007). *Essentials of cross battery assessment* (2nd ed.). Hoboken, NJ: Wiley.

Fletcher, J. M., Lyon, G. R., Fuchs, L. S., & Barnes, M. A. (2007). *Learning disabilities: From identification to intervention*. New York, NY: Guilford Press.

Francis, D. J., Fletcher, J. M., Stuebing, K. K., Lyon, G. R., Shaywitz, B. A., & Shawitz, S. E. (2005). Psychometric approaches to the identification of LD: IQ and achievement scores are not sufficient. *Journal of Learning Disabilities, 38*, 98–108. doi:10.1177/00222194050380020101

Francis, D. J., Rivera, M., Lesaux, N., Kieffer, M., & Rivera, H. (2006). *Research-based recommendations for instruction and academic interventions*. Portsmouth, NH: Center on Instruction.

Gersten, R., & Baker, S. (2003). English-language learners with learning disabilities. In H. L. Swanson, K. R. Harris, & S. Graham (Eds.), *Handbook of learning disabilities* (pp. 94–109). New York, NY: Guilford Press.

Geva, E. (2000). Issues in the assessment of reading disabilities in L2 children—Beliefs and research evidence. *Dyslexia, 6*, 13–28. doi:10.1002/(SICI)1099-0909(200001/03)6:1<13::AID-DYS155>3.0.CO;2-6

Geva, E., & Siegel, L. S. (2000). Orthographic and cognitive factors in the concurrent development of basic reading skills in two languages. *Reading and Writing, 12*, 1–30. doi:10.1023/A:1008017710115

González, J. E., González, C. J., Monzo, A. E., & Hernandez-Valle, I. (2000). Onset-rime units in visual word recognition in Spanish normal readers and children with reading disabilities. *Learning Disabilities Research & Practice, 15*, 135–141.

Good, R. H., Bank, N., & Watson, J. M. (Eds.). (2003). *Indicadores Dinámicos del Exito en la Lectura (Dynamic indicators of reading success)*. Eugene, OR: Institute for the Development of Educational Achievement.

Good, R. H., & Kaminski, R. A. (Eds.). (2002). *Dynamic indicators of basic early literacy skills* (6th ed.). Eugene, OR: Institute for the Development of Educational Achievement.

Gorman, B. (2009). Cross-linguistic universals in reading acquisition with applications to English-language learners with reading disabilities. *Seminars in Speech and Language, 30*, 246–260. doi:10.1055/s-0029-1241723

Graves, A. W., Plasencia-Peinado, J., Deno, S. L., & Johnson, J. R. (2005). Formatively evaluating the reading progress of first grade English learners in multiple-language classrooms. *Remedial and Special Education, 26*, 215–225. doi:10.1177/07419325050260040401

Guan, C. Q., Liu, Y., Chan, D. H. L., Ye, F., & Perfetti, C. A. (2011). Writing strengthens orthography and alphabetic-coding strengthens phonology in learning to read Chinese. *Journal of Educational Psychology, 103*, 509–522. doi:10.1037/a0023730

Gunn, B., Biglan, A., Smolkowski, K., & Ary, D. (2000). The efficacy of supplemental instruction in decoding skills for Hispanic and non-Hispanic students in early elementary school. *The Journal of Special Education, 34*, 90–103. doi:10.1177/002246690003400204

Hernandez, A. E., & Li, P. (2007). Age of acquisition: Its neural and computational mechanisms. *Psychological Bulletin, 133*, 638–650.

Hoeft, F., Ueno, T., Reiss, A. L., Meyler, A., Whitfield-Gabrieli, S., Glover, G. H., . . . Gabrieli, J. D. (2007). Prediction of children's reading skills using behavioral, functional, and structural neuroimaging measures. *Behavioral Neuroscience, 121*, 602–613. doi:10.1037/0735-7044.121.3.602

Individuals With Disabilities Education Improvement Act of 2004, Pub. L. No. 108-446, § 614, 118 Stat. 2707 (2004).

Ives Wiley, H. I., & Deno, S. L. (2005). Oral reading and maze measures as predictors of success for English learners on a state standards assessment. *Remedial and Special Education, 26*, 207–214. doi:10.1177/07419325050260040301

Juel, C., & Minden-Cupp, C. (2000). Learning to read words: Linguistic units and instructional strategies. *Reading Research Quarterly, 35*, 458–492. doi:10.1598/RRQ.35.4.2

Klingner, J. K., Artiles, A. J., & Barletta, L. M. (2006). English language learners who struggle with reading. *Journal of Learning Disabilities, 39*, 108–128. doi:10.1177/00222194060390020101

Kovelman, I., Baker, S. A., & Petitto, L. A. (2008). Age of first bilingual language exposure as a new window into bilingual reading development. *Bilingualism: Language and Cognition, 11*, 203–223. doi:10.1017/S1366728908003386

Koyama, S., Kakigi, R., Hoshiyama, M., & Kitamura, Y. (1998). Reading of Japanese Kanji (morphograms) and Kana (syllabograms): A magnetoencephalographic study. *Neuropsychologia, 36*(1), 83–98. doi:10.1016/S0028-3932(97)00097-3

Kuhl, P. (2011). Early language learning and literacy: Neuroscience implications for education. *Mind, Brain, and Education, 5*, 128–142. doi:10.1111/j.1751-228X.2011.01121.x

Lesaux, N. K., Lipka, O., & Siegel, L. S. (2006). Investigating cognitive and linguistic abilities that influence the reading comprehension skills of children from diverse linguistic backgrounds. *Reading and Writing, 19*, 99–131. doi:10.1007/s11145-005-4713-6

Lesaux, N. K., Rupp, A., & Siegel, L. S. (2007). Growth in reading skills of children from diverse linguistic backgrounds: Findings from a 5-year longitudinal study. *Journal of Educational Psychology, 99*, 821–834. doi:10.1037/0022-0663.99.4.821

Lesaux, N. K., & Siegel, L. S. (2003). The development of reading in children who speak English as a second language. *Developmental Psychology, 39*, 1005–1019. doi:10.1037/0012-1649.39.6.1005

Limbos, M. M., & Geva, E. (2001). Accuracy of teacher assessments of second-language students at risk for reading disability. *Journal of Learning Disabilities, 34*, 136–151. doi:10.1177/002221940103400204

Linan-Thompson, S., & Hickman-Davis, P. (2002). Supplemental reading instruction for students at risk for reading disabilities: Improve reading 30 minutes at a time. *Learning Disabilities Research & Practice, 17*, 242–251. doi:10.1111/1540-5826.00049

Lindgren, S. D., DeRenzi, E., & Richman, L. C. (1985). Cross-national comparisons of developmental dyslexia in Italy and the United States. *Child Development, 56*, 1404–1417. doi:10.2307/1130460

Mann, V. A. (2003). Language processes: Keys to reading disability. In H. L. Swanson, K. R. Harris, & S. Graham (Eds.), *Handbook of learning disabilities* (pp. 213–228). New York, NY: Guilford Press.

Mathes, P. G., Pollard-Durodola, S. D., Cárdenas-Hagan, E., Linan-Thompson, S., & Vaughn, S. (2007). Teaching struggling readers who are native Spanish speakers: What do we know? *Language, Speech, and Hearing Services in Schools, 38*, 260–271. doi:10.1044/0161-1461(2007/027)

McCardle, P., Mele-McCarthy, J. M., & Leos, K. (2005). English language learners and learning disabilities: Research agenda and implications for practice. *Learning Disabilities Research & Practice, 20*, 68–78. doi:10.1111/j.1540-5826.2005.00122.x

McDougall, S., Brunswick, S., & de Mornay Davies, P. (2010). An introduction and overview. In S. Brunswick, S. McDougall, & P. de Mornay Davies (Eds.), *Reading and dyslexia in different orthographies* (pp. 3–21). New York, NY: Psychology Press.

National Association for Bilingual Education & ILIAD Project. (2002). *Determining Appropriate Referrals of English Language Learners to Special Education: A self-assessment guide for principals*. Washington, DC: National Association for Bilingual Education and Arlington, VA: Council for Exceptional Children.

National Early Literacy Panel. (2009). *Developing early literacy: Report of the National Early Literacy Panel, a scientific synthesis of early literacy development and implications for intervention*. Washington, DC: National Institute for Literacy.

Norton, E. S., Kovelman, I., & Petitto, L. A. (2007). Are there separate neural systems for spelling? New insights into the role of rules and memory in spelling from MRI. *Mind, Brain, and Education, 1*, 48–59. doi:10.1111/j.1751-228X.2007.00005.x

Ochoa, S. H., González, D., Galarza, A., & Guillemard, L. (1996). The training and use of interpreters in bilingual psycho-educational assessment: An alternative in need of study. *Diagnostique, 21*, 19–22.

Ochoa, S. H., Rivera, B. D., & Powell, M. P. (1997). Factors used to comply with the exclusionary clause with bilingual and limited-English-proficient pupils: Initial Guidelines. *Learning Disabilities Research & Practice, 12*, 161–167.

Ortiz, S. O., & Ochoa, S. H. (2005). Intellectual assessment: A nondiscriminatory interpretive approach. In D. P. Flanagan & P. L. Harrison (Eds.), *Contemporary intellectual assessment* (2nd ed., pp. 234–250). New York, NY: Guilford Press.

Pasquarella, A., Chen, X., Lam, K., Luo, Y. C., & Ramirez, G. (2011). Cross-language transfer of morphological awareness in Chinese–English bilinguals. *Journal of Research in Reading, 34*(1), 23–42. doi:10.1111/j.1467-9817.2010.01484.x

Paulesu, E., Demonet, J., Fazio, F., McCrory, E., Chanoine, V., Brunswick, N., . . . Frith, U. (2001). Dyslexia: Cultural diversity and biological unity. *Science, 291,* 2165–2167. doi:10.1126/science.1057179

Petitto, L. A. (2009). New discoveries from the bilingual brain and mind across the life span: Implications for education. *Mind, Brain, and Education, 3,* 185–197. doi:10.1111/j.1751-228X.2009.01069.x

Samson, J. F., & Lesaux, N. K. (2009). Language-minority learners in special education: Rates and predictors of identification for services. *Journal of Learning Disabilities, 42,* 148–162. doi:10.1177/0022219408326221

Sánchez, M. T., Parker, C., Akbayin, B., & McTigue, A. (2010). *Processes and challenges in identifying learning disabilities among students who are English language learners in three New York State districts* (Issues & Answers Report, REL 2010–No. 085). Newton, MA: Educational Development Center.

Sandberg, K. L., & Reschly, A. L. (2011). English learners: Challenges in assessment and the promise of curriculum-based measurement. *Remedial and Special Education, 32,* 144–154. doi:10.1177/0741932510361260

Shapiro, E. S. (2011). *Academic skills problems: Direct assessment and intervention* (4th ed.). New York, NY: Guilford Press.

Shu, H., McBride-Chang, C., Wu, S., & Liu, H. (2006). Understanding Chinese developmental dyslexia: Morphological awareness as a core cognitive construct. *Journal of Educational Psychology, 98,* 122–133. doi:10.1037/0022-0663.98.1.122

Siegel, L. S. (2011). Reducing reading difficulties in English L1 and L2: Early identification and intervention. In P. McCardle, B. Miller, J. R. Lee, & O. J. L. Tzeng (Eds.), *Dyslexia across languages* (pp. 294–304). Baltimore, MD: Paul H. Brookes.

Siok, W. T., Perfetti, C. A., Jin, Z., & Tan, L. H. (2004). Biological abnormality of impaired reading is constrained by culture. *Nature, 431,* 71–76. doi:10.1038/nature02865

Snow, C., Burns, M. S., & Griffin, P. (1998). *Preventing reading difficulties in young children.* Washington, DC: National Academy.

Tan, L. H., Spinks, J. A., Feng, C. M., Siok, W. T., Perfetti, C. A., Xiong, J., . . . Gao, J. H. (2003). Neural systems of second language reading are shaped by native language. *Human Brain Mapping, 18,* 158–166. doi:10.1002/hbm.10089

Temple, E., Poldrack, R. A., Salidis, J., Deutsch, G. K., Tallal, P., Merzenich, M. M., & Gabrieli, D. E. (2001). Disrupted neural responses to phonological and orthographic processing in dyslexic children: An fMRI study. *NeuroReport, 12,* 299–307. doi:10.1097/00001756-200102120-00024

U.S. Department of Education, Institute of Education Sciences, National Center for Education Statistics. (2011). *NAEP data explorer.* Retrieved from http://nces.ed.gov/nationsreportcard/naepdata/

Vaughn, S., Linan-Thompson, S., Mathes, P., Cárdenas-Hagan, E., Pollard-Durodola, S. D., & Francis, D. (2005). Interventions for 1st grade English language learners with reading difficulties. *Perspectives, 31,* 31–35.

Vaughn, S., Linan-Thompson, S., Mathes, P., Cirino, P., Carlson, C., Pollard-Durodola, S. D., . . . Francis, D. (2006). Effectiveness of a Spanish intervention for first-grade English language learners at risk for reading difficulties. *Journal of Learning Disabilities, 39,* 56–73. doi:10.1177/00222194060390010601

Vaughn, S., Mathes, P. G., Linan-Thompson, S., Cirino, P., Carlson, C., Pollard-Durodola, S. D., . . . Francis, D. J. (2006). Effectiveness of an English intervention for first-grade English language learners at risk for reading problems. *The Elementary School Journal, 107,* 153–180. doi:10.1086/510653

Vaughn, S., Mathes, P. G., Linan-Thompson, S., & Francis, D. J. (2005). Teaching English language learners at risk for reading disabilities to read: Putting research into practice. *Learning Disabilities Research & Practice, 20,* 58–67. doi:10.1111/j.1540-5826.2005.00121.x

Wang, M., Cheng, C., & Chen, S. (2006). Contribution of morphological awareness to Chinese–English biliteracy acquisition. *Journal of Educational Psychology, 98,* 542–553. doi:10.1037/0022-0663.98.3.542

Warger, C., & Burnette, J. (2000). *Five strategies to reduce overrepresentation of culturally and linguistically diverse students in special education.* Arlington, VA: ERIC Clearinghouse on Disabilities and Gifted Education.

Waxman, H. C., Padrón, Y. N., & García, A. (2007). Educational issues and effective practices for Hispanic students. In S. J. Paik & H. J. Walberg (Eds.), *Narrowing the achievement gap* (pp. 131–151). New York, NY: Springer. doi:10.1007/0-387-44611-7_8

Wilkinson, C. Y., Ortiz, A. A., Robertson, P. M., & Kushner, M. (2006). English language learners with reading-related LD: Linking data from multiple sources to make eligibility determinations. *Journal of Learning Disabilities, 39,* 129–141. doi:10.1177/00222194060390020201

Woodcock, R. W. (1991). *Woodcock Language Proficiency Battery–Revised.* Chicago, IL: Riverside.

Woodcock, R. W., & Muñoz-Sandoval, A. F. (1995). *Language survey: Comprehensive manual.* Chicago, IL: Riverside.

You, H., Gaab, N., Wei, N., Cheng-Lai, A., Wang, Z., Jian, J., . . . Ding, G. (2011). Neural deficits in second language reading: fMRI evidence from Chinese children with English reading impairment. *NeuroImage, 57,* 760–770. doi:10.1016/j.neuroimage.2010.12.003

11

AN INTEGRATED APPROACH TO THE ASSESSMENT OF THE REFUGEE STUDENT

KAREN LEE SEYMOUR

Refugee children are a uniquely identifiable group in schools because they have typically experienced war, displacement, trauma, and loss, in addition to poor living conditions, food scarcity, and limited or disrupted schooling (Ehntholt, Smith, & Yule, 2005; Kaplan, 2009; Miller, Mitchell, & Brown, 2005). These numerous and significant stressors increase the risk of health, emotional, behavioral, cognitive, and academic difficulties while in temporary housing and later, when they are resettled.

School psychologists typically work with refugee children upon resettlement, when children must adapt to a new environment in a different culture, learn a new language, and navigate a distinct school system. Therefore, school psychologists must be culturally competent clinicians, particularly in relation to refugee children who are vulnerable to the effects of premigration, migration, and resettlement and who attend schools across the globe (Ecklund & Johnson, 2007). This chapter provides an overview of the refugee experience;

http://dx.doi.org/10.1037/14320-012
Assessing Bilingual Children in Context: An Integrated Approach, A. B. Clinton (Editor)

describes unique factors, stressors, and hardships that affect refugee children's development; and offers the practitioner tools to address the complexities in evaluation of refugee children.

REFUGEE ORIGINS AND RESETTLEMENT

The number of refugees across the world has remained relatively stable since the late 1990s, fluctuating between 13 million and 16 million people (United Nations High Commissioner for Refugees [UNHCR], 2011). The number of internally displaced persons globally was estimated to be 27.5 million at the end of 2010 (UNHCR, 2011). There is no obligation for a state to resettle refugees; however, those that do allow entry to refugees allocate budgets, develop and provide programs, and have annual resettlement quotas. The number of states offering specific refugee resettlement programs has increased over the last several years from 14 in 2005 to 26 in 2012, with the United States, Australia, and Canada being the top three resettlement countries (Executive Committee of the High Commissioner's Programme [EC], 2012).

The United Nations General Assembly 1951 Convention Relating to the Status of Refugees is the foundation of international refugee protection. A *refugee* is defined as

> [Any person who] owing to well-founded fear of being persecuted for reasons of race, religion, nationality, membership of a particular social group or political opinion, is outside the country of his nationality and is unable, or owing to such fear, is unwilling to avail himself of the protection of that country; or who, not having a nationality and being outside the country of his former habitual residence as a result of such events, is unable or, owing to such fear, is unwilling to return to it. (p. 137)

Resettlement in third countries, one of the three durable solutions of the UNHCR to resolve the problem of refugees, remains an important solution for many. Resettlement however, is granted to a mere 1% of the world's refugees (EC, 2012). Voluntary repatriation and local integration in the country of first asylum are the other two solutions. The national origins of refugees who have been resettled have shifted over time: The 1980s and 1990s registered large numbers of refugees from Eastern Europe, the Middle East, and Southwest Asia, with a smaller number from Africa. The early 2000s witnessed substantial increases in refugees from Africa, the Middle East, and Southwest Asia (EC, 2012). These changes reflect conflict zones and war.

Children younger than 18 years of age, with fairly equal gender distribution, comprise close to 50% of refugee populations. Approximately 11% of these are under the age of 5 years (Reed, Fazel, Jones, Panter-Brick, & Stein,

2012). Refugees hailing from urban areas are likely to have lived in dispersed or individual type accommodation, collective centers, or settlements, whereas those from rural regions probably resided in refugee camps and settlements (UNHCR, 2011). Children and their families are frequently confined to camps for several years prior to relocation, during which time they rely on the international community for education, medical care, and other basic needs (Werker, 2007).

THE REFUGEE JOURNEY

The stressors to which most refugees are exposed occur at three different stages: (a) in the country of origin, (b) during the flight to safety, and (c) on resettlement in a host country (Hodes, 2000). Although each refugee's experience is unique, there are common elements, including preflight chaos at home (e.g., violence, torture, harassment, oppression, disappearances of family members), deprivation of basic needs and rights, persecution, and fear and anxiety (Berman, 2001).

The departure stage, also called *flight* or *migration*, usually occurs without preparation and often with no specific destination. During flight to the country of asylum, refugees often encounter long, difficult, and dangerous travel across hazardous terrain and under extremely adverse conditions (Geltman et al., 2005). Malnutrition and food insecurity, poverty, inadequate shelter, illness and infectious diseases, poor sanitation, limited access to potable water, and further violence become additional compounding factors of the refugee migration experience (Moss et al., 2006).

The final stage of the journey, for some, is resettlement in a third country, which brings with it the challenges of many postmigration stressors: a distinct cultural environment with unfamiliar customs; language barriers; complex health, education, and legal systems; changes in social and gender status and parental role; financial difficulties and unemployment; and potentially, exposure to discriminatory behaviors (Porter & Haslam, 2005; Thomas & Lau, 2002; Victorian Foundation for Survivors of Torture, 2012).

PSYCHOLOGICAL IMPLICATIONS FOR REFUGEE CHILDREN

There is considerable evidence that refugee children are at significant risk of developing psychological disturbance as a result of their experiences (Fazel & Stein, 2003; Leavey et al., 2004; Lustig et al., 2004; Shaw, 2003). Children's needs in times of crisis are likely to be multifaceted and closely connected with the basic needs of security, food, shelter, education, and family connection (Jones, 2008). The combinations of conditions of adversity and exposure to violence in countries of origin, followed by migration and subsequent resettlement, expose children to many risks to their physical, emotional, and social development and functioning.

The prevalence rates of mental health problems in refugee children vary widely across studies because of distinct research methods and uniqueness of samples (Henley & Robinson, 2011; Murray, Davidson, & Schweitzer, 2008). Despite these variations, it is accepted that the many challenges faced by refugee children over significant periods are likely to overwhelm their resources. The prevalence of posttraumatic stress disorder and a range of other mental health problems, including depression and anxiety, is higher in refugee children than control populations (Fazel, Wheeler, & Danesh, 2005; Thomas & Lau, 2002). *Unaccompanied minors*, defined as "those who are separated from both parents and are not being cared for by an adult who, by law or custom, is responsible to do so" (UNHCR, 1994, p. 52), and *asylum-seeking children*, defined as "people who have requested international protection and whose claim for refugee status has not yet been determined" (UNHCR, 2008, p. 13), without caregivers are at particularly high risk and are reported to have high frequencies of mental health problems (Leavey et al., 2004; Wiese & Burhorst, 2007).

TRAUMA AND THE REFUGEE CHILD

Posttraumatic Stress Disorder

Posttraumatic stress disorder (PTSD) is characterized by exposure to an extremely stressful or catastrophic event or situation. *Traumatic stress* refers to the emotional and physical response to an event that threatens the life or physical or psychological well-being of the child or someone important to the child and is unexpected, unpredictable, uncontrollable, and terrifying (Sargent, 2009). Traumatic stress persists after an incident has ended and continues to affect the child's capacity to function. Children's reactions to traumatic events can include repeated reliving of the trauma, repetitive traumatic play, nightmares, disturbed sleep, concentration problems, irritability, hyperarousal, underarousal or dissociation, psychosomatic symptoms (e.g., stomach and headache pain), enuresis, and affective difficulties (e.g., crying, depression, withdrawal from peers).

Symptoms of PTSD are commonly seen among children of different cultures from war-affected countries (Shaw, 2003). In a rigorous systematic review, Fazel and colleagues (2005) analyzed a sample of 260 refugee children from Bosnia, Central America, Iran, Kurdistan, and Rwanda. They found a prevalence rate for PTSD of 11%, with a range of 7% to 17%. Morgos, Worden, and Gupta (2007–2008) assessed the psychosocial effects of guerrilla-style warfare in 331 displaced children in Southern Darfur, finding 75% of the children met criteria for PTSD, whereas 38% exhibited clinical symptoms of depression, and 20% were found to have significant levels of grief symptoms.

Preschool children are particularly sensitive to traumatic events because they have limited cognitive resources and consequent difficulties in comprehending and processing their experiences (Montgomery, 1998). Thabet, Karim, and Vostanis (2006) examined the relationship between exposure to war trauma (home invasions, beatings, shootings, and death) on the behavior and emotional well-being of preschool children living in the Gaza Strip. High levels of exposure to traumatic events were related to more severe behavioral and emotional symptoms. Preschool children were likely to respond through nonspecific behavioral problems, such as increased episodes of temper tantrums, overactivity, and attention-seeking, and they were more likely to demonstrate underlying anxiety, as seen in poor concentration and elevated fears. Kithakye, Morris, Terranova, and Myers (2010) examined pre- and postconflict data from Kenyan children between 3 and 7 years old who experienced destruction of their homes, death of a parent, or harm to parents or themselves. Experiences of these events were associated with adjustment difficulties, increased aggression, and decreased prosocial behavior.

Several studies have also demonstrated the persistence of PTSD in young refugees up to 12 years subsequent to resettlement (Almqvist & Brandell-Forsberg, 1997; Sack, Him, & Dickason, 1999). Kinzie, Sack, Angell, Clarke, and Ben (1989) found that 48% of young Cambodian refugees still presented with PTSD 3 years after resettlement, which was almost identical to the percentage found at the initial interview, and 41% met the criterion for depression. Even 6 years later, PTSD was still evident, and evidence indicated that traumatized children may be more vulnerable to subsequent traumatic experiences.

Depression, Anxiety, and Other Mental Health Consequences

Children who experience severe trauma may suffer from additional difficulties that may affect their overall functioning. These include anxiety and depression (Thabet, Abed, & Vostanis, 2004), somatic complaints, sleep problems, generalized fears, delinquent and aggressive behaviors (Qouta & Odeh, 2005; Rostami, Babapour-Kheiroddin, Shalchi, Badinloo, & Hamzavi-Abedi, 2009), impulse control problems, attention-deficit/hyperactivity disorder (Weinstein, Staffelbach, & Biaggio, 2000), social regression and peer difficulties (Almqvist & Brandell-Forsberg, 1997), pessimism (Lavi & Solomon,

2005), and brief psychotic episodes and suicidal ideation (Famularo, Fenton, Kinscherff, & Augustyn, 1996; Yule, 1999).

Effects of Trauma on the Developing Child

Trauma has the potential to affect every aspect of the child's development and functioning, including brain development, psychosocial adaptation, and responses to stress and other life experiences (Hodas, 2006). This section includes a discussion of the associated structural and functional alterations in brain development affected by trauma, such as that frequently endured by refugee children. It begins with how trauma affects the brain and continues with the brain–body systems involved in adaptive responses to threat. Finally, the section concludes with a discussion of the critical importance of a secure attachment relationship, because the strength and quality of the relationship between parents and their children are fundamental to the effective development of children's brain architecture, functions, and capacity (Fogel, King, & Shanker, 2008). This section also reviews key protective and resilience factors and how these may buffer the adverse effects of trauma and increase the child's chances of positive adaptation.

Psychological trauma involves complex physiological systems and multiple structures within the brain, which are affected through a series of chemical activations and feedback loops (Hodas, 2006). In reacting to trauma the body uses two brain–body systems to deal with stress. The first response to fear involves a fast-acting stress system, known as the *fight-or-flight* or *hyperarousal* response, which rapidly mobilizes resources the body can use immediately to act on stress. For most individuals, this process ends shortly after the danger has passed. However, children exposed to severe and chronic trauma are often unable to move back down the arousal continuum and instead remain in a hyperaroused physiological state that interferes with their internal comfort level, ability to complete daily tasks, and capacity to listen, reason, acquire information, and learn new skills (Hodas, 2006).

The second major adaptation to threat when fight or flight is not possible, a common situation for young children, involves avoidant and psychological fleeing mechanisms that are *dissociative* or implicate "disengaging from stimuli in the external world and attending to an 'internal' world" (Perry, Pollard, Blakley, Baker, & Vigilante, 1995, p. 6). Dissociation is a defense against fear or pain and allows children to escape mentally from frightening or painful experiences (Moroz, 2005). Initially, as in the fight-or-flight response, catecholamines are released. Next, however, a largely opposite neurobiological process unfolds that results in decreased blood pressure and heart rate, decreased movement, high compliance, avoidance, numbing, and restricted affect, resulting in protective mental and physiological responses (Perry et al., 1995).

The primary adaptive response to threat varies according to a number of factors. A hyperarousal response is more common in males, older children, and when the individual has witnessed or played an active role in the traumatic event (Perry, 2003). A dissociative response is more common in younger children, females, and during traumatic experiences that are characterized by pain, helplessness, or an inability to escape (Perry, 2003). In most traumatic events, the individual uses a combination of these two primary adaptive response patterns (Perry, 2003). Trauma shocks the body and dysregulates the parasympathetic and sympathetic nervous systems, with the child's initial neurophysiologic response to stress establishing a pattern of response that will be triggered repetitively and at lower and lower levels of threat (Moroz, 2005).

MacMillan and colleagues (2009) reported that chronically elevated cortisol levels in trauma-affected children result in hypervigilance that interferes with their capacity to react to new situations, manage their emotions, and engage in learning. High-stress hormone levels contribute to limited attention span and concentration difficulties and have been associated with eating and sleeping problems that further affect the child's capacity to positively engage with learning opportunities (Australian Childhood Foundation, 2010). The prolonged stimulation of the hypothalamic–pituitary–adrenal axis may also result in conditions including dysthymia, persistent mild depression, major depression, oppositional defiant disorder, and attention-deficit/hyperactivity disorder (MacMillan et al., 2009).

Trauma and Brain Development: Physiology and Neurobiology

In the response to trauma there are specific brain pathways and structures that are affected. These include the hypothalamic–pituitary–adrenal axis, the brain stem, the right amygdala of the limbic system, the left hippocampus, the prefrontal cortex, the vermis of the cerebellum, the corpus callosum, and the cerebral cortex, with left cortex underdevelopment, referred to as hemispheric lateralization (van der Kolk, 2003). The effects of trauma in children may be multiplied because critical brain structures are developmentally susceptible to disruption (Australian Childhood Foundation, 2010).

Neurochemical changes affect structural brain maturation across the sensitive periods by altering developmental processes such as neurogenesis, myelination, synaptic overproduction, and pruning (Glaser, 2000). Magnetic resonance imaging studies of brains of children with a diagnosis of PTSD have shown that, compared with normal controls, children with a trauma history have smaller cerebral and prefrontal cortex volumes, smaller corpus callosum size (particularly in males), and larger lateral ventricles and frontal lobe cerebrospinal fluid volumes (De Bellis et al., 1999).

Extreme stress and psychological trauma trigger an increase in cortisol (the "stress hormone") levels to facilitate survival responses (MacMillan et al., 2009). At extreme levels cortisol can cause alterations in a child's brain development and, ultimately, destruction of brain cells, resulting in structural and functional brain changes (Delima & Vimpani, 2011). High levels of cortisol can disrupt cell differentiation, cell migration, and critical aspects of central nervous system integration and functioning (Moroz, 2005). In sum, excessive or prolonged stress can be toxic to the developing brain, particularly in the absence of moderating effects such as protection afforded by supportive relationships with caregivers (Shonkoff, 2009).

Memory, Learning, and Cognition

Research has revealed that children with chronic stress exposure or trauma are likely to have changes in brain development that further affect their neuropsychological functioning and undermine learning performance. These include attention and concentration, language comprehension, working and long-term memory, shifting from the abstract to the concrete and from the concrete to the abstract, and general cognitive flexibility and problem solving (Elliott, 2000). Refugee children, therefore, are likely to be compromised in their ability to engage successfully in learning experiences because of high stress levels and trauma experiences.

A number of studies of chronically traumatized children have demonstrated lower overall cognitive functioning, with specific deficits on standardized intelligence measures and in academic achievement, particularly in reading and mathematics. Exposure to stress or complex trauma affects the effectiveness of key brain structures involved in integration of the different dimensions of memory, which may compromise learning (Australian Childhood Foundation, 2010). Crozier and Barth (2005) examined the cognitive and academic abilities of chronically traumatized children, finding that these children were more likely than the normative sample to score significantly below average on standardized measures of intelligence and achievement in reading, writing, and mathematics. Similarly, a study of Sri Lankan children exposed to war showed significantly impaired cognitive development as well as negative impacts on memory and language abilities in the children's native Tamil and second language, English (Elbert et al., 2009).

Executive Functions

Studies have found performance deficits in executive function ability and attention to be associated with a trauma history. Located in the prefrontal regions of the frontal lobe and connected with other cortical, subcortical, and brainstem regions, *executive functions* refer to a set of cognitive abilities that control and regulate other skills and behaviors that are necessary for goal-directed behavior (Alvarez & Emory, 2006). These diverse abilities include directing attention (including shifting, inhibiting, and focusing attention), problem solving, manipulating information in working memory, and self-monitoring (DePrince, Weinzierl, & Combs, 2009). Children with problems in executive functioning may be impulsive, disorganized, and distracted; they may have difficulties delaying gratification and may demonstrate poor judgment, dysregulated behavior, and amotivation (Gabowitz, Zucker, & Cook, 2008; Hughes, 2002).

Children with PTSD were found to have difficulties with frontal lobe functioning, indicated by weakness in the areas of abstract reasoning and executive function, problem solving, learning and memory, and attention (Beers & De Bellis, 2002). Children with PTSD demonstrated greater distractibility and impulsivity as well. On emotion-laden, socially oriented tasks requiring applying past experience to future decision making, Cook et al. (2005) documented inappropriate prefrontal functioning and executive functioning deficits in self-awareness, lack of meaningful involvement with others, and difficulties assessing complex emotional experiences. The following case study illustrates the impact of trauma on the developing child.

Case Study: Trauma in a Refugee Child

> When Joy[1] was age 4, she and her older sibling were exposed to substantial ongoing violence and harassment, including witnessing their own mother's beating, suffering injuries from shrapnel, and observing harm and death come to their neighbors in their African village. Separated earlier from their father, who was thought to be detained in jail, Joy and her sibling were without protective and effective caregivers in the aftermath of the violence. They had to remain within their distressed community and had to seek medical assistance for their mother, later becoming separated from her. The family later resided for 3 years in a refugee camp before being resettled in Australia when Joy was 8 years old.
>
> On enrollment in school, Joy presented with significant adjustment difficulties, including aggressive and poor prosocial behaviors. She was frequently observed to be in a hyperaroused state, as shown by uncontrollable laughing without provocation. She also showed poor emotional regulation, as demonstrated by angry outbursts and screaming at peers; impulsivity, such as frequently leaving the classroom to wander around the school, kicking or punching buildings and equipment; and frequent

---

[1]The details of the case studies have been changed to preserve the anonymity of the individuals involved.

temper tantrums. At other times, Joy appeared to be in a dissociative state, remaining frozen in one position or being largely withdrawn and highly compliant. On one occasion, Joy became extremely distressed when seeing a doll's clothing item that was of army camouflage colors.

Despite a calm classroom, a structured and predictable routine with consistent behavioral management, and caring teachers and adults, Joy continued to demonstrate psychological and psychosocial distress and had difficulty in concentration and learning. Comprehensive trauma assessment provided diagnoses of PTSD with comorbid anxiety.

Trauma and Attachment

From pregnancy through early childhood, the quality of children's relationships with adults and caregivers has a significant impact on the child's cognitive, emotional, and social development (http://www.developingchild.harvard.edu). *Attachment* refers to an emotional tie between an infant or child and a caregiver and results in numerous behaviors on the part of both that help in establishing the relationship (Landy, 2009). According to John Bowlby (1958), the quality of the attachments is critical to the child's personality and particularly to his or her emotional and social development.

Refugee Children and Attachment

Refugee children are at particular risk of experiencing adverse effects of disrupted attachment patterns due to the conditions that result in seeking refuge and resettlement (Kaplan, 2009). Refugee families typically incur many different, and often prolonged, types of stressors that may influence and challenge the ability of the parent or caregiver to establish and maintain a secure relationship with their children. A positive attachment bond, crucial to the child developing capabilities in emotional regulation, relationships, cognition, motor development, and language, may be weakened in such instances and have a significant impact on the refugee child's development, including school-based performance. Although little data are available regarding the number of refugee children who have deceased or missing parents, the UNHCR (2011) reported that more than 15,500 asylum applications were lodged by unaccompanied or separated children from 69 countries in 2010 alone; these were mostly from Afghanistan and Somalia.

Children's early development depends on the health and well-being of their parents. Children up to 18 months of age need caregivers to soothe them so that their brains learn to self-regulate. Nurturing relationships build pathways of neural connections. A secure attachment results in infants being better able to soothe themselves in periods of stress because of the increased connections in the brain that decrease the amount of cortisol released when stressed (Southwick, Rasmusson, Barron, & Arnsten, 2005). For this reason, infants and toddlers may be particularly affected by the upheaval caused by the refugee experience, which may compromise their ability to self-regulate. The development of a significant number of young refugee children is affected by multiple, interrupted, and cumulative risk factors (Shonkoff & Phillips, 2000) that may give rise to negative changes in the attachment between children and their parents. Typically, parents are refugees themselves and may also suffer from PTSD, depression, and extreme stress. In addition, refugees are likely to experience events that deprive them of existing support structures, such as a supportive family or extended family network that is lost through death, separation, and displacement. Further, disempowering experiences such as victimization, abuse, and helplessness are common experiences in refugee camps (Ekblad, 1993). Protracted war and conflict, perilous flight, food insecurity, poverty, and adverse refugee camp conditions are likely to disrupt parent–child relationships. A parent with poor attachment capabilities is less able to pass on healthy attachment to the child, and this can be exacerbated if the parent is experiencing preoccupying life experiences. Many refugee parents may not be attuned, for example, to their children's emotional state and may have reduced capacity to develop a nurturing, sensitive, and healthy attachment and provide the significant protective factors necessary for normal brain development (Qouta, Punamaki, & El Sarraj, 2005).

It is important to consider the risk of *secondary trauma*, or children being raised by traumatized refugee parents, and the consequences of possible poor attachment on the child's life and development. Weise (2007) indicated that young children of traumatized mothers seem to perceive, directly or indirectly, their mother's traumas, and this affects the child's psychological development. Similarly, Qouta and colleagues (2005) reported a significant link between the mental health of mothers and that of their children, such that when mothers' psychological problems increased, children's problems did as well. In the presence of traumatic events, children often mimic their caregivers' responses, and the more disorganized the parent, the more likely the child will be disorganized as well (Streeck-Fischer & van der Kolk, 2000). Children may also respond to their caregiver's distress by avoiding or suppressing their own feelings or behaviors, by avoiding the parent altogether, or by becoming "parentified" in an attempt to reduce parental distress (Cook et al., 2005).

Finally postsettlement stressors, previously described, may affect the safe, supportive environment and stable, caring relationships that children need. Birman and colleagues (2005) indicated that parents preoccupied upon resettlement with finding shelter and employment and meeting their basic needs may neglect the emotional needs of their children. The following case study highlights the impact of disrupted attachment on the developing child.

Case Study: Attachment in a Refugee Child

Zara, age 3, and her two siblings were orphaned at very young ages when their parents were killed in war in Sudan. With the loss of their primary caregivers, the children were sent to a neighboring country and were looked after by a distant relative for a short period before being cared for by the friend of a maternal aunt who also had several of her own children. Zara was often unsupervised, experienced food insecurity, and lacked adequate protection.

Three years later, the children were resettled in Australia to live with another distant relative. This relationship was interrupted by an extended absence of the caregiver. On attending school for the first time, Zara, now 7 years old, presented as emotionally labile; she withdrew from peers and teachers, had poor social skills, was frequently noncompliant, and had problems in regulating her food intake, often taking food from others and family members. These difficulties were also evident in the home environment. Zara was observed to be chronically aroused and easily overstimulated and experienced difficulties in modulating strong emotions. She had problems focusing attention on classroom instruction and made limited academic progress.

Little is known of the quality of Zara's attachment to her mother in infancy and early childhood. However, it is likely that war conditions compromised her mother's ability to securely attach with her. The subsequent changes in caregivers at an early age may have interrupted the opportunity for her to form a secure attachment with any adult. Zara was assessed as being insecurely attached in light of her history of loss of parents, disrupted attachment patterns, and interrupted secure relationships, with likely periods of prolonged stress without consistent care affecting her social, emotional, and cognitive development.

Protective and Risk Factors

Both protective and risk factors interact in complex ways in the life of a child. In terms of protective factors, refugee children and adolescents are often extremely resilient and resourceful, despite the many adversities they face (Rutter, 2003). *Risk factors* are those factors associated with increased probability of negative outcomes, such as debilitating symptoms or failure to achieve potential, and *protective factors* are those associated with resistance to stress (Moroz, 2005). As previously noted, refugee children face numerous risk factors. Table 11.1 provides a framework for conceptualizing risk and protective factors.

TABLE 11.1
Protective and Risk Factors in Child Development

Protective factors	Risk factors
• Positive attachment and connections to emotionally supportive and competent adults within a child's family or community • Family adaptability and cohesion • Development of cognitive and self-regulation abilities • Positive beliefs about oneself (self-concept) and about the world as safe, predictable, fair • Behavioural control and internal locus of control • Positive temperament and easygoing disposition • Intelligence • Self-efficacy and motivation to take positive action on one's own behalf • Religious and spiritual belief systems	• Insecure attachment • Unaccompanied by family members • Gender and age • Preexisting mental disorders • Developmental disability, previous chronic physical illness, and malnutrition • Parental stress and distress including depression, PTSD, and other mental health conditions, especially maternal distress and depression • Psychological proximity of the threat to the child and child's subjective experience at the time of exposure • Parental or caregiver response to the trauma or threat and altered parenting patterns as a result of threat • Intensity and duration of exposure, including severity of the trauma • Degree of life threat and witnessing the event • Political persecution and imprisonment of father • Separation from loved ones, parents, and siblings • Knowing someone who was killed or injured • History of exposure to traumatic events, either experienced or witnessed • Family dissolution, violence, lack of cohesion, and ineffective organisation • Negative caregiver–child interactions • Low levels of social support • Postmigration stressors (e.g., housing, financial hardship, unemployment, language problems, social isolation, racial discrimination)

Note. PTSD = posttraumatic stress disorder.

Trauma and the Refugee Child Summary

Children exposed to multiple ongoing traumatic experiences, such as those experienced by refugee children growing up in a camp or war zone or living with parents who have been traumatized through torture or imprisonment, are likely to suffer negative emotional, behavioral, and cognitive consequences. Trauma results in a heightened biological stress response with subsequent neurobiological changes and, ultimately, impairs a child's learning capacity and executive functioning, resulting in an inability to achieve the academic functioning and skills needed to underpin adult function (Beers & De Bellis, 2002). Experiences of physical and emotional trauma and loss and perceived or actual abandonment may give rise to negative developmental consequences (Hamilton, Anderson, Frater-Mathieson, Loewen, & Moore, 2005).

Insecure attachments alter the normal developmental process for children, which can severely affect a child's ability to communicate and interact with others and form healthy relationships throughout life (Bacon & Richardson, 2001). Frequently, children with a trauma history are referred to the school's special education services because of a failure to progress socially and academically at a rate commensurate with their peers, and many are diagnosed with learning or emotional and behavioral disorders (Shonk & Cicchetti, 2001). Knowledge and identification of the diverse life experiences the refugee child has had that may affect learning is critical and informs meaningful assessments and assists in determining appropriate educational programs and interventions. As a result of their experiences, refugee children may manifest psychological difficulties, distress, and functional impairment and demonstrate delays or deficits in their ability to achieve age-appropriate behavioral development and emotional regulation. Table 11.2 provides an overview of screening and assessment measures that may be appropriate for use in schools.

HEALTH CONCERNS AND THE REFUGEE CHILD

Malnutrition

The World Health Organization (WHO; as cited in Infonet-Biovision, 2012) defines *malnutrition* as "the cellular imbalance between the supply of nutrients and the energy and the body's demand for them to ensure growth, maintenance and specific functions" (para. 1). Malnutrition is responsible for the death of over half of the world's children (Pelletier & Frongillo, 2003) and is a major risk factor for illness and death in refugee children. Malnutrition alters various events in the brain, potentially resulting in behavioral and cognitive abnormalities (Morgane, Mokler, & Galler, 2002). Because of the

TABLE 11.2
Measures Developed, Adapted, and Used With Refugee Populations

Name of scale	Domains assessed	Author	Informant/reporter	Age range
Behavioral Assessment System for Children (BASC, BASC–2)	Behaviors, thoughts, emotions; also adaptive and maladaptive behaviors in home, school, and community	Reynolds & Kamphaus (1992, 2004)	Self-report, teacher rating, parent rating, structured developmental history, classroom observation	2 years–21 years, 11 months
Child Behavior Checklist (CBCL)	Behavior problems and social competencies	Achenbach (1991)	Teacher and parent report, youth self-report	2–18 years
Achenbach System of Empirically Based Assessment		Achenbach & McConaughy (1997)		
Child PTSD–Reaction Index (CPTSD–RI)	Symptoms of PTSD	Frederick, Pynoos, & Nader (1992)	Self-report	7–18 years
Depression Self-Rating Scale (DSRS)	Depression	Birleson, (1981)	Self-report	8–14 years
Hopkins Symptom Check-list (HSCL)	Anxiety and depression	Derogatis, Lipman, Rickels, Uhlenhuth, & Covi (1974)	Self-report	Adults and adolescents
Impact of Events Scale (R–IES)	PTSD	Smith, Perrin, Dyregrov, & Yule (2003)	Self-report	8 years and older
Revised Children's Manifest Anxiety Scale (RCMAS)	Anxiety	Reynolds & Richmond (1978)	Self-report	6–19 years

(continues)

TABLE 11.2
Measures Developed, Adapted, and Used With Refugee Populations *(Continued)*

Name of scale	Domains assessed	Author	Informant/reporter	Age range
Strengths and Difficulties Questionnaire (SDQ)	Positive and negative behavioural symptoms	Goodman, Meltzer, & Bailey (1998)	Teacher and parent report, youth self-report	4–17 years
Trauma Symptom Checklist for Children (TSCC)	Distress and symptoms related to trauma	Briere (1996)	Self-report	8–16 years
Trauma Symptom Checklist for Young Children (TSCYC)	PTSD and related symptoms (intrusion, avoidance, arousal, sexual concerns, dissociation, anxiety, depression, anger/aggression)	Briere (2005)	Caregiver report	3–12 years
UCLA PTSD Index for DSM–IV (PTSD–I)	PTSD symptoms	Pynoos, Rodriquez, Steinberg, Stuber, & Frederick (1998)	Self-report, parent report	7–18 years
War Trauma Questionnaire (WTQ)	War trauma exposure	Macksoud (1992)	Self-report	Children and adolescents
War Trauma Screening Scale (WTSS)	Violence and adversity experienced in war exposure	Layne, Stuvland, Saltzman, Djapo, & Pynoos (1999)	Self-report	Adolescents

Note. PTSD = posttraumatic stress disorder.

critical role played by proper nutrition in development and the frequency of malnutrition experienced by refugee children, the following section specifically addresses the issue of malnutrition on learning and the brain. The adequacy of diet from conception across childhood, particularly while the brain is rapidly growing, has significant and lasting implications for children's functioning in all domains.

Nutrients and growth factors regulate brain development during fetal and early postnatal life, with the brain being particularly vulnerable to nutritional insults. All nutrients are important for neuronal cell growth and development, with certain nutrients such as protein, energy, certain fats (n-6 and n-3), iron, zinc, copper, iodine, selenium, vitamin A, choline, and folate having greater effects on brain development than do others (Georgieff, 2007). Early nutritional insult at a critical period, which represents a once-only developmental window, can neither be repeated nor reversed (Morgane et al., 2002) and may result in brain dysfunction. A growing body of evidence asserts that the effects of insult on the developing brain may be long-lasting and lead to permanent deficits in learning and behavior (Galler & Barrett, 2001; Strupp, & Levitsky, 1995).

Micronutrient malnutrition is the world's most prevalent nutritional problem (Murray-Kolb et al., 2012). *Micronutrients* are those essential nutrients required in small amounts for growth, health, and behavioral functioning. A diet low in plant-based foods, such as dark green leafy vegetables and orange-colored fruits and vegetables, and animal source foods, such as liver, egg yolk, dairy products, and fish, may result in a vitamin A deficiency that manifests behaviorally as night blindness, growth retardation, anemia, impaired immune system, and severe infections (Neumann, Gewa, & Bwibo, 2004). Iron deficiency is a major cause of anemia and can have adverse functional consequences on cognitive development and learning, behavior, and psychomotor development. Lozoff and colleagues (Lozoff et al., 2006; Lozoff, Jimenez, Hagen, Mollen, & Wolf, 2000; Lozoff, Jimenez, & Wolf, 1991) have demonstrated the persistence of cognitive deficits in young children subsequent to iron deficiency anemia treatment in a widely cited longitudinal analysis of cognitive and motor effects. A group of malnourished children tested in early childhood and again in adolescence showed persistent arithmetic, writing, and motor function deficits as well as more frequent referrals to special education. Affective and social and emotional difficulties and attention problems were also observed.

Iodine deficiency disorders constitute the single major cause of preventable fetal and infant brain damage and retarded psychomotor development in young children (Delange, 2001). It has been estimated that iodine deficiency may also result in lowered intellectual ability where at least 15 IQ points may be forfeited (United Nations System Standing Committee on Nutrition

[UNSCN], 2004). Even a marginal deficiency may reduce a child's mental development by 10%, which then adversely affects school performance. Iodine deficiency disorders can be eliminated by the addition of iodine to cooking salt (UNSCN, 2004).

Vitamin D deficiency is highly prevalent in refugee children, particularly those originally from sub-Saharan Africa (Bwibo & Neumann, 2003). A deficiency of vitamin D and/or calcium, combined with reduced exposure to sunlight, which converts 7-dehydrocholesterol in the skin to vitamin D3, may result in varying conditions. Vitamin D is found in a few foods such as oily fish, goat and cow's milk, and some fortified cereals. Vitamin D deficiency conditions include rickets, low height for age, delayed walking, leg bowing, and seizures; failure to thrive and muscle weakness and pain are also associated with the insufficiency.

Laus, Vales, Costa, and Almeida (2011) offered some possible explanations for the impact of malnutrition in early life on cognitive development. During critical periods of central nervous system development, malnutrition may affect chemical reactions such as cell division (neurogenesis and gliogenesis), migration of neurons and glial cells, cellular differentiation, myelinization, synapse formation, and synthesis and release of neurotransmitters. Nutritional insult from the final third gestational phase to the first 2 years of life has the potential to cause irreversible morphological, neurophysiological, neurochemical, and functional damages. Cortical involvement may be impaired—for example, changes in the right parietal cortex, which is related to visuospatial functions, and changes in hippocampal functioning may result in deficits in memory and spatial learning. Alterations in the central nervous system are associated with motor and cognitive function delays, such as problems with attention, impaired school performance, decreased IQ scores, memory and learning deficiencies, and reduced social skills.

Severe, as well as mild to moderate malnutrition, affects all aspects of a child's development, with malnourished children exhibiting health, growth, cognition, motor, social, and behavioral changes. Developmental delays, delays meeting key milestones, delayed mental development, and permanent cognitive deficits, which affect school performance and the ability to learn and grow to full potential, are the lifelong sequelae of malnutrition. Growth deficit as a result of malnutrition is not only associated with mortality but also compromises a child's resistance to infectious diseases, contributes to delayed psychomotor development, and affects cognitive and language functioning and academic achievement. The brain areas affected by malnutrition may also result in socioemotional sequelae. In classrooms, behavioral and attitudinal presentations may encompass reduced motivation, low energy levels, irritability, anxiety, apathy, attention deficits, and reduced social responsiveness and interaction with the environment (Jukes, 2005; Meeks Gardner,

Grantham-McGregor, & Chang, 1993). The extent of delay and resultant deficit depends on both the severity and duration of compromised nutrition and the age at which malnutrition occurred, with younger-aged children likely to be most vulnerable and at risk (Shashidhar, 2011) because insult on the brain may be irreversible if occurrence was during a critical period of rapid brain growth (Benton, 2010; de Souza, Fernandes, & Taveres do Carmo, 2011; Nassar, Shaaban, Nassar, Younis, & Abdel-Mobdy, 2012).

The following case study highlights the cumulative threats to the health and nutritional status of young children from conception through the early years of development, particularly the impact of mild to moderate malnutrition on cognitive development.

Case Study: Malnutrition in a Refugee Child

Poh was born an underweight baby in a remote village in Burma. Her mother's nutritional intake during pregnancy was described as multideficient. She was unable to produce breast milk when Poh was born and, because of the family's extreme poverty and food insecurity, Poh was fed the liquid from boiled rice mixed with sugar. Poh continued to be undernourished throughout infancy and early childhood. Her developmental milestones were substantially delayed. Poh produced some speech sounds at age 3 and single words at age 5. She experienced coordination problems and did not begin walking until after age 3. Rudimentary schooling was available in the village, but Poh was considered too delayed to be able to access it. When Poh was 7, the family was forced to relocate to a refugee camp along the Thailand–Burma border, where they lived for several years before being resettled in Australia. As a student at her new school in Australia, Poh presented as quiet and compliant and lacking in curiosity. She did not initiate conversation or interaction with others, answered questions in one-word sentences in her first language, and demonstrated limited adaptive functioning and self-help skills, which required adult support.

A language assessment confirmed Poh's poor language skills. A comprehensive nonverbal cognitive assessment revealed Poh to be of very delayed cognitive ability. Medical evaluations resulted in diagnoses of significant global developmental delay, latent tuberculosis infection, persisting vitamin D deficiency, recurrent severe bilateral otitis media, and moderate to severe bilateral hearing loss. It is likely that Poh's prenatal and postnatal mal- or undernutrition, as reported by her mother, had a deleterious impact on her cognitive functioning. Her mother was likely to have been malnourished herself across the pregnancy; poor stores of iron, zinc, vitamin A, and iodine may have contributed to compromised fetal growth and development. Nutrients normally provided through breast milk to the infant, assuming an adequate diet in the lactating mother, would have not been available in the rice formula, hence there was poor nutrition across the period of rapid brain growth, limiting development of important aspects of her brain architecture.

Malaria

Malaria, a parasitic disease caused by plasmodium parasites that spread to humans through bites from infected mosquitoes (WHO, 2011), constitutes a major threat to child survival (WHO, 2008). *Plasmodium falciparum* (*P. falciparum*), one of the four malarial parasites that infect humans, is responsible for the majority of malaria deaths globally. *P. falciparum* produces a range of acute neurological manifestations and sequelae through direct contact with the central nervous system; cerebral malaria is the severe point of the clinical spectrum (Newton, Hien, & White, 2000). This section describes the impact of infection on children's neurocognitive functioning and subsequent educational outcomes.

Cerebral malaria (CM), defined as malaria prostration, multiple seizures or severe anaemia, has been estimated to affect over 785,000 children, with peak incidence in preschool children in sub-Saharan Africa annually (John et al., 2008). *P. falciparum* can cause anemia through the destruction of red blood cells and can damage the brain and other body organs by blocking the capillaries that supply essential blood to these organs (Tjitra et al., 2008). Children surviving CM often sustain brain injury that results in long-term neurocognitive, neurological, and behavioral impairments. Impairments may occur in motor functioning, including coordination; speech, hearing, and vision; cognitive and language functioning; and behavioral abnormalities or difficulties, such as hallucinations and psychosis (Kihara, Carter, & Newton, 2006). The influence of CM often does not end when children recover from the disease's acute symptoms. It has been reported that malaria in childhood is likely to have subtle to profound long-term effects on cognition, behavior, and school performance (Holding & Snow, 2001; Price, Douglas, & Anstey, 2009).

John and colleagues (2008) investigated the long-term effects of malaria on cognitive functioning. Six months following an episode of CM, 21.4% of infected Ugandan children, ages 5 to 12 years, demonstrated significantly poorer performance on measures of working memory, attention, and tactile learning as compared with healthy community children. At 2-year follow-up, cognitive impairment was present in 26.3% of children who had had CM as compared with 8% of the community children, indicating a 3.67% increased risk of cognitive impairment, after adjustment for age, gender, nutrition, home environment, and level of schooling. Although one child with diagnosed deficit at 6 months was not found to have deficit at 24 months, four additional children were found to have deficit at the follow-up period. The research suggests that cognitive impairment may continue to unfold developmentally across the years subsequent to a CM episode.

Behavioral and neuropsychiatric disorders have been demonstrated to occur after CM. Research with Ugandan children demonstrated behavioral problems, including hyperactivity, impulsiveness, and inattentiveness, similar to those observed in children diagnosed with attention-deficit/hyperactivity disorder and conduct disorders with aggressive, self injurious, or destructive behavior where no prior behavioral problems existed (Idro et al., 2010). Two patterns were observed: The first pattern demonstrated immediate onset of deficits, and the second pattern showed late-onset deficits, behavior problems developing within months, and epilepsy developing within months to years after the injury. The study also clearly documented that deficits arose in motor function, vision, speech, and hearing as long-term sequelae following CM.

Although some insults to the brain and some neurologic deficits related to malaria improve over time, with most changes occurring within the first 1 to 2 years (Mung'Ala-Odera, Snow, & Newton, 2004), other impairments—such as less severe motor deficits, hearing and visual impairments, speech and language difficulties, behavior difficulties, and learning problems including memory and attention—may only become evident as the child grows older. This is because school tasks become more complex cognitively and much of what is taught is encoded in literate language, with most basic academic skills being delivered through verbal expression (Levine, 1999). Careful and comprehensive exploration of a refugee child's developmental history is both essential and critical in determining the occurrence of infection and illness, subsequent neurological sequelae, and the possible effects on the child's development and functioning. The following case study illustrates the impact of malarial infection on neurocognitive functioning.

Case Study: Malaria in a Refugee Child

Deng was reported by his parents to have suffered from untreated malaria at approximately 3 years of age because of the absence of available medical assistance in the African refugee camp in which he was born. Developmental milestones, as reported by his parents, were considered age appropriate: Deng crawled at 6 months, walked at 12 months, and babbled by 12 months. When he was 3, Deng experienced high fever for several days and, according to his parents, minor convulsive movements of his limbs, irregular breathing, and episodes of apparent unconsciousness. At age 6, Deng and his family resettled in Western Australia. Shortly after arrival, Deng was hospitalized with severe malaria. According to medical records, his hearing and vision were in the normal range.

Deng commenced school in an intensive English center and presented with challenging behaviors, including physical aggression and withdrawal, retention and memory difficulties, attention and concentration problems, limited prosocial and self-help skills, and deficits in fine-motor control and coordination. The parents reported difficulties at home, which included limited self-help skills, aggression, and delayed first language speech and language skills. Over a 2-year period Deng received intensive teacher and educational assistant support, an individualized education plan with teaching adjustments and behavioral intervention. Deng continued to have difficulties with his individualized education plan, making limited progress; he evidenced memory and retention problems and had poor skills in social interaction. Further neurological assessment was indicated, and epilepsy was diagnosed. Cognitive assessment through the Universal Nonverbal Intelligence Test (Bracken & McCallum, 1998) indicated very delayed intellectual functioning.

CONCLUSION

Students from refugee backgrounds are often referred to school psychologists for significant learning and behavior difficulties, including assessment of intellectual disability and social, emotional, and behavioral problems (Fraine & McDade, 2009). It is critical that school psychologists possess a comprehensive understanding and appreciation of the complexity of factors experienced by refugee children prior to and after resettlement and how these may influence the student's performance within a school setting. When the factors discussed throughout this chapter are carefully and systematically explored and evaluated, the school psychologist can better understand the impact of being a refugee on a child's learning and behavior in order to adequately assess and intervene with this population. The school psychologist must carefully consider the most appropriate assessments to employ with refugee children when it has been determined that a formal evaluation is required. Table 11.3 lists several nonverbal measures used with culturally and linguistically diverse students that purport to decrease cultural factors and bias and to decrease language-dependent or environmentally dependent content. Appendix 11.1 provides a checklist of the constellation of factors that require careful evaluation of the extent to which they may be present and affect the refugee student's learning; it is intended to complement a complete academic, language, and adaptive functioning evaluation. Table 11.4 provides a framework for obtaining information about the refugee child's psychosocial history and developmental and attachment history, the history of exposure to violence and traumatic events, medical and health history, current family functioning and acculturative stress, and the cultural expectations and norms of the refugee child and his or her family.

TABLE 11.3
Nonverbal Intelligence Tests

Intelligence test	Timed bonus items	Age range	Administration time	Authors
Comprehensive Test of Nonverbal Intelligence (C–TONI)	No	6–adult	60 minutes	Hammill, Pearson, & Wiederholt (1996)
Leiter–R		2–20 years, 11 months	25–40 minutes	Roid & Miller (1997)
Naglieri Non-Verbal Ability Test–Individual (NNAT–Individual)	No	5–17 years, 11 months	25–35 minutes	Naglieri & Ronning (2000)
Raven's Progressive Matrices (RPM)	No	5–adult	15–45 minutes	Raven (1992)
Universal Nonverbal Intelligence Test (UNIT)	Yes	5–17 years, 11 months	Extended battery: 30–45 minutes	Bracken & McCallum (1998)
Wechsler Nonverbal Scale of Ability (WNV)	No	4–21 years, 11 months	45 minutes	Wechsler & Naglieri (2006)

TABLE 11.4
Premigration, Migration, and Resettlement History: Parent Interview (Developmental, Psychosocial, Trauma, and Postsettlement)

Prenatal/early development history	Key areas to investigate
Mother's health	Health, nutrition, medical conditions, illnesses, drugs, and medicines prenatal and postpartum (e.g., malaria, neurological conditions, anemia) Living conditions (e.g., refugee camp, war zone, flight, postsettlement) Note: Chronic stress, drugs or alcohol, insufficient nutrition in pregnancy may harm a baby's developing brain. Pregnancy problems and availability of antenatal care (including labor and delivery) Maternal stress, depression, PTSD, torture or trauma, rape, and postpartum depression Note: Adverse environments can be particularly damaging to the young child's developing brain and affect attachment. Hospital or midwifery assistance or unassisted

(continues)

TABLE 11.4
Premigration, Migration, and Resettlement History: Parent Interview
(Developmental, Psychosocial, Trauma, and Postsettlement)   *(Continued)*

Prenatal/early development history	Key areas to investigate
	Birth trauma or difficult birth (e.g., long birth, breech, head or neck injury, forceps, difficulties due to female genital mutilation: reinfibulation)
	Number of children (previous miscarriages, reproductive loss, death of children), birth order
	Age of mother, risk of birth anomalies or genetic disorders (e.g., consanguinity, sickle-cell disease, diabetes), whether father was present or absent or whether involuntarily separated
Baby's health	Premature, carried to term, gestation period
	Complications after delivery (e.g., fetal distress, including birth defects, health, illness, and sickness)
	Birth weight and weight gain (e.g., failure to thrive and affecting factors, healthy)
	Breastfeeding or alternative feeding (including problems, insufficient lactation, length of time, mother's nutrition)
Developmental milestones	Motor skills: age at sitting up, crawling, standing, walking (including problems, abnormalities, or delays)
Important to inquire if the parent feels the child's skills were late, on track, or early and if they were achieved at a similar time to siblings (through their specific cultural lens)	Skills in: balance, catching and throwing, running, body coordination and strength
	Social smiling, subsequent social skill development
	Language milestones: age at babbling, single words, pointing, couple words, speaking in sentences (including how well or whether there were deficits: stuttering, unusual speech tone, hard to understand, limited conversation, listening skills)
	Languages spoken (i.e., primary or dominant language[s], languages exposed to in refugee camp or host country)
	Toilet training: age introduced, age at bladder and bowel control day and night and occurrence of accidents or bedwetting (e.g., cultural expectations differ and practices may be affected by availability of hygiene equipment and materials, latrines)
	Feeding: breast fed or bottle fed, weaning, introduction of solids, amount of and nutritional quality of foods or food insecurity
	Sleeping patterns: nightmares, disturbances, difficulties, and fears of separation

(continues)

TABLE 11.4
Premigration, Migration, and Resettlement History: Parent Interview
(Developmental, Psychosocial, Trauma, and Postsettlement)   *(Continued)*

Prenatal/early development history	Key areas to investigate
	Growth progression: height and weight, stunting, rickets
	Note: cultural physical differences (e.g., Dinka: tall, lithe; Burmese: small, slim)
	Developmental delays or disabilities: chronic infections, recurrent illnesses, environmental deprivation or adversities
Health, illnesses, medical history	Nutritional status: availability of foods, rations, food insecurity, malnutrition (severe or chronic, iodine deficiency, water availability and quality)
Additional risk factors to consider due to the refugee experience	Eating patterns: poor appetite, feeding problems, overeating, hoarding, or stealing foods
	Consider interplay of malnutrition and infection
	Hospital admissions or medical assistance: availability (e.g., cerebral malaria Pl. falciparum, encephalitis, infectious diseases, seizures, fevers and vomiting, anemia, dehydration, diarrhea, loss of consciousness, coma
	Health and treatment of child and sequelae, with or in absence of medical intervention (e.g., traditional medicines and treatment)
	Accidents, injuries, and head trauma
	Vision and hearing (e.g., delays; deficits; middle ear disease; deafness due to head trauma, shelling, explosions; refractive errors; visual acuity problems)
	Note: likely to have not been assessed prior to resettlement
	Temperament: including fussy, irritable, difficult to soothe, withdrawn, overactive or underactive, passive, enjoyed or rejected cuddles, contact
	Attachment and mother–child relationship: parental distress, psychological well-being, emotional unavailability, parenting capacity to provide protection, care, nurturing of child, child's attachment behaviors, seeking comfort, stranger wariness
	Periods of prolonged separation during early years and availability of a replacement caregiver, including child's emotional reactions: distress, withdrawal, separation fears, anxiety, anger
	Note: Healthy brain development is dependent on loving, stable, and protective attachments with caregivers.

(continues)

TABLE 11.4
Premigration, Migration, and Resettlement History: Parent Interview
(Developmental, Psychosocial, Trauma, and Postsettlement) *(Continued)*

Prenatal/early development history	Key areas to investigate
Trauma history Note: Traumatic stress can derive from a single life-threatening or horrifying event or through repeated exposures. Note: Factors or responses that may have mitigated or intensi-fied the child and family's trau-matic responses Note: a dose–effect relationship between cumulative trauma and symptoms of emotional distress	Sensitive inquiry about the circumstances of any traumatic event(s): age (consider "critical periods" of brain development); fam-ily members involved and how they were affected; physical injury; nature of abuse or trauma (violence, war, sexual or physical assault); direct experience or witnessing of events; death, loss, or separation from par-ents and family; parent ability to protect and comfort child(ren); and timing and duration (i.e., preflight, migration, and resettlement and parent, family, community responses and level of support and subsequent indi-vidual and family functioning, cohesion Note: A useful approach is, "Some people have had bad things happen to themselves and their families. Has anything happened to you or your family that could be affecting your health or the way you are feeling now?" (Victorian Foundation for Survivors of Tor-ture, 2012, p. 17)
Emotional and behavioral functioning Note: as an infant, toddler, early childhood, and current age	Somatic complaints, fears and anxieties, excessive dependency or fierce self-suffi-ciency, depression or withdrawal, crying, enuresis, sleep problems, nightmares, irri-tability, anger, aggression, impulsivity, peer and sibling relationship difficulties and dif-ficulties relating to others, avoiding contacts, not wanting to attend school, regressive behaviors, conduct disorders, grief reac-tions, dissociation, hypervigilance, difficul-ties in emotional regulation, preoccupation with the traumatic event (e.g., through play, drawing, risk-taking behavior)
Settlement history and stressors Note: Knowledge of the time of arrival, country of origin, flight, and asylum will provide prelimi-nary information pertaining to the nature of conflict, war, and possible traumatic experiences (e.g., visa documentation).	Sensitively track migration and movement and reasons and conditions and age of child across each move Members comprising the family unit includ-ing involuntary separation, death, members remaining in country of origin and asylum

(continues)

TABLE 11.4
Premigration, Migration, and Resettlement History: Parent Interview
(Developmental, Psychosocial, Trauma, and Postsettlement)   *(Continued)*

Prenatal/early development history	Key areas to investigate
Postsettlement stressors Note: Consider the cumulative effect of a number of stressors experienced.	Cultural distance between the original and resettlement culture and cultural and traditional dislocation Social support, extended family members, community supports Acculturative stress: asylum-seeking process, access to employment, education, housing and frequent moves, utility costs, welfare and legal difficulties, socioeconomic stressors, racism, language barriers Role and gender changes and responsibilities and intergenerational conflict

Note. From "A Bilingual (English and Spanish) Psychoeducational Assessment MODEL Grounded in CHC Theory: A Cross Battery Approach," by P. Olvera and L. Gómez-Cerrillo, 2011, *Contemporary School Psychology, 13,* p. 122. Copyright 2011 by California Association of School Psychologists. Reprinted with permission.

APPENDIX 11.1: CHECKLIST FOR ASSESSMENT OF REFUGEE CHILDREN

(Intended to complement a complete, academic, language, and adaptive functioning evaluation)

Birth date
- ☐ Specific or general (12/31 or 1/1)
  - ○ If general—such as last or first day of year—likely actual birthdate is unknown
  - ○ Attempt to validate or refer for wrist x-ray when clearly much younger or older than recorded date

Developmental history
- ☐ Nutrition:
  - ○ Mother's nutrition during pregnancy? Meals? Vitamins?
  - ○ Postnatal: Mother able to produce breast milk or availability of nutritionally adequate replacement fluid or formula?
  - ○ Early months: Diet included necessary vitamins and minerals (iron, iodine, zinc, vitamin A, B complex, D)?
  - ○ Nutritional adequacy of child's diet post weaning and early childhood? Typical meal? Frequency of meals?
- ☐ Birth:
  - ○ Gestation period, delivery, health, trauma
- ☐ Milestones:
  - ○ Motor Skills: sitting, crawling, walking
  - ○ Language: babbling, words, sentences
  - ○ Toileting: bladder and bowel control
  - ○ Growth: height and weight progression, head circumference
- ☐ Medical:
  - ○ Hearing and vision
  - ○ Malaria, infection, anemia, injury, head trauma, accidents
  - ○ Chronic conditions (often unrecognized)
  - ○ Developmental delays or disabilities, including dental health
  - ○ Any medical attention available
    Refer for pediatric or medical investigation. Neuropsychological assessment may be required to investigate brain–behavior relationships
- ☐ Attachment:
  - ○ Quality of mother–child relationship and factors affecting the capacity to provide care, safety, emotional availability, and nurturance
  - ○ Changes in caregiver or periods of prolonged separation

Trauma history
- ☐ Exposed to war or violence? Conditions of refugee camp? If indicated recommend
  - ○ Referral for specialist assessment or
  - ○ Skilled school psychologist assessment
  - ○ Referral for culturally appropriate mental health services or programs

Language
- ☐ Parents literate in first language
- ☐ Determine language proficiency, language dominance, and language preference
- ☐ Determine developmental stage child is functioning at in second language acquisition
- ☐ Determine competence in basic interpersonal communication skills and cognitive academic language proficiency in first language and second language (language disorder must be present in both to be considered disordered)
- ☐ Consider stage and proficiency levels and compare with length of current instruction

School history
- ☐ Schooling availability and/or disruptions (exposure and opportunity to learn)
- ☐ Formality/quality: teacher qualification, language(s) of instruction, class size, literacy and numeracy skill levels, subjects learned

Resettlement schooling history
- ☐ Appropriateness of the type of educational placement
- ☐ Effectiveness of the teaching methodology: instruction, strategies, intervention, evidence-based programs, specialist teachers
- ☐ Adequate length of time, assistance, and support in English language instruction before exiting program or special education referral
- ☐ Student's achievement levels and progress has been tracked and monitored and also compared with like peers to assist in discerning ESL related factors from disability
- ☐ Difficulties in acclimating to school: routines, teaching style, expectations, and norms of behavior, discipline, lack of experience with materials or equipment

Acculturation

- [ ] Determine the level of acculturation to new culture and structured schooling, social system with higher demands than refugee camp
- [ ] Determine if acculturative stress is affecting self-esteem, socialization, behavior, language development and learning (by-products may look similar to emotional or behavioral difficulties)

Behavioral and social assessment

- [ ] Indicated when student presents with ongoing and persistent behavioral difficulties and social impairment (beyond adjustment period, failure to respond to behavior management). Multiple informants: Parent, teacher, and self-reporting (if applicable). Measures: For example, BASC, CBCL, SDQ (adapted and used with refugee populations)

Intellectual and cognitive assessment

- [ ] Indicated when student has not made expected progress and when all potential causes for learning difficulties, behavior problems, or low performance have been systematically explored and been ruled out
- [ ] Selection of most appropriate assessment instruments (few measures normed on diverse cultural groups). Review psychometric properties and use with specialised groups. Several nonverbal measures purport decrease in cultural factors and bias and language and environmentally dependent content
- [ ] Assessment should identify strengths and weaknesses, indicate how student adapts to new learning, and application of new skills in a variety of contexts
- [ ] Determine adaptive functioning if student suspected of intellectual disability

Parental input essential to discern how well child meets the personal and social demands unique to their culture.

- [ ] Memory: assess if noted to be problematic and deficits persist (i.e., visual recall, spatial memory, verbal retrieval, working memory)
- [ ] Interpret results by integration of all available formal, informal, and psychometric assessment results, across all domains

REFERENCES

Achenbach, T. M. (1991). *Manual for Child Behavioral Checklist.* Burlington, VT: University of Vermont.

Achenbach, T. M., & McConaughy, S. H. (1997). *Empirically based assessment of child and adolescent psychopathology: Practical applications* (2nd ed.). Thousand Oaks, CA: Sage.

Almqvist, K., & Brandell-Forsberg, M. (1997). Refugee children in Sweden: Post-traumatic stress disorder in Iranian preschool children exposed to organized violence. *Child Abuse & Neglect, 21,* 351–366. doi:10.1016/S0145-2134(96)00176-7

Alvarez, J. A., & Emory, E. (2006). Executive function and the frontal lobes: A meta-analytic review. *Neuropsychology Review, 16*(1), 17–42. doi:10.1007/s11065-006-9002-x

Australian Childhood Foundation. (2010). *Making space for learning: Trauma informed practice in schools.* Retrieved from http://www.childhood.org.au/~/media/Files/Fundraising%20files/Fundraising%20resource%20files/Making%20space%20for%20learning%20ACF.ashx

Bacon, H., & Richardson, S. (2001). Attachment theory and child abuse: An overview of the literature for practitioners. *Child Abuse Review, 10,* 377–397. doi:10.1002/car.718

Beers, S. R., & De Bellis, M. D. (2002). Neuropsychological function in children with maltreatment-related posttraumatic stress disorder. *The American Journal of Psychiatry, 159,* 483–486. doi:10.1176/appi.ajp.159.3.483

Benton, D. (2010). The influence of dietary status on the cognitive performance of children. *Molecular Nutrition & Food Research, 54,* 457–470. doi:10.1002/mnfr.200900158

Berman, H. (2001). Children and war: Current understandings and future directions. *Public Health Nursing, 18,* 243–252. doi:10.1046/j.1525-1446.2001.00243.x

Birleson, P. (1981). The validity of depressive disorder in childhood and the development of a self-rating scale: A research report. *Journal of Child Psychology and Psychiatry, 22,* 73–88. doi.org/10.1111/j.1469-7610.1981.tb00533.x

Birman, D., Ho, J., Pulley, E., Batia, K., Everson, M. L., Ellis, H., . . . Gonzalez, A. (2005). *Mental health interventions for refugee children in resettlement.* Retrieved from http://www.nctsnet.org/nctsn_assets/pdfs/materials_for_applicants/MH_Interventions_for_Refugee_Children.pdf

Bowlby, J. (1958). The nature of the child's tie to his mother. *The International Journal of Psychoanalysis, 39,* 350–373.

Bracken, B. A., & McCallum, R. S. (1998). *Universal Nonverbal Intelligence Test (UNIT).* Itasca, IL: Riverside.

Briere, J. (1996). *Trauma Symptom Checklist for Children (TSCC).* Odessa, FL: Psychological Assessment Resources.

Briere, J. (2005). *Trauma Symptom Checklist for Young Children (TSCYC)*. Odessa, FL: Psychological Assessment Resources.

Bwibo, N. O., & Neumann, C. G. (2003). The need for animal source foods by Kenyan children. *The Journal of Nutrition, 133*, 3936S–3940S.

Cook, A., Spinazzola, J., Ford, J., Lanktree, C., Blaustein, M., Cloitre, M., . . . van der Kolk, B. (2005). Complex trauma in children and adolescents. *Psychiatric Annals, 35*, 390–398.

Crozier, J. C., & Barth, R. P. (2005). Cognitive and academic functioning in maltreated children. *Children & Schools, 27*(4), 197–206. doi:10.1093/cs/27.4.197

De Bellis, M. D., Keshavan, M. S., Clark, D. B., Casey, B. J., Giedd, J. N., Boring, A. M., . . . Ryan, N. D. (1999). Developmental traumatology part II: Brain development. *Biological Psychiatry, 45*, 1271–1284. doi:10.1016/S0006-3223(99)00045-1

Delange, F. (2001). Iodine deficiency as a cause of brain damage. *Postgraduate Medical Journal, 77*, 217–220. doi:10.1136/pmj.77.906.217

Delima, J., & Vimpani, G. (2011). The neurobiological effects of childhood maltreatment: An often overlooked narrative related to the long-term effects of early childhood trauma? *Family Matters, 89*, 42–57.

DePrince, A. P., Weinzierl, K. M., & Combs, M. D. (2009). Executive function performance and trauma exposure in a community sample of children. *Child Abuse & Neglect, 33*, 353–361. doi:10.1016/j.chiabu.2008.08.002

Derogatis, L. R., Lipman, R. S., Rickels, K., Uhlenhuth, E. H., & Covi L. (1974). The Hopkins Symptom Checklist (HSCL). A measure of primary symptom dimensions. *Modern Problems in Pharmacopsychiatry, 7*, 79–110.

de Souza, A. S., Fernandes, F. S., & Taveres do Carmo, M. d. G. (2011). Effects of maternal malnutrition and postnatal nutritional rehabilitation on brain fatty acids, learning, and memory. *Nutrition Reviews, 69*, 132–144. doi:10.1111/j.1753-4887.2011.00374.x

Ecklund, K., & Johnson, W. B. (2007). Toward cultural competence in child intake assessments. *Professional Psychology: Research and Practice, 38*, 356–362. doi:10.1037/0735-7028.38.4.356

Ehntholt, K. A., Smith, P. A., & Yule, W. (2005). School-based cognitive behavioural therapy group intervention for refugee children who have experienced war-related trauma. *Clinical Child Psychology and Psychiatry, 10*, 235–250. doi:10.1177/1359104505051214

Ekblad, S. (1993). Psychosocial adaptation of children while housed in a Swedish refugee camp: Aftermath of the collapse of Yugoslavia. *Stress Medicine, 9*, 159–166. doi:10.1002/smi.2460090306

Elbert, E., Schauer, M., Schauer, E., Huschka, B., Hirth, M., & Neuner, F. (2009). Trauma-related impairment in children—A survey in Sri Lanka provinces affected by armed conflict. *Child Abuse & Neglect, 33*, 238–246. doi:10.1016/j.chiabu.2008.02.008

Elliott, J. G. (2000). The psychological assessment of children with learning difficulties. *British Journal of Special Education, 27,* 59–66. doi:10.1111/1467-8527.00161

Executive Committee of the High Commissioner's Programme. (2012). *Progress report on resettlement.* Retrieved from http://www.unhcr.org/5006a6aa9.pdf

Famularo, R., Fenton, T., Kinscherff, R., & Augustyn, M. (1996). Psychiatric comorbidity in childhood posttraumatic stress disorder. *Child Abuse & Neglect, 20,* 953–961. doi:10.1016/0145-2134(96)00084-1

Fazel, M., & Stein, A. (2003). Mental health of refugee children: Comparative study. *BMJ, 327,* 134. doi:10.1136/bmj.327.7407.134

Fazel, M., Wheeler, J., & Danesh, J. (2005). Prevalence of serious mental disorder in 7,000 refugees resettled in Western countries: A systematic review. *The Lancet, 365,* 1309–1314. doi:10.1016/S0140-6736(05)61027-6

Fogel, A., King, B. J., & Shanker, S. (2008). *Human development in the 21st century: Visionary policy ideas from systems scientists.* Cambridge, England: Cambridge University Press.

Fraine, N., & McDade, R. (2009). Reducing bias in psychometric assessment of culturally and linguistically diverse students from refugee backgrounds in Australian schools: A process approach. *Australian Psychologist, 44,* 16–26. doi:10.1080/00050060802582026

Frederick, C., Pynoos, R., & Nader, K. (1992). *Child Posttraumatic Stress Reaction Index (CPTS-RI).* Retrieved from http://www.ptsd.va.gov/professional/pages/assessments/cpts-ri.asp

Gabowitz, D., Zucker, M., & Cook, A. (2008). Neuropsychological assessment in clinical evaluation of children and adolescents with complex trauma. *Journal of Child & Adolescent Trauma, 1,* 163–178. doi:10.1080/19361520802003822

Galler, J. R., & Barrett, L. R. (2001). Children and famine: Long-term impact on development. *Ambulatory Child Health, 7,* 85–95. doi:10.1046/j.1467-0658.2001.00109.x

Geltman, P. L., Grant-Knight, W., Mehta, S., Lloyed-Travaglini, C., Lustig, S., Landgraf, J., & Wise, P. (2005). The "Lost Boys of Sudan": Functional and behavioural health of unaccompanied refugee minors resettled in the United States. *Archives of Pediatrics & Adolescent Medicine, 159,* 585–591. doi:10.1001/archpedi.159.6.585

Georgieff, M. K. (2007). Nutrition and the developing brain: Nutrient priorities and measurement. *The American Journal of Clinical Nutrition, 85,* 614–620.

Glaser, D. (2000). Child abuse and neglect and the brain—A review. *Journal of Child Psychology and Psychiatry, 41,* 97–116. doi:10.1017/S0021963099004990

Goodman, R., Meltzer, H., & Bailey, V. (1998). The Strengths and Difficulties Questionnaire: A pilot study on the validity of the self-report version. *European Child & Adolescent Psychiatry, 7,* 125–130. doi.org/10.1007/s007870050057

Hamilton, R. J., Anderson, A., Frater-Mathieson, K., Loewen, S., & Moore, D. W. (2005). *Interventions for refugee children in New Zealand Schools: Models, methods, and best practice.* Retrieved from http://www.educationcounts.govt.nz/publications/schooling/5463

Hammill, D. D., Pearson, N. A., & Wiederholt, J. L. (1996). *Comprehensive Test of Nonverbal Intelligence.* Austin, TX: Pro-Ed.

Henley, J., & Robinson, J. (2011). Mental health issues among refugee children and adolescents. *Clinical Psychologist, 15,* 51–62. doi:10.1111/j.1742-9552.2011.00024.x

Hodas, G. R. (2006). *Responding to childhood trauma: The promise and practice of trauma informed care.* Harrisburg, PA: Pennsylvania Office of Mental health and Substance Abuse Services.

Hodes, M. (2000). Psychologically distressed refugee children in the United Kingdom. *Child Psychology & Psychiatry Review, 5,* 57–68. doi:10.1017/S136064170000215X

Holding, P. A., & Snow, R. W. (2001). Impact of Plasmodium falciparum on performance and learning: A review of the evidence. *The American Journal of Tropical Medicine and Hygiene, 64,* 68–75.

Hughes, C. (2002). Executive functions and development: Why the interest? *Infant and Child Development, 11,* 69–71. doi:10.1002/icd.296

Idro, R., Kakooza-Mwesige, A., Balyejjussa, S., Mirembe, G., Mugasha, C., Tugumisirize, J., & Byarugaba, J. (2010). Severe neurological sequelae and behaviour problems after cerebral malaria in Ugandan children. *BMC Research Notes, 3.* doi:10.1186/1756-0500-3-104

Infonet-Biovision. (2012). *Malnutrition.* Retrieved from http://www.infonet-biovision.org/default/ct/817/nutrition

John, C. C., Bangirana, P., Byarugaba, J., Opoka, R. O., Idro, R., Jurek, A. M., . . . Boivin, M. J. (2008). Cerebral malaria in children is associated with long-term cognitive impairment. *Pediatrics, 122*(1), e92–e99. doi:10.1542/peds.2007-3709

Jones, L. (2008). Responding to the needs of children in crisis. *International Review of Psychiatry, 20,* 291–303. doi:10.1080/09540260801996081

Jukes, M. (2005). The long-term impact of preschool health and nutrition on education. *Food and Nutrition Bulletin, 26,* 193–200.

Kaplan, I. (2009). The effects of trauma and the refugee experience on psychological assessment processes and interpretation. *Australian Psychologist, 44,* 6–15. doi:10.1080/00050060802575715

Kihara, M., Carter, J. A., & Newton, C. R. (2006). The effect of Plasmodium falciparum on cognition: A systematic review. *Tropical Medicine & International Health, 11,* 386–397. doi:10.1111/j.1365-3156.2006.01579.x

Kinzie, J. D., Sack, W., Angell, R., Clarke, G., & Ben, R. (1989). A three-year follow-up of Cambodian young people traumatized as children. *Journal of the American Academy of Child & Adolescent Psychiatry, 28,* 501–504. doi:10.1097/00004583-198907000-00006

Kithakye, M., Morris, A., Terranova, A., & Myers, S. (2010). The Kenyan political conflict and children's adjustment. *Child Development, 81,* 1114–1128. doi:10.1111/j.1467-8624.2010.01457.x

Landy, S. (2009). *Pathways to competence: Encouraging healthy social and emotional development in young children.* Baltimore, MD: Paul H. Brookes.

Laus, M. F., Vales, L. D. M. F., Costa, T. M. B., & Almeida, S. S. (2011). Early post-natal protein-calorie malnutrition and cognition: A review of human and animal studies. *International Journal of Environmental Research and Public Health, 8,* 590–612. doi:10.3390/ijerph8020590

Lavi, T., & Solomon, Z. (2005). Palestinian youth of the intifada PTSD and future orientation. *Journal of the American Academy of Child & Adolescent Psychiatry, 44,* 1176–1183. doi:10.1097/01.chi.0000177325.47629.4c

Layne, C. M., Stuvland, R., Saltzman, W., Steinberg, A., & Pynoos, R. S. (1999). *War Trauma Exposure Scale.* Sarajevo, Bosnia: UNICEF Bosnia and Hercegovina.

Leavey, G., Hollins, K., King, M., Barnes, J., Papadopoulos, C., & Grayson, K. (2004). Psychological disorder amongst refugee and migrant schoolchildren in London. *Social Psychiatry and Psychiatric Epidemiology, 39,* 191–195. doi:10.1007/s00127-004-0724-x

Levine, M. D. (1999). Neurodevelopmental variation and dysfunction among school-aged children. In M. D. Levine, W. B. Carey, & A. C. Crocker (Eds.), *Developmental–behavioural pediatrics* (3rd ed., pp. 520–535). Philadelphia, PA: Saunders.

Lozoff, B., Beard, J., Connor, J., Felt, B., Georgieff, M., & Schallert, T. (2006). Long lasting neural and behavioural effects of iron deficiency in infancy. *Nutrition Reviews, 64,* 34–43. doi:10.1301/nr.2006.may.S34-S43

Lozoff, B., Jimenez, E., Hagen, J., Mollen, E., & Wolf, A.W. (2000). Poorer behavioral and developmental outcome more than 10 years after treatment for iron deficiency in infancy. *Pediatrics, 105,* E51. doi:10.1542/peds.105.4.e51

Lozoff, B., Jimenez, E., & Wolf, A. W. (1991). Long-term developmental outcome of infants with iron deficiency. *The New England Journal of Medicine, 325,* 687–694. doi:10.1056/NEJM199109053251004

Lustig, S. L., Kia-Keating, M., Knight, W. G., Geltman, P., Ellis, H., Kinzie, J. D., . . . Saxe, G. N. (2004). Review of child and adolescent refugee mental health. *Journal of the American Academy of Child & Adolescent Psychiatry, 43,* 24–36. doi:10.1097/00004583-200401000-00012

Macksoud, M. (1992). Assessing war trauma in children: A case study of Lebanese children. *Journal of Refugee Studies, 5,* 1–15. doi.org/10.1093/jrs/5.1.1

MacMillan, H. L., Georgiades, K., Duku, E. K., Shea, A., Steiner, M., Niec, A., . . . Schmidt, L. A. (2009). Cortisol response to stress in female youths exposed to childhood maltreatment: Results of the Youth Mood Project. *Biological Psychiatry, 66,* 62–68. doi:10.1016/j.biopsych.2008.12.014

Meeks Gardner, J. M., Grantham-McGregor, S. M., & Chang, S. M. (1993). Behaviour of stunted children and the relationship to development [Abstract]. *The Proceedings of the Nutrition Society, 52,* 36A.

Miller, J., Mitchell, J., & Brown, J. (2005). African refugees with interrupted schooling in the high school mainstream: Dilemmas for teachers. *Prospect: An Australian Journal of Teaching TESOL, 20*(2), 19–33.

Montgomery, E. (1998). Refugee children from the Middle East. *Scandinavian Journal of Social Medicine, 54,* 1–152.

Morgane, P. J., Mokler, D. J., & Galler, J. R. (2002). Effects of prenatal protein malnutrition on the hippocampal formation. *Neuroscience and Biobehavioral Reviews, 26,* 471–483. doi:10.1016/S0149-7634(02)00012-X

Morgos, D., Worden, J. W., & Gupta, L. (2007–2008). Psychosocial effects of war experiences among displaced children in Southern Darfur. *Omega: The Journal of Death and Dying, 56,* 229–253.

Moroz, K. J. (2005). *The effects of psychological trauma on children and adolescents.* Waterbury: Vermont Agency of Human Services.

Moss, W. J., Ramakrishnan, M., Storms, D., Henderson Siegle, A., Weiss, W. M., Lejnev, I., & Muhe, L. (2006). Child health in complex emergencies. *Bulletin of the World Health Organization, 84,* 58–64. doi:10.2471/BLT.04.019570

Mung'Ala-Odera, V., Snow, R. W., & Newton, C. R. (2004). The burden of the neurocognitive impairment associated with Plasmodium falciparum malaria in sub-Saharan Africa. *The American Journal of Tropical Medicine and Hygiene, 71*(2), 64–70.

Murray, K. E., Davidson, G. R., & Schweitzer, R. D. (2008). *Psychological wellbeing of refugees resettling in Australia: A literature review prepared for the Australian Psychological Society.* Melbourne: Australian Psychological Society.

Murray-Kolb, L. E., Khatry, S. K., Katz, J., Schaefer, B. A., Cole, P. M., LeClerq, S. C., . . . Christian, P. (2012). Preschool micronutrient supplementation effects on intellectual and motor function in school-aged Nepalese children. *Archives of Pediatrics & Adolescent Medicine, 166,* 404–410. doi:10.1001/archpediatrics.2012.37

Naglieri, J. A., & Ronning, M. E. (2000). The relationship between general ability using the Naglieri Nonverbal Ability Test (NNAT) and Stanford Achievement Test (SAT) reading achievement. *Journal of Psychoeducational Assessment, 18,* 230–239. doi:10.1177/073428290001800303

Nassar, M. F., Shaaban, J. Y., Nassar, J. F., Younis, N. T., & Abdel-Mobdy, A. E. (2012). Language skills and intelligence quotient of protein energy malnutrition survivors. *Journal of Tropical Pediatrics, 58,* 226–230. doi:10.1093/tropej/fmr081

Neumann, C. G., Gewa, C., & Bwibo, N. O. (2004). Child nutrition in developing countries. *Pediatric Annals, 33,* 658–674.

Newton, C. R. J. C., Hien, T. T., & White, N. (2000). Cerebral malaria. *Journal of Neurology, Neurosurgery, and Psychiatry, 69,* 433–441. doi:10.1136/jnnp.69.4.433

Olvera, P., and Gómez-Cerrillo, L. (2011). A bilingual (English and Spanish) psycho-educational assessment MODEL grounded in Cattell-Horn Carroll (CHC) Theory: A cross battery approach. *Contemporary School Psychology, 13,* 117–127.

Pelletier, D. L., & Frongillo, E. A. (2003). Changes in child survival are strongly associated with changes in malnutrition in developing countries. *The Journal of Nutrition, 133,* 107–119.

Perry, B. D. (2003). *Effects of traumatic events on children: An introduction.* Retrieved from http://www.mentalhealthconnection.org/pdfs/perry-handout-effects-of-trauma.pdf

Perry, B. D., Pollard, R., Blakley, T., Baker, W., & Vigilante, D. (1995). Childhood trauma, the neurobiology of adaptation and "use-dependent" development of the brain: How "states" become "traits." *Infant Mental Health Journal, 16,* 271–291. doi:10.1002/1097-0355(199524)16:4<271::AID-IMHJ2280160404>3.0.CO;2-B

Porter, M., & Haslam, N. (2005). Predisplacement and postdisplacement factors associated with mental health of refugees and internally displaced persons: A meta-analysis. *JAMA, 294,* 602–612. doi:10.1001/jama.294.5.602

Price, R. N., Douglas, N. M., & Anstey, N. M. (2009). New developments in Plasmodium vivax malaria: Severe disease and the rise of chloroquine resistance. *Current Opinion in Infectious Diseases, 22,* 430–435. doi:10.1097/QCO.0b013e32832f14c1

Pynoos, R., Rodriguez, N., Steinberg, A., Stuber, M., & Frederick, C. (1998). *UCLA PTSD Index for DSM–IV.* Los Angeles, CA: UCLA Trauma Psychiatry Program.

Qouta, S., & Odeh, J. (2005). The impact of conflict on children. The Palestinian Experience. *The Journal of Ambulatory Care Management, 28,* 75–79.

Qouta, S., Punamaki, R. L., & El Sarraj, E. (2005). Mother-child expression psychological distress in acute war trauma. *Clinical Child Psychology and Psychiatry, 10,* 135–156. doi:10.1177/1359104505051208

Raven, J. C. (1992). *Raven manual: Standard Progressive Matrices.* Oxford, England: Oxford Psychologists Press.

Reed, R. V., Fazel, D. M., Jones, L., Panter-Brick, C., & Stein, A. (2012). Mental health of displaced and refugee children resettled in low-income and middle-income countries: Risk and protective factors. *The Lancet, 379,* 250–265. doi:10.1016/S0140-6736(11)60050-0

Reynolds, C. R., & Kamphaus, R. W. (1992). *Behavior Assessment System for Children.* Circle Pines, MN: American Guidance Service.

Reynolds, C. R., & Kamphaus, R. W. (2004). *BASC–2: Behaviour Assessment System for Children, manual* (2nd ed.). Circle Pines, MN: American Guidance Service.

Reynolds, C. R., & Richmond, B. O. (1978). What I think and feel: A revised measure of children's manifest anxiety. *Journal of Abnormal Child Psychology, 6,* 271–280. doi:10.1007/BF00919131

Roid, G. H., & Miller, L. J. (1997). *Leiter International Performance Scale–Revised: Examiner's manual.* Wood Dale, IL: Stoelting.

Rostami, R., Babapour-Kheiroddin, J., Shalchi, B., Badinloo, F., & Hamzavi-Abedi, F. (2009). Emotional and behavioural problems of Afgan refugees and war-zone adolescents. *Iranian Journal of Psychiatry, 4,* 36–40.

Rutter, J. (2003). *Supporting refugee children in 21st century Britain* (2nd ed.) Stoke-on-Trent, England: Trentham Books.

Sack, W. H., Him, C., & Dickason, D. (1999). Twelve-year follow-up study of Khmer youths who suffered massive war trauma as children. *Journal of the American Academy of Child & Adolescent Psychiatry, 38,* 1173–1179. doi:10.1097/00004583-199909000-00023

Sargent, J. (2009). *Traumatic stress in children and adolescents: Eight steps to treatment.* Retrieved from http://www.psychiatrictimes.com/articles/traumatic-stress-children-and-adolescents-eight-steps-treatment

Shashidhar, H. S. (2011). *Malnutrition.* Retrieved from Emedicine.medscape.com/article/985140-overview#showall

Shaw, J. A. (2003). Children exposed to war/terrorism. *Clinical Child and Family Psychology Review, 6,* 237–246. doi:10.1023/B:CCFP.0000006291.10180.bd

Shonk, S. M., & Cicchetti, D. (2001). Maltreatment, competency deficits, and risk for academic and behavioural maladjustment. *Developmental Psychology, 37,* 3–17. doi:10.1037/0012-1649.37.1.3

Shonkoff, J. P. (2009). *Investment in early childhood development lays the foundation for a prosperous and sustainable society.* Retrieved from http://www.child-encyclopedia.com/documents/ShonkoffANGxp.pdf

Shonkoff, J. P., & Phillips, D. A. (2000). *From neurons to neighborhoods: The science of early childhood development.* Washington, DC: National Academy Press.

Smith, P., Perrin, S., Dyregrov, A., & Yule, W. (2003). Principal components analysis of the impact of event scale with children in war. *Personality and Individual Differences, 34,* 315–322. doi.org/10.1016/S0191-8869(02)00047-8

Southwick, S. M., Rasmusson, A., Barron, J., & Arnsten, A. (2005). Neurobiological and neurocognitive alterations in PTSD: A focus on norepinephrine, serotonin, and the hypothalamic–pituitary–adrenal axis. In J. J. Vasterling & C. R. Brewin (Eds.), *Neuropsychology of PTSD: Biological, cognitive, and clinical perspectives* (pp. 27–58). New York, NY: Guilford Press.

Streeck-Fischer, A., & van der Kolk, B. A. (2000). Down will come baby, cradle and all: Diagnostic and therapeutic implications of chronic trauma on child development. *Australian and New Zealand Journal of Psychiatry, 34,* 903–918. doi:10.1080/000486700265

Strupp, B. J., & Levitsky, D. A. (1995). Enduring cognitive effects of early malnutrition. *The Journal of Nutrition, 125,* 2221S–2232S.

Thabet, A. A. M., Abed, Y., & Vostanis, P. (2004). Comorbidity of post-traumatic stress disorder and depression among refugee children during war conflict. *Journal of Child Psychology and Psychiatry, 45,* 533–542. doi:10.1111/j.1469-7610.2004.00243.x

Thabet, A. A. M., Karim, K., & Vostanis, P. (2006). Trauma exposure in pre-school children in a war zone. *British Journal of Psychiatry, 188,* 154–58. doi.org/10.1192/bjp.188.2.154

Thomas, T., & Lau, W. (2002). *Psychological well being of child and adolescent refugee and asylum seekers: Overview of major research findings of the past ten years*. Sydney, Australia: Human Rights and Equal Opportunity Commission.

Tjitra, E., Anstey, N. M., Sugiarto, P., Warikar, N., Kenangalem, E., Karyana, M., . . . Price, R. N. (2008). Multidrug-resistant Plasmodium vivax associated with severe and fatal malaria: A prospective study in Papua, Indonesia. *PLoS Medicine, 5*, e128. doi:10.1371/journal.pmed.0050128

United Nations General Assembly. (1951). *Convention relating to the status of refugees*. Retrieved from http://www.refworld.org/docid/3be01b964.html

United Nations High Commissioner for Refugees. (1994). *Refugee children: Guidelines on protection and care*. Retrieved from http://www.unicef.org/violencestudy/pdf/refugee_children_guidelines_on_protection_and_care.pdf

United Nations High Commissioner for Refugees. (2008). *2007 Global trends: Refugees, asylum-seekers, returnees, internally displaced and stateless persons*. Retrieved from http://www.unhcr.org/4852366f2.html

United Nations High Commissioner for Refugees. (2011). *UNHCR Global Trends 2010*. Retrieved from http://www.unhcr.org/4dfa11499.html

United Nations System Standing Committee on Nutrition. (2004). *5th report on the world nutrition situation: Nutrition for improved development outcomes*. Retrieved from http://www.unscn.org/layout/modules/resources/files/rwns5.pdf

van der Kolk, B. (2003). The neurobiology of childhood trauma and abuse. *Child and Adolescent Psychiatric Clinics of North America, 12*, 293–317. doi.org/10.1016/S1056-4993(03)00003-8

Victorian Foundation for Survivors of Torture. (2012). *Caring for refugee patients in general practice: A desk-top guide* (4th ed.). Retrieved from http://www.foundationhouse.org.au/resources/publications_and_resources.htm

Wechsler, D., & Naglieri, J. A. (2006). *Wechsler Nonverbal Scale of Ability*. New York, NY: Psychological Corporation.

Weinstein, D., Staffelbach, D., & Biaggio, M. (2000). Attention-deficit hyperactivity disorder and posttraumatic stress disorder: Differential diagnosis in childhood sexual abuse. *Clinical Psychology Review, 20*, 359–378. doi:10.1016/S0272-7358(98)00107-X

Werker, E. (2007). Refugee camp economies. *Journal of Refugee Studies, 20*, 461–480. doi:10.1093/jrs/fem001

Wiese, E. B. P. (2007). "I think he is still inside me": Mother/child psychotherapy and Sandplay with a Kosovar woman and her infant son. In J. P. Wilson & B. Drozdek (Eds.), *Voices of trauma: Treating survivors across cultures* (pp. 271–294). New York, NY: Springer.

Wiese, E. B. P., & Burhorst, I. (2007). Transcultural psychiatry: A mental health program for asylum-seeking and refugee children and adolescents in the Netherlands. *Transcultural Psychiatry, 44*, 596–613. doi:10.1177/1363461507083900

World Health Organization. (2008). World malaria report 2008. Retrieved from http://whqlibdoc.who.int/publications/2008/9789241563697_eng.pdf

World Health Organization. (2011). *Malaria fact sheet no. 94*. Retrieved from http://www.who.int/mediacentre/factsheets/fs094/en/index.html

Yule, W. (1999). Post-traumatic stress disorder. *Archives of Disease in Childhood, 80*, 107–109. doi:10.1136/adc.80.2.107

AFTERWORD

AMANDA B. CLINTON

Evaluation in human psychology represents a particular challenge for mental health and education professionals because of the inherent complexities associated with the fact that no two people are alike. Even the "most clear-cut" case hovers more in gray areas than at the black-and-white ends of extremes. As the number of variables related to any referral increase, so too do the challenges associated with assessment. Experts agree that assessment of the bilingual child, particularly within contexts in which immigration, acculturation, poverty, and/or trauma are involved, is particularly complex. Various challenges and potential solutions related to the evaluation of bilingual children have been presented by authors of the preceding chapters in this book. The purpose of this concluding section is to consider these issues as a whole.

THE BILINGUAL CHILD IN CONTEXT

Although learning a second language adds complexity to cognitive processes, acquiring more than one language is certainly a manageable task for children. The human brain appears to be wired to learn language from a very young age (Garcia-Sierra et al., 2011). In fact, the infant brain is capable of processing sounds from all languages at birth. Only when there is a lack of exposure to specific tones and sounds are neurons pruned, ultimately disappearing because of inactivity (Garcia-Sierra et al., 2011). In the early elementary years, however, the young brain is still engaged in significant interhemispheric communication that, in part, reflects active language learning centers (see Chapter 3, this volume). As such, children's brains continue to be molded in terms of language, and, by consequence, they are responsive to a linguistically rich environment for a significant period of time.

Because the human brain is designed for language acquisition, relatively few children who learn two or more languages in optimal conditions are referred for psychological evaluation. More typically, youngsters whose histories are more complex because of environmental, learning, and mental health challenges are those who are ultimately recommended for assessment. Key contextual issues that may influence first and/or second language acquisition include, but are not limited to, the health of the child's mother, nutrition in infancy and childhood, trauma and stress, poverty, low levels of parental education, immigration and acculturation, organic factors, and even the structure of the child's native and acquired languages. Often, more than one of these co-occurs, creating a pattern of complex relationships to which adding instruction in a second language is particularly difficult.

Specific assessment tools, such as standardized tests, and many procedures, such as response to intervention, make important contributions to deciphering and understanding the bilingual child who has been referred for assessment. However, on their own, these instruments and methods lack the sensitivity and depth required to address the myriad complexities that are present, and they cannot independently provide answers. In our highly technical world, bilingual assessment may remain an exception to current trends in that in lieu of programmed materials or computer assessments offering insights and diagnoses, it is highly trained and well-informed clinicians who are critical to making meaningful determinations. Psychologists must be knowledgeable about the complex contexts within which many second language learners are developing. These professionals have to be capable of integrating numerous sources of scientific information and relating that to the interpretation of data and analysis of behavioral observation and interview findings. In this manner, meaningful assessment of the bilingual child is conducted and effective intervention plans are designed and implemented.

Developmental, Social, and Familial Factors

As discussed throughout this volume, a healthy developmental trajectory is key to positive long-term outcomes. The brain grows rapidly before birth and during infancy, establishing innumerable neuronal connections and pruning unused nervous system cells by 2 years of age. In facilitative contexts, early childhood—an important period for motor, language, and sensory development, largely as a result of increasing myelination of axons in these areas—sets the stage for future growth. As the frontal cortex initiates its course of development—one lasting through adolescence and early adulthood—thinking and self-control processes advance as well (Kolb & Whishaw, 2008). Notable progress in language and social comprehension also occurs throughout childhood (Kagan & Herschkowitz, 2005; Stassen Berger, 2012).

Poverty, however, can have a significant negative impact on the development of language in childhood (Adams, 1990; Campbell & Ramey, 1994). Children hailing from homes with limited economic resources tend to be those who begin school with lower levels of preliteracy, and they rarely catch up with their peers (Hart & Risley, 1995). This is particularly problematic given that most second language learners are from families that have recently immigrated and are living at or below the poverty level (U.S. Census Bureau, 2012). When poverty is combined with stress and trauma, as is the situation with refugee children, the consequences may be particularly dire (see Chapter 11, this volume). When children are stressed for an extended time, not just language but also related functions, such as memory, attention, problem solving, and reasoning abilities, tend to suffer (Elliott, 2000). Emotional centers of the brain may further be affected by trauma and stress, resulting in behavioral symptomology as well (Siegel, 1999).

In sum, second language learners are often those whose families confront poverty, immigration, or refugee status issues and live in high-stress environments. These factors can affect language and overall cognitive development. Often, these developmental, social, and familial factors can result in low literacy in a child's native language. When a second language is added, semilingualism—or partial development of both the native and acquired language—may be observed (see Chapter 4, this volume).

Language Structure and Transfer

The structure of a language may influence the way in which it is learned. Transfer of knowledge from one's native language to a second language relies on how the sounds of language are represented (e.g., alphabetic or logographic, phoneme or syllable, transparent or opaque; see Chapter 2, this volume). A language that is relatively orthographically transparent, such as Spanish or Italian, may be relatively accessible because there is a virtual one-to-one correspondence between letters and their sounds. Other alphabetic languages, such as English and French, are considered orthographically opaque. This is because letter–sound correspondence may vary considerably, depending on the particular word. For example, in English, the *a* sounds different in the words *cake, back, above,* and *meat,* to name a few.

The differences in cross-language transfer depending on the orthographic structure of the original language and the second language represent an important consideration for assessment of the bilingual child. If a child's acquired language is orthographically more complex than his or her native tongue, transfer of direct knowledge may be limited. However, if the alphabet is the same (e.g., Spanish to English), it is likely that some phoneme–grapheme combinations will be the same. For those whose first language is alphabetic but different (e.g., Russian to English), phoneme–grapheme combinations will not transfer, but the idea of alphabetic representation of sounds will. In logographic languages, such as Chinese, transfer appears to occur, but at different levels (McBride-Chang et al., 2008). Furthermore, linguistic complexities may be particularly critical in cases of low literacy, poor developmental supports, and high stress, where a child encounters a variety of risk factors that affect learning. Acquiring a particularly distinct and/or opaque second language could be cognitively overwhelming for the child who is already struggling. Expectations for the type and degree of transfer should, then, incorporate structural aspects of language and contextual considerations of the child.

Assessment and Intervention

Assessment is particularly complicated in the case of bilingualism because few measures have been developed for this purpose, and those that have do not have norms for bilingual children (see Chapter 5, this volume). For this reason, it is important to carefully consider the validity of assessment tools and procedures when they are selected. Alternatives such as nonverbal measures, dynamic assessment, or response to intervention (see Chapter 6, this volume) may be helpful in illuminating the bilingual child's strengths and weaknesses and developing appropriate interventions. However, each of these methods also has limitations. To date, no adequate norm-referenced, standardized measure has been developed that incorporates a child's native language acquisition processes along with the experience and processes involved in learning a second language. Response to intervention models that aim to determine and provide appropriate instruction for bilingual students have yet to be clearly delineated (Gersten et al., 2006), and determining the cause of failure to respond to instruction and intervention is still difficult (Barrera & Liu, 2010).

CONCLUSION

Human beings are wired to socialize and communicate with one another. They accomplish this largely through the use of language. The bilingual child who is referred for assessment is often the youngster who must adjust to a variety of critical contextual influences in conjunction with her or his own individual uniqueness while trying to negotiate two languages. Arguably, the majority of bilingual children seen by psychologists have not been granted optimal environmental conditions for overall development. These less-than-favorable situations typically have a significant impact on language. Not only in the United States but also in many regions across the globe, second language learners who need support are those whose histories are complicated by a web of factors ranging from refugee experiences to poverty, low parental literacy, unsafe neighborhoods, and even professionals who misunderstand normative native and second language acquisition processes. Although progress has been made in understanding the relationships between experience and biology as they manifest in academic and social environments, much remains to be learned. At present, the best practices with bilingual children rely on a highly knowledgeable team of professionals able to integrate and apply data from neuroscience to mental health to culture and political history to linguistic structure of languages in order to develop meaningful and flexible treatment plans that respond to the needs of the bilingual child.

REFERENCES

Adams, M. J. (1990). *Beginning to read: Thinking and learning about print*. Cambridge, MA: MIT Press.

Barrera, M., & Liu, K. K. (2010). Challenges of general outcomes measurement in the RTI progress monitoring of linguistically diverse exceptional learners. *Theory Into Practice, 49*, 273–280. doi:10.1080/00405841.2010.510713

Campbell, F. A., & Ramey, C. T. (1994). Effects of early intervention on intellectual and academic achievement: A follow-up study of children from low-income families. *Child Development, 65*, 684–698. doi:10.2307/1131410

Elliott, J. G. (2000). The psychological assessment of children with learning difficulties. *British Journal of Special Education, 27*, 59–66. doi:10.1111/1467-8527.00161

Garcia-Sierra, A., Rivera-Gaxiola, M., Percaccio, C. R., Conboy, B. T., Romo, H., Klarman, L., . . . Kuhl, P. K. (2011). Bilingual language learning: An ERP study relating early brain responses to speech, language input, and later word production. *Journal of Phonetics, 39*, 546–557. doi:10.1016/j.wocn.2011.07.002

Gersten, R., Baker, S., Shanahan, T., Linan-Thompson, S., Chiappe, P., & Scarcella, R. (2006). *Effective literacy and language instruction for English learners in the elementary grades: An IES practice guide.* Washington, DC: IES, Department of Education.

Hart, B., & Risley, T. (1995). *Meaningful differences in the everyday experiences of young American children.* Baltimore, MD: Paul H. Brookes.

Kagan, J., & Herschkowitz, N. (2005). *A young mind in a growing brain.* Mahwah, NJ: Erlbaum.

Kolb, B., & Whishaw, I. (2008). *Fundamentals of human neuropsychology* (6th ed.). New York, NY: Worth.

McBride-Chang, C., Tong, X., Shu, H., Wong, A. M.-Y., Leung, K.-w., & Tardif, T. (2008). Syllable, phoneme, and tone: Psycholinguistic units in early Chinese and English word recognition. *Scientific Studies of Reading, 12,* 171–194. doi:10.1080/10888430801917290

Siegel, D. J. (1999). *The developing mind: Toward a neurobiology of interpersonal experience.* New York, NY: Guilford Press.

Stassen Berger, K. (2012). *The developing person through childhood.* New York, NY: Worth.

U.S. Census Bureau. (May, 2012). *The foreign-born population in the United States: 2010.* Retrieved from http://www.census.gov/prod/2012pubs/acs-19.pdf

INDEX

Hammill, D. D., 125
Hanley, J. R., 30
Hart, B., 82
Health concerns, 278, 281–286
Hemispheres (brain), 221–222
Heredia, R. R., 65
Hindi (language), 65
Hispanic Neuropsychology Society, 72
Holahan, J. M., 61
Homae, F., 54–55
Home Language Survey, 117
Homes, of students, 118
Home visit, 92
Honeymoon stage (acculturation), 197–199
Hopkins Symptom Checklist (HSCL), 279
Huang, H. S., 30
Hudson, R. F., 151
Hunley, S. A., 111
Hyperarousal response, 270
Hypothalamic–pituitary–adrenal axis, 271
Hypothesis-testing approach, 129

IDEIA (Individuals With Disabilities Education Improvement Act), 145
IDEIA Oral Language Proficiency Test, 121
Idioms, 65
IEPs (individual education plans), 118
Illinois, 110, 138
"Immigrant paradox," 165
Immigrant students, 90
Immigration
    and bilingual assessment, 10–12
    and educational attainment, 193
Immigration status, acculturation and, 195
Impact of Events Scale (R–IES), 279
Increasing participation stage (acculturation), 200–202
Indicadores Dinámicos del Éxito en la Lectura, 250
Individual education plans (IEPs), 118
Individuals With Disabilities Education Improvement Act (IDEIA), 145
Inflections
    in alphabetic languages, 31–32
    in Chinese, 32

Informal assessments
    of language proficiency, 121–122
    of literacy, 250–253
    for semilingualism, 91–92
Inhibitory control, 57
Initial literacy (phase), 224, 233
Instruction
    appropriate for ELs, 146
    increasing the intensity of, 143
Integration
    in acculturation matrix, 197
    as category of adaptation, 202
Intellectual assessment, 109–131
    and academic performance, 113–116
    approaches to, 123–128
    and bilingualism, 111–113
    contextual factors in, 116–119
    and demographics, 110–111
    Educational File Language Review Checklist, 131
    and language proficiency assessment, 119–123
Intellectual functioning
    effect of bilingualism on, 112–113
    nonverbal tests of, 94–95
Interhemispheric communication (brain)
    and corpus callosum, 60
    and language development, 55
    in young brains, 306
Interpreters
    in assessment process, 139
    in bilingual assessments, 17
    in clinical interviews, 167
    and intellectual assessment, 127
Interventions
    for bilingual children, 308
    culturally competent, 205–206
    limitations of, 306
Interviews
    clinical, 167
    of parents, 287–291
    semistructured, 172, 180, 182
    for social, emotional, and behavioral assessments, 172
    structured, 172
    unstructured, 172
Iodine deficiency, 281–282
IQ, Brief vs. Full-Scale, 126
Iron deficiency, 281
Isel, F., 59
Ives Wiley, H., 151

Japanese kanji, 243
Jimerson, S., 150
John, C. C., 284
Journey, of refugees, 267

KABC–2 (Kaufman Assessment Battery
    for Children–Second Edition),
    94, 126–127
Kane, M. J., 27
Kang, J., 30
Kang, S.-J., 35
Karim, K., 269
Kaufman, A. S., 126–127
Kaufman Assessment Battery for
    Children–Second Edition
    (KABC–2), 94, 126–127
Kellogg, R. T., 222–223
Kester, Ellen Stubbe, 71
Kim, B. S. K., 203
Kim, K. H. S., 40
Kindler, A. L., 110
Kinzie, J. D., 269
Kithakye, M., 269
Klein, D., 40
Klein, J., 150
Knowledge
    domain, 225, 230
    metaknowledge, 230, 231
    procedural, 230
    of universal text attributes, 230
Knowledge crafting (phase), 223
Knowledge telling (phase), 223
Knowledge transforming (phase), 223
Korean (language), 37
Korean Hangul (language), 30
Kovelman, I., 245
Kumar, U., 65

L1. See Native language
L2. See Second language
Language
    academic, 9
    and acculturation process, 192–193
    for assessments, 92, 121, 139
    conversational, 9, 168
    structure and transfer of, 307–308
Language acquisition
    and brain, 54, 305–306
    language transfer in, 38
    and semilingualism, 83–89

Language continuum (term), 113
Language development
    and home environment, 93
    neuropsychology of, 54–60
Language disorder assessment, 63–66
Language Dominance Checklist,
    74–75
Language proficiency
    assessment of, 113–114, 119–123
    development of, 114–116
    and membership in culture, 179–180
Language-reduced assessment, 125
Language switching, 57–58
Language transfer
    and bilingual assessment, 16–17
    defined, 16
    and language structure, 307–308
Language variables, in interventions,
    205
Laus, M. F., 282
Learning disabilities, 147
Lebel, C., 61
Lehtonen, M., 58
Leiter–Revised (test)
    for intellectual assessment, 126
    and refugee students, 287
Lenses, of evaluators, 226
Lervåg, A., 29
Lesaux, N. K., 253
Levitt, V., 166
Lexical tone, 31
Li, T., 37
Lichtenstein, R., 118
Limbos, M. M., 254
Limited bilingualism, 82
Linan-Thompson, S., 96
Lingual/calcarine cortex, 245
Linklater, D. L., 151
Literacy
    at home, language development
        and, 85
    informal assessments of, 250–253
    in L1, to assist in L2 acquisition, 88
    and learning trajectory, 82
    and orthography, 243–244
    phases of, 224
Literacy acquisition, 35
Literacy roots (phase), 224
Liu, Y., 145
Locke, J. L., 73

ABOUT THE EDITOR

Amanda B. Clinton, PhD, is an associate professor of psychology at the University of Puerto Rico, where her work focuses on neuropsychology, dual language learning, and social–emotional skill development within a cultural framework. She earned her MEd at the University of Washington and her PhD at the University of Georgia. She is a credentialed school psychologist and a licensed psychologist. As a Fulbright Scholar in Medellín, Colombia, Dr. Clinton researched relationships between language structure and reading acquisition processes. Dr. Clinton has worked with second language learners from various regions of the world, including Central and South America as well as the United States, and has published and presented her work nationally and internationally.